History and Culture of Tamil Nadu

Reconstructing Indian History & Culture
(ISSN 0971-3824)

1. Society in Ancient India; by Sures Chandra Banerji
2. Political Thought in Ancient India; by G.P. Singh
3. Early Indian Historical Tradition and Archaeology; by G.P. Singh
4. Vasantotsava: The Spring Festivals of India; by Leona M. Anderson
5. Ecological Readings in the Veda; by M. Vannucci
6. Vṛndāvana in Vaiṣṇava Literature; by Maura Corcoran
7. Social History of the Tamils (1707-1947); by P. Subramanian
8. Ancient Indian Coinage; by Rekha Jain
9. Buddhism and Socio-Economic Life of Eastern India; by Bimal Chandra Mohapatra
10. Chandragupta Maurya; by P.L. Bhargava
11. Mṛtyu: Concept of Death in Indian Traditions; by Gian Giuseppe Filippi
12. Yama: The Glorious Lord of the Other World; by Kusum P. Merh
13. Sacred Complex of Ujjain; by D.K. Samanta
14. Vedic View of the Earth; by S.R.N. Murthy
15. Society in the Atharvaveda; by B.S. Kharade
16. Orissan History, Culture and Archaeology; by S. Pradhan
17. Education in Ancient India; by Mitali Chatterjee
18. Surā: The Liquor and the Vedic Sacrifice; by M.B. Kolhatkar
19. Human Ecology in the Vedas; by Marta Vannucci
20. Governance in Ancient India; by Anupa Chandra Pandey
21. The Cultural Glory of Ancient India: A Literary Overview; by Sures Chandra Banerji
22. Kauṭilya's Arthaśāstra in the Light of Modern Science & Technology; by Sunil Sen Sarma
23. History of Jainism: With Special Reference to Mathurā; by V.K. Sharma
24. Cultural Tourism in India: Museums, Monuments & Arts — Theory and Practice; by S.P. Gupta; Krishna Lal; Mahua Bhattacharya
25. Ancient Indian Historiography: Sources and Interpretations; by G.P. Singh
26. Republics, Kingdoms, Towns and Cities in Ancient India; by G.P. Singh
27. Facets of Ancient Indian History and Culture: New Perception; by G.P. Singh
28. Kamakhya: A Socio-cultural Study; by Nihar Ranjan Mishra
30. Life Style of the Vedic People; by Pranati Ghosal
31. History and Culture of Tamil Nadu: As Gleaned from the Sanskrit Inscriptions Vol. 2 (up to c. AD 1310 - *c.* AD 1885); by Chithra Madhavan
32. Matrimonial Alliances and Ancient Indian Polity (*c.* 600 BCE to *c.* 650); by Preeti Prabhat
33. Artisans and Craftsmen of Northern India; by Kuldeep Singh Thind
34. The Evolution of Historiographical Tradition in Ancient and Medieval India; by G.P. Singh
35. Warfare in Ancient India, Theory and Practice; by Soma Basu
36. Sanskrit Education and Literature in Ancient and Medieval Tamil Nadu by Chithra Madhavan
37. Rājadharma in Mahābhārata; by Priyanka Pandey

Reconstructing Indian History & Culture, no. 29

History and Culture of Tamil Nadu

— As Gleaned from the Sanskrit Inscriptions —

Volume - 1

(Up to *c.* AD 1310)

by

Chithra Madhavan

with a Foreword by

K.V. Raman

PRINTWORLD

Publishers of Indian Traditions

Cataloging in Publication Data — DK
[Courtesy: D.K. Agencies (P) Ltd. <docinfo@dkagencies.com>]

Madhavan, Chithra, 1966- **author.**
History and culture of Tamil Nadu : as gleaned from the Sanskrit inscriptions / by Chithra Madhavan ; with a foreword by K.V. Raman. – Fourth impression.
volumes cm. – (Reconstructing Indian history & culture ; no
"First published in India in 2005" – Title page verso.
Includes bibliographical references.
Contents: volume 1. Upto c. AD 1310

1. Tamil Nadu (India) – History – Sources. 2. Inscriptions, Sanskrit – India – Tamil Nadu. I. Title. II. Series: Reconstructing Indian history & culture ; no. 29.

LCC DS485.M28M33 2019 | DDC 411.7095482 23

ISBN 13: 978-81-246-0308-6 (vol. 1) (Hardbound)
ISBN 13: 978-81-246-0369-7 (vol. 2) (Hardbound)
ISBN 13: 978-81-246-0370-3 (set) (Hardbound)
ISBN 13: 978-81-246-0380-2 (vol. 1) (Paperback)
ISBN 13: 978-81-246-0395-6 (vol. 2) (Paperback)
ISBN 13: 978-81-246-0396-3 (set) (Paperback)

First published in India in 2005
Second impression in 2008
Third impression in 2013
Fourth impression in 2019

Printed and published by:
D.K. Printworld (P) Ltd.
Regd. office : *Vedaśrī*, F-395, Sudarshan Park
(Metro Station: ESI Hospital) New Delhi - 110 015
Phones : (011) 2545 3975, 2546 6019
e-mail : indology@dkprintworld.com
Web : www.dkprintworld.com

For
my parents

Foreword

Sanskrit is often described as the *lingua franca* of ancient India and served as a unifying link-language of all the regions therein. The rulers of various dynasties all over India issued inscriptions in Sanskrit and this was the same in the case of the ancient Tamil country as well although they are seen in lesser numbers than those composed in Tamil. The Sanskrit epigraphs of the Pallavas, Pāṇḍyas and Coḷas are a very valuable and authentic source of data for reconstructing the ancient history of Tamil Nadu. The lithic epigraphs in Sanskrit found etched on the walls of temples, as well as the Sanskrit portions or *praśasti*s of the bi-lingual copper-plate records offer a wealth of information about civil and military administration, social, economic and religious life and in particular about education and literature of the ancient Tamil country which are not forthcoming from any other source. While the data from the Tamil inscriptions have been properly utilized in reconstructing the history of Tamilnadu, the Sanskrit epigraphs have not received adequate attention and have not been comprehensively analysed till now.

This work deals with an in-depth study of these epigraphs of the Pallavas, Pāṇḍyas and the Coḷas upto the early part of the 14th century AD and also includes the Sanskrit records of chieftains and those of kings from outside the Tamil country who ruled over this region. This study by Dr. Chithra Madhavan is a significant contribution to the history and culture of Tamil Nadu, bringing to light many hitherto unknown details especially with regard to the cultural and educational aspects. There has been a long felt need for such a work and it has been done with commendable competence. I am sure the scholarly world will welcome and appreciate this interesting study.

14.10.2004

K.V. Raman
Professor and Head (Retd.)
Dept. of Ancient History and Archaeology
University of Madras
Chennai

Preface

THE present work embodies the result of the research carried out by me from 1996-99 for which I was awarded the Ph.D degree by the University of Mysore.

I am greatly indebted to Dr. M.S. Krishna Murthy, Professor, Department of Studies in Ancient History and Archaeology, University of Mysore, Mysore who has helped and encouraged me at every stage of this work. I feel proud and happy to have worked under his guidance.

I am extremely obliged to Dr. K.V. Raman, Professor and Head (Retd.), Department of Ancient History and Archaeology, University of Madras, Chennai, for advising me to explore this topic, for encouraging me at every stage of this study and for his personal interest in this work. I am indeed fortunate to have had the benefit of his scholarly advice. I also thank him for kindly contributing the foreword to this book.

My sincere thanks to Dr. S. Sankaranarayanan, Dy. Superintending Epigraphist (Retd.), Archaeological Survey of India and Hon. Director, Adyar Library and Research Centre, Chennai for his substantial help and encouragement. I thank Dr. M.D. Sampath, Director (Retd.), Epigraphy, Archaeological Survey of India, Mysore for giving me access to the transcripts of the inscriptions. I also thank Dr. S. Swaminathan, Assistant Superintending Epigraphist, Archaeological Survey of India, Mysore for all his help.

I wish to thank my parents for their support and encouragement throughout the period of this work. My special thanks to my mother who has helped me in the reading and translation of many of the Sanskrit epigraphs.

My heartfelt thanks to Shri. L.J. Krishnamurthi and Smt. Shobha Jayaraman for all their help throughout the period of this study.

This work (Vol. I) deals with the Sanskrit inscriptions of Tamil Nadu upto *c.*1310 AD. Vol II which is to be published soon is a study of the Sanskrit inscriptions from *c.*1310 AD – *c.* 1885 AD.

Chithra Madhavan

Contents

Abbreviations

ABORI:	Annals of the Bhandarkar Oriental Research Institute
ALB :	*Adyar Library Bulletin*
ARE :	*Annual Reports on Epigraphy*
ASIAR :	Archaeological Survey of India Annual Report
ASLP :	*Administration and Social Life under the Pallavas* by C. Minakshi
BITCM:	*Bulletin of the Institute of Traditional Culture,* Madras
EHAII :	*Evolution of the Hindu Administrative Institutions in India,* by S.K. Aiyangar
DCVP :	*The Dalavāipuram copper-plate grant of Parāntaka Vīra Nārāyaṇa Pāṇḍya* by T.N. Subramaniam
EI :	*Epigraphia Indica*
ECPR :	*Esālam Copper plates of Rājendra Choḷa I* by R. Nagaswamy
HSVK :	*Historical Sculptures of the Vaikuṇṭhaperumāḷ Temple, Kāñchī* by C. Minakshi
Ind. Ant.:	*Indian Antiquary*
IHQ :	*Indian Historical Quarterly*
IOP :	*Inscriptions of the Pallavas* by T.V. Mahalingam
JMU :	*Journal of the Madras University.*
JOR :	*Journal of Oriental Research.*
KA :	*Kauṭilīyam Arthaśāstram,* edited by K.P. Kangle

KPPN :	*Kumaraḍimaṅgalam plates of the Pallava king Nandivarman III* by N. Ramesan
KTPR :	*Karandai Tamil Sangam Plates of Rājendra Choḷa I* by K.G. Krishnan
MASI :	*Memoirs of the Archaeological Society of India*
MS :	*Manusmṛti*, Edited by Ganganatha Jha
PCM :	*Pallavar Ceppetukal Muppatu*
PCP :	*Pandiyar Ceppetukal Pattu*
PJCG :	*Paḷḷankovil Jaina Copper-plate Grant of the early Pallava Period* by T.N. Subramaniam
PGCC :	*Political Geography of the Chola Country*, by Y. Subbarayalu
QJMS :	*Quarterly Journal of the Mythic Society*
SCVP :	*Śivakāśi Copper-Plate Grant of Vīra-Pāṇḍya* by T.N. Subramaniam and P.R. Srinivasan
SII :	*South Indian Inscriptions*
SITI :	*South Indian Temple Inscriptions*
TAS :	*Travancore Archaeological Series*
TASSI :	*Transactions of the Archaeological Society of South India*
TVCP :	*Tiruttani and Veḷāñjeri Copper Plates*, by R. Nagaswamy
VGPS :	*Vesanta Grant of Siṁhavarman Pallava* by N. Ramesan

Key to Transliteration

अ *a* (but)	ङ *ṅa* (sing)[1]	न *na* (numb)[4]
आ *ā* (palm)	च *ca* (chunk)[2]	प *pa* (spin)[5]
इ *i* (it)	छ* *cha* (catch him)[2]	फ* *pha* (philosophy)[5]
ई *ī* (beet)	ज *ja* (john)[2]	ब *ba* (bin)[5]
उ *u* (put)	झ *jha* (hedgehog)[2]	भ *bha* (abhor)[5]
ऊ *ū* (pool)	ञ *ña* (bunch)[2]	म *ma* (much)[5]
ऋ *ṛ* (rhythm)	ट *ṭa* (start)[3]	य *ya* (young)
ए *e* (play)	ठ* *ṭha* (anthill)[3]	र *ra* (drama)
ऐ *ai* (high)	ड *ḍa* (dart)[3]	ल *la* (luck)
ओ *o* (toe)	ढ* *ḍha* (godhead)[3]	व *va* (vile)
औ *au* (loud)	ण *ṇa* (under)[3]	श *śa* (shove)
क *ka* (skate)[1]	त *ta* (path)[4]	ष *ṣa* (bushel)
ख* *kha* (blockhead)[1]	थ *tha* (thunder)[4]	स *sa* (so)
ग *ga* (gate)[1]	द *da* (that)[4]	ह *ha* (hum)
घ *gha* (ghost)[1]	ध* *dha* (breathe)[4]	

ं *ṁ anusvāra* (nasalisation of preceding vowel)

: *ḥ visarga* (aspiration of preceding vowel)

Tamil characters:

ற* ṟ ள* ḷ ழ* ḻ ண* ṇ

* No exact English equivalents for these letters.

[1] guttural [2] palatal [3] lingual [4] dental [5] labial

Introduction

THERE are many sources for studying about the history of the Tamil country in the ancient and medieval periods such as literary works, numismatics, epigraphy, folklore and legends. Among all these sources, the most important one for reconstructing the history of the Tamil country in the above-mentioned periods is epigraphy. In the words of D.C. Sircar,

> The great importance of inscriptions lies in the fact that they generally offer information about personages and events of Indian history about which nothing is known from any other source.[1]

The Pallavas, Pāṇḍyas and the Coḷas, who ruled over the Tamil country from the fifth century AD upto the early part of the 14th century AD have left behind a very rich legacy of thousands of inscriptions which are a storehouse of authentic information about the political, social, economic, administrative, religious and cultural conditions which existed at that time. A proper reconstruction of the history of the Tamil country in the ancient and medieval periods is not possible without an in-depth study and analysis of the inscriptions of those periods, which offer detailed information not provided by any other source.

Most of the inscriptions of the Tamil country belonging to the ancient and medieval periods are in the Tamil language.

1. D.C. Sircar, *Indian Epigraphy*, Delhi, 1965, p. 17.

However, a large number of epigraphs are also bilingual, i.e., they are written in Sanskrit as well as in Tamil. In addition to this, there are also plenty of copper-plate as well as lithic inscriptions found written only in Sanskrit. These inscriptions, composed in Sanskrit and Tamil and those written wholly in Sanskrit serve as very valuable sources of historical data. Since Sanskrit was the court language of the Pallava kingdom, many of the official documents namely the copper-plate grants and the royal edicts on stone were written in this language.

Since these Sanskrit copper-plate grants and stone inscriptions serve as such authentic and informative sources for the study of the history of these periods, a concerted and integrated study of these Sanskrit epigraphs is necessary. This is the main objective of this work.

The attention of the early pioneering epigraphists and historians was focused mainly on the information collected from these inscriptions which pertained to the genealogy and the connected chronology of these hitherto unknown dynasties. This was justifiably so since these epigraphists and historians had first to build up the historical framework from the data culled from these inscriptions. Thus, their writings reveal less emphasis on the social, cultural and administrative aspects contained in these valuable copper-plate grants and stone inscriptions. It is this feeling of inadequacy which impelled me to take up these aspects as the main focus of study in this work. The Sanskrit epigraphs of the Tamil country starting from the fourth-fifth centuries AD upto 1310 AD have been dealt with in this work since the former marks the beginning of the Pallava rule in the Tamil country and the latter marks the end of the second Pāṇḍyan empire.

These inscriptions fall into various categories. Some record political events such as wars and conquests and mention the various military achievements of the rulers. Some epigraphs record commercial agreements and sale and purchase of land. Most of the inscriptions are, however, donative in character. They record the gift of land, money or other valuables by the rulers as well as by private individuals to temples, to other religious institutions and to the brāhmaṇas learned in the traditional scriptures. Most of these gifts, especially the gift of lands were made in the form of permanent endowments and hence the need for engraving them on a permanent medium such as stone or copper-plates, for the benefit of future generations of donees.

The earliest inscriptions of the Pallavas, such as the Mañcikallu,[2] Hīrahadagalli[3] and Mayidavōlu[4] copper-plate charters are in the Prakṛt language, and the Sanskrit charters are later in date. Although many of the early Pallava records, both in Prākṛt and Sanskrit have been discovered in the present-day state of Andhra Pradesh, I have included the information culled from these records in this work as these epigraphs have some vital bearing on the topic and cannot be ignored.

Some of the important copper-plate epigraphs of the Pallavas which provide plenty of data about this period such as the Kūram plates of Parameśvaravarman I,[5] Reyūru plates of Rājasiṁha,[6] Kaśākuḍi,[7] Udayendiram[8] and Taṇḍantoṭṭam plates[9] of Nandivarman Pallavamalla and Velūrpāḷaiyam plates of Nandivarman III[10] are bi-lingual, being written in Sanskrit and Tamil, the Sanskrit *praśasti* always preceding the Tamil portion. There are also numerous lithic inscriptions of the Pallavas, written in Sanskrit found on the walls of the temples built by them in their capital city, Kāñcīpuram, Māmallapuram and other places.

---

2. *EI*, vol. XXXII, no. 2, pp. 89-90 (Mañcikallu Inscription).
3. *EI*, vol. I, no. 1, pp. 5-7 (Hīrahadagallī plates).
4. *EI*, vol. VI, no. 8, pp. 86-88 (Maidavōlu inscription).
5. *SII*, vol. I, no. 151, pp. 148-50 (Kūram plates).
6. *E.I.* vol. XXIX, no. 11, pp. 95-97 (Reyūru grant).
7. *SII*, vol. II, no. 73, pp. 346-51 (Kaśākuḍi plates).
8. *SII*, vol. II, no. 74, pp. 365-70 (Udayendiram plates).
9. *SII*, vol. II, no. 99, pp. 520-21 (Taṇḍantōṭṭam plates).
10. *SII*, vol. II, no. 98, pp. 507-10 (Velūrpāḷaiyam plates).

Similarly, with regard to the period of the Pāṇḍyas, most of their important copper-plate charters such as the Veḷvikuḍi[11] and Śrīvaramaṅgalam[12] plates of Neḍuñjaḍaiyaṉ, Daḷavāipuram plates of Parāntaka Vīranārāyaṇa,[13] Larger Siṉṉamaṉūr plates of Rājasiṁha II[14] and the Śivakāśi plates of Vīra Pāṇḍya[15] are bi-lingual, while many of their lithic epigraphs are found to be either bi-lingual or fully in the Sanskrit language.

The Coḷas, who have issued the largest number of inscriptions among the rulers of the Tamil country engraved most of their inscriptions in Tamil, but the number of bi-lingual and inscriptions written fully in the Sanskrit language belonging to their period are also numerous. The most important Coḷa inscriptions dealt with in this study are the Veḷāñjeri plates of Parāntaka I,[16] Anbil plates of Sundara Coḷa,[17] Larger Leiden plates of Rājarāja I,[18] Tiruvālaṅgāḍu,[19] Karandai,[20] and Esālam plates[21] of Rājendra I, and the Kanyākumārī lithic inscription of Vīra Rājendra[22] (the Sanskrit portion of which is identical, verse for verse with the Cārāla plates[23] of the same ruler found at Cittoor district in Andhra Pradesh).

Although the bulk of the epigraphical records, starting from the Pallava period and gradually increasing in later periods are in Tamil, the rulers had all along patronized

11. *EI*, vol. XVII, no. 16, pp. 298-304 (Veḷvikuḍi plates).
12. *PCP*, pp. 56-62 (Śrīvaramaṅgalam plates).
13. T.N. Subramaniam, *DCVP*, pp. 13-31.
14. *SII*, vol. III, no. 206, pp. 451-56 (Larger Siṉṉamaṉūr plates).
15. T.N. Subramaniam and P.R. Srinivasan: *SCVP*, pp. 43-52.
16. R. Nagaswamy, *Tiruttani and Veḷañjeri Copper-plates*, Madras, 1979.
17. *EI*, vol. XV, no. 5, pp. 58-66 (Anbil plates).
18. *EI*, vol. XXII, no. 34, pp. 238-54 (Larger Leiden plates).
19. *SII*, vol. III, no. 205, pp. 393-412 (Tiruvālaṅgāḍu plates).
20. K.G. Krishnan, *KTPR*, pp. 69-193.
21. R. Nagaswamy, *ECPR*, pp. 31-51.
22. *TAS*, vol. I, no. 34, pp. 129-49 (Kanyākumārī Inscription).
23. *EI*, vol. XXV, no. 25, pp. 251-65 (Cārāla plates).

Sanskrit learning and the Sanskrit language was freely used in the administrative records and transactions. Even in the records which were written in Tamil, Sanskrit expressions have been freely used, especially for technical terms.

Since the time of scholars of Pallava and Coḷa history like R. Gopalan,[24] C. Minakshi[25] and K.A. Nilakanta Sastri,[26] many new inscriptions have come to light such as the Veḷāñjeri inscription of Aparājita Pallava[27] the Veḷāñjeri plates of Parāntaka I[28] and the Esālam plates of Rājendra Coḷa I.[29] In this work I have paid particular attention to the Sanskrit epigraphs, especially those which have been discovered recently in great detail to show the importance of Sanskrit sources for writing about the socio-cultural history of Tamil Nadu.

Apart from the Sanskrit inscriptions of the Pallava, Coḷa and Pāṇḍya periods, other Sanskrit records of rulers from outside the Tamil country have also been found in Tamil Nadu. To this category belong the epigraphs of the Hoysala king Vīra-Rāmanātha (AD 1254-95), who, after the death of his father Vīra-Someśvara ruled over the southern part of his dominion including the Tamil provinces, while his half-brother, Narasiṁha III ascended the throne at the Hoysala capital Dvārasamudra (modern Halebiḍ in Karnataka). Some of Rāmanātha's Sanskrit records have been found at the Raṅganāthasvāmī temple at Śrīraṅgam (Tiruchirāpaḷḷi district, Tamil Nadu)[30] and Hosūr[31] (Dharmapurī district).

Sanskrit and bi-lingual epigraphs of the illustrious Keraḷa king, Ravivarman Kulaśekhara (AD 1299-1314) who ruled over

24. R. Gopalan, *History of the Pallavas of Kanchi*, Madras, 1928.
25. C. Minakshi, *ASLP*, Madras, 1977.
26. K.A. Nilakanta Sastri, *The Coḷas*, Madras, 1984.
27. R. Nagaswamy, *TVCP*.
28. *Ibid*.
29. R. Nagaswamy, *ECPR*.
30. *SII*, vol. XXIV, no. 274, pp. 294-95; nos. 275 and 276, p. 295.
31. *ARE*, 275 of 1969/70.

the Tamil country for some time during the early years of the fourteenth century AD (and who according to a Tamil inscription found in the Varadarājasvāmi temple, Kāñcīpuram, performed his second coronation in this city on the banks of river Vegavatī in AD 1312-13), have been discovered in different parts of Tamil Nadu like Śrīraṅgam,[32] Kāñcīpuram[33] and Tiruvaḍi (South Arcot district).[34]

It is known that the Kākatiya rule under Pratāparudra II, spread southwards into the Tamil country in the first quarter of the fourteenth century. A bi-lingual epigraph of this ruler dated AD 1316 has been found in Kāñcīpuram.[35]

The data collected from these Sanskrit records of the Hoysalas, Ravivarman Kulaśekhara and Pratāparudra II found in Tamil Nadu have also been included in this work.

These Sanskrit inscriptions provide us with cultural links with various other dynasties of south India and even beyond, with regard to judicial and administrative terms, social institutions and language and literature. The Sanskrit epigraphs of this study reveal that the terms and terminologies which were used all over India were used in this part of the country also. One of the main objectives of this work is to bring out the linkages of Tamil Nadu with the pan-Indian heritage and to show how the Sanskrit inscriptions place Tamil Nadu in the mainstream of Indian historical and cultural inheritance.

This book is divided into seven chapters. The first deals with the political geography of the period under study as gleaned from the Sanskrit inscriptions. For purposes of administration, the kingdoms were divided into small units which were again sub-divided into still smaller ones. The names of these different administrative units as well as the

---

32. *EI*, vol. IV, no. 18, pp. 149-50.
33. *EI*, vol. IV, no. 17, pp. 146-47.
34. *EI*, vol. VIII, no. 2, pp. 8-9.
35. *EI*, vol. VII, no. 18, p. 130.

names of many of the areas in India and also outside the boundaries of India can be gleaned from these Sanskrit epigraphs.

The next chapter deals with the administrative system as it existed in the days of the Pallava, Pāṇḍya and Coḷa rulers. The Sanskrit inscriptions provide an authentic account of the position of the kings of the Tamil country. These rulers, as elsewhere in ancient and medieval India were the heads of government. Monarchy was the system of government which prevailed and the king was the undisputed head of the state.

The duties of the kings can be gleaned from these epigraphs and they correspond to the injunctions given in the *Dharmaśāstras* which clearly outline the responsibilities of the head of state. The main duty of these kings, as elsewhere in the world, was the protection of the subjects and this has been repeatedly emphasised in many of the copper-plate and lithic inscriptions of the period under study. Another important duty of the rulers was safeguarding the *varṇāśramadharma* or the order of the castes. The kings, as the heads of justice and revenue administration enshouldered onerous responsibilities and these can be well understood from the information offered by the Sanskrit epigraphs.

The third chapter discusses in-depth the system of military administration in the Tamil country. The Tamil kings were frequently engaged in wars with the neighbouring powers and this necessitated the maintenance of a strong and efficient army. Many of the inscriptions such as the Kūram, Tiruvālaṅgāḍu and Karandai copper-plates offer a graphic description of the wars waged by these rulers. From these inscriptions, an accurate picture of the military administration of those times can be gleaned. The part played by the kings, generals, infantry, cavalry and elephant corps in the wars, the various weapons of warfare, the nature of wars, the rules and regulations according to which the battles were conducted, and the role of the navy can be gauged from the epigraphs of these kings.

In the next chapter, the aspects of economic life as gleaned from the Sanskrit copper-plate charters and stone inscriptions have been discussed. Agriculture was the main occupation of the people of the Tamil country in the ancient and medieval periods as it was in the rest of India also.

The Tamil kings, realizing the need for making suitable arrangements for the storage of water for purposes of irrigation in case of failure of rains on which the farmers were totally dependent, did their best in this direction. The efforts taken by the rulers to aid the farmers, helped increase the agricultural yield and thereby contributed to the overall economic prosperity of the state.

The temple during the days of the Pallava, Pāṇḍya and Coḷa rulers was a centre of socio-economic activity and the Sanskrit inscriptions reveal that numerous employment opportunities were created by this religious institution for the common people. The existence of guilds of agriculturists and of craftsmen are also known from the bi-lingual inscriptions.

The epigraphs of the period provide plenty of data regarding the social conditions as they existed in the period under study and these are discussed in the fifth chapter of this work, "Social Life." The four-fold division of society usually found in ancient and medieval India, probably existed in the Tamil country during this age. The brāhmaṇas occupied a very respectable position in society and were honoured by the kings as well as by the common people as can be seen from the inscriptions. Information about the queens of the Pallava, Pāṇḍya and Coḷa dynasties and the role played by them are also forthcoming from the inscriptions.

With regard to the field of education and literature, the Sanskrit inscriptions provide a lot of information and these are dealt with in the next chapter titled, "Education and Literature." The rulers gifted lands to brāhmaṇas to live in and these *agrahāras* or brāhmaṇa settlements, along with temples, *maṭhas* and institutions known as *ghaṭikās* were the important centres of learning.

The names of various Vedic scholars and teachers, who were the donees of the land-grants and the subjects they had specialized in such as Vedas, Vedāṅgas, Itihāsas, Purāṇas and the different systems of philosophy are contained in detail in the inscriptions.

The names of many poets of very high calibre who composed the Sanskrit *praśasti*s of the epigraphs, who would otherwise have faded into anonymity are known only from their inscriptions. Their names as well as a few details about their family and their educational achievements are contained at the very end of the inscriptions composed by them. Their compositions in various metres and styles compare favourably with the best in Sanskrit poetry.

Many of the kings of the Tamil country, as revealed by their inscriptions appear to have been very well-read. Their love of poetry and the fine-arts are also revealed by the epigraphs. Kings like Mahendravarman I, Rājasiṁha, Nandivarman Pallavamalla, Rājarāja I and Rājendra I, to mention only a few among a host of rulers of the Tamil country were themselves well-educated and also contributed substantially to the spread of education and learning in their kingdom.

The inscriptions also make it known that apart from the rulers, many officials of the state and even the common people made many endowments for the cause of education.

The last chapter deals with the data collected from the epigraphs with regard to the religious conditions pertaining in the Tamil country in the period of this study under the title, 'Religion and culture'.

The kings of the Tamil country judging from the evidence provided by the Sanskrit inscriptions of the period under study, appear to have been extremely religious. The epigraphs, especially the copper-plate charters reveal that these rulers gave numerous grants of lands (*devadāna*) to various temples, as well as gifts of invaluable jewels and other ornaments made of gold and encrusted with different types of precious stones.

Many of the inscriptions reveal that these ornaments given to the deities were made from the gold accumulated from the various wars waged by these kings.

The inscriptional evidence makes it very clear that the Pallava, Pāṇḍya, and Coḷa rulers followed the Vedic religion. Both Viṣṇu and Śiva were worshipped by them along with other Gods and Goddesses of the Hindu pantheon. Although many of the kings, especially those belonging to the Coḷa dynasty were great devotees of Śiva, they were not intolerant towards the Vaiṣṇavite sect and even constructed shrines of Viṣṇu and donated liberally to the Viṣṇu temples.

These rulers were also tolerant of religions other than their own, such as Jainism and Buddhism as can be seen from their records. Apart from the rulers, high officials of the state and even the common people contributed to the upkeep and maintenance of the temple by making gifts to it.

In this work, while referring to the Tamil portions of the bi-lingual grants or to some Tamil inscriptions which have some bearing on the topics covered, I have specifically stated as such so that there may be no confusion with the Sanskrit part of the bi-lingual records or with the inscriptions which are wholly in Sanskrit. For unavoidable reasons, I have retained the old district names as given in the volumes of the Annual Reports on Epigraphy and South Indian Inscriptions, despite many changes having taken place with regard to the names of the districts in recent years.

1

Political Geography

ALL the kingdoms in ancient India were divided into many administrative units, which were again sub-divided into smaller ones for facilitating the work of the rulers. Territorial divisions such as *rāṣṭra, viṣaya* and *grāma* were found in many of the kingdoms both of north and south India such as the Mauryas and the Guptas as well as the Cāḷukyas and the Viṣṇukuṇḍīs.

The Sanskrit inscriptions of the Pallavas supply the names of a number of provinces (*rāṣṭras*) such as Muṇḍa-rāṣṭra,[1] Karma-rāṣṭra or Karmāṅka-rāṣṭra,[2] Vengo-rāṣṭra,[3] Sendarka-rāṣṭra[4] and Mānyavantara-rāṣṭra.[5] S.S. Ramachandra Murthy has identified Muṇḍa-rāṣṭra with part of the modern Nellore district in Andhra Pradesh,[6] Karma (or Karmāṅka)-rāṣṭra with parts of Guṇṭūr and Prakāsam districts (Andhra Pradesh)[7] and Vengo-rāṣṭra with modern Peda Vegi in the West Godāvarī

1. *EI*, vol. VIII, no. 15, l. 14, p. 162. (Pikira plates); *EI*, vol. XXIV, no. 43, l. 13, p. 302 (Viḷāvaṭṭi plates).
2. *EI*, vol. VIII, no. 23, l. 14, p. 235. (Cendalūr plates); *EI*, vol. XV, no. 11, l. 18, p. 255. (Oṁgoḍu II plates); *EI*, vol. XXIV, no. 18, l. 16, p. 142 (Cura plates).
3. *Ind. Ant.*, vol. V (May, 1876), no. 15, l. 17, p. 155 (Maṅgalūr plates).
4. *SII*, vol. II, no. 73, l. 98, p. 351 (Kaśākuḍi plates).
5. *SII*, vol. I, no. 151, l. 49, p. 150 (Kuram plates).
6. S.S. Ramachandra Murthy, *A Study of Telugu Place-Names*, Delhi, 1985, pp. 102-03.
7. *Ibid.*, pp. 71-76.

district of Andhra Pradesh.[8] Members of the royal family such as the crown-prince were sometimes placed in charge of the provincial governments. According to C. Minakshi,

> The working of the central government, of the provinces and the districts resembled the one projected in the *Arthaśāstra* conforming to the Maurya, Gupta and Sātavāhana type, rather than those prevalent in the Tamil country.[9]

Sub-divisions called the *koṣṭhaka*s (*koṭṭam*s) are also mentioned in the Sanskrit epigraphs. According to D.C. Sircar, a *koṭṭam* was a district within a province.[10] Toṇḍaimaṇḍalam was traditionally believed to have been divided into twenty-four such *koṭṭam*s. It is interesting to note that in Toṇḍaimaṇḍalam the administrative divisions which were divided into *koṭṭams* and existed in the land prior to the Pallavas were maintained even after they came to rule the kingdom.[11] These *koṭṭam*s such as Uṇḍivana-koṣṭhaka (*koṭṭam*),[12] Antah-koṭṭa,[13] and Ūṟṟukkāṭṭu-koṭṭa[14] are some of the names given in the Sanskrit portions of some of the bi-lingual inscriptions.

The names of many of the villages are mentioned in the Sanskrit portions of the bi-lingual grants of the Pallavas. These villages mentioned therein are mostly those granted as *brahmadeya* to the learned brāhmaṇas of the period or as *devadāna* to the temples of their choice.

Many of the *agrahāra*s (called *maṅgalam* or *caturvedi-maṅgalam*) were named after the rulers or the vassal chiefs and officials who granted these villages. Some of the names found in the Sanskrit inscriptions of the Pallavas are

---

8. S.S. Ramachandra Murthy, *A Study of Telugu Place-Names*, Delhi, 1985, pp. 71-76.
9. C. Minakshi, *ASLP*, p. 140.
10. D.C. Sircar, *Indian Epigraphical Glossary*, Delhi, 1966, p. 161.
11. C. Minakshi, *op. cit.*, p. 46.
12. Kaśākuḍi plates, *op. cit.*, I.98, p. 351.
13. R. Nagaswamy, *TVCP*, *Veḷāñjeri plates of Aparājita*, plate III, p. 2.
14. Kuram plates, *op. cit.*, I.49 p. 150.

Parameśvaramaṅgalam,[15] Ekadhīramaṅgalam,[16] Udayacandramaṅgalam,[17] Dayāmukhamaṅgalam,[18] Nayadhīramaṅgalam,[19] Kumaraḍimaṅgalam[20] and Meliṟuñjeru.[21] Names like Siṁhaviṣṇu-caturvedimaṅgalam, Avaninārāyaṇa caturvedimaṅgalam, Pallavanārāyaṇa-caturvedimaṅgalam, Uttarameru-caturvedimaṅgalam, Rājamalla-caturvedimaṅgalam and Aparājita-caturvedimaṅgalam are found in numerous Tamil inscriptions.

With regard to the period of the Coḷas, some information is forthcoming from the Sanskrit inscriptions about the territorial divisions which existed in the Tamil country at that time. As in most cases, the village was the smallest unit of government. Since most of the Sanskrit inscriptions of the Coḷas mention only the grant of land to brāhmaṇas, the names of many of the *agrahāra*s (called *maṅgalam*s or *caturvedimaṅgalams*) are given therein. Some of these are as follows: Karuṇākaramaṅgalam,[22] Rājarāja-caturvedimaṅgalam,[23] Siṁhaḷāntaka-caturvedimaṅgalam,[24] Nityavinoda-caturvedimaṅgalam,[25] and Tribhuvanamahādevī-caturvedimaṅgalam.[26] In many cases these new *agrahāra*s were created by the kings by clubbing together many villages. Other names such as Keraḷāntaka-caturvedimaṅgalam, Rājāśraya-caturvedimaṅgalam, Jayamkoṇḍacoḷa-caturvedimaṅgalam, Muḍikoṇḍacoḷa-caturvedimaṅgalam and Rājādhirāja-caturvedimaṅgalam are forthcoming from a large number of Tamil epigraphs.

---

15. Kuram plates, *op. cit.*, I.49 p. 150.
16. Kaśākuḍi plates, *op. cit.*, p. 351.
17. *SII*, vol. II, no. 74, p. 368 (Udayendiram plates).
18. *SII*, vol. II, no. 99, p. 520 (Taṇḍantoṭṭam plates).
19. *EI*, vol. XXXVI, no. 20, p. 153 (Pullūr plates).
20. N. Ramesan: *KPPN*, p. 201.
21. R. Nagaswamy, *TVCP*, *op. cit.*
22. *EI*, vol. XV, no. 5, v. 39, p. 63 (Anbil plates).
23. R. Nagaswamy, *ECPR*, v. 21, p. 32.
24. Tiruvālaṅgāḍu plates, *op. cit.*, v. 130, p. 401.
25. *Ibid.*, v. 131, p. 401.
26. K.G. Krishnan, *KTPR*, v. 67, p. 75.

Nāḍu

Territorial divisions called the *nāḍu* are found in many of the Coḷa records. According to Y. Subbarayalu, the *nāḍu* (with its synonym, *kūṟṟam*), was an important limb of the administrative system of the Coḷas.[27] These *nāḍu*s were composed of smaller villages. The fertility and favourable irrigation conditions in a *nāḍu*, it seems, determined the number of villages it contained.[28] The Sanskrit portion of the Esālam charter of Rājendra I states that he gave two villages named Nannāḍu and Erpākkam in Panaiyūrnāḍu to a temple of Lord Śiva.[29]

Vaḷanāḍu

The territorial division called the *vaḷanāḍu* is mentioned in many of the inscriptions of the Coḷas. Although it is mainly in the Tamil inscriptions that this term regularly occurs, a few of the Sanskrit portions of the bi-lingual charters also mention this same Tamil term. According to Y. Subbarayalu, the *vaḷanāḍu* as a territorial element was peculiar and confined to Coḷa times and Coḷa territory.[30] He has suggested that since the *nāḍu*s were too small in area to serve as viable administrative units, the *vaḷanāḍu*s were created by Rājarāja I.[31]

Many of the inscriptions which mention the *vaḷanāḍu*s, reveal that they were named after one or the other of the surnames of the rulers or of their consorts. The Larger Leiden plates of Rājarāja I (AD 1006) mention that Nāgapaṭṭinam, where the Cūḷāmaṇivihāra was built was situated in a division called Paṭṭanakūṟṟam which was included in a big group of districts named Kṣatriyaśikhāmaṇi-vaḷanāḍu.[32] The Karandai inscription also mentions two more of these territorial divisions, namely,

27. Y. Subbarayalu: *PGCC*, p. 19.
28. *Ibid.*, p. 22.
29. R. Nagaswamy, *ECPR*, v. 7, p. 33.
30. Y. Subbarayalu, *PGCC*, p. 56.
31. *Ibid.*, p. 67.
32. *EI*, vol. XXII, no. 34, ll. 76-77, p. 241 (Larger Leiden plates).

Vīracoḷa-vaḷanāḍu and Nityavinoda-vaḷanāḍu in connection with the conferment of land-grants to learned brāhmaṇas by Rājendra I.[33]

Although these are the few names provided by the Sanskrit inscriptions, a number of the names of such *valanāḍus* such as Keraḷāntaka-vaḷanāḍu, Pāṇḍikulanāśani-vaḷanāḍu, Rājāśraya-vaḷanāḍu, and Uttamacoḷa-vaḷanāḍu, situated in the Coḷa country are found in many Tamil epigraphs.

Maṇḍalam

The *maṇḍalam* or province was the largest unit of administration and was above the *vaḷanāḍu*. The Coḷa empire at the height of its glory consisted of a number of such *maṇḍalams*. The Tamil inscriptions mention the names of *maṇḍalams* such as Jayamkoṇḍa-coḷamaṇḍalam, Rājarājamaṇḍalam, Nigariḻi-coḷamaṇḍalam, and Mummaḍi-coḷamaṇḍalam. The Tiruvālaṅgāḍu plates of the 6th year of Rājendra I (AD 1018), mention that in his reign a land-grant was made to a Śiva temple in Purāṇagrāma (Paḻayaṉūr in Tamil), which was the ornament of Jayamkoṇḍa-coḷamaṇḍalam.[34] Similarly, the Esālam plates also mention that the *agrahāra* named Rājarājacaturvedimaṅgalam was situated in Jayamkoṇḍa-coḷamaṇḍalam.[35]

A study of the inscriptions of the Pāṇḍyas reveals that their territorial-divisions were similar to those found in the Pallava and Coḷa countries such as *kūṟṟam*, *vaḷanāḍu* and *nāḍu* and the villages (*grāmam*) usually ending with the suffix *maṅgalam*, *kuḍi* or *ūr*. The term *nāḍu* was used as equivalent to that of the *rāṣṭra* as seen from the Larger Siṉṉamaṉūr plates (*c.* AD 926-27), in which the place Vaḍa-Kaḷavaḷi-rāṣṭra mentioned in the Sanskrit section is called as Vaḍa-Kaḷavaḷi-nāḍu in the Tamil section.[36]

33. K.G. Krishnan, *KTPR*, v. 68, p. 75.
34. Tiruvālaṅgāḍu plates, *op. cit.*, v. 128, p. 401.
35. R. Nagaswamy, *ECPR*, v. 21, p. 32.
36. *SII*, vol. III, no. 206, v. 27, p. 453 and l. 143, p. 456; see K.A. Nilakanta Sastri, *The Pandyan Kingdom (From the Earliest Times to the Sixteenth Century)*, Madras, 1972, pp. 77-78.

Some of the names of the *agrahāras* mentioned in the Sanskrit inscriptions of the Pāṇḍyas are Maṇiyāci renamed as Tiśaiccuḍarmaṅgalam, Śrīvallabhamaṅgalam, Śrīmaṅgalam, Śrīvaramaṅgalam and Śāsanamaṅgalam.

Capital Cities

The Sanskrit epigraphs of the period of this study reveal the names of the capital cities of the ruling powers of these periods.

KĀÑCĪPURAM

Among all the important cities in the Tamil country, Kāñcīpuram, the capital city of the Pallavas stands out as one of the most important ones in the political and cultural fields. The Sanskrit inscriptions refer to Kāñcīpuram very often. Many of the early Pallava charters of the fourth-sixth centuries AD in Prākṛt and in Sanskrit such as the Mayidavolu,[37] Hīrahaḍagalli,[38] Vesanta,[39] Udayendiram (I)[40] and the Cendalūr[41] plates were issued by the kings of this dynasty from Kāñcīpuram. This city continued to be an important one in the subsequent periods also. The Esālam copper-plate grant states that Rājendra Coḷa I, while residing at Kāñcīpuram in the palace (*mahāśāla*), gifted wealth to brāhmaṇas.[42] This city is described here as "the ornament of the whole world" (*sakalabhūvanitāvibhūṣām*).

The Sanskrit portions of some of the Pallava and the Coḷa bi-lingual charters such as the Velūrpaḷaiyam,[43] Madras Museum plates of Uttama Coḷa[44] and the Larger Leiden plates[45]

37. *EI*, vol. VI, no. 8, l. 1, p. 86 (Mayidavolu plates).
38. *EI*, vol. I, no. 1, l. 1, p. 5 (Hīrahaḍagalli plates).
39. N. Ramesan, *VGPS*, I.1, p. 95.
40. *EI*, vol. III, no. 23, l. 1, p. 145 (Udayendiram I plates).
41. *EI*, vol. VIII, no. 23, l. 1, p. 234 (Cendalūr plates).
42. R. Nagaswamy, *ECPR*, v. 24, p. 33.
43. *SII*, vol. II, no. 98, v. 31, p. 510 (Velūrpāḷaiyam plates).
44. *SII*, vol. III, no. 128, p. 269 (Madras Museum plates of Uttama Coḷa).
45. *EI*, vol. XXII, no. 34, vv. 45-48, p. 243 (Larger Leiden plates).

reveal the names of many artisans such as carpenters, weavers and painters who hailed from Kāñcīpuram (called in Tamil as Kaccippeḍu), thus revealing Kāñcīpuram to be a great cultural centre also.

Some of the rulers took special pride in their association with this city. One of the titles of Narasiṁhavarman II (Rājasiṁha), was *srī kāñcī-mahāmaṇiḥ* (the great jewel of Kāñcī).[46] The Kāḍava chieftain Kopperuñjiṅga bore the title *kāñcīpura-kānta* (protector of Kāñcīpuram).[47]

TAÑJĀVŪR

Tañjāvūr was the capital of the line of the imperial Coḷas from the time of Vijayālaya, who captured this city from the Muttaraiyar chieftains in the ninth century AD, up to the twelfth century AD when Rājendra I made Gangaikoṇḍacoḷapuram his capital-city. The Tiruvālaṅgāḍu plates in a very poetic manner, state that Vijayālaya took possession of Tañcāpuri (Tañjāvūr) just as he would seize (by the hand), his own wife (*ātma-vadhūm=iv=āsau-jagrāha*).[48] This verse also describes Tañjāvūr as being pituresque to the sight and as beautiful as Alakā (*sadṛṅ=vicitrām=alakābhirāmām*), and which (by its high turrets) had reached the sky (*vyāptāmbarām*). In some Tamil inscriptions, Vijayālaya is mentioned as *Tañjai-koṇḍa-Parakesari* (*Parakesari*, the captor of Tañjāvūr). The Kanyākumārī inscription also states that Vijayālaya built, in the Coḷa country a town named Tañcāpurī which had all the advantages of a new city.[49] Prior to the capture of this city by this king, Uraiyūr, on the banks of the Kāverī was the ancient capital of this dynasty.

The Esālam plates of Rājendra Coḷa I refer to this city as Tañjānagarī in connection with the construction here of the great Śiva temple (Rājarājeśvaram) by Rājarāja I.[50]

46. *SII*, vol. I, no. 25, p. 15.
47. *SII*, vol. XII, no. 120, p. 58.
48. Tiruvālaṅgāḍu plates, *op. cit.*, v. 45, p. 395.
49. *TAS*, vol. I, no. 34, v. 54, p. 142 (Kanyākumārī inscription).
50. R. Nagaswamy: *ECPR*, v. 13, p. 32.

GAṄGAIKOṆḌACOḶAPURAM

It was Rājendra I, the son and successor of Rājarāja I and who himself bore the title Gaṅgaikoṇḍacoḷa, on account of his having brought the waters of the river Gaṅgā to the Coḷa country after a campaign to the north, who established a new capital named Gaṅgaikoṇḍacoḷapuram also mentioned in some records as Gaṅgāpurī. This city, was probably built to commemorate this event and was the capital of this dynasty for almost two-hundred and fifty years. The Tiruvālaṅgāḍu plates poetically mention that after his conquests, Rājendra I "entered his own (capital) town, which, by its prosperity, despised all the merits of the abode of the Gods."[51] The Esālam plates state that Rājendra I brought the pure water of the Gaṅgā to his country and established the city Gaṅgaikoṇḍacoḷapuram after his name.[52]

MADURAI

With regard to the period of the Pāṇḍyas, whose ancient capital was the famous city of Madurai, the Sanskrit inscriptions of this dynasty do not offer any description. However, some Coḷa records mention the titles of many of the Coḷa monarchs as *maduraikoṇḍa* (one who conquered Madurai) and *madurāntakaḥ* (the destroyer of Madurai) in connection with their victory over the Pāṇḍya rulers and the capture of their capital-city.

In addition to these flourishing capital cities, there must also have existed other big cities which were the headquarters of petty chieftains and which must have been important centres both from the political and cultural point of view. The Sanskrit inscriptions of this study mention a few of these.

The Udayendiram plates of Nandivarman Pallavamalla (*c.* AD 752), mention the city of Vilvala, ruled by Udayacandra, a vassal of this king.[53] R. Gopalan has identified this place with

51. Tiruvālaṅgāḍu plates, *op. cit.*, v. 12, p. 393.
52. R. Nagaswamy, *op. cit.*, vs. 17-18, p. 32.
53. Udayendiram plates, *op. cit.*, no. 74, l. 37, p. 367.

Vilvaḷanagara-viḻḻivalam in Chingleput district.[54] The Pullūr inscription (*c.* AD 764-65), also of the same ruler mentions Avanicandra Yuvarāja, the lord of Vilvalapura.[55] It is likely that this Vilvalapura was the same as Vilvala of the Udayendiram plates and that Avanicandra was the son of Udayacandra.[56]

A Sanskrit inscription of a feudatory of the Coḷas, Bhūti Vikrama Kesari, mentions that this chieftain lived in a palace on a hill in the city of Koḍumbāḷur.[57] Although no information about this city is forthcoming from the inscriptions of this period, it is possible that this city was an important one as there existed strong bonds of friendship between the Coḷa rulers and the Koḍumbāḷur chiefs. Vikrama Kesari himself was the son of a Coḷa princess named Anupamā who was married to a Koḍumbāḷūr chieftain.[58]

Port Cities

MĀMALLAPURAM

Māmallapuram, named after the title *māmalla* borne by Narasimhavarman I, was the main sea-port during the Pallava period. The celebrated Vaiṣṇava saint, Tirumaṅgai Āḻvār has also mentioned that Māmallapuram was a busy port, stating that ships with elephants and gems came to that place.[59] However, it is diappointing to note that none of the Sanskrit inscriptions of the period of this study make any mention of Māmallapuram as a busy port city although numerous inscriptions of the Pallavas have been found there. A bi-lingual

---

54. R. Gopalan, *History of the Pallavas of Kanchi*, Madras, 1928, p. 124.
55. Pullūr plates, *op. cit.*, no., 20, l. 12, p. 152.
56. M.S. Govindasamy, *The Role of Feudatories in Pallava History*, Annamalainagar, 1965, p. 143.
57. K.A. Nilakanta Sastri, "The Koḍumbāḷur Inscription of Vikrama-Kesari" *JOR*, vol. VII, v. 6, p. 9.
58. *Ibid.*, v. 3.
59. *Nalāyira Divya Prabhandam*, ed. K. Venkatasami Reddiyar, Madras, 1981, *Periya Tirumoḷi; Kaḍanmallai hymns*, 6.

inscription of the Kāḍava ruler, Kopperuñjiṅga mentions one of his birudas *mallāpuri-vallabha* (friend of Mallāpuri), thus revealing his connections with this port town.[60]

NĀGAPAṬṬINAM

Nāgapaṭṭinam also appears to have been a busy port even during the Pallava period. Rājasiṁha constructed a Buddha *vihāra* at Nāgapaṭṭinam at the request of the Chinese emperor for the use of the Buddhist community visiting the place for commercial purposes.[61]

The Larger Leiden plates mention that the Śailendra ruler, Māravijayottuṅgavarman built a Buddhist *vihāra* at Nāgapaṭṭinam.[62] According to K.V. Raman, Nāgapaṭṭinam was the first port on the mainland touched by vessels from the east bound for south India as mentioned from Itsing's account and this must have been one of the reasons for the construction of the *vihāra* at Nāgapaṭṭinam.[63]

Many of the Sanskrit inscriptions, especially of the Coḷas, give the names of the countries conquered by them during their numerous campaigns and also some of the important cities therein, and an identification of these places is possible.

VĀTĀPI

Vātāpi, now known as Bādāmī (Bījāpur district of Karnataka) was the capital city of the Cāḷukyas and finds mention in some Pallava epigraphs. An inscription of Narasiṁhavarman I (*c.* AD 642), records his victory over Vātāpi and the construction of a pillar of victory (*dvajasthambha*) by him at that place.[64] His destruction of Vātāpi is also mentioned in other Pallava inscriptions such as the Kūram plates of Parameśvaravarman

60. *SII*, vol. XII, no. 120, p. 58.
61. C. Minakshi, *ASLP*, p. 24.
62. Larger Leiden plates, *op. cit.*, 173-86, pp. 241-42.
63. K.V. Raman, "Religious Trends during Rajaraja's Reign" from *Rajaraja, The Great* (*Seminar Proceedings*), Bombay, 1987, p. 106.
64. *SII*, vol. XI, no. 1, p. 1.

I (seventh century AD),[65] Udayendiram plates (*c.* AD 752)[66] and Kaśākuḍi[67] plates (*c.* AD 753-54) of Nandivarman Pallavamalla.

MĀNYAKHEṬA

The frequent wars of the Coḷas with the Cāḷukyas are mentioned in many of their Sanskrit and Tamil inscriptions and their famous city of Mānyakheṭa (Malkhed, near Gulbargā in Karnataka) which had once been the capital of the Rāṣṭrakūṭas is mentioned therein. The Karandai Tamil Saṅgam plates of the 8th regnal year of Rājendra I (AD 1021), mention that Rājendra I captured and destroyed Mānyakheṭa.[68] The Kanyākumārī inscription, dated in the 7th regnal year of Vīra-Rājendra (AD 1069), also mentions that Rājendra I made Mānyakheṭa "a playground for his armies."[69] According to K.A. Nilakanta Sastri, soon after this invasion, the Cāḷukyas transferred their capital to Kalyāṇī or Kalyāṇapura, 48 miles to the north-east of Malkhed.[70] The Kanyākumārī record also mentions that Rājādhirāja, the son of Rājendra I set fire to Kalyāṇapura after conquering its overlords.[71]

It is known from a Tamil inscription that after the sack of Kalyāṇapura, Rājādhirāja assumed the title of Vijayarājendra and performed a *vīrābhiṣeka* (coronation of victor) in the city.[72] A fine image of a *dvārapālaka* which used to be at the entrance to the Dārāsuram temple (Tañjāvūr district) and has since been removed to the Tanjavur Art Gallery bears the Tamil inscription: "the *dvārapālaka* brought by Uḍayār Śrī Vijayarājendradeva after burning Kalyāṇapuram."[73]

65. Kūram plates, *op. cit.*, no. 151, l. 17, p. 148.
66. Udayendiram plates, *op. cit.*, l. 14, p. 366.
67. Kaśākuḍi plates, *op. cit.*, v. 22, p. 349.
68. K.G. Krishnan, *KTPR*, vv. 51-55, pp. 73-74.
69. Kanyākumārī inscription, *op. cit.*, v. 70, pp. 145-46.
70. K.A. Nilakanta Sastri, *The Coḷas*, Madras, 1984, p. 198.
71. Kanyākumārī inscription, *op. cit.*, pp. 146-47.
72. *ARE*, 244 of 1925.
73. K.A. Nilakanta Sastri, *A History of South India*, Madras, 1988, p. 186.

Keraḷa

The region of Keraḷa has often been mentioned in the Sanskrit inscriptions of the Coḷas, once again in the context of the wars waged by the Coḷa rulers against the kings of this area. The Karandai copper-plate inscription mentions that Parāntaka I conquered Keraḷa.[74] These plates also mention that Rājarāja I conquered the Keraḷa country[75] and this fact is mentioned in the Tiruvālaṅgāḍu plates also.[76] Rājendra I, too has been glorified as conquering Keraḷa.[77]

Utkala and Kaliṅga

These areas which correspond to the region of Orissa have been mentioned in the Kanyākumārī[78] and the Karandai[79] epigraphs as having been conquered by Rājendra I.

Overseas Contacts

The Sanskrit inscriptions, especially those of the Coḷas, contain some names of countries overseas. It is obvious that these rulers had established trade-contacts with and also conquered many of the countries outside the limits of India.

The Vāyalūr inscription of Rājasiṁha states, "may he exercise the royal prerogative and take up the vow of administering his subjects up to the extremities of his kingdom, as even to include the thousand islands" (*dvīpalakṣam*).[80] H. Krishna Sastri has suggested that this could perhaps be a reference to the Lakṣadvīp islands.[81]

SRI LANKA

One of the places outside the shores of India mentioned most often in the Sanskrit inscriptions is Sri Lanka. Some Pallava

74. K.G. Krishnan, *KTPR*, v. 17, p. 70.
75. *Ibid.*, v. 27, p. 71.
76. Tiruvālaṅgāḍu plates, *op. cit.*, v. 31, p. 241.
77. *Ibid.*, v. 83, p. 398.
78. Kanyākumārī inscription, *op. cit.*, v. 71, p. 146.
79. K.G. Krishnan, *KTPR*, v. 27, p. 71.
80. *EI*, vol. XVIII, no. 18, pp. 145-52 (Vāyalūr Pillar inscription).
81. *Ibid.*, p. 152.

kings are known to have conquered Laṅkā.[82] The epigraphs of the Coḷas such as the Larger Leiden,[83] Tiruvālaṅgāḍu,[84] and Karandai plates[85] also mention the conquest of the Siṁhaḷa kings by Parāntaka I, Rājarāja I and Rājendra I.

KĀMBOJA

There is only one reference to Kāmboja (modern-day Kampuchea) in the Sanskrit inscriptions. The Karandai record mentions that the king of Kāmboja (*Kāmbhojarāja*) sent Rājendra I a chariot in order to win his friendship.

KAṬĀHA

Kaṭāha, called as Kaḍāram in Tamil, the Sanskrit name given to Malaysia, is mentioned in the Larger Leiden plates in which Rājarāja I is mentioned as having permitted the construction of a *vihāra* in Nāgapaṭṭinam by Śrī Māravijayottuṅgavarman, of the Śailendra dynasty (*śailendra-vaṁśa-saṁbhūtena*), who was the lord of Śrī Vijaya (*śrīviṣayādhipati*), and who was conducting the rule of Kaṭāka (*kaṭāh-ādhipatyam=ātanvata*).[87] Rājendra I's conquest of Kaṭāha also finds mention in a few Coḷa inscriptions.[88]

---

82. Kaśākuḍi plates, *op. cit.*, vv. 20 and 22, p. 349.
83. Larger Leiden plates, *op. cit.*, v. 31, p. 241.
84. Tiruvālaṅgāḍu plates, *op. cit.*, v. 80, p. 421.
85. K.G. Krishnan, *KTPR*, v. 17, p. 70.
86. *Ibid.*, v. 48, p. 73.
87. Larger Leiden plates, *op. cit.*, l. 180, p. 242.
88. Tiruvālaṅgāḍu plates, *op. cit.*, v. 123, p. 400; Kanyākumārī plates, *op. cit.*, v. 72, p. 146; K.G. Krishnan, *KTPR*, v. 62, p. 74.

2

Administration (Civil)

THE Sanskrit inscriptions of the Pallavas, Coḷas and Pāṇḍyas are invaluable for studying about the manner in which the administration of the state was conducted during these periods in the Tamil country. A systematic analysis of their administrative institutions is possible only through an in-depth study of their copper-plate grants and lithic inscriptions. A detailed picture regarding the position of the king, the manifold duties and responsibilities of the ruler, the names and duties of the ministers and various other officials associated with the administrative machinery, systems of revenue and expenditure, judicial and military administration can be gleaned from these epigraphs.

The King

Monarchy was the most common form of government in ancient and medieval India, although other forms of government such as republics were also known. In the Tamil country, starting from the Saṅgam period, no other form of government other than monarchy was known.

The works on political thought written in ancient India such as the *Arthaśāstra* of Kauṭilya have stated that the state consists of seven limbs (*saptāṅga*) of which the king is the most important one.[1] The *Kuraḷ*, a work of the Saṅgam period, has underlined the importance of the king by stating that the army,

1. *KA*, 6, 1, 1.

subjects, food, ministers, allies and forts are all subject to the ruler.[2]

It is known from the Saṅgam works that the king was the highest authority in the land and was the pivot of administration. The exalted position of the king was maintained during the succeeding periods in the history of the Tamil country also as can be seen from the epigraphs of the Pallavas, Coḷas and the Pāṇḍyas.

Qualities of a King

The *Dharmaśāstras* give a good guideline as to the qualities which a king was supposed to possess. The *Manusmṛti* clearly states that a king should possess qualities such as wisdom, enthusiasm, personal ability, modesty and humility.[3] The *Arthaśāstra* mentions a very long list of such qualities, among them being intelligence, seeking the advice of elders, piety, truthfulness and bravery.[4] The *Kuraḷ*, which devotes an entire chapter to the subject of kingship, also stresses these virtues which a king was to possess.[5] In a similar manner, these texts make a mention of many vices which the rulers were to avoid cultivating, namely, anger, lust, drunkenness and gambling and urged them to become self-possessed.

The Sanskrit inscriptions of the period of this study truly reflect the high ideals enshrined in this tradition as given by the ancient works. These epigraphs, either directly or indirectly, refer to these qualities possessed by the kings. Almost all the records praise the Pallava, Pāṇḍya and Coḷa rulers as being righteous, well-educated, truthful and who ruled with the welfare of their subjects as their main aim.

An inscription of Rājasiṁha describes the kings born in the Pallava race as those who spoke the truth (*satyavācāṁ*),

---

2. *The Kuraḷ*, (tr. and ed.) by P.S. Sundaram, New Delhi, 1990, Ch. 39, v. 382.
3. *MS*, Ch. VII. 7.
4. *KA*, 6, 1, 3.
5. *Kuraḷ*, *op. cit.*, Ch. 39.

who assiduously honoured the aged (*vṛddhasevāparāṇām*), who forcibly subdued lust and the other internal enemies (*kāmādy-antascarā-ri-prasabha-vijayinām*), who were firm (*dhirāṇām*), mighty (*ūrjitānām*) and endowed with polity and modesty (*naya-vinayavatām= pallavānān=nṛpāṇām*).[6]

Although these descriptions of the rulers as given by the poets might be exaggerated versions, yet it can be seen that these kings were expected, as stated in the *Dharmaśāstras*, to possess and develop certain qualities which would help them in discharging their duties in a proper manner.

Divine Origin

The law-givers of ancient India have elevated the status of the king to that of God, The *Manusmṛti*[7] and the *Arthaśāstra*[8] have laid stress on the divine origin of the ruler. In the Tamil country also, the kings of the Pallava, Pāṇḍya and Coḷa dynasties assigned a divine origin to their race. This was perhaps done to increase the prestige of the ruler in the eyes of the people and also because such a theory was advocated in the ancient law-books.

The Pallava inscriptions, especially the copper-plate grants[9] describe the divine origin of the Pallava race. The Vāyalūr lithic inscription[10] also gives details about the mythical progenitors of the Pallava dynasty. The inscriptions mention Lord Viṣṇu, Brahmā, Aṅgiras, Bṛhaspati, Saṁyu, Bharadvāja, Droṇa and Aśvatthāman as their ancestors. To Aśvatthāman was born Pallava, from whom the race of the Pallavas began.

---

6. *SII*, vol. I, no. 24, v. 4, p. 12.
7. *MS*, VII. 4-8.
8. *KA*, I.13, 10.
9. *SII*, vol. I, no. 151, l. 9, p. 148 (Kūram plates); *SII*, vol. II, no. 73, vv. 10-19, p. 347 (Kaśākuḍi plates); *SII*, vol. II, No. 74, l. 8, p. 366 (Udayendiram plates); *EI*, vol. XVIII, no. 14, v. 3, p. 120 (Paṭṭa-ttāḷmaṅgalam plates); *SII*, vol. II, no. 98, v. 3, p. 507 (Velūrpāḷaiyam plates); *EI*, vol. XVIII, no. 2, vv. 2-6, pp. 9-10 (Bāhūr plates).
10. *EI*, vol. XVIII, no. 18, ll. 1-2, p. 150 (Vāyalūr Pillar inscription).

The details given in these inscriptions regarding this divine origin are beautifully sculptured in a panel running around the inner-courtyard of the Vaikuṇṭhaperumāḷ temple at Kāñcīpuram. This series of historical sculptures depicts all the mythical ancestors of the Pallavas up to the birth of the first Pallava, after which all the historical details regarding the Pallava dynasty are given.

According to S. Sankaranarayanan, Rājasiṁha was probably the first to introduce to south India a clear-cut theory of divinity of the ruling king.[11] In an epigraph from the Kailāśanātha temple, Kāñcīpuram, he is described as Puruṣottama (the best male, i.e., Lord Viṣṇu) in incarnation.[12]

With regard to the race of the Pāṇḍyas, their inscriptions reveal that these rulers prided themselves as belonging to the lunar race with the moon as their divine ancestor.[13] The inscriptions refer to the kings of this dynasty by epithets such as *śaśikula-tilakaḥ* (the ornament of the lunar race), *śaśikula bhūṣaṇaḥ* (the jewel of the lunar race) and *candrakula-pradīpaḥ* (light of the lunar race).

In a similar manner, the Coḷa rulers also adopted a mythical ancestry and claimed to belong to the Solar dynasty with the Sun as their ancestor as revealed by their inscriptions.[14]

These epigraphs refer to the kings of the Coḷa dynasty by epithets such as *ravivaṁśa-dīpaḥ* (the light of the Solar race), *ravikula-tilakaḥ* (the ornament of the Solar race), *ravivaṁśa-śikhāmaṇiḥ* (the head-jewel of the Solar dynasty) and *ravikula-śekharaḥ* (the head of the Solar family).

---

11. S. Sankaranarayanan, "A Pallava Inscriptional Poem in Sanskrit," *ALB*, vol. LV, 1991, pp. 84-85.
12. *Ibid.*, pp. 81-85.
13. *EI*, vol. XVII, no. 16, v. 4, p. 298 (Veḷvikuḍi plates); *SII*, vol. III, no. 206, l.3, pp. 462-63. (Smaller Siṉṉamaṉūr plates); *PCP*; Śrīvara-maṅgalam plates of Neḍuñjaḍaiyan, v. 4, pp. 56-57.
14. *EI*, vol. XV, no. 5, vv. 5-7, p. 59 (Anbil plates); *EI*, vol. XXII, no. 34, v. 3, p. 238 (Larger Leiden plates); *SII*, vol. III, no. 205, v. 4, p. 393 (Tiruvālaṅgāḍu plates); K.G. Krishnan: *KTPR*, v. 2, p. 69.

Duties of the Kings

The kings, as the sole head of the territories over which they ruled, have been assigned duties of various types, some of paramount importance and others secondary in nature. The most important duty of kings has always been the protection of their people and their territories from external invasions so as to maintain peace and stability within their state. The *Manusmṛti*, which lays down the duties of the different *varṇas*, states explicitly that the highest duty of the kṣatriya is the protection of his subjects.[15] The *Arthaśāstra* also states that "the duty of a ruler consists in protecting his subjects according to the law."[16]

The Sanskrit epigraphs of the period under study reveal that the kings of the Tamil country considered it as their primary duty to ensure the protection of their subjects. Many of the early Pallava charters[17] refer to the kings of this dynasty as the fifth *lokapāla*, thus putting them on par with the four *lokapāla*s or guardians of the four cardinal points of the compass, namely Indra of the East, Yama of the South, Varuṇa of the West and Kubera of the North, known in Indian mythology.

Protection of the subjects (*prajā pālana*) is repeatedly referred to in many of the early Pallava copper-plates as one of the duties of the rulers.[18]

Many of the titles (*biruda*s) of these kings found in their Sanskrit epigraphs show their commitment towards ensuring the security and protection of their subjects. The *biruda*s of Rājasiṁha such as *śrī āśrayāṅkaraḥ* (the granter of safety), *śrī*

---

15. *MS*, Ch.VII.2.
16. *KA*, 3, 1, 41.
17. *Ind. Ant.* (February 1876), p. 51 (Uruvapaḷḷi plates); *EI*, vol. XXXVIII, no. 18, p. 104 (Sakrepaṭṇa plates); *EI*, vol. XV, no. 11, p. 254 (Oṁgoḍu II plates), *EI*, vol. XXIV, no. 18, p. 141 (Cura plates); *EI*, vol. VIII, no. 15, p. 161 (Pikira plates).
18. Uruvapaḷḷi plates, *op. cit.*, p. 51; Sakrepaṭṇa plates, *op. cit.*, p. 104; Pikira plates, *op. cit.*, p. 161; Oṁgoḍu II plates, *op. cit.*, p. 254; *EI*, vol. XXIV, no. 43, p. 301, (Viḷvaṭṭi plates).

rakṣāmaṇiḥ (the jewel of protection), and *śrī deśavardhanaḥ* (the bestower of prosperity on his country) reveal the commitment of this king towards the protection and welfare of his country and his people.[19]

Nandivarman Pallavamalla is described as *śaraṇyaḥ prajānām* (the refuge of his subjects) in the Udayendiram copper-plates.[20] The Taṇḍantoṭṭam plates of the same ruler (*c.* AD 789), poetically state that "wise men praise him as Hari (Viṣṇu) because he offers protection to all living beings" (*yaḥ khalu narakānt-ātma hari-iti bahu manyate vibudaiḥ*).[21]

Among the Pāṇḍyan rulers, Jaṭila Parāntaka Neḍunjaḍaiyan is described in the Veḷvikuḍi copper-plate grant (*c.* AD 770), as "giving to the subjects who sought refuge in him, his promise of protection" (*abhayam śaraṇāgata prajābhyaḥ*).[22]

Paternal Aspect of Kingship

It was another important duty for the kings to care for their subjects as a father. The Mauryan ruler Aśoka has stated in his edicts that all men were his children.[23] Kālidāsa, in his *Raghuvaṁśa* also echoes a similar sentiment.[24]

That this concept was also respected in the Tamil country can be seen from the information provided by the Veḷāñjeri copper-plate inscription of Parāntaka Coḷa I which states that the subjects treated him as their parent (*praṇayinaḥ pitaram = prajās-ca*).[25] This ruler is described in the Tiruvālaṅgāḍu copper-plates as "the embodiment of the boundless joy of his subjects" (*ānanda-sandoha iva prajānān=tadīya=sūnus=tanumān=babhūva*).[26]

---

19. *SII*, vol. I, no. 25, pp. 14-18.
20. Udayendiram plates, *op. cit.*, v. 4, p. 367.
21. *SII*, vol. II, no. 99, v. 8, p. 520 (Taṇḍantoṭṭam plates).
22. *EI*, vol. XVII, no. 16, v. 16, p. 299 (Veḷvikuḍi plates).
23. D.C. Sircar, *Inscriptions of Aśoka*, Delhi, 1975, p. 54.
24. Venkataraghavacharya, (ed.), *Raghuvaṁśa*, Madras, 1952, I. 24.
25. R. Nagaswamy, *TVCP*, *Veḷāñjeri plates of Parāntaka I*, v. 13, plate II, p. 2.
26. Tiruvālaṅgāḍu plates, *op. cit.*, v. 50, p. 396.

Kings as Upholders of Dharma

The works on polity written in ancient India emphasize that one of the main aims of the rulers was the promotion of *dharma*. The rulers of the Tamil country seemed very concerned about administering their kingdoms according to the rules laid down in the law-books, especially that of Manu and prided themselves on upholding *dharma*, as can be gleaned from some of their Sanskrit inscriptions.

Many of the rulers of the Tamil country took great pride in comparing themselves with Manu. An inscription of Mahendravarman I describes this king as "one who resembled Manu in his manner of ruling" (*manuprakhyo rājye*).[27] *śrī manucaritaḥ* (one who resembles Manu by his deeds) was one of the titles of Rājasiṁha.[28]

The Velūrpāḷaiyam plates of Nandivarman III (*c.* AD 852), record very poetically that "there came into existance the race of the Pallavas who followed the law of protection by which even the slightest sufferings of their subjects was removed" (*vaṁśas=tato=varttata pallavānāṁ rakṣā-vidi-dhvasta vipallavānāṁ*).[29] These plates add that Parameśvaravarman II "governed the earth according to the laws laid down by Manu" and that he was "the chastiser of the dark age" (*mānavena kramen=orvīm=aśād=yaḥ kaliśāsanaḥ*).[30]

According to an inscription of the Pāṇḍyas, the kings of this dynasty ruled the country by "strictly following the rules set by Manu" (*manvayātān=apy=ācarān*).[31] The Tamil portion of the Larger Siṉṉamaṉūr plates (AD 926-27), refers to Parāntakan Vīranārāyaṇa (Parāntakan Saḍaiyan) as the king whose conduct (followed the rules) prescribed by Manu (*manucaritaḥ*).[32]

27. *SII*, vol. I, no. 34, p. 30.
28. *SII*, vol. I, no. 25, p. 16.
29. Velūrpāḷaiyam plates, *op. cit.*, v. 4, p. 507.
30. *Ibid.*, v. 14, p. 508.
31. T.N. Subramaniam, *DCPV*, v. 6, p. 14.
32. *SII*, vol. III, no. 206, l. 115, p. 461. (Larger Siṉṉamaṉūr plates).

The Coḷa epigraphs like the Larger Leiden,[33] Tiruvālaṅgāḍu,[34] Karandai,[35] Esālam[36] and Kanyākumārī[37] inscriptions mention Manu, the son of Sūrya as one of the legendary ancestors of the Coḷa dynasty. The Kanyākumarī record describes Manu as the expounder of the *dharmas*.

The Tiruvālaṅgāḍu plates state that the people of the Coḷa country considered their ruler, Parāntaka I to be Manu himself, reborn to establish his own laws which had degenerated in the *Kali* age (*kaler=balāt praskalitam=sva-śāstram punaḥ=vyavasthāpayitum-pr̥thivyām,* | *prapta=manuṁ yam=manute jana-oghaḥ pravr̥tta-cāritra-ratim nr̥pendram*).[38]

The Karandai charter praises Rājarāja I as *manuvaṁśa-ketuḥ* (the banner of the race of Manu).[39] The same epigraph refers to his son, Rājendra I as *manu-kulābharaṇam* (the ornament of the race of Manu).[40]

The epigraphs also contain direct references to these rulers upholding *dharma* or righteousness and ruling in accordance with the laws given in the *Dharmaśāstras*. Many of the early Pallava copper-plate charters[41] mention *dharma mahārāja* and *dharma mahārājādhirāja*, as the titles borne by some of the Pallava monarchs.

The Vesanta grant of Siṁhavarman II (*c.* fifth century AD), describes Śrī Vijaya Vīravarman as "the abode of *dharma*" (*āśrayo dharmasya*),[42] while the Pallāvaram inscription of

33. Larger Leiden plates, *op. cit.*, v. 3, p. 238.
34. Tiruvālaṅgāḍu plates, *op. cit.*, v. 4, p. 393.
35. K.G. Krishnan, *KTPR*, v. 3, p. 69.
36. R. Nagaswamy, *ECPR*, v. 3, p. 31.
37. *TAS*, vol. I, no. 34, v. 9, p. 132 (Kanyākumārī inscription).
38. Tiruvālaṅgāḍu plates, *op. cit.*, v. 57, p. 396.
39. K.G. Krishnan, *KTPR*, v. 35, p. 72.
40. *Ibid.*, v. 39, p. 72.
41. *EI*, vol. I, no. 1, p. 5 (Hīrahadagalli plates); Sakrepaṭṇa plates, *op. cit.*, p. 104.; *EI*, vol. XV, no. 11, p. 251 (Oṁgoḍu I plates); Uruvapaḷḷi plates, *op. cit.*, p. 51.
42. N. Ramesan, *VGPS*, p. 95.

Mahendravarman I refers to him as "the protector of *dharma*" (*dharmapālakaḥ*).[43]

Some of the titles of Rājasiṁha which reveal his commitment in upholding *dharma* are *śrī dharma nityaḥ* (the constantly just), *śrī dharma kavacaḥ* (whose armour is *dharma*), and *śrī dharma setuḥ* (the reservoir of *dharma*) and *śrī adharma bhīruḥ* (one who is afraid only of injustice).

The Pallava ruler, Dantivarman is described in the Bāhūr copper-plate inscription (*c*. AD 877), as "ruling the earth according to *dharma* even in the *kali* age" (*dharmmeṇa pālanāḍ-bhūmiṁ kalāv=api yuge nṛpaḥ*).[45]

The numerous inscriptions of the Coḷas also reveal that these rulers adhered to the laws given in the *Dharmaśāstras* and strove to be righteous in their rule. Āditya Coḷa I has been described in the Tiruvālaṅgāḍu charter as "one who was always bent upon removing evil, adhering himself to the path of the righteous and protecting the earth" (*doṣāpanītau satatam pravṛttaḥ sanmārga-vartti kṣitim=anvarakṣat*).[46] Parāntaka Coḷa I is mentioned in the Larger Leiden plates as "the follower of *dharma*" (*dharmānuyāte*).[47]

The Karandai inscription of Rājendra I praises this ruler as having "reached the eminence of *dharma*" (*labdha dharmm-odāya*).[48] This epigraph adds that during his reign, "the subjects were devoted to *dharma* and to their own duties" (*loko dharmaparāḥ=sva-karma-nirataḥ*).[49] According to an epigraph of Vīra Rājendra, this king "ruled his country according to the prescribed laws" (*rājyam vyadhita vidhivaṭ*).[50]

43. *SII*, vol. XII, no. 13, p. 7 (Pallāvaram inscription).
44. *SII*, vol. I, no. 25, pp. 14-18.
45. *EI*, vol. XVIII, No. 2, v. 10, p. 10 (Bāhūr plates).
46. Tiruvālaṅgāḍu plates, *op. cit.*, v. 47, p. 396.
47. Larger Leiden plates, *op. cit.*, v. 19, p. 240.
48. K.G. Krishnan, *KTPR*, v. 47, p. 73.
49. *Ibid.*, v. 46, p. 73.
50. Kanyākumārī inscription, *op. cit.*, v. 75, p. 147.

Kings as Upholders of Social Order

Another important duty of the kings in ancient and medieval India was the maintenance of the social order. Society in India was based on the fundamental principles of *varṇāśrama,* i.e., the division of society into different groups, with each group having to follow their own separate and complimentary functions or duties. The king was to aid and encourage the smooth functioning of this system.

The *Manusmṛti* clearly states that "the king has been created to be the protector of the castes (*varṇa*) and orders, who, all according to their rank, discharge their several duties."[51] The *Arthaśāstra* also states that "the ruler shall promulgate laws to guard the right conduct of the four castes."[52]

The kings of the Tamil country, as elsewhere in India, during the ancient and medieval periods, seem to have followed these precepts regarding *varṇāśramadharma* laid down in the ancient law books. The Kūram charter records that the Pallava ruler, Parameśvaravarman I "throughly enforced the laws of the castes and the orders" (*supraṇīta-varṇa-āśrama-dharmasya*).[53] The Kasākuḍi charter mentions that the kings of the Pallava dynasty "protected the special rules of all castes and orders" (*paripālita-sakala-varṇa-āśrama-vyavastā-viśesaḥ*).[54]

These rulers had various other duties such as organizing the judicial, revenue and military departments and taking measures to encourage agriculture and industry. All these activities of these kings in the period of our study are discussed in the following pages.

Succession

Kingship appears to have been hereditary during the ancient days in the Tamil country as it was in many other monarchical

51. *MS,* VII.35.
52. *KA,* 3, 1, 38.
53. Kūram plates, *op. cit.,* l. 17, p. 148.
54. Kaśākuḍi plates, *op. cit.,* l. 35, pp. 347-48.

states in India. The evidence offered by the Sanskrit inscriptions under study reveal that the law of primogeniture or the succession of the eldest son to the throne was in vogue. The Sanskrit charters of the early Pallava kings provide the names of four generations of rulers, namely, the donor himself, his father, grandfather and great-grandfather, thus indicating that during this period, the son followed the father to the throne.

However, during the Pallava period in the eighth century AD, there was a departure from the usual system, with Nandivarman Pallavamalla, a member of a collateral branch of the Pallava race being elected to the throne. The Kaśākuḍi plates record that this king was "chosen by the subjects" (*vr̥taḥ prajābhiḥ*) as the king.[55] This epigraph adds that his sixth ancestor was Bhīmavarman, who was the younger brother of Siṁhaviṣṇu.[56] The Paṭṭattāḷmaṅgalam plates of this king state that he ascended the throne while he was "still young" (*yuvaiva*).[57]

Further detailed information regarding the accession of Nandivarman Pallavamalla to the throne at Kāñcīpuram are provided by the series of historical sculptures depicting the main events of the rule of the Pallava dynasty, accompanied by labelled panels in Tamil in the Vaikuṇṭhaperumāḷ temple at Kāñcīpuram which explain the events leading to his election.[58] This epigraph states that when Parameśvaravarman II died, and anarchy prevailed in the kingdom, the important men of the realm, namely, the *mātra*s, the *ghaṭikaiyār* and the *mūla prakr̥ti*s requested Hiraṇyavarman Mahārāja (of the collateral branch of the Pallava dynasty) to become the king. He, in turn, asked four of his sons, among whom only Pallavamalla *alia*s Parameśvara, who was only twelve years old agreed to go. The inscription further states that he was anointed king

55. Kaśākuḍi plates, *op. cit.*, v. 27, p. 349.
56. *Ibid.*, v. 28.
57. Paṭṭattāḷmaṅgalam plates, *op. cit.*, v. 7, p. 121.
58. *SII*, vol. IV, No. 135, pp. 10-12.

under the name Nandivarman and was invested with all the royal insignia.

Other than this episode, there are no other instances in Pallava history to mark any departure from the accepted norm of the kingdom being handed down from father to son.

During the Coḷa period also, sons succeeded their father to the throne as can be seen from the numerous records of this period. However, once again, there was one instance where there was a change from the routine system, in the tenth century AD. Although Aruḷmoḻivarman (Rājarāja I) ought to have succeeded to the throne following the death of his father Parāntaka Coḷa II (Sundara Coḷa), it was his paternal uncle and son of Gaṇḍarāditya, Uttama Coḷa, who became king. The Tiruvālaṅgāḍu plates state that though he was requested by the subjects (*prārthyamāna prajābhiḥ*) to occupy the Coḷa throne, Aruḷmoḻivarman, who understood the essence of royal conduct (*kṣatradharmārthavedi*), did not desire the kingdom for himself even in his mind (*manasāpi*) while his paternal uncle coveted it.[59] The very next verse states that Madurāntaka (Uttama Coḷa) installed him in the office of the heir-apparent (*abhiṣicya yauvarājye*) and (himself) ruled the kingdom.[60]

With regard to the period of the Pāṇḍyas, the Sanskrit epigraphs do not provide any information to show any change from the system of primogeniture.

Coronation Ceremony

The coronation ceremony marking the accession of a ruler was a very important and solemn one. The Tiruvālaṅgāḍu plates give some details regarding the coronation of Rājarāja I.[61] This inscription states that Aruḷmoḻivarman was installed in the administration of the kingdom and the custom of pouring water on the king's head during the coronation ceremony is alluded to. The musical instruments traditionally

59. Tiruvālaṅgāḍu plates, *op. cit.*, v. 69, p. 397.
60. *Ibid.*, v. 70.
61. Tiruvālaṅgāḍu plates, *op. cit.*, v. 72.

played during this auspicious function such as the war-drums (*paṭaha*), rows of bells (*ghaṇṭa*), kettle-drums (*bheri*), tambourines (*muraja*) and conches (*śaṅkha*) are mentioned as being played during the coronation of this king.

The series of historical sculptures found in the Vaikuṇṭha-perumāḷ temple, Kāñcīpuram, reveal that the coronation ceremony was a very important one although the Pallava inscriptions do not mention these at all. C. Minakshi has identified several sculptures as those depicting the coronation ceremonies of different Pallava rulers.[62]

Yuvarāja

Many of the inscriptions of the ancient and medieval Tamil country reveal that kings selected their eldest sons to become the *yuvarāja* or heir-apparent even during their own lifetime so that there would be no problems regarding succession afterwards. Another important reason for nominating a son as crown-prince was that he could be trained in the affairs of administration at an early age, which would be of great use to him when he eventually ascended the throne.

Many of the Sanskrit inscriptions provide the names of the crown-princes. The Prākr̥t Mayidavolu charter of Pallava Śivaskandavarman (fourth century AD), refers to him as *yuvamahārāja*.[63] Again, another Prākr̥t inscription of the Pallava queen Cārudevī records that her husband, Vijaya Buddhavarman was a *yuvamahārāja*.[64] The Uruvapaḷḷi[65] and the Neḍungarāya[66] charters which were issued by Viṣṇu-gopavarman refer to him a *yuvamahārāja*.

A copper-plate grant of the fifth century AD, found at Peddamudiyam (Andhra Pradesh) issued by Siṁhavarman

62. C. Minakshi, *HSVK*, p. 58.
63. *EI*, vol. VI, no. 8, l. 1, p. 88 (Mayidavolu plates).
64. *EI*, vol. VIII, no.12, l. 2, p. 145 (Guṇapadeya plates).
65. Uruvapaḷḷi plates, *op. cit.*, p. 51.
66. T.V. Mahalingam, *IOP*, p. 50 (Neḍungarāya plates).

mentions his title as *dharmma-yuvamahārāja-kumāra*, thus indicating that he was a prince when he issued this charter.[67] The mention of the word *kumāra* in this title reveals that he was a prince under a prince, namely, his father Viṣṇugopavarman who himself was known as *yuvarāja* because he was serving as the governor of a territory under his elder brother and king, Siṁhavarman II. Since Siṁhavarman of the Peddamudiyam charter, in addition is called *avara* (junior), it may be assumed that he had an elder brother.[68]

It appears from the data gleaned from these inscriptions that the crown prince was involved in the process of the administration of the kingdom to a very great extent. The Mayidavolu inscription is a royal order from *yuvamahārāja* Śivaskandavarman issued from Kāñcīpuram to an official (*vyāpṛta*) at Dhannakaḍa (modern Amarāvatī) conferring a gift of land on two brāhmaṇas. The Uruvapaḷḷi charter (*c.* fifth century AD) was issued by *yuvamahārāja* Viṣṇugopa from Palakkaḍa granting land in the village of Uruvapaḷḷi to a Viṣṇu temple, while the Neḍungarāya copper-plates (*c.* fifth century AD), record a grant of the village of Neḍungarāya to three brāhmaṇas by the same crown-prince, again from Palakkaḍa.

The Peddamudiyam plates record that the junior-prince Siṁhavarman made a royal grant to a few brāhmaṇas and that he addressed his orders to the villagers of Pulusuluru and officials like the *naiyogika*s and *vallabha*s stationed there.[69]

The practice of selecting the crown-prince during the lifetime of the king was followed during the Coḷa period also. The Tiruvālaṅgāḍu plates record that Uttama Coḷa (Madurāntaka) installed Rājarāja in the office of the heir-apparent (*abhiṣicya yauvarājye*) and himself ruled the kingdom.[70]

---

67. K.V. Ramesh, "A Pallava Charter and Two Copper Medallions from Peddamudiyam" (From *Sri Ramachandrika, Prof. Oruganti Ramachadriah Festschrift*), pp. 117-21.
68. *Ibid.*
69. *Ibid.*, p. 121.
70. Tiruvālangāḍu plates, *op. cit.*, v. 70, p. 397.

Although the Sanskrit inscriptions do not give any more information on this subject, the Tamil epigraphs reveal that Rājarāja I himself made his son Rājendra as his heir-apparent in the closing years of his reign and the latter, in turn, made his son Rājādhirāja as co-ruler to administer the affairs of the state. This custom was carried on in the dynasty of the Coḷas from that time onwards.

Imperial Titles

The kings of the Tamil country adopted many imperial titles as can be gleaned from their Sanskrit inscriptions. *Mahārāja, dharma-mahārāja, mahārājādhirāja*, and *dharmamahārājādhirāja* were some of the titles borne by the early Pallava rulers.

Apart from titles such as these, the Pallava kings also adopted certain *biruda*s from the time of Mahendravarman I which are mostly found on the walls of the rock-cut cave and structural temples of these periods. These kinds of titles which glorify these rulers, and at the same time reveal their achievements and personal tastes were also adopted by the Coḷas and Pāṇḍyas.

An analysis of the *biruda*s of the kings shows the different categories of titles which they assumed which describe their military prowess, heroism, religious devotion and love for the arts and the learned.

Some of the rulers assumed new names when they were annointed as kings. A Tamil inscription mentions that Pallavamalla *alia*s Parameśvara was given the name Nandivarman when he was crowned king.[71] Rājasiṁha had the *abhiṣekanāma* Narasiṁhavarman[72] and Aruḷmoḻivarman assumed the royal title Rājarāja on ascending the throne.

The Coḷa rulers adopted the titles of *rājakesari* and *parakesari* alternatively on ascending the throne. The Karandai plates specifically mention this stating that "the name *rājakesarin* and (that) of *parakesarin* became alternately the order of kings born

71. *SII*, vol. IV, no. 135, p. 11.

72. C. Minakshi, *ASLP*, p. 54.

in their family."[73] Some of the other copper-plate charters of the Coḷas also mention this custom.[74]

Royal Emblems

All the ruling dynasties in ancient and medival India chose a particular symbol as their royal crest or emblem. These emblems usually adorned all the official documents of the state used for purposes of administration to give them authenticity.

The Sanskrit inscriptions provide some information about the royal emblems of the ruling powers of the Tamil country. The figure of the bull was the official symbol of the dynasty of the Pallavas. An inscription of Rājasiṁha mentions two of his titles *śrī ṛṣabha darpaḥ* (he who boasts of the bull) and *śrī ṛṣabha lāñchanaḥ* (he whose sign is the bull).[75] An epigraph of the Pallava queen, Raṅgapatākā, the consort of Rājasiṁha describes her husband as *vṛṣadhvaja* (he who has the bull as his flag).[76]

The Kaśākuḍi copper-plates refer to Parameśvaravarman I as *vṛṣāṅkaḥ* (one who has the bull as his sign).[77] Nandivarman Pallavamalla has been referred to in this same epigraph as *śākvaraketanaḥ* (one whose crest is the bull).[78] The stanzas of the Vaiṣṇava saint, Tirumaṅgai Āḻvār on the Parameśvara Viṇṇagar (i.e., Vaikuṇṭhaperumāḷ temple) contains references to the *ṛṣabhalāñchana* i.e., "vidal-velkoḍi," the victorious bull-banner.[79]

This bull emblem of the Pallava rulers also appears on the seals found on several of the Pallava copper-plate charters, thus confirming that this symbol was indeed the royal crest of the Pallava dynasty. The figure of the couchant bull is found

73. K.G. Krishnan, *KTPR*, v. 9, p. 70.
74. Larger Leiden plates, *op. cit.*, v. 8, p. 239; Tiruvālaṅgāḍu plates, *op. cit.*, vv. 31-32, p. 395.
75. *SII*, vol. I, no. 25, p. 15.
76. *SII*, vol. I, no. 29, v. 1, p. 23.
77. Kaśākuḍi plates, *op. cit.*, v. 24, p. 349.
78. *Ibid.*, v. 9, p. 347.
79. C. Minakshi, *ASLP*, p. 57.

on the seals of the copper-plate inscriptions of the early Pallava kings such as the Mayidavolu, Guṇapadeya, Udayendiram, Viḷavaṭṭi, Cura, Paḷḷankovil, Rāyakoṭṭah, Vunnaguruvapalem, and also the later records like the Reyūru, Paṭṭattāḷmaṅgalam, Kūram, Pullūr, Kaśākuḍi, Velūrpāḷaiyam, Taṇḍantoṭṭam and Veḷāñjeri charters. The bull symbol also appears on the obverse of many of the coins belonging to the Pallava dynasty.

Some of the other copper-plate grants of the Pallavas, such as the Uruvapaḷḷi and the Pikira grants bear the symbol of the lion instead of the bull on their seals. C. Minakshi has suggested that since these grants which have the lion on the seal were issued from victorious camps, it is possible that this lion-crest was used only to mark the victories of the Pallava rulers.[80]

Apart from the symbol of the bull found on the seals of the copper-plate grants, on coins and the references to it contained in the inscriptions, the *khaṭvāṅga* or club also seems to have been used by the Pallava rulers as a symbol on their flags. The *khaṭvāṅga* is a club or staff with a skull at the top considered as a weapon of Śiva, and carried by ascetics and *yogins*.[81]

Parameśvaravarman I is described as *khaṭvāṅgaketuḥ* (one whose banner is the *khaṭvāṅga*) in the Kaśākuḍi plates.[82] Although this is the only Sanskrit epigraph of the Pallavas which mentions the *khaṭvāṅga* as a royal symbol, a Tamil inscription mentions that during the coronation of Nandivarman Pallavamalla, he was bestowed with all the insignia of royalty, and one of these was the *khaṭvāṅga* flag.[83]

Just as the bull and the *khaṭvāṅga* were the royal insignia of the Pallava rulers, the tiger was the crest of the dynasty of the Coḷa kings, even during the Saṅgam period. Several of the

80. C. Minakshi, *ASLP*, p. 54.
81. V.S. Apte, *The Student's Sanskrit-English Dictionary*, Delhi, 1986, p. 174.
82. Kaśākuḍi plates, *op. cit.*, v. 24, p. 349.
83. *SII*, vol. IV, no. 135, pp. 10-12.

Saṅgam works mention the tiger as the royal crest of the Coḷas.

Unfortunately, the Sanskrit epigraphs of the period of the imperial Coḷas do not supply any information about their royal emblem. However, the seals of several of the copper-plate charters of the Coḷa kings such as the Veḷāñjeri, Anbil, Larger Leiden, Tiruvālaṅgāḍu and Karandai plates bear the figure of the tiger.

Many of the coins issued by the Coḷa rulers, also contain the figure of the tiger along with several other signs, thus confirming that the tiger symbol was indeed the royal emblem of this ruling house in the Tamil country.

Similarly, the Pāṇḍya rulers starting from the Saṅgam period, used the figure of the fish as their royal emblem. The Sanskrit inscription of the Pāṇḍya ruler Jaṭāvarman Sundara Pāṇḍya I (thirteenth century AD), found in the Raṅganāthasvāmi temple at Śrīraṅgam is shown flanked by two fish, one on either side of this epigraph.[84]

This inscription states that the fish was the emblem on this king's banner.[85] In the panegyrical introductions of the Tamil inscriptions of the Pāṇḍya kings, it is stated that their banner had the symbol of the two fishe.[86] The Pāṇḍyan coins also depict this royal emblem. The seal of the Daḷavāipuram bi-lingual copper-plates contains the figure of two carps below which are a tiger and a bow.

The Nesarika plates of the Rāṣṭrakūṭa king, Govinda III, gives a list of the crests of the kings of the Tamil country which he took away from them. The crests of the Pallava, Pāṇḍya and the Coḷa kings of the Tamil country are mentioned in this epigraph as *vṛṣabha* (bull), *matsya* (fish) and *vyāghra* (tiger) respectively.[87]

A Sanskrit inscription of the Keraḷa ruler Ravivarman Kulaśekhara (who ruled in the early part of the fourteenth

---

84. *EI*, vol. III, no. 2, p. 8.
85. *Ibid.*, v. 27, p. 14.
86. *Ibid.*, p. 17 and no. 3.
87. *EI*, vol. XXXIV, no.19, p. 131.

century AD), from Śrīraṅgam[88] as well as the Sanskrit portions of two bi-lingual records of this ruler from Kāñcīpuram[89] and Tiruvaḍi[90] (South Arcot district) mention that this king had the Garuḍa emblem on his banner. All three epigraphs which contain the same string of *biruda*s of this king praise him in a poetic manner as "the establisher of his Garuḍa banner on the (seven) principal mountains" (*kulaśikhari-pratiṣṭhāpita-garuḍadhvaja*).

The Udayendiram plates of the Western Gaṅga chief Pṛthivīpati II, who was a dependent of Parāntaka I, mention that his banner bore the figure of a blackbuck (*kṛṣṇa-dhvajaḥ*).[91]

An inscription of the Kāḍava ruler Kopperuñjiṅga mentions that his banner was painted with the emblem of a sword.[92]

Ministers

The kings of ancient India were the heads of vast administrative systems and thus had to shoulder many responsibilities. In discharging these onerous duties, they required the assistance of able and efficient men on whom they could depend.

Political thinkers like Kauṭilya have pointed out the necessity of appointing ministers for helping the ruler in the task of administration. According to him, "Rulership can be successfully carried out only with associates; one wheel alone does not turn, therefore the king should appoint ministers and listen to their opinion."[93] Many of the ancient texts also stress that the ministers thus appointed should possess various qualities such as learning, intelligence, bravery and foresight.[94]

---

88. *EI*, vol. IV, no. 18, l. 3, p. 149.
89. *EI*, vol. IV, no. 17, l. 5, p. 147.
90. *EI*, vol. VIII, no. 2, l. 2, p. 8.
91. *SII*, vol. II, no. 76, v. 24, p. 384.
92. *TTD* Inscriptions, vol. I, no. 10, p. 18.
93. *KA*, I.7, 9.
94. *MS*, VII. 54; *KA*, II; *Kuraḷ*, Ch. 62.

The Sanskrit inscriptions provide plenty of information regarding the ministers of the Pallava, Pāṇḍya and Coḷa rulers. They are referred to in these epigraphs as *amātyas*, *mantris* and *sacivas*. The descriptions of these ministers as given in the inscriptions reveal the qualities and capabilities which they possessed. It is obvious that the rulers of the Tamil country took great care in the selection of their ministers and did so only after carefully assessing their qualities and suitability for the office.

Amātyas

The earliest Pallava inscription which refers to the *amātya* is the Hīrahadagalli charter of Śivaskandavarman in Prākṛt.[95] This epigraph mentions the *amātyas* (*amācce*) among many of the other officials of the Pallava king. However, this grant does not mention the duties which this official was supposed to discharge.

Some of the epigraphs of the Coḷa kings mention the *amātyas*. Naralokavīra, the famous general of Kulottuṅga Coḷa I is described in one of this king's inscriptions of the eleventh century AD as his *amātya*.[96]

Although Naralokavīra was one of the most renowned generals of Kulottuṅga I who won numerous wars for his king, he seems to have served him in the capacity of a minister (*amātya*) also. In the higher branches of the king's service there was then no separation between the civil and military functions of officials.[97] Another record of Kulottuṅga I mentions an *amātya* named Vāṇādhirāja.[98]

95. Hīrahadagalli plates, *op. cit.*, p. 5.
96. *SII*, vol. XXVI, no. 388, pp. 252-53.
97. K.A. Nilakanta Sastri, *Studies in Coḷa History and Administration*, Madras, 1932, p. 177.
98. *SII*, vol. XXIV, no. 26, p. 21.

Mantris

Mantris are mentioned in many of the copper-plate grants of the Pallava kings. Although the names and the qualities of these ministers are described, sometimes in great detail in these epigraphs, the exact nature of their work in connection with the administration of the kingdom are not mentioned.

The earliest Pallava copper-plate inscription which mentions the *mantri* is the Paḷḷankovil charter of Siṁhavarman III.[99] This epigraph states that a minister (*mantri*) of this king was a person named Narabhaya who was "wise" (*sudhiḥ*) and "the abode of good qualities" (*guṇasaṁghāspadam*). This Narabhaya was the executor (*ājñapti*) of this grant.

A very gifted minister of Nandivarman Pallavamalla was Brahmaśrīrāja, mentioned in the Kaśākuḍi grant.[100] This epigraph mentions that he was the *mukhya-mantri* or chief minister of the king just as Bṛhaspati was to Indra and that he was well-educated and loyal to his king.

Another versatile minister of Nandivarman Pallavamalla is mentioned in the Pullūr plates of this king which states that the executor of this grant was a minister (*mantri*) named Nāgaśarma Brahmādhirāja.[101] This minister is described as the best among brāhmaṇas *(dvijavaraḥ)*, Bṛhaspati in person (*pratyakṣa bṛhaspatiṁ*) and well-versed in the science of weapons and warfare (*kṣatravidyā*).

A minister (*mantri*) of Nṛpatuṅgavarman named Uttamaśīla is mentioned in the Bāhūr grant.[102] In the Tamil portion of this inscription his name is given as Viḍelviḍugu-Kāḍupaṭṭi-Tamiḻa-peraraiyaṉ. The same person was the *ājñapti* of the Ciṟṟūr plates of Nṛpatuṅgavarman.[103]

---

99. T.N. Subramaniam, *PJCG*, p. 76.
100. Kaśākuḍi plates, *op. cit.*, l. 87, p. 350.
101. *EI*, vol. XXXVI, no. 20, l. 13, p. 153 (Pullūr plates).
102. Bāhūr plates, *op. cit.*, v. 28, p. 11.
103. T.V. Mahalingam, *IOP*, p. 442 (Ciṟṟūr plates of Nṛpatuṅgavarman); see also R. Nagaswamy, "Ciṟṟūr Plates of Nṛpatunga" *from Studies in Ancient Tamil Law and Society*, Madras, 1978, pp. 32-33.

A Ministerial Council (*mantri-maṇḍala*) also functioned during the Pallava period. A Tamil record from the Vaikuṇṭhaperumāḷ temple of the period of Nandivarman II Pallavamalla mentions the *mantri-maṇḍala*.[104]

Such ministerial councils which adviced the king existed in other ancient kingdoms of south India such as the Kadambas, Cāḷukyas, Rāṣṭrakūṭas Yādavas and Kākatiyas.[105]

The epigraphs of the Coḷas also contain some information about the ministers who helped the kings to discharge their duties. The Tiruvālaṅgāḍu plates record the name of a *mantri* of Rājendra Coḷa I named Jananātha, son of Rāma, who is described in glowing terms as "the foremost among scholars" (*viduśāmagre*), "the storehouse of virtues" (*guṇanidhiḥ*) and "the birthplace of compassion" (*dayā-janmabhūmiḥ*).[106] He is mentioned as Narākkaṉ-Mārāyaṉ Jananāthaṉ *alias* Rājendraśoḷa Brahmādhirājan of Keraḷāntakacaturvedimaṅgalam in Venāḍu (a subdivision) of Uyyakoṇḍārvaḷanāḍu in the Tamil portion of this grant.[107]

The Karandai epigraph also mentions this minister (*mantri*) Jananātha and praises him in glowing terms as "a second body of the king" (*narapater-asya dvitīyam vapuḥ*), "chief of the pious following the path of virtue" (*sanmārgāśrayiṇām satām-adhipatiḥ*) and "an ocean for the streams of learning" (*vidyānadī-vāridhiḥ*). He was the *vijñapti* of this grant.[108] The Tamil portion refers to him as Narākkaṉ Mārāyaṉ Jananāthaṉ *alias* Rājendraśoḷa Brahmādhirājaṉ from the same village as is mentioned in the Tiruvālaṅgāḍu grant. He is designated as the officer who "examines our (i.e.) the king's affairs" (*nam karmam ārāyum*).[109] In this record Rājendra I is said to have camped in the *maṇḍapa*

---

104. *SII*, vol. IV, no. 135, p. 11; see also T.V. Mahalingam, *South Indian Polity*, Madras, 1955, pp. 105-06.
105. *Ibid.*, p. 106.
106. Tiruvālaṅgāḍu plates, *op. cit.*, v. 127, p. 401.
107. *Ibid.*, p. 411.
108. K.G. Krishnan, *KTPR*, v. 70, p. 75.
109. *Ibid.*, p. 92.

called Rājendraśoḷa Brahmādhirājaṉ. This *maṇḍapa* was evidently named after this high-ranking brāhmaṇa official.[110]

The Esālam epigraph, also of Rājendra I mentions this Jananātha, son of Rāman, in the Sanskrit section (Narākkaṉ Mārāyaṉ Jananāthaṉ in the Tamil part) as the *ājñapti* of this grant.[111] He was probably the same person mentioned in the Tiruvālaṅgāḍu and the Karandai plates. He was one of the sons of Kṛṣṇaṉ Rāmaṉ, also called Rājendra-Coḷa-Brahmamārāyaṉ, the great commander-in-chief of Rājarāja I, who erected the enclosure to the Tañjāvūr temple and served under Rājendra I also.[112]

The epigraphs of the Pāṇḍyas also mention ministers (*mantri*) of these rulers. The Larger Siṉṉamaṉūr copper-plate grant records that the *vijñapti* (the person who requested the grant to be made) of this inscription was a *mantri* named Jaṭila.[113] He is described in this charter as being "of respectful descent" (*tuṅgābhijātyaḥ*), "a storehouse of prosperity" (*śrīnidhiḥ*), and a poet (*kavi*), belonging to the Atri *gotra*.

A Sanskrit epigraph (AD 770), found in the rock-cut Narasiṁha shrine at Āṉaimalai near Madurai, mentions that a person named Madhurakavi, the son of Māra (*mārasūnuḥ*) who was pre-eminently charming in manners (*maduratara*ḥ), hailing from a family of *vaidyas*, who was a resident of Karavandapura (*karavandapura-nivāsinaḥ*), and who was very wise (*matimān*) was the minister (*mantri*) of the Pāṇḍyan king Neḍuñjaḍaiyan.[114]

A Tamil record at the very same place mentions the actual name of this minister as Māraṅgāri, who bore the title Mūvendamaṅgalapperaraiyaṉ of Kaḷakkuḍi and describes him as the prime-minister (*uttara-mantri*) of the king.

This Tamil epigraph also mentions that his younger brother, Māraṉ Eyinaṉ who bore the title Pāṇḍimaṅgala-

110. K.G. Krishnan, *KTPR*, p. 18.

111. R. Nagaswamy, *ECPR*, v. 32, p. 33.

112. *Ibid.*, p. 11.

113. Larger Siṉṉamaṉūr plates, *op. cit.*, v. 33, p. 453.

114. *EI*, vol. VIII, no. 33, pp. 319-20 (Āṉamalai Inscription).

viśaiyaraiyaṉ became the *uttara-mantri* after his brother passed away.[115]

A Sanskrit verse in the Veḷvikuḍi grant issued by Neḍuñjaḍaiyan mentions Māran-Kāri (*mangaḷarājo maduratarah̤*) as the *ājñapti* of this grant.[116]

The place Karavaṇḍapura *alias* Kaḷakkuḍi has been identified with Uggirankoṭṭai in Tirunelveli district.[117]

The Sanskrit portion of the Śivakāśi copper-plate inscription of Vīra-Pāṇḍya records that the executor (*ājñapti*) of this grant was the minister Teṉṉavaṉ *uttara mantri* who held the post of *sandhivigraha*.[118]

An important minister of Māravarman Sundara Pāṇḍya I, named Gurukulataraiyaṉ *alias* Śoraṉ Uyyaniṉrāḍuvāṉ, who made many benefactions to a Viṣṇu temple at Tiruttangal (Rāmnād district) is mentioned in a record (AD 1227), found in this temple.[119]

Saciva

The inscriptions of the Pallavas do not mention the *saciva*, but this term can be found in the Coḷa and the Pāṇḍya epigraphs. The Anbil plates of Parāntaka II (Sundara Coḷa) record that a person named Aniruddha described in this grant as "the abode of wisdom" (*prajñādhāma*), "the home of liberality" (*vadānyatānilayanam*) and "a mansion of right conduct" (*ācāravāso mahān*) was his respected *saciva*.[120]

The Larger Siṉṉamaṇūr plates contain a reference to a *saciva* of the Pāṇḍyan king Rājasiṁha named Nakkankumāṉ.[121] He is described as the son of a nobleman of Kīḻ-vemba-nāḍu, the

115. *EI*, vol. VIII, no. 33, p. 320.
116. Veḷvikuḍi plates, *op. cit.*, v. 18, p. 303.
117. *EI*, vol. XXIII, no. 45, p. 285.
118. T.N. Subramaniam and P.R. Srinivasan, *SCVP*, v. 20, p. 46.
119. *ARE*, 554 of 1922.
120. Anbil plates, *op. cit.*, no. 5, vv. 31-32, p. 62.
121. Larger Siṉṉamaṇūr plates, *op. cit.*, v. 35, p. 453.

master of an elephant (*nāthaḥ kariṇyāḥ*) and a warden (*kuḍikāval*).

A *saciva* named Jayasiṁha who served Vikrama Pāṇḍya (*vikrama-pāṇḍya-deva sacivaḥ*) described as brave (*śūraḥ*) and prosperous (*nidhi-śreyasām*) has been mentioned in an epigraph found at Dalavānūr.[122]

Although there certainly must have been differences between the *amātyas*, *sacivas* and the *mantris* with regard to their duties, it is not possible to know what these actually were during the period of our study in the Tamil country as the epigraphs unfortunately do not specify their responsibilities and duties. However, the *Manusmṛti* mentions that the *amātya* was the chief minister, while the word *saciva* has only been denoted in a general sense.[123] Kauṭilya also differentiates between *mantrins* and the *amātyas*, stating in one context that persons may be appointed as *amātyas* and as *mantrins* according to their capacity for doing work.[124]

Mahāmātras

A class of officers called the *mahāmātras* are mentioned in a Pallava inscription, the Vesanta plates.[125] This inscription records a gift of the village of Vesanta as *brahmadeya* to a brāhmaṇa from Siṁhavarman together with eighteen *parihāras* adding that the officers of the king such as *mahāmātras*, should ensure that the orders of the king with regard to the immunities were maintained.

The Kumaraḍimaṅgalam copper-plates mention that king Nandivarman III gave a land-grant to learned brāhmaṇas following a request by a chief named Nayabhara Maṅgaḷa-mahārāja, who is poetically described as "a sun in the sky of *mahāmātras*" (*mahā-mātrakula gagana gataḥ*).[126]

122. *ARE*, 54 of 1905.
123. *MS*, VII. 54.
124. *KA*, 1.8.27.
125. N. Ramesan, *VGPS*, p. 96.
126. N. Ramesan, *KPPN*, p. 201.

The *Arthaśāstra* mentions the *mahāmātras* and this term has been translated by Shama Sastri as "minister."[127] The edicts of Aśoka also mention the *mahāmātras* in connection with spreading his ideology. V.R. Ramachandra Dikshitar has stated that apart from the fact that the *mahāmātras* were ministers or high officials of the state, no other definite functions of theirs can be gleaned from the *Arthaśāstra*.[128]

Adhyakṣas

The *adhyakṣas* are mentioned in a few early Pallava inscriptions, like the Vesanta,[129] Maṅgaḷūr[130] and Viḻavaṭṭi[131] epigraphs in connection with carrying out the orders of the rulers with regard to gift of land-grants. The *Arthaśāstra* refers to the *adhyakṣas* who were the superintendents in charge of various departments.[132] C. Minakshi has stated that the *adhyakṣas* were officers of the district in the nature of superintendents.[133]

Many other officials are mentioned in various early Pallava grants in Prākṛt and in Sanskrit such as the *bhojakas*, *vallabhas*, *govallabhas* and *āyuktas*, but their exact duties have not been specified. C. Minakshi has opined that these officials were also officers of the district who were in the nature of superintendents and were directly placed under the control of the central government.[134]

Treasurer

The treasury (*kośa*) was so vital for the existence of a kingdom that Kauṭilya has mentioned it as one of the seven limbs of the state.[135]

127. R. Shama Sastri (tr.), *Kauṭilīyam Arthaśāstram*, Mysore, 1923, I.12.
128. V.R.R. Dikshitar, *The Mauryan Polity*, Delhi, 1993, p. 209.
129. N. Ramesan, *VGPS*, p. 96.
130. *Ind. Ant.*, vol. v (1876), p. 155.
131. Viḻavaṭṭi plates, *op. cit.*, p. 302.
132. *KA*, 1.5.8 and 1.19.12.
133. C. Minakshi, *ASLP*, p. 140.
134. *Ibid.*
135. *KA*, II.5.

The Sanskrit portion of the Taṇḍantoṭṭam plates record that a person named Dayāmukha, with the permission of his king, Nandivarman II Pallavamalla, caused a village to be granted to three hundred and eight brāhmaṇas calling it Dayāmukhamaṅgalam.[136] This same person, also called as Kumāra was the executor (*ājñapti*) of this grant and held the important post of treasurer (*kośādhyakṣa*).[137]

This official has been praised in glowing terms in this charter as "a wise man" (*matimān*), "who had stood the test of honesty" (*upadha*), "who was pure in enjoying religious merit" (*dharma*), "wealth" (*artha*), and "desires" (*kāma*), "who was the receptacle of right conduct" (*śuddha cāritra pātram*), "who was devoted solely to the service of his master" (*svāmyeka bhaktivrataḥ*), "who seeks refuge in virtue" (*dharmaśaraṇaḥ*) and "who is clever in discharging the duties of a treasurer" (*kośādhyakṣa-niyoga-karma-kuśalaḥ*).

The post of a treasurer must have indeed been a very responsible one and only persons with proper credentials and capabilities must have been appointed to this office as the description of the treasurer in the Taṇḍantoṭṭam plates reveals.

SPIES

An efficient system of espionage was maintained by the rulers of ancient and medieval India. The rulers, by means of the information obtained through their spies, came to know about the happenings in their own kingdoms as well as in the kingdoms of the enemies.

Many of the writers of ancient India have mentioned the importance of spies and provided a detailed picture of the type of people the rulers were to appoint as spies.[138] The inscriptions of the Tamil country reveal that the kings followed the system of appointing spies to help them in their work.

---

136. Taṇḍantoṭṭam plates, *op. cit.*, v. 9, p. 520.
137. *Ibid.*, v. 10.
138. *MS*, VII.154; *KA*, I.11; *Kuraḷ*, Ch. 59.

The very first reference to spies in the Pallava kingdom are contained in the Hīrahadagalli plates (*c.* fourth century AD).[139] The word *sañcārāntaka* mentioned in this inscription has been taken by G. Bühler to refer to spies.[140]

The Uruvapaḷḷi grant of Viṣṇugopavarman (*c.* fifth century AD), also records the name *sañcārāntaka*.[141] This epigraph records that this king gave the village of Uruvapaḷḷi as *devabhoga* to a Viṣṇu temple and that various officials including the *sañcārāntakas* were to ensure that they and others were to treat that village with immunity from taxation. Other Pallava inscriptions[142] mention the *sañcārāntaka* in the same context as the Uruvapaḷḷi charter.

The Viḷavaṭṭi grant (*c.* fifth century AD), mentions the licensed spies (*pravarāñcara*) in connection with the taxes payable by them to the king.[143]

Apart from the Pallava inscriptions, a Sanskrit record of the Kadamba king Kakutsthavarman, namely the Tāḷagunda Pillar inscription provides some information about spies in the Pallava kingdom.[144] This inscription states that Mayūraśarman, the founder of the Kadamba dynasty went to the *ghaṭikā* at Kāñcīpuram to study the sacred scriptures, but could not complete his education there because of his quarrel with a *pallavāśvasaṁstha*. According to R. Sathianathaier this term means a mounted spy, since the term *saṁstha* meaning spy has been mentioned by Kauṭilya.[145]

The practice of appointing spies was present in the Coḷa period also. The Udayendiram plates of Pṛthivīpati II (AD 922), mentions that Āditya I "learned about the true state (of the

139. Hīrahadagalli plates, *op. cit.*, p. 5.

140. *Ibid.*, p. 8.

141. Uruvapaḷḷi plates, *op. cit.*, p. 52.

142. Cura plates, *op. cit.*, p. 142; N. Ramesan, *VGPS*, p. 96.

143. Viḷavaṭṭi plates, *op. cit.*, p. 303.

144. *EI*, vol. VIII, no. 5, pp. 31-33 (Tāḷaguṇḍa Inscription).

145. R. Sathianathaier, *Studies in the Ancient History of Toṇḍaimaṇḍalam*, Madras, 1987, pp. 49-50.

affairs of his enemies) from his spies" (*cāra*).[146]

Rahasyādhikṛt

Another official mentioned very often in the copper-plate charters of the Pallavas was the *rahasyādhikṛt*. G. Bühler has understood this term to be that of a Privy Councillor.[147] T.V. Mahalingam has taken this official to be confidential minister who was charged with the duty of the drafting of a manual or the writing of a record and who was an important member of the Ministerial Council.[148]

The *rahasyādhikṛt* is mentioned in several of the early Pallava grants. His duty, as can be gleaned from these inscriptions, was to put into writing the orders of the king. The Prākṛt Hīrahadagalli plates state that this charter was prepared in his own handwriting by the *rahasyādhikṛt* Bhaṭṭiśarman of Kolivāla (*kolivāla-bhojakasa rahasādhikata-bhaṭṭisammassa sahatthalikhiteṇa paṭṭika kadatti*).[149]

The Vesanta plates of Siṁhavarman II record that his royal order addressed to the villagers of Vesanta granting that village as a *brahmadeya* together with immunities to a learned brāhmaṇa was engraved on copper-plates as it was issued orally by the king by a person named Kūlipottan, who was a *rahasyādhikṛt* of the king (*rahasyādhikṛtena kūlipottena likhiteyam tāmrapaṭṭiketi*).[150]

The Viḷavaṭṭi charter of Siṁhavarman mentions that the order for the gift of the village of Viḷavaṭṭi to a brāhmaṇa name Viṣṇuśarman which was issued orally by the king was committed to writing by the *rahasyādhikṛt* named Acyuta (*rahasyādhikṛten-ācyutena likhitaṁ śāsanaṁ*).[151]

---

146. *SII*, vol. II, no. 76, p. 382.
147. *EI*, vol. I, no. 1, p. 9.
148. T.V. Mahalingam, *South Indian Polity*, Madras, 1955, p. 122.
149. Hīrahadagalli plates, *op. cit.*, p. 7.
150. N. Ramesan, *VGPS*, p. 96.
151. Viḷavaṭṭi plates, *op. cit.*, no. 43, p. 303.

Sandhivigraha

An official named *sandhivigraha* is mentioned in only one Sanskrit inscription of the period of this study, namely, the Śivakāśi copper-plate grant. This charter records that the *ājñapti* of this grant was the minister Teṉṉavan Uttara-mantri who was holding the post of *sandhivigraha* (*ājñaptir=asmin=nṛpateḥ kurvāṇas=sandhivigraham*).[152] Since he is called *uttara-mantri*, it may be assumed that he was an official of high standing.

Officials known as *sandhivigrahika* are known from records of dynasties such as the Guptas and other rulers of north India and also figure in the epigraphs of the Cāḷukyas and Rāṣṭrakūṭas. The *sandhivigrahin* was a high-ranking officer of the state to whom were entrusted the important problems of peace (*sandhi*), war (*vigraha*), neutrality (*āsana*), marching (*yāna*), seeking refuge (*saṁśrayaṇa*) and dual policy (*dvaidhibhāvaḥ*).[153] In the days of the Cāḷukyas and the Rāṣṭrakūṭas, their charters appear to have been drafted by the *sandhivigrahin* or foreign-minister.[154]

Some Tamil inscriptions such as the Smaller Leiden plates of Kulottuṅga I mention this officer.[155] In this record, the *sandhivigrahin* named Rājavallabha-Pallavaraiyaṉ was given the work of drafting the copper-plate charter of a royal order of Kulottuṅga I in favour of the *saṁgha* of the Cūlāmaṇivihāra at Nāgapaṭṭinam as requested by two ambassadors of the king of Kaḍāram.

It is therefore probable that the *sandhivigrahin* mentioned in the Śivakāśi plates had the duty of drafting the official records, although it is not explicitly mentioned in this inscription.

---

152. T.N. Subramaniam, *SCVP*, v. 20, p. 46.
153. D.K. Ganguly, *Aspects of Ancient Indian Administration*, New Delhi, 1979, p. 188.
154. T.V. Mahalingam, *South Indian Polity*, Madras, 1955, p. 143.
155. *EI*, vol. XXII, no. 35, pp. 276-77.

Kāraṇika

There seem to have been a class of officials called *kāraṇika* as seen from the evidence found in several Pallava charters. The Kūram copper-plates state that the *ājñapti* of this record was Uttarakāraṇika-mahāsenadatta.[156] The Sanskrit *praśasti* of the Taṇḍantoṭṭam plates was composed by Parameśvara surnamed Uttarakāraṇika, the son of Paramottārakāraṇika.[157] According to C. Minakshi, in the name Uttarakāraṇika, *kāraṇika* is not a proper name, but the designation of an official, since a few copper-plates from north India reveal the *kāraṇika* to be an official who figures as the composer or writer of the contents of these grants.[158] The term *uttarakāraṇika* must be taken to denote the office which was above that of the *kāraṇika* and *paramottārakāraṇika* must have been the chief of all *kāraṇika*s, the head of this class of officers.[159]

Gajādhyakṣa (Superintendent of Elephants)

A large number of war-elephants were maintained by the Tamil kings and the training and maintenance of these elephant forces must have called for very experienced personnel who could handle these animals. The *Arthaśāstra* devotes one full section to the work of the superintendent of elephants called *gajādhyakṣa,* who was to perform duties such as looking after the elephant stables, bathing, feeding and training of the elephants.[160]

The inscriptions of the Pallavas, Pāṇḍyas and Coḷas reveal that they maintained a very strong elephant corps, which often participated in wars. It is obvious that these elephant brigades were looked after and trained by an officer in charge of them.

---

156. Kūram plates, *op. cit.*, p. 150.
157. Taṇḍantoṭṭam plates, *op. cit.*, v. 14, p. 521.
158. C. Minakshi, *op. cit.*, pp. 78-79.
159. *Ibid.*
160. *KA*, I.31.

The Śivakāśi copper-plate grant of Vīra-Pāṇḍya (AD 940-41), mentions the *gajādhyakṣa* in the Sanskrit portion of the charter.[161] This grant states that the circumambulation of the female elephant (in connection with the custom of demarcating the land given to the donees) was conducted by the *ājñapti* (executor) of the deed who was under the supervision of the superintendent of the elephant corps (*gajādhyakṣa*) named Śrī Teṉṉavaṉ anuttara — Pallavadyaraiya. The Śrīvaramaṅgalam copper-plate grant of Pāṇḍyan Neḍuñjaḍaiyan (*c.* AD 785), mentions an official designated "overseer of elephants" (*matta-gajādhyakṣa*) in the Tamil section.[162]

These inscriptions, while referring to these officials, do not give any information about the exact duties carried out by them. However, it may be safely assumed that their duties would mostly conform with the detailed description of the jobs the *gajādhyakṣa* was expected to perform as outlined in the *Arthaśāstra*.

Members of the Royal Family

It appears from the epigraphical sources that members of the royal family also helped the king in matters of administration. Apart from the crown-prince (*yuvarāja*) who assisted the ruler as seen earlier, other princes also served the kingdom.

The Tiruvālaṅgāḍu plates reveal that Rājendra I, having defeated the Pāṇḍyan ruler, appointed his own son, Coḷa-Pāṇḍya, to protect the Pāṇḍya country.[163] Again, the same epigraph records that after Rājendra had conquered the Keraḷa country, he appointed his son Coḷa Pāṇḍya to protect this place.[164]

Vassal Chiefs

In addition to the ministers and other officials, the chieftains

---

161. T.N. Subramaniam, *SCVP*, v. 22, p. 46.
162. *PCP*, *Śrīvaramaṅgalam copper-plate grant of Neḍuñjaḍaiyan*, l. 72, p. 60.
163. Tiruvālaṅgāḍu plates, *op. cit.*, v. 93, p. 399.
164. *Ibid.*, v. 99.

must have also been of assistance to the king in the sphere of administration.

Chieftains were known in the Tamil country even during the Saṅgam age, when they aligned themselves with one or the other of the three important powers which existed at that time, namely the Coḷas, Ceras and Pāṇḍyas, and also tried to free themselves of the shackles when opportunity was provided.

In the subsequent periods of Tamil history also, these chiefs played an important role by teaming up with one or the other of the major powers such as the Pallavas, Coḷas and the Pāṇḍyas in order to enhance their own standing and prestige. The Sanskrit inscriptions provide the names of many of the feudatories of the period who, apart from influencing the political scenario, also played an important role in the administrative sphere.

A few of the copper-plate grants of the Pallava rulers reveal the names of some of their vassals. The Udayendiram grant of Nandivarman Pallavamalla provides details about Udayacandra, his vassal who was the ruler of a place named Vilvala (*vilvalābhidhānasya nagarasyādhipatiḥ*) and who rendered great help to his master.[165] In this inscription, Udayacandra is described as having been born in the race of Pūcān (*Pūcānkule*), which had been handed down by (i.e., had been in the hereditary service of) the uninterrupted succession of the Pallava race (*pallavakulaḥ paraṁparāgate*).

It was on the request made by Udayacandra and to honour this loyal general for the services which he had rendered, that Nandivarman Pallavamalla gave the village named Kumāramaṅgala-Veḷḷaṭṭūr to a hundred and eight brāhmaṇas, renaming it as Udayacandramaṅgalam. This place has been identified with the village of Udayendiram on the banks of the river Pālār in North Arcot district.[166]

---

165. Udayendiram plates, *op. cit.*, l. 37, p. 367.

166. *Ibid.*, p. 365.

The Pullūr record of the same ruler mentions another vassal named Avanicandra Yuvarāja in the Sanskrit portion.[167] He is described as being devoted to his king and as "the lord of Vilvalapura" (*vilvalapureśa*). Evidently, Avanicandra was the son and heir-apparent of Udayacandra and his father was still ruling the principality when this grant was made.[168]

The Paṭṭattāḷmaṅgalam plates mention in the Sanskrit portion, the name of a chieftain of Nandivarman Pallavamalla called Mangaḷarāṣṭra-bhartri (the lord of the district called Maṅgala-rāṣṭra) and Maṅgaḷajanapadabhartuḥ (the ruler of the country of Maṅgala).[169] He is described as the servant of the Pallava king (*pallavendra bṛtyaḥ*). This epigraph mentions that he gave to a concourse of brāhmaṇas their desired object, which was a gift of land, after having petitioned the king for this repeatedly.

The Velūrpāḷaiyam plates record that a Coḷa chieftain named Kumarāṅkuśa, apparently a feudatory of the Pallavas, made a request to the Pallava king Nandivarman III for gifting the village named Tirukāṭṭupaḷḷi for maintaining the various services connected with the temple of Śiva in that village.[170]

The Bāṇas were important chiefs who were first vassals of the Pallavas and later of the Coḷas in the Tamil country. The Ciṟṟūr plates of Nṛpatuṅgavarman mention a Bāṇa chief named Parañjaya who is described as the "sun in the sky of the Bāṇa family" (*balikulāmbara bhānumāli*).[171] He was requested by his wife, Pṛthivīmāṇikkā to grant lands to certain brāhmaṇas and at Parañjaya's request, his king Nṛpatuṅgavarman gifted a village, Pṛthivīmahādevīcaturvedimaṅgalam to the brāhmaṇas. Parañjaya, the *vijñapti* of this grant is called in the Tamil portion of this record as Kāḍupaṭṭi Muttaraiyaṉ.

---

167. Pullūr plates, *op. cit.*, l.10, p. 152.
168. *Ibid.*, p. 147.
169. Paṭṭattāḷmaṅgalam plates, *op. cit.*, pp. 115-24.
170. Velūrpāḷaiyam plates, *op. cit.*, vv. 25-26, p. 509.
171. T.V. Mahalingam, *IOP*, p. 442 (Ciṟṟūr plates of Nṛpatuṅgavarman).

The information about the vassals available from the epigraphical sources are partially supplemented by the series of sculptures found in the Vaikuṇṭhaperumāḷ temple at Kāñcīpuram which depict the main events of the Pallava rule. C. Minakshi has identified many of the figures found in these panels as those of the vassal chiefs of the Pallava rulers who are often seen paying homage to their overlord.[172] These chiefs are also shown in the panels preceding the election of Nandivarman Pallavamalla, meeting him with the royal paraphernalia and taking part in the actual coronation ceremony.

The Sanskrit inscriptions of the Coḷas also mention many of the vassals of this dynasty. An epigraph found at Mūvarkovil at Koḍuṁbāḷur of the period of Bhūti Vikrama Kesari who was a contemporary of Āditya I and his son Parāntaka I, gives some informaion about the lineage of the Koḍuṁbāḷur chiefs termed in this inscription as belonging to the Yaduvaṁśa.[173]

Another Koḍuṁbāḷur chief named Śiriya Veḷār *alias* Pirāntakaṉ Iruṅgoḷaṉ a vassal of Sundara Coḷa, figures in an inscription from Tiruviśalūr which records a grant made by this chief, called in this epigraph as Śiruveḷā, to the Śiva temple at this place.[174]

The Udayendiram copper-plates of Pṛthivīpati II Hastimalla[175] provide some information about this Western Gaṅgā vassal of Parāntaka Coḷa I. According to this inscription, Parāntaka I conferred on Pṛthivīpati II, the title of *bāṇādhirāja* (lord of the Bāṇas) after this Coḷa king had conquered the Bāṇas, probably with the help of this vassal.

The Sholingūr Rock inscription[176] also mentions this

172. C. Minakshi, *HSVK*, p. 61.

173. *JOR*, vol. VII, pp. 8-9.

174. *SII*, vol. III, no. 121, pp. 257-58; see also K.V. Subrahmanya Aiyer, *Historical Sketches of the Ancient Dekhan, vol. II*, Coimbatore, 1967, p. 194.

175. *SII*, vol. II, no. 76, pp. 375-90.

176. *EI*, vol. IV, no. 32, pp. 223-24.

dependent of Parāntaka I in connection with a grant made for the maintenance of a tank (see chapter on Economic Life).

A Gaṅga chieftain named Sīyagaṅga, son of Coḷendra Siṁha and a vassal of Kulottuṅga III figures in an inscription found in the Varadarājasvāmi temple, Kāñcīpuram. In this record which mentions a benefaction of this chief to this shrine, he is called as *kūvaḷālāpura-parameśvara-gaṅga-kulodbhava*, i.e., "the lord of Kolār" (near Mysore) and "one who was born of the Gaṅga family."[177]

The chieftains of Milāḍu, known as the Milāḍuḍaiyars who ruled over the Tirukkoyilūr region in South Arcot district were subordinates of the Coḷas. A bi-lingual inscription from Tirukkoyilūr provides some information about a Milāḍu chieftain called Narasiṁhavarman *alias* Raṇakesari Rāman, described as belonging to the family of Bhārgava and residing at Śrīkovalūr (Tirukkovalūr).[178] This record, dated in the sixth year of Rājendra Coḷa II (AD 1057-58), mentions this king accompanying his elder brother Rājādhirāja in the conquest of Raṭṭapāḍi. The title of the Milāḍu chief, Raṇakesari and the context in which the campaign against the Western Cāḷukyas is mentioned in the record, suggests that this chieftain too must have participated in the fight with success.[179]

A few Sanskrit inscriptions of the Telugu-Coḍas, vassals of the imperial Coḷas are available and these belong to the reign of Tammusiddhi, son of Eṟisiddhi and brother of Manuma Siddhi of Nellore, who held a subordinate position under Kulottuṅga III.

A record of this chief found at Śrīraṅgam mentions his genealogy,[180] while other inscriptions mention his gifts to

177. *ARE*, 589 of 1919; K.V. Raman, *Śrī Varadarājaswāmi Temple*, Kāñcī, Delhi, 1975, p. 16.

178. *EI*, vol. VII, no. 20 (K), pp. 145-46.

179. M.S. Govindasamy, *The Role of Feudatories in Later Coḷa History*, Annamalainagar, 1979, p. 40.

180. *ARE*, 367 of 1953/54.

various temples in the Tamil country.[181]

A Bāṇa chieftain, Rājarājadevan *alias* Magadaipperumāḷ also known as Magadesan, Ponparappināṉ and Magadainā̤ḍālvaṉ, a vassal of Kulottuṅga III is known from a number of Sanskrit and bi-lingual epigraphs found at various place like Tiruvaṇṇāmalai, Tiruvānaikkāval, Nārattāmpūṇḍi, Arakaṇḍanallūr and Tirupparaṅkuṉṟam.[182]

An inscription found at the Bilvanātheśvara temple at Tiruvaḷḷam (North Arcot district) of the fourteenth century AD mentions a chief named Vīra Campa, the son of a Coḷa king.[183] Another inscription of the same chief of the same date from the Varadarājasvāmi temple, Kāñcīpuram mentions his name as Campa, son of Vīra-Coḷa.[184] Probably, he was Vīra-Camparāja *alias* Sambuvarāya who figures in the inscriptions in North Arcot as the subordinate of Jaṭāvarman Sundara Pāṇḍya I.[185] The Sambuvarāya chiefs were in charge of the Toṇḍaimaṇḍalam area during the period of the decline of the Pāṇḍyas, Telugu-Coḍas, and Hoysalas till they were overrun by the Vijayanagara power.

Justice

The ruler was the highest judicial authority in his kingdom in ancient India. The *Manusmṛti* emphasizes the duty of the king in dispensing proper justice and in punishing the guilty.[186]

The ruler, though he was the supreme judge in the land, had to dispense justice strictly according to the injunctions laid down in the *Dharmaśāstras*. In this work, he was assisted by scholarly ministers who were well-versed in these texts.

The kings of the Saṅgam period prided themselves in

181. *ARE*, 395 of 1958/59; *EI*, vol. VII, no. 21A, pp. 148-50; *Ibid.*, 21B, pp. 152-55.
182. *ARE*, 554 of 1902; *SII*, vol. VIII, no. 135, pp. 63-64; 482 of 1908; 369, 370 and 371 of 1925; 117 of 1934-35; 247 of 1941-42.
183. *EI*, vol. III, no. 12(A), p. 70.
184. *Ibid.*, no. 12(B), p. 71.
185. K.V. Raman, *op. cit.*, p. 25.
186. *MS*, VIII, 16-22.

dispensing impartial justice. The Saṅgam works such as the *Śilappadikāram*[187] contain an account of the king Manu Nīti Coḷan, so called because he was totally impartial while giving the verdicts.

The Sanskrit drama *Mattavilāsaprahasana* by king Mahendravarman I mentions a judicial court named *Adhikaraṇa* at the Pallava capital-city, Kāñcīpuram.[188] The corruption which existed in this court at that period is also brought out in this work.

The Sanskrit terms *karaṇadaṇḍam* and *adhikaraṇadaṇḍam* mentioned in the Tamil section of the Kaśākuḍi plates have been analysed by C. Minakshi, who has opined that the *adhikaraṇadaṇḍam* was the fine imposed on offenders by the district or chief court (*adhikaraṇa*) while the *karaṇadaṇḍam* was the fine imposed by a court inferior in rank.[189]

The bi-lingual Daḷavāipuram copper-plate grant of Pāṇḍya Parāntaka Vīra Nārāyaṇa (AD 910), provides an instance of a king settling a land dispute.[190] According to the Sanskrit portion of this inscription, a Pāṇḍya king, Kaṭunkoṉ, gave away the village of Śrīmaṅgalam to twelve brāhmaṇas. Another ruler, whose name is not mentioned, gave a village named Somasikuṟichchi to a person named Kāṭhaka Somayāji. A portion of this village was at a later period, appropriated by śūdras and named Madhurasthāna satgrāma. A person named, Keśava, born in Somasikuṟichchi, son of Nārāyaṇa, grandson of Māyā and belonging to the *Vana-gotra*, made a petition to the ruler that these two villages of Śrīmaṅgalam and Somāsikuṟichchi be combined into one and granted to the brāhmaṇas. This was done by the king and the edict written on a copper-plate.

Apart from the royal court, there were many organizations

187. *Śilappadikaram*, Ch. 20, 53-55.
188. *Mattavilāsasprahasana*, ed. N.P. Unni, Trivandrum, 1974, p. 43.
189. C. Minakshi, *ASLP*, p. 70.
190. T.N. Subramaniam, *DCPV*, pp. 16-18.

which settled their own disputes such as trade and agricultural guilds which managed their own affairs. A bi-lingual inscription of the Coḷa period mentions that an agricultural guild called *Cittirameḻi-periyanāḍu* used to dispense justice for the good of the whole world (*sarva-loka-hitān-nyāyām*).[191] Local disputes were settled locally at the village level through the good offices of the *sabhā*.

Punishments

The establishment of a proper and efficient system of justice in any society necessarily requires the awarding of some kind of punishment to the person committing the offence. The works written in the Sanskrit language in ancient India, such as the Purāṇas, Dharmaśāstras and Smṛtis lay stress on the importance of punishing the offenders with the aim of deterring others from committing similar crimes and also with the motive of reforming the offender.

The *Manusmṛti* clearly states,

> Punishment alone governs all created beings, punishment alone protects them, punishment watches over them when they sleep; the wise declare punishment (to be identical with) the law.[192]

The necessity of using punishment as a means of establishing law and order in the state was well-understood by the kings of the Tamil country. A study of the epigraphs of the period under study clearly reveals that these rulers felt that the use of force was vital for the maintenance of law and order.

During the period of the Pallavas, corporal punishment for offenders of the law seems to have been in vogue. One of the earliest copper-plate inscriptions of the Pallavas, the Hīrahadagalli charter of Śivaskandavarman, which records a gift of land to brāhmaṇas, clearly mentions at the end of this epigraph that any person causing any problem to the donees

191. *SII*, vol. VII, no. 129, p. 54.
192. *MS*, VII.18.

of the grant would be restrained by punishment.[193] Some other copper-plate inscriptions,[194] all recording gifts of land, contain Sanskrit verses at the end which state that any person transgressing the order given in the edicts or causing disturbance to the donees will be subject to corporal punishment (*śarīra daṇḍam*).

Some of the titles of Rājasiṁha reveal that this king gave severe punishment to offenders.[195] The *birudas śrī ugra daṇḍa* (one whose punishments are terrible), and *śrī caṇḍa daṇḍa* (he whose punishments are fierce), show that punishments, probably corporal ones, were utilized by the king as a deterrent against crimes.

The inscriptions of the Coḷas and Pāṇḍyas, however, do not contain any threat of corporal punishment to those who transgressed the edicts issued by the rulers. These charters of land grants only contain a request by the donors to the future generations to protect the charity given by them. The absence of the threat of corporal punishment in their charters does not imply that such types of punishment were not meted out in the later periods.

Marco Polo states that the Pāṇḍyan rulers were "very strict in executing justice upon criminals" and that death was sometimes the punishment for a transgressor against right and justice.[196]

Imprecatory Verses

The kings of the Tamil country considered it a great virtue in giving gifts of land to learned brāhmaṇas as *brahmadeya* and to temples as *devadāna*, and considered it their duty to see that their gifts were adequately safeguarded. Apart from the

193. Hīrahadagalli plates, *op. cit.*, p. 7.
194. Mayidavolu plates, *op. cit.*, l. 21, p. 87; Uruvapaḷḷi plates, *op. cit.*, p. 52; Viḷavaṭṭi plates, *op. cit.*, p. 303; *Ind. Ant.*, vol. v (May 1876), p. 156, (Mangalūr plates); Reyūrū plates, *op. cit.*
195. *SII*, vol. I, no. 25, pp. 16-18.
196. K.A. Nilakanta Sastri, *The Pāṇḍyan Kingdon*, Madras, 1972, p. 175.

threat of corporal punishment to those who transgressed their orders which are contained in their copper-plate inscriptions, some imprecatory verses in Sanskrit are also found at the end of these charters to ensure that even future generations did not bring any trouble to the family of the donees and law and order should be maintained in the state.

These stanzas usually extoll the merit accruing to gifts in general, particularly to gifts of land, especially those made in favour of brāhmaṇas and also denounce the resumption of gift-land in the possession of brāhmaṇas in particular.[197] These verses are found in many of the early Pallava copper-plate inscriptions[198] and in some of the Pāṇḍyan epigraphs.[199]

These verses reveal the importance which was attached to the gift of land (*bhūmi-dāna*) by the rulers and the measures taken by them to prevent theft or confiscation of the land given to the donees.

Revenue Administration

Revenue administration was one of the most important duties of the kings and the most convenient and lawful means of acquiring revenue was the imposition of taxes on the people. The ideal king in the Indian tradition was one who was moderate in tax-collection. The *Dharmaśāstras* too permit the rulers to collect taxes from the people in a just manner. According to Manu, "Just as the leech, the calf and the bee take their food little by little, even so must the king draw from his realm moderate annual taxes."[200] Oppression by the rulers has also been condemned in the *Kuraḷ*.[201] Taxes were

---

197. D.C. Sircar, *Indian Epigraphy*, Delhi, 1965, p. 176.
198. Oṁgoḍu II plates, *op. cit.*, p. 255; Uruvapaḷḷi plates, *op. cit.*, p. 52; Sakrepaṭṇa plates, *op. cit.*, p. 105; Maṅgalūr plates, *op. cit.*, p. 156; Cura plates, *op. cit.*, p. 142.
199. Veḷvikuḍi plates, *op. cit.*, vv. 19-23, pp. 303-04; Smaller Siṉṉamaṉūr plates, *op. cit.*, p. 464; Śrīvaramaṅgalam plates, *op. cit.*, p. 61.
200. *MS*, VII, 129.
201. *Kuraḷ*, Ch. 56, vv. 555-56.

levied by the rulers of the Saṅgam period, the most important and common type being that of land-tax.

The kings during the Pallava, Pāṇḍya and Coḷa periods also levied taxes on their subjects. Tax remissions were granted by the kings in many instances. The types of taxes levied by the rulers on different sections of the society can be understood from the numerous Sanskrit epigraphs issued during those periods, which mention the gifts given by the rulers in the form of land either to brāhmaṇas or to temples and made "tax-free."

The Viḻavaṭṭi copper-plates provide information about various taxes which were imposed on different sections of the people.[202] These include taxes due from the metal and leather workers (*loha-carmmakāra*), the shop-keeping cloth dealers (*āpaṇa-paṭṭa-kāra*), licensed spies (*pravarāñcara*) rope jugglers or dancers (*rajju-pratihāra*), those that live by shops or shop-keepers (*āpan-ājīvika*), the taxes payable by barbarians or outcastes (*nāhala*), mask-actors (*mukhadhāraka*), water-diviners (*kūpadarśaka*), from weavers (*tantravāya*), from gambling (*dyūta*), from marriage (*vivāha*), from barbers (*nāpita*) and the taxes payable by the artisans. The term *rajju-pratihāra* means rope-jugglers or dancers, but *rajju-pratihāra-āpanājīvika* may be a tax for maintaining surveyors and gate-keepers (toll-collectors) and from shop-keepers.[203]

This record reveals that Siṁhavarman granted the village of Viḻavaṭṭi to a brāhmaṇa named Viṣṇuśarman stating that all the above-mentioned taxes which belonged to him should henceforth be given to Viṣṇuśarman.

Apart from this inscription, no other Sanskrit epigraph of the period of the Pallavas gives the names of taxes which were levied on the people. It is the Tamil section of many of the bi-lingual copper-plate charters which are the actual operative part of these epigraphs which supply a list of taxes payable to the state.

202. Viḻavaṭṭi plates, *op. cit.*, p. 303.

203. D.C. Sircar, *Indian Epigraphical Glossary*, Delhi, 1966, p. 274.

Some of the Pallava epigraphs praise the kings of this dynasty as imposing very light taxes on their subjects. The Pullūr plates of Nandivarman Pallavamalla mention that during his reign, taxation was very mild (*param mṛdu-karo rāja*).[204] The Veḷāñjeri plates of Aparājita Pallava very poetically mention that like Rāma who destroyed the demons Khara and Dūṣaṇa at Janasthāna, this king destroyed the burden of taxation and hardship in his country (*dāśarathi iva janasthāna vinihita khara dhūśaṇo*).[205]

Parihāras

A very large number of Pallava epigraphs which record the gift of land to learned brāhmaṇas mention that it was exempted from taxes (*parihāra*). The meaning of *parihāra* is a special grant, immunity, privilege or exemption from taxes.[206]

The *Arthaśāstra* clearly mentions that those who perform sacrifices (*ṛtvik*), the spiritual teachers (*ācāryas*), priests (*purohita*) and those well-versed in the Vedas (*śrotriyas*) should be gifted *brahmadeya* lands yielding sufficient produce (*abhirūpadāyaka*) and exempted from taxes and fines (*adaṇḍa hāra*).[207]

Many of the Pallava inscriptions such as the Mayidavolu,[208] Hīrahaḍagalli,[209] Guṇapadeya,[210] Oṁgoḍu,[211] Neḍungarāya,[212] Vesanta,[213] Sakrepaṭṇa,[214] Udayendiram plates of Nandivarman

---

204. Pullūr plates, *op. cit.*, p. 152.
205. R. Nagaswamy, *TVCP*, *Veḷāñjeri plates of Aparājita*, Plate III, p. 1.
206. V.S. Apte, *Students Sanskrit-English Dictionary*, Delhi, 1986, p. 324.
207. *KA*, II, 1, 7.
208. Mayidavolu plates, *op. cit.*, p. 87.
209. Hīrahadagalli plates, *op. cit.*, pp. 6-7.
210. Guṇapadeya plates, *op. cit.*, p. 146.
211. Oṁgoḍu (I) plates, *op. cit.*, p. 251.
212. T.V. Mahalingam, *IOP*, p. 51.
213. N. Ramesan, *VGPS*, p. 96.
214. Sakrepaṭṇa plates, *op. cit.*, p. 105.

I,[215] Cendalūr,[216] Pikira,[217] Maṅgaḷūr,[218] Cura[219] and Kaśākuḍi[220] epigraphs mention that lands were gifted along with exemptions, in some cases with all the eighteen *parihāras*. Some of the *parihāra*s mentioned in the Hīrahadagalli inscription include exemption from supplying food, water, firewood, cots, etc., to the officers visiting the place, exemption from giving milk and curd, from digging the land for salt, from tapping palm-wine, from supplying bullocks, from supplying grass, wood, vegetables, flowers, etc.

The Anbil plates record that Sundara Coḷa gave to his trusted minister Aniruddha, the village called Karuṇākara-maṅgalam with all privileges, inclusive of the taxes, *kārāṇmai* and *miyāṭci*.[221] According to K.A. Nilakanta Sastri, the terms *kārāṇmai* and *miyāṭci* correspond to the cultivator's and landlord's rights respectively.[222] The Esālam plates state that Rājendra I gave a village named Vikramacoḷanallūr tax-free to a Śiva temple.[223]

The Larger Siṉṉamaṉūr plates state that Pāṇḍya Rājasiṁha III gave to a brāhmaṇa, Parāntakaśarman the *agrahāra* named Narcheygai-Puttūr also called Maṇḍaragauravamaṅgalam as a *brahmadeya* together with (its) *kārāṇmai* and *miyāṭci*.[224]

According to the Śivakāśi plates, Vīra-Pāṇḍya gave as a *brahmadeya* gift to a poet Pītāmbara, the village Śāsanamaṅgalam with the *kārāṇmai* and *miyāṭci* rights bestowed on the donee.[225]

An important source of revenue by which the treasury of

---

215. Udayendiram (I) plates, *op. cit.*, p. 146.
216. Cendalūr plates, *op. cit.*, p. 235.
217. Pikira plates, *op. cit.*, p. 162.
218. Maṅgalūr plates, *op. cit.*, p. 156.
219. Cura plates, *op. cit.*, p. 142.
220. Kaśākuḍi plates, *op. cit.*, p. 351.
221. Anbil plates, *op. cit.*, v. 40, p. 63.
222. K.A. Nilakanta Sastri, *The Coḷas*, Madras, 1984, p. 577.
223. R. Nagaswamy, *ECPR*, v. 28, p. 33.
224. Larger Siṉṉamaṉūr plates, *op. cit.*, vv. 28-32, p. 453.
225. Śivakāśi plates, *op. cit.*, v. 16, p. 45.

the kings of the Tamil country must have been enlarged was the booty captured from the vanquished kings and their country following the conquests.

The epigraphs of the Pallava, Pāṇḍya and the Coḷa rulers are full of accounts of their various successful campaigns and the war-booty seized in the form of gold, jewellery, elephants and horses from the conquered rulers. The Udayendiram grant of Nandivarman Pallavamalla records that his capable general, Udayacandra seized faultless necklaces of excellent lusture, and an immeasurable heap of gold and elephants (*niravadya-pramukh-āṁśuhārān aparimita suvarṇa-saṁcayam kuñjarān=api yo=jagrāha*) after having defeated a chief of the Niṣādas named Pṛthivīvyāghra.[226]

The epigraphs of the Coḷas, especially their copper-plate records contain accounts of the war-booty which was captured following the defeat of various enemy kings. The Karandai plates[227] give a very detailed list of the property captured from the Siṁhaḷa king who was defeated by the Coḷa army of Rājendra I thus, "the strong (Rājendra) having conquered the mighty Siṁhaḷa king by a fierce army, captured in battle his territory (*tad bhūmiṁ*), his crown (*tan mukuṭam*), his queen (*tadīya mahiṣīn*), her crown (*tasyāś=ca maulim*), his daughter (*tat putrīn*), his mass of properties (*tadīya vastu nivahan*), his vehicles (*tad vahanāny*), the garland of Indra (*indrahāram*) and the spotless crown of the Pāṇḍya king (*amalam pāṇḍyasya mauliṁ*) which was preserved by him."

The epigraphs of the Pāṇḍyas also contain accounts of the war-booty captured from the kings whom they defeated. The Śrīraṅgam inscription of Jaṭāvarman Sundara Pāṇḍya I contains information about the crowns captured from the treasuries of his enemies, the wealth he had carried away from the king of Kāṭhaka and the masses of gold which he had brought from numerous wars.[228]

---

226. Udayendiram plates, *op. cit.*, p. 368.
227. K.G. Krishnan, *KTPR*, v. 58, p. 74.
228. *EI*, vol. III, no. 2, pp. 11-14.

Expenditure

The income earned by the state by means of collecting taxes from the subjects, by accumulating wealth through conquests and the like must have been spent in different directions. A considerable amount of the wealth accumulated by the kings of the Tamil country must have been spent on defence. The frequent wars which took place necessitated the maintenance of large armies. The payment given to the soldiers and generals, the procurement and maintenance of horses and war-elephants and the supply of food and weapons to the soldiers must have amounted to a very large sum of money.

In addition to the army officials, the Sanskrit as well as the Tamil epigraphs mention various officials in-charge of different departments concerned with the administration of the state. A considerable amount of money must have been spent on the salaries of these officials.

The Sanskrit inscriptions reveal that these kings performed various types of sacrifices such as the *aśvamedha, rājasūya* and *tulābhāra* ceremonies. Each of these religious rites was an elaborate and complicated ceremony and would have cost the state very large sums of money.

However, the greater part of the expenditure of the state would, undoubtedly, have been spent for the betterment of the people. The numerous inscriptions reveal that the kings spent money on works of public utility such as construction of wells, constructing and repairing tanks, establishing educational institutions and hospitals and building temples. A lot of money was also given by kings to the learned and the needy as repeatedly mentioned by the inscriptions of this period.

The maintenance of the numerous palaces of the rulers, their personal retinue and the allowances given to the queens and other members of the royal family was also a part of the state expenditure.

3

Administration (Military)

WARS have, from time immemorial, been a part and parcel of any organized state. The maintenance of a strong army was an essential feature of every kingdom, helping to check invasions, quelling internal revolts and aiding the ruler in expanding his territory. The *Arthaśāstra* has mentioned the army (*daṇḍa*) as one of the seven elements of the state.[1] The *Kuraḷ* also mentions the army (*paḍai*) as one of the limbs of the state,[2] adding that the greatest wealth of a ruler is an army which is well-manned and fearless.[3]

All the kingdoms in ancient and medieval India possessed well-equipped armies and the kingdoms of the Tamil kings were no exception to this. The inscriptions of these periods reveal that these kingdoms possessed large and powerful armies which participated in numerous wars.

During these periods, the king was the head of the army. In most cases, the kings themselves were at the forefront of the army, leading their soldiers to war against the enemy. The Kūram plates state that Parameśvaravarman I was at the head of the Pallava troops in their battle against the Cāḷukyas.[4] According to the Karandai plates, Rājarāja I led the Coḷa army against the Western Cāḷukyas, fighting on horse-back.[5]

1. *KA*, VI.1.1.
2. *The Kuraḷ*, (tr. and ed.) P.S. Sundaram, New Delhi, 1990, Ch. 39, v. 381.
3. *Ibid.*, Ch. 77, v. 761.
4. *SII*, vol. I, no. 151, p. 148 (Kūram plates).
5. K.G. Krishnan, *KTPR*, v. 29, p. 71.

The kings themselves appear to have been excellent warriors and extremely skilled in the use of various weapons as indicated by many of their inscriptions. An epigraph of Rājasiṁha describes the Pallava kings as "those who excelled in the knowledge of weapons" (*heti-vidyāvarāṇām*).[6] The Kaśākuḍi charter mentions that the early Pallava rulers won major battles because of "a knowledge of the science of all weapons" (*samasta-śastra-śāstra-nirjjit-orijjita-samitayaḥ*).[7]

Siṁhaviṣṇu is described in the Paḷḷankovil grant (*c.* AD 550), as being like Arjuna (*balena jiṣṇuḥ*).[8] Another inscription of Rājasiṁha contains many of his *biruda*s (titles) such as *śrī citrakārmukaḥ* (the wonderful archer), *śrī yuddhārjunaḥ* (he who resembles Arjuna in battle) and *śrī ekadhanurdharaḥ* (the unrivalled archer) which proclaim the skill of this Pallava ruler in wielding the bow.[9]

Nandivarman Pallavamalla is also praised as an excellent archer and compared to Droṇa and Arjuna in the Udayendiram plates (*arjuna iva kārmukhe droṇa iva dhanurvede*).[10] The Taṇḍantoṭṭam plates state that this ruler was "praised for (his knowledge in) the use of all weapons in battle" (*samiti-mahitaḥ-sarva-śastra-prayogaiḥ*).[11] Interestingly, another inscription states that Aparājita Pallava destroyed the enemy elephants with an elephant goad (*aṅkuśa*), an unusual weapon to be used in wars.[12]

Rājarāja's skill in using the mace, one of the most widely used weapons of war in those days, is attested to by the Tiruvālaṅgāḍu plates which state that this king killed a ruler of Āndhra named Bhīma with a mace (*daṇḍa*).[13] The epigraphs reveal that some of the kings were adept in sword-fighting.

---

6. *SII*, vol. I, no. 24, p. 12.
7. *SII*, vol. II, no. 73, l. 46, p. 348 (Kaśākuḍi plates).
8. T.N. Subramaniam, *PJCG*, v. 4, p. 76.
9. *SII*, vol. I, no. 25, pp. 14-18.
10. *SII*, vol. II, no. 74, ll. 26-27, p. 366 (Udayendiram plates).
11. *SII*, vol. II, no. 99, v. 2, p. 520 (Taṇḍantoṭṭam plates).
12. R. Nagaswamy, *TVCP*, *Veḷāñjeri plates of Aparājita*, v. 10, plate II, p. 2.
13. *SII*, vol. III, no. 205, v. 82, p. 398 (Tiruvālaṅgāḍu plates).

The Karandai plates record that Rājarāja withstood the assault of the Western Cāḷukyan army led by Satyāśraya holding a sword (*asi*) while seated on horse-back.[14]

An interesting but damaged epigraph from Viriñcipuram (North Arcot district) praises the valour and greatness of the sword of Sundara Coḷa.[15] The Kāḍava chief Kopperuñjiṅga also appears to have excelled in sword-fighting as revealed by his titles *khaḍgamalla*[16] and also *kṛpaṇamalla,*[17] both meaning "excellent swordsman." In a Tamil inscription he is called *vāḷvaḷḷapperumāḷ*[18] again a reference to his skill with the sword.

It appears from the evidence gathered from the inscriptions that the royal princes were trained in the martial arts from a very young age. The Karandai epigraph reveals that even when he was a young boy, Rājendra Coḷa I was well trained in riding on horses (*turaṅga*), elephants (*mātaṅga*) and chariots (*ratha*) and was adept in the use of arms and weapons.[19] The Tiruvālaṅgāḍu plates allude to the immense physical strength of Rājendra I.[20]

Some of the kings seem to have been very skilled wrestlers as indicated by their titles. Narasiṁhavarman I's famous title was *māmalla* (*mahāmalla* or the great wrestler). An inscription bearing this name is found in the Dharmarāja Ratha, begun during his reign at Māmallapuram.[21] This title is also found in a record of this ruler from Bādāmi (Bījāpur district, Karnataka).[22] In a Tamil inscription also he is described as *māmalla*.[23] Rājasiṁha has been glorified in many of his

14. K.G. Krishnan, *KTPR*, v. 29, p. 71.
15. *ARE*, 185 of 1939-40.
16. *SII*, vol. XII, no. 120, p. 58.
17. *SII*, vol. XII, no. 246, p. 154.
18. *ARE*, 480 of 1902.
19. K.G. Krishnan, *op. cit.*, v. 42, p. 72.
20. Tiruvālaṅgāḍu plates, *op. cit.*, v. 121, p. 400.
21. K.R. Srinivasan, *The Dharmarāja Ratha and its Sculptures, Mahābalipuram*, New Delhi, 1975, p. 7.
22. *SII*, vol. XI, no. I, p. 1 (Bādāmi inscription).
23. *SII*, vol. VII, no. 42, p. 16.

inscriptions as being a very talented wrestler — *śrī amitramallaḥ* (the wrestler with his foes), *śrī apratimallaḥ* (the unrivalled wrestler) and *śrī mahāmallaḥ* (the great wrestler) are some of the titles of this king.[24]

Nandivarman II has been called *kṣatriyamalla* (the best of wrestlers among the kṣatriyas) and *pallavamalla* (the best of wrestlers among the Pallavas) in the Kaśākuḍi plates.[25]

Army Generals

The vital role played by the army in safeguarding the lives of the common people had been realized from very early times in ancient India and great importance was paid to the selection and appointment of the officers in charge of the army. The *Manusmṛti* states that "the army depends on the official (placed in charge of it) and the due control of the subjects on the army."[26] Kauṭilya mentions the commander of the army (*senāpati*) and states that he should be well trained in the science of all (kinds of) fights and weapons and he should be renowned for riding on elephants, horses and chariots and with the direction of the work done by the fourfold troops.[27] The *Kuraḷ* also states that an army without leaders will melt away even though it has many good soldiers.[28]

The numerous Sanskrit inscriptions of the Tamil country reveal that the armies were under the command of very loyal and capable generals who were known as *senāpati, daṇḍanātha, daṇḍādinātha* and *sainyanātha*.

The Hīrahadagalli charter mentions among other officials, the *neyikas*.[29] G. Bühler has taken this word to mean a corrupted form of the Sanskrit term *nāyaka* which would indicate a military officer of the rank of a corporal or general.[30] The

---

24. *SII*, vol. I, no. 25, pp. 14-18.
25. Kaśākuḍi plates, *op. cit.*, l. 78, p. 350.
26. *MS*, VII, 65.
27. *KA*, II. 33, 9.
28. *Kuraḷ, op. cit.*, Ch. 77, v. 770.
29. *EI*, vol. I, no. I, p. 5 (Hīrahadagalli plates).
30. *Ibid.*, p. 8.

Uruvapaḷḷi grant mentions a general (*senāpati*) of Viṣṇugopavarman, named Viṣṇuvarma.[31]

The inscriptions of the Coḷas, especially the Tiruvālaṅgāḍu copper-plates repeatedly mention the generals in command of the Coḷa army in connection with the various military exploits of these kings and also their unswerving loyalty. The Tiruvālaṅgāḍu inscription records that the general (*daṇḍanātha*) of Rājarāja I captured the town of Viḷinda which was surrounded by a moat and which was impregnable to the enemies.[32] This general has been glorified in this epigraph as being "the hereditary home of the Goddess of Victory" (*viḷindam vijayaramā-kula mandirañ=jigāya*). These plates also state that the general (*daṇḍanātha*) of Rājendra I attacked a Pāṇḍyan king and his powerful army and drove him out his country.[33]

The same inscription states that Rājendra I, wanting to purify the Coḷa country with the sacred waters of the river Gaṅgā, ordered his general (*daṇḍādinātha*) to conquer the enemy kings of the kingdoms situated on the banks of the Gaṅgā.[34] This general, although his name is not mentioned in the inscription, is glorified as possessing many powerful battalions (*balavad bal-augham*) under his control, as being the resort of heroism (*śaury=āspadaḥ*) and the foremost of diplomats (*nītimad=agragaṇyam*). This inscription describes the exploits of the Coḷa army led by this general (*sainyanātha*), consisting of numerous powerful elephants, horses and foot-soldiers in great detail. Having conquered the enemy kings, enroute to the Gaṅgā, this general brought the sacred waters of this river to his master, carried by the kings he had defeated on his way. The Kanyākumārī inscription also records this feat accomplished by the generals of Rājendra Coḷa I.[35]

---

31. *Ind. Ant.*, vol. V (February 1876), p. 52 (Uruvapaḷḷi plates).
32. Tiruvālaṅgāḍu plates, *op. cit.*, v. 79, p. 398.
33. *Ibid.*, v. 91, pp. 398-99.
34. *Ibid.*, v. 109, p. 400.
35. *TAS*, vol. I, no. 34, v. 71, p. 146 (Kanyākumārī inscription).

According to the Karandai epigraph, this king captured the city of Mānyakheṭa (Maṇṇaikkaḍakkam in the Tamil part), while he remained in his own capital.[36] Thus, it appears that Rājendra I must have sent one of his trusted generals on this campaign, his own presence in his capital city having been necessary.

The services of Naralokavīra, a famous general of Kulottuṅga Coḷa I and who also served his son and successor, Vikrama Coḷa in many wars are known from many Tamil inscriptions and from the Tamil work *Vikramaśoḷan-ulā*. He was a highly respected official who had a large fief at Manavil in North Arcot district which he perhaps obtained as a reward for his distinguished services in the southern campaigns of Kulottuṅga I.[37]

There are a number of beautiful Sanskrit inscriptions of this well-known general, but these proclaim his benefactions to various temples rather than glorify his exploits as a general (see chapter on Religion).

Another famous general of Kulottuṅga I was Karuṇākara Toṇḍaimān. A Sanskrit inscription from Drākṣārāma[38] (Andhra Pradesh) mentions the exploits of a general, called in this epigraph by various names such as Vaṇḍuvarāja, Pallavarāja and Tiruvaraṅga who annihilated the whole of the Kaliṅga country, defeated the Gaṅga ruler and other kings and thus raised the prestige of his master. K.V. Subrahmanya Aiyer has stated that this army chief is the same as the army general Karuṇākara Toṇḍaimān who has been glorified in the *Kaliṅgattuparaṇi* of Jayaṁkoṇḍar, a Tamil work composed in the reign of Kulottuṅga Coḷa I.[39]

Some of the overseas expeditions of the Coḷas to countries such as Sri Lanka and Kaṭāha (Malaysia) seem to have been

---

36. K.G. Krishnan, *KTPR*, v. 55, p. 74.
37. K.A. Nilakanta Sastri, *Studies in Coḷa History and Administration*, Madras, 1932, pp. 183-85, and also p. 188.
38. *EI*, vol. XXII, No. 23, pp. 143-44 (Drākṣārāma inscription).
39. *Ibid.*, p. 140.

under the charge of their generals. The Tiruvālaṅgāḍu plates record that the general of Rājarāja I crossed the ocean by ships and defeated the king of Laṅkā, thereby indicating that this king assigned this task to one of his able generals and did not proceed to Sri Lanka himself.[40] The composer of this inscription praises this general in a very poetic manner thus:

> The Lord of the Rāghavas (Rāma) constructing a bridge across the water of the ocean with the help of able monkeys killed with great difficulty the king of Laṅkā: (but) this terrible general (of Rājarāja) crossed the ocean by ships and burnt the Lord of Laṅkā. Hence Rāma is surely surpassed by this (Coḷa general).

The Kanyākumārī inscription reveals that Parāntaka I "caused his army to cross the sea and subdue the king of Siṁhaḷa."[41] This epigraph also states that Rājendra I made his army, which had defeated several enemy kings cross the sea and capture Kaṭāha.[42] Since these inscriptions do not state that the rulers themselves went on these long sea-voyages, it is possible that it was the generals who were in charge of these overseas expeditions.

T.V. Mahalingam has suggested that the king himself did not lead the army unless it was vital, since his life was too precious to be risked in battles.[43] Instances such as the capture of the Pallava ruler Nandivarman II by enemy kings[44] and the death of the Coḷa crown prince Rājāditya, the son of Parāntaka I, while leading his army seated on the back of an elephant, against the Rāṣṭrakūṭa king, Kṛṣṇa III at Takkolam,[45] show the grave dangers to which these kings exposed themselves while leading the army on the battle-field.

40. Tiruvālaṅgāḍu plates, *op. cit.*, v. 80, p. 398.
41. Kanyākumārī inscription, *op. cit.*, v. 59, p. 143.
42. *Ibid.*, v. 72, p. 146.
43. T.V. Mahalingam, *South Indian Polity*, Madras (1955), p. 271.
44. Udayendiram plates, *op. cit.*, l. 37, p. 367.
45. Larger Leiden plates, *op. cit.*, v. 20, p. 240.

It is also possible that these kings deputed their generals on long expeditions and did not go themselves as their presence in the capital city was imperative for purposes of administration and to protect the kingdom from invasions.

The loyalty and attachment of a Coḷa general is revealed in a very interesting epigraph found in the Ādhipurīśvara temple at Tiruvoṟṟiyūr.[46] This general, named Vallabha, the son of the chief of Vallabharāṣṭra named Rājaśekhara, who was probably a subordinate or general of the king of Keraḷa, came to the Coḷa country and became the general of Rājāditya (the son and crown-prince of Parāntaka Coḷa I). Unfortunately, Vallabha was not present at the battle of Takkolam where Rājāditya lost his life. This general, stricken with grief at not having been with his master at that time and "feeling that his act was unworthy of his class, himself, his family and his master" lost interest in worldly attachments and ultimately became a monk and settled at Tiruvoṟṟiyūr.

V. Raghavan has identified Vallabha with a Keraḷa general of Rājāditya called Vellaṅ-Kumāra or Vellaṅ-Kumāran, who is mentioned in two Tamil records from Grāmam (South Arcot district),[47] and described as an eminent Malayāḷi (*uttamaḥ keraḷānām*), a grand-general of Rājāditya (*avicalita-camūnāyaka* and *perumpaḍai-nāyakar*).

A bi-lingual epigraph of the 14th century AD found in the Varadarājasvāmi temple, Kāñcīpuram records that Muppiḍi, a general (*nāyaka*) of the Kākatīya ruler, Pratāparudra II of Ekaśilānagarī (Warrangal) came to Kāñcī and installed a certain Mānavīra as the governor of Kāñcī.[48] Mānavīra mentioned in this inscription was probably a member of the Telugu-Coḍa family which was connected with Kāñcī.[49]

---

46. *EI*, vol. XXVII, no. 47, pp. 301-02 (Tiruvoṟṟiyūr inscription).
47. *Ibid.*, n. 1.
48. *EI*, vol. VII, no. 18, vv. 2-4, p. 130.
49. *Ibid.*, pp. 129-30.

Composition of the army

It is possible that the army of the Tamil kings was composed of members from all castes. According to K.A. Nilakanta Sastri,

> We can form no idea of the methods of recruitment or of the numbers of the troops permanently employed in the army. It is remarkable that many of the leaders (*senāpatis*) in the army were of brahmin extraction, and when sufficiently distinguished, bore the title Brahmādhirāja.[50]

An example of a brāhmaṇa excelling in warfare is provided by the Pullūr record which states that a minister of Nandivarman Pallavamalla named Nāgaśarma Brahmādhirāja excelled in the science of weapons and warfare (*kṣatravidyā-vicakṣaṇaḥ*).[51] This brāhmaṇa minister, extolled in this inscription as "the most excellent of brāhmaṇas" (*dvijavaraḥ*), must obviously, have been an extremely able general or commander to have been the recipient of the title *brahmādhirāja*. The Anbil plates also record that Sundara Coḷa conferred upon his minister Aniruddha, the title *brahmādhirāja*.[52]

A bi-lingual epigraph of the tenth century AD, mentions in the first Sanskrit verse that a person named Nārāyaṇa who was a *brahmādhirāja* made a grant of lamps as well as a grant of paddy to the Viṣṇu temple at Pārthivaśekharapuram (Pārthivapuram, near Kanyākumārī).[53] The Tamil section of this inscription states that his full name was Pañcavaṉ Brahmādhirājan *alias* Kumāran Nārāyaṇan. The word Pañcavaṉ is known to be the title of the Pāṇḍyas, thus suggesting that the donor was a senior officer under the Pāṇḍyas and that he had adopted the title or was conferred with the same as a mark of his devoted subordination to the then Pāṇḍya king.[54]

---

50. K.A. Nilakanta Sastri, *The Coḷas*, pp. 457-58.
51. *EI*, vol. XXXVI, no. 20, p. 153 (Pullūr plates).
52. *EI*, vol. XV, no. 5, v. 42, p. 63 (Anbil plates).
53. *EI*, vol. XLI, no. 1, p. 6 (Pārthivapuram inscription).
54. *Ibid*., p. 3.

Since the donor happens to be a high ranking officer under the Pāṇḍyas, it is not unlikely that the region including Pārthivapuram where this officer was possibly present in AD 923 to make this grant was under the influence of Rājasiṁha, the contemporary Pāṇḍyan king.[55]

Princes of the royal family and the feudatories of the kings also seem to have participated in the wars. The Amarāvatī Pillar inscription states that on one of his marches, the Pallava ruler, Siṁhavarman was guarded on his back, flanks and front by his brave vassals and feudatories (*māṇḍalika sāmanta*).[56]

The Udayendiram plates give a very vivid picture of the role played by the brave and loyal feudatory of Nandivarman Pallavamalla named Udayacandra, the "lord of the city of Vilvala."[57] This chieftain is praised in this epigraph as "the chastiser of hostile enemies" (*paracakradaṇḍi*) and "the excellent hero" (*dhīravaraḥ*).[58] Many of the services rendered by Udayacandra such as rescuing Pallavamalla when he was besieged in Nandipura by his enemies, the killing of the Pallava king, Citramāya, defeating enemies at the battle-fields of Nimbavana, Cūtavana, Śaṅkaragrāma, Nellūr, Nelveli and Sūrāvarundūr, killing of the Śabara king, chasing a Niṣāda chief named Pṛthivivyāghra who was following his *aśvamedha* horse out of the territory of Viṣṇurāja which he then subjected to his own king, destroying a fort named Kāḷīdurga and defeating the Pāṇḍya king at the battle of Maṇṇaikuḍi are mentioned in this epigraph.

The Karandai plates record that Rājendra I was always accompanied by princes hailing from good families and by the feudatories of the king.[59] These feudatories are described

---

55. *EI*, vol. XLI, no. 1, (Pārthivapuram inscription)., pp. 3-4.
56. *SII*, vol. I, no. 32, p. 27 (Amarāvatī Pillar inscription).
57. Udayendiram plates, *op. cit.*, l. 44, p. 367.
58. *Ibid.*, l. 61, p. 368.
59. K.G. Krishnan, *KTPR*, v. 56, p. 74.

as experts in warfare and who possessed arms befitting their rank and who never retreated from the battle-fields.[60]

A Sanskrit record[61] of the Kāḍava chieftain, Kopperuñjiṅga found at the Vṛṣabheśvara temple in Chengam (North Arcot district) mention the exploits of his *sāmanta* named Gāṅgeya, while another inscription at the same place extolls his valour.[62]

Divisions in the Army

The army in ancient India was traditionally divided into four units, namely, chariots, elephants, horses and foot soldiers, collectively known as *caturaṅga* or *caturaṅgabala*. This military arrangement was common throughout ancient and medieval India and the numerous Sanskrit inscriptions of the Pallavas, Pāṇḍyas and the Coḷas reveal that these army divisions were maintained in the Tamil country also. These epigraphs provide a graphic picture of the part played by these military units in the wars.

Chariots

Chariots (*rathas*) were used in ancient India in wars as well as a mode of transport for royalty. Chariots were used in the Tamil country also as early as the Saṅgam age as can be seen from the Saṅgam work such as the *Maduraikkāñci* which states that a Coḷa ruler possessed a large number of beautiful war-chariots and was famous because of that.[63]

The use of the chariot seems to have declined by the days of the Pallavas, Pāṇḍyas and Coḷas. Although a number of inscriptions describe the numerous battles of these kings, the use of war-chariots has not been mentioned in any of them. Even the Kūram plates which give a very graphic description of the war of Peruvaḷanallūr and mention the parts played by the other three divisions in the army do not make any reference

---

60. K.G. Krishnan, *KTPR*, v. 57, p. 74.
61. *ARE*, 65 of 1974-75.
62. *ARE*, 68 of 1974-75.
63. *Maduraikkānci*, (ed.) U.V. Swaminatha Iyer, Madras, 1920, l. 752.

to war-chariots.[64] The historical sculptures found in the Vaikuṇṭhaperumāḷ temple, Kāñcīpuram which depict the achievements of the kings of the Pallava dynasty and which contain various battle scenes in which elephants, horses and foot-soldiers are seen actively participating, do not depict any war-chariots.

The inscriptions of the Coḷas such as the Larger Leiden and the Tiruvālaṅgāḍu inscriptions which repeatedly mention the role played by the elephant corps, cavalry and infantry in their wars, fail to mention the use of chariots. The Karandai plates, however, do contain a few references to chariots but not in the context of wars. This inscription mentions that as a boy, Rājendra I was well trained in the art of riding chariots.[65] The same epigraph also records that the king of Kāmboja, in order to win Rājendra's friendship sent him a chariot with which he had triumphed over the armies of his enemies in battle.[66]

Thus it seems likely that starting from the period of the Pallavas, war-chariots were not in any significant use in the Tamil country, although they may have been used as a mode of transport for royalty and high officials of the state.

Elephants

The practice of using trained elephants in wars as well as part of the royal entourage was very common in all parts of India during the ancient and medieval periods. The Tamil country was no exception to this practice and the Saṅgam works provide accounts of the role played by elephants in the battles of that period. The *Puraṇānūru* very poetically describes the elephants as standing in the middle of a large army like the navy in the ocean,[67] and that they butted against the strong gates of the forts due to the impact of which, the bolts were twisted out of shape and the gates forced open.[68]

64. Kūram plates, *op. cit.*, pp. 148-50.
65. K.G. Krishnan, *KTPR*, v. 42, p. 72.
66. *Ibid.*, v. 48, p. 73.
67. *Puranānūru*, (ed.) U.V. Swaminatha Iyer, Madras, 1923, v. 13.
68. *Ibid.*, v. 14.

The Sanskrit inscriptions reveal that the elephant corps played a major role in the armies of the Tamil kings. The Pallava rulers seem to have had a special preference for elephants and maintained a large and powerful elephant force. The elephants are referred to in the epigraphs by the terms *gaja, mātaṅga, nāga, kari, ibha, vāraṇa, kuñjara* and *sindūra*. Some of the Pallava kings were noted for their knowledge of the *Gajaśāstra* or the science of elephants. Many titles of Rājasiṁha, such as *śrī ibha vidyādharaḥ* (one who possesses the knowledge of elephants), *śrī ibha vatsarājaḥ* (he who resembles the king of Vatsa in the knowledge of elephants), *śrī nāga priyaḥ* (one who is fond of elephants) and *śrī vāraṇa bhāgadattaḥ* (he who resembles Bhāgadatta in the knowledge of elephants) reveal his interest in elephants.[69] Another title of this king found in Māmallapuram reads *śrī vāmānkuśaḥ* (bearer of a handsome elephant-goad).[70]

Nandivarman Pallavamalla also possessed an excellent knowledge of elephants. The Udayendiram copper-plates record that this king resembled the king of Vatsa in the knowledge and science of elephants (*vatsarāja iva kuñjareṣu*)[71] while the Kaśākuḍi plates also echo the same idea (*vāraṇa tantravādya viṣaye vatseśvaraḥ*).[72]

The interest which the rulers of the Pallava dynasty evinced in elephants indicates that these kings must have maintained a very large and strong elephant force and this is attested to by epigraphical evidence.

---

69. *SII*, vol. I, no. 25, pp. 14-18.
    The reference to Vatsarāja is to Udayana, the king of Vatsa, who was an expert on elephants, while the reference to Bhāgadatta is to the ruler of Prāgjyotiṣa, an ally of Duryodhana in the *Mahābhārata* war who was well-versed in elephant lore and whose elephant Supratīka caused havoc in the Pāṇḍava army.
70. *SII*, vol. XII, no. 23, p. 11.
71. Udayendiram plates, *op. cit.*, l. 19, p. 366.
72. Kaśākuḍi plates, *op. cit.*, v. 29, pp. 349-50.

The Kūram copper-plates, which give an account of the war between the Pallava ruler Parameśvaravarman I and the Cāḷukyan king Vikramāditya give a detailed description of the part played by the elephant corps in this battle.[73] The Udayendiram plates also reveal that elephants formed a large section of the armies of the Pallavas as well as that of their enemies during that period.[74] An inscription of Aparājita Pallava reveals that he conquered a Coḷa ruler in the battle of Ciṟṟāṟṟūr with the help of his elephant forces.[75]

The epigraphs reveal that the Pallava rulers took personal interest in their elephants. The Kūram grant gives a detailed picture of the personal elephant of Parameśvaravarman I named Arivāraṇa.[76] This grant states that this elephant appeared like the king of mountains himself (*adrināthasākṣādiva*), that he was followed by thousands of other elephants (*dvīpa-sahasra-kṛtānuyānam*) and that this king had a golden saddle studded with jewels fitted on the back of this elephant (*ratna-prabhā-khacita-kāñcana-śāri-bandham samnāhya nāgam=arivāraṇa-nāmadeyam*).

A Tamil inscription of the Bāṇa chief Rājarājadevan[77] *alias* Magadaipperumāḷ states that his personal elephant was called by the Sanskrit name Airāvata. This was evidently after the divine white elephant which arose from the milk-ocean mentioned in a very large number of Sanskrit works such as the *Mahābhārata*[78] and the *Bhāgavata Purāṇa*.[79]

The accounts of the role played by elephants in the battle between the Pallava armies and their enemies given in the Pallava inscriptions are corroborated by the panel of historical

73. Kūram plates, *op. cit.*, pp. 148-50.
74. Udayendiram plates, *op. cit.*, pp. 365-70.
75. R. Nagaswamy, *TVCP*, *op. cit.*
76. Kūram plates, *op. cit.*, v. 5, p. 149.
77. *SII*, vol. VIII, no. 97, pp. 50-51.
78. M.N. Dutt (tr.), *Mahābhārata* (vol. I, Ādi Parva), Delhi, 1997, Ch.XVIII, v. 41, p. 40.
79. Swami Tapasyananda (tr.), *Śrīmad Bhāgavatam* (vol. II), Madras, 1982, Ch. 8, v. 4, p. 327.

sculptures found in the Vaikuṇṭhaperumāḷ temple, Kāñcīpuram. A large number of panels show the elephant forces of the Pallavas marching with soldiers mounted on their backs. The panels which depict the actual battle scenes between the Pallavas and their enemies show the elephants of either side locked in combat with one another and trying to push through each other's defences.

The inscriptions of the Coḷas reveal that the practice of maintaining a strong elephant force was continued in this period also. The Anbil plates praise the capability of the personal elephant of Sundara Coḷa on the battlefield.[80]

The Larger Leiden plates state that the Coḷa prince Rājāditya was killed in battle while seated on the back of an excellent elephant.[81] The strength and brute force of the elephant corps of the Coḷa army are described in the Anbil, Larger Leiden and the Tiruvālaṅgāḍu plates.

The composer of the Karandai inscription poetically describes the elephant brigade of the army of Rājarāja I on one of their marches thus: "the traces of the tusks of the elephants caused due to playful butting are seen even today on the mounds on the banks of the waters of Tuṅgabhadrā river" (*yad-danti-danta-kṣatayo rājante-=dy=āpi sarvataḥ, tungabhadrā-nadī-toya-rodho jaghana-bhūmiṣu*).[82]

The Tiruvālaṅgāḍu inscription states that the army of Rājendra I crossed the rivers by way of bridges formed by the herds of elephants (*kari-nikara-nibaddha-setu-mārgair= balam=atarat=saritas-=tadīyam=agryam*).[83]

The Kanyākumārī inscription also records the strength of the elephant corps of the army of Rājendra Coḷa I. The composer of this inscription states in a poetic manner that "the banks of the Gaṅgā slipped down this river through the

80. Anbil plates, *op. cit.*, v. 29, p. 62.

81. Larger Leiden plates, *op. cit.*, v. 20, p. 240.

82. K.G. Krishnan, *KTPR*, v. 28, p. 71.

83. Tiruvālaṅgāḍu plates, *op. cit.*, v. 112, p. 400.

destruction of his roaring elephant brigade (*gaṅgām=udgarjan-nija-kari-ghaṭa-pātita-taṭām*)."[84]

These rulers also added to their existing forces by forcibly taking over the elephant corps of their vanquished enemies. Instances of this practice have been recorded in inscriptions such as the Udayendiram, Larger Leiden, Tiruvālaṅgāḍu, Karandai and the Śrīvaramaṅgalam plates of Pāṇḍyan Neḍuñjaḍaiyan. The Taṇḍantoṭṭam plates record details about one particular elephant which Nandivarman Pallavamalla captured from a Gaṅga king. This elephant, named Paṭṭavardhana is described in this epigraph as "an excellent one, which in arrogance was like its master, like victory in appearance and which moved about like a high mountain" (*sva-bhartur=iva yam=mado jaya iv=āṅgavāñ=jaṅgamo girīndra iva paṭṭavardhana iti dvipendro=bhajat*).[85] The elephants thus captured from the enemy ranks must have considerably strengthened the armies of the Tamil kings.

The Karandai plates state that the king of Cakragoṣṭha presented Rājendra Coḷa I with a large number of elephants belonging to the *bhadra* type (*asamkhyair-bhadrair gajaiḥ*) which were worthy of being used for coronation (*abhiṣeka-yogyaiḥ*) and thereby pleased this king.[86]

In addition to the epigraphical references to the strength of the elephant brigade in the Coḷa army, there are the accounts written by foreign travellers. A Chinese author, writing about the Coḷa army in AD 1178, has recorded that,

> The government owns sixty thousand war-elephants, everyone seven or eight feet high. When fighting, these elephants carry on their backs, houses and these houses are full of soldiers who shoot arrows at long range and fight with spears at close quarters. When victorious, the elephants are granted honorary names

84. Kanyākumārī inscription, *op. cit.*, v. 71, p. 146.
85. Taṇḍantoṭṭam plates, *op. cit.*, v. 7, p. 515.
86. K.G. Krishnan, *KTPR*, v. 48, p. 73.

> to signalize their merit, and there are some who bestow upon them embroidered housing and golden mangers. Everyday, the elephants are taken into the presence of the king.[87]

Seven ways of training elephants are mentioned in the *Arthaśāstra* among which are *vadhāvadha* (destruction or capture of horses, men, etc.) and *hastiyuddha* (pitting elephants against one another).[88] The Sanskrit inscriptions reveal that such training must have been given to the elephants in the Tamil country as they have often been described as attacking the enemy troops in this manner. The Kūram plates state that in the battle against the Cāḷukyas, "troops of furious elephants impaled each other's faces with their tusks" (*anyonya-liśa-radana-kuliśa-sthira-kīlita-vadana-matta-gaja-bṛnde*),[89] while the Tiruvālaṅgāḍu plates mention that "the fire generated by the tusks of huge infuriated elephants dashing against each other burnt all the banners (*uttuṅga-matta-gaja-danta-vighaṭṭan-odyad-vahnīr=dhvajāni*).[90]

The *Arthaśāstra* gives the names of different classes of elephants,[91] while another work, the *Mṛgapakṣiśāstra* lists thirteen classes of elephants.[92] Another Sanskrit work, the *Gajaśāstra* also describes the special characteristics of different types of elephants.[93]

Some of these names find mention in the epigraphs. The name *ibha* found in one of the *biruda*s of Rājasiṁha (*śrī ibha vatsarājaḥ*) is a reference to one class of elephant.[94] Again, the

87. K.A. Nilakanta Sastri, *Foreign Notices of South India*, Madras, 1939, p. 144.
88. *KA*, II. 32, n. 4.
89. Kūram plates, *op. cit.*, p. 149.
90. Tiruvālaṅgāḍu plates, *op. cit.*, v. 104, p. 399.
91. *KA*, II. 31.
92. *Mṛgapakṣiśāstra*, (tr.) M. Sundaracharya, Kalahasti, 1927, pp. 16-23.
93. K.S. Subrahmanya Sastri (ed.), *Gajaśāstra of Pālakāpya Muni*, Tanjore, 1958.
94. *SII*, vol. I, no. 25, pp. 14-18.

name *bhadra* used in the Karandai plates to describe the elephants presented to Rājendra I is a reference to the *bhadra* or most excellent variety of elephants.[95]

Unfortunately, many of these well-trained war-elephants met their end in the battlefields. The composer of the Kūram plates describes the pathetic scene where "the brave warriors marched on the backs of rows of fallen elephants which formed a bridge over the flood of blood" (*rudhir-augha-pālikāyita-patita-gaja-śreṇi-pṛṣṭha-vicarat-subhaṭe*).[96]

Thus, it can be seen from the evidence provided by the Sanskrit inscriptions that the elephant corps constituted a vital and much valued part of the armies of the kings of the Tamil country, marching at the head of the troops, fording rivers, trampling down the enemy troops and engaging in other such activities which made the work much easier for the other sections of the army.

Cavalry

Cavalry was another important division of the army during the ancient and the medieval periods in the Tamil country. The works of the Saṅgam period reveal that horses were used in the wars of that age and played an important role in battles. The *Maduraikkāñci* states that the horses were specially selected for their swiftness of movement.[97] The epigraphs of the Pallavas and Coḷas are full of references to the strength of the cavalry forces in their armies and horses are referred to by the terms *aśva*, *turaga*, *haya* and *vāji*.

It was mandatory for the princes of ancient and medieval India to learn horse-riding. The *Arthaśāstra* clearly states that princes should be well-trained in using horses.[98] The Sanskrit epigraphs reveal that the Tamil kings were experts in horse-riding and evinced great interest in caring for these animals.

95. K.G. Krishnan, *KTPR*, v. 49, p. 73.
96. Kūram plates, *op. cit.*, p. 149.
97. *Maduraikkāñci*, *op. cit.*, ll. 48-52.
98. *KA*, 1, 5, 12.

An epigraph of Rājasiṁha refers to one of his *birudas śrī aśva priyaḥ* (one who is fond of horses).[99] The Udayendiram plates state that Nandivarman Pallavamalla was as skilled as Nakula in the management of horses (*nakula iva turaṅgameṣu*).[100] The Karandai plates record that even when he was a boy, Rājendra I was well-trained in horse-riding.[101]

The earliest mention of the role played by horses in the battles appears in the Kūram inscription, which states that the Pallava army which Parameśvaravarman I led against the Cāḷukyas consisted of "countless troops of horses" (*haya-lakṣaiḥ*).[102] This king's own horse which is described in this inscription as belonging to a noble breed was named *atiśaya* (eminence) and this horse was fitted with a saddle covered with jewels (*ratna palyāṇavantam*).

The armies of the Coḷas also had very powerful cavalry divisions. The Tiruvālaṅgāḍu plates repeatedly refer to the large numbers of horses in the army of Rājendra I.[103] The Coḷa rulers also added to their existing cavalry forces by capturing large numbers of horses from the enemies they defeated. The Larger Leiden plates[104] as well as the Karandai plates[105] record that Rājendra I, having defeated many of his enemies captured their horses along with their territories and wealth. Rājendra I is said to have defeated the Siṁhaḷa king and captured all his property including his vehicles, probably referring to his horses and elephants.[106]

---

99. *SII*, vol. I, no. 25, p. 16.
100. Udayendiram plates, *op. cit.*, l. 19, p. 366.
    The reference to Nakula made in this record is to the Pāṇḍava prince who was an expert on horses.
101. K.G. Krishnan, *KTPR*, v. 42, p. 72.
102. Kūram plates, *op. cit.*, p. 148-50.
103. Tiruvālaṅgāḍu plates, *op. cit.*, pp. 393-401.
104. Larger Leiden plates, *op. cit.*, v. 31, p. 241.
105. K.G. Krishnan, *KTPR*, v. 27, p. 71; v. 35, p. 72.
106. *Ibid.*, v. 58, p. 74.

The cavalrymen seem to have fought in these wars with weapons such as swords and spears. The Kūram inscription records that the cavalrymen of the opposing Pallava and Cāḷukyan armies attacked each other's heads with swords.[107] The panels of historical sculptures in the Vaikuṇṭhaperumāḷ temple at Kāñcīpuram corroborate the accounts given in the inscriptions. Many panels depicting scenes of the army going to war show sculptures of horses with soldiers on them.[108]

Import of Horses

The inscriptions do not reveal whether the horses in the armies of the kings of the Tamil country were imported or bred in India, but it is clear from the information offered by these epigraphs that the kings and princes rode only on superior breeds of horses. The Kūram inscription states that the personal horse of Parameśvaravarman I called *atiśaya* was of noble breed (*kalyāṇa jātim*).[109] The Karandai epigraph records that Rājendra I rode upon a horse "of noble breed" (*ajāneyam*), "as fast as the wind" (*pavana-sama-javam*) and that he was accompanied by other princes who also rode on similar horses (*āruhya tādrig-vidha turaga-gataiḥ*).[110]

The import of horses into the Tamil country was in practice even during the Saṅgam period. The Saṅgam work *Paṭṭinapālai* refers to the import of horses.[111] The practice of importing horses was prevalent in the later periods also. The strong cavalry divisions referred to in the epigraphs show that large numbers of horses of good breed must have been imported. Some Tamil inscriptions refer to the *kudirai-ceṭṭi*s who were dealers in horses.[112] According to K.A. Nilakanta Sastri, these traders must have imported horses from places such as Arabia

107. Kūram plates, *op. cit.*, v. 6, p. 149.
108. C. Minakshi, *HSVP*.
109. Kūram plates, *op. cit.*, v. 6, p. 149.
110. K.G. Krishnan, *KTPR*, v. 56, p. 74.
111. *Paṭṭinapālai*, (ed.) U.V. Swaminatha Iyer, Madras, 1918, l. 185.
112. *ARE*, 556 of 1904.

and Pegu and distributed them among the princes and nobles in the land.[113]

The fact that large numbers of horses were imported into the Pāṇḍyan country is known from the writings of Marco Polo and Wassaf.[114] According to Marco Polo, large sums of the revenue of the kingdom were spent on buying imported horses for the king and for the army. The number of horses imported annually into south India was estimated to be around ten thousand animals. These two writers also confirm that the climate of this part of the country was unfavourable for breeding horses. They add that the Indians did not know how to maintain or train horses as a result of which these animals became unfit, necessitating fresh import of horses from Arabia very often.

All these epigraphical and literary evidences therefore reveal that the references to horses "of noble breed" found in the Sanskrit inscriptions of the Tamil country must have certainly alluded only to the superior breed of horses imported from countries such as Arabia.

Infantry

Infantry or foot-soldiers were the next most important division of the army and must have comprised the largest section among the army divisions. The Sanskrit inscriptions contain numerous references to foot-soldiers. According to the Kūram plates, the foot-soldiers fought with various weapons such as bows, swords and clubs and protected themselves with shields.[115] They also indulged in hand-to-hand fights. The Tiruvālaṅgāḍu plates repeatedly mention that the army of Rājendra I was composed of innumerable foot-soldiers.[116]

---

113. K.A. Nilakanta Sastri, *The Coḷas*, Madras, 1984, p. 607.
114. K.A. Nilakanta Sastri, *The Pāṇḍyan Kingdom*, Madras, 1972, pp. 169-71.
115. Kūram plates, *op. cit.*, pp. 148-59.
116. Tiruvālaṅgāḍu plates, *op. cit.*, pp. 413-26.

These soldiers were grouped under different battalions each of which must have been under the control of a high official who in turn was under the control of the commander-in-chief of the army. According to the Tiruvālaṅgāḍu plates, Rājendra I gave orders to the commander of his army who is described as having many powerful battalions under his control.[117]

The rate of casualities among the soldiers in these wars seems to have been very high. The Kūram plates vividly describe the plight of the soldiers who had been wounded and had lost various limbs and who lay either dying or dead with weapons still clutched in their hands and with their ornaments broken.[118]

The Karandai plates record that the destruction caused by the army of Rājarāja Coḷa I in the wars against his enemies was so enormous that there were no soldiers to be seen on the battlefield who had not lost one limb or another.[119]

Large numbers of foot-soldiers are seen in the panels of the Vaikuṇṭhaperumāḷ temple in Kāñcīpuram. They are depicted holding weapons of war such as spears and swords and holding shields to protect themselves.

Military Ethics

War in India was governed by certain ethical codes in the ancient and medieval periods. Warfare was divided into two varieties — *dharma-yuddha* or that which was carried on according to the law of *dharma* and *adharma yuddha* or *kūṭa-yuddha* which was unrighteous warfare. The *Manusmṛti* clearly mentions the ethical codes which should be followed by the warriors on the battlefield and also gives a list of persons who should not be killed such as those who are bereft of weapons and the wounded.[120]

---

117. Tiruvālaṅgāḍu plates, *op. cit.*, v. 110, p. 400.
118. Kūram plates, *op. cit.*, l. 23, p. 149.
119. K.G. Krishnan, *KTPR*, v. 33, p. 72.
120. *MS*, VII, 90-98.

In the Tamil country also, ethical codes in warfare were stressed upon from the Saṅgam period. Although wars were undertaken primarily for gaining territory and for the accumulation of wealth, yet certain restrictions were placed upon the means of acquiring them. The works written during the Saṅgam age mention some of those moral codes. The *Tolkāppiam* states that prior warning should be given to persons such as old and feeble-hearted men before war is declared.[121] However, judging by the instances given in the Saṅgam works themselves, it appears that such ethical codes were not always practised by the warrior class. The *Paṭṭinappālai* gives an account of the women who were taken as captives and their ill-treatment at the hands of the captors.[122]

The violation of the military ethics followed in the Saṅgam period continued in the later periods also. The inscriptions of the Tamil kings reveal that there was bitter enemity between the opposing armies on the battlefield. Not only were large numbers of soldiers killed and maimed in war, but even generals and the kings of the opposing armies were captured and slain and in many instances ill-treated in violation to the norms of *dharma-yuddha*.

The kings who ruled on the banks of the Gaṅgā and who were defeated by the army of Rājendra I were made to carry the waters of the Gaṅgā in pots according to the account given in the Tiruvālaṅgāḍu plates of this king.[123] The Kanyākumārī inscription of his son Vīra-Rājendra, mentions that Karikāla Coḷa constructed an embankment to the river Kāverī and made the kings who refused to surrender to him carry earth for this purpose with baskets in their hands.[124]

---

121. *Tolkkāpiam*, (ed.) V.U. Chidambaram Pillai, Madras, 1941, Porul, v. 10.
122. *Paṭṭinapālai*, *op. cit.*, ll. 246-49.
123. Tiruvālaṅgāḍu plates, *op. cit.*, v. 117, p. 399-400.
124. Kanyākumārī inscription, *op. cit.*, v. 49, p. 141.

The inscriptions also mention that in many instances the enemy country was wantonly destroyed, sometimes by setting fire to them. According to the Kanyākumārī inscription, Parāntaka I, after vanquishing the Pāṇḍyan ruler, burnt his capital Madurai.[125] Rājendra I is mentioned as having conquered Keraḷa and completely destroyed the country of this ruler in the Tiruvālaṅgāḍu plates.[126] The Karandai plates record that the army of this ruler set fire to the city of Mānyakheṭa.[127]

Women were also not spared by the invading armies of the Coḷas, although this was contrary to the codes of the *Dharmaśāstras*. The inscriptions reveal the ill-treatment meted out to the women of the enemies.

The Karandai plates describe the plight of the women of Mānyakheṭa, who were caught in the burning mansions of this city when the army of Rājendra I set fire to it.[128] The same inscription records that when Rājendra I defeated the king of Laṅkā, his queen (*mahiṣī*) and his daughter (*putrī*) were also taken as captives by him.[129]

Some of these cruel acts committed by the Coḷa armies and which have been mentioned in their own inscriptions have also been recorded in the epigraphs and chronicles of the enemies who suffered at their hands. An inscription of the Cāḷukya ruler Satyāśraya from Hoṭṭūr (Dharwar) dated AD 1007, records that the army of the Coḷas murdered even women, children and brāhmaṇas after ravaging the Cāḷukyan country.[130]

Thus, it is clear that the armies of the Tamil country did not always comply with the ethical codes of warfare found in

---

125. Kanyākumārī inscription, *op. cit.*, v. 57, p. 143.
126. Tiruvālaṅgāḍu plates, *op. cit.*, v. 97, p. 399.
127. K.G. Krishnan, *KTPR*, v. 53, p. 73.
128. *Ibid.*
129. *Ibid.*, v. 58, p. 74.
130. *EI*, vol. XVI, p. 75 (Hoṭṭur inscription).

the law-books and plundered and ravaged the land of the enemies at will.

Character of the Soldiers

The soldiers of the Tamil country have been praised even in the ancient works of the Saṅgam period as being heroic in nature and willing to lay down their lives for their kings. It was common for soldiers to fight the enemy and die on the battlefield rather than to retreat even in the face of adversity. According to a Saṅgam work, the *Purāṇānūru*, a mother of a soldier was heart-broken when she heard the news that her son, while fighting the enemy had retreated, but when she found that her son had been killed on the battlefield and his body cut into two, she felt happy.[131]

The Sanskrit inscriptions give numerous examples of soldiers being killed while fighting. The Karandai plates state that the feudatories (*sāmanta*), who always accompanied Rājendra I, bore the strokes of weapons on their limbs on the foreside, thereby indicating that they had never shown their backs to the war-front.[132]

Weapons of War

Various kinds of weapons were used in the wars waged by the kings of the Tamil country. The Saṅgam literature provides a good idea about the types of weapons used in the battles of that period. The lance or spear (*vel*), the sword (*vāḷ*), the bow (*vil*) and the arrow (*pahali, ambu, kavai* or *kol*) seem to have been the weapons most commonly used by the warriors.[133]

The inscriptions of the Pallavas, Pāṇḍyas and Coḷas also mention the kinds of weapons used by the warriors. The soldiers, generals and kings are mentioned in the epigraphs as using swords (*asi, khaḍga*), bows (*śarāsana, dhanuṣ*), arrows (*patatru*), javelins (*tomara*), maces (*daṇḍa, gadā*), spears (*śakti*),

131. *Puranānūru, op. cit.*, 279.

132. K.G. Krishnan, *KTPR*, vv. 56-57, p. 74.

133. N. Subrahmanian, *Sangam Polity*, Madurai, 1980, p. 157.

darts (*prāsa*), lances (*kaṇaya*) and discus (*cakra*). The historical sculptures of the Vaikuṇṭhaperumāḷ temple at Kāñcīpuram, show the soldiers fighting with various weapons such as javelins, different varieties of swords, shields and staves. The mahouts of the elephants are shown holding the *aṅkuśa* or elephant goads in their hands.[134]

Musical Instruments Used in Wars

Musical instruments were used in wars from very ancient times and the Vedas and epics also refer to names of different varieties of these instruments. Tamil literature also contains the names of these instruments such as *parai, muraśu* and *paṇḍil.*

The terrific noise made by these musical instruments on the battlefield was probably meant to make the warriors cheerful and enthusiastic and to make them fight with spirit and vigour.

The Kūram plates which graphically describe the battle at Peruvaḷanallūr between the Pallava and the Cālukyan armies mention the war-drums (*paṭaha*) and the conches (*śaṅkha*) and state that the sound of these drums was like thunder (*paṭaha-rava-garjjit-ogre*) and that the conches which were incessantly blown (*aviraḷam=udīrṇa-śaṅkhe*) resembled the sound of the ocean (*vijṛmbamāṇe samudra iva*).[135]

Certain musical instruments such as the *kaṭumukhavāditra* and the *samudraghoṣa* were used by the Pallava kings in warfare. A Tamil epigraph found in the Vaikuṇṭhaperumāḷ temple in Kāñcīpuram of the reign of Nandivarman Pallavamalla states that prince Parameśvara was anointed king under the name Nandivarman and was invested with all the insignia of royalty among which one was the *samudraghoṣa* (conch blowing with the sound of the sea).[136]

---

134. C. Minakshi, *HSVK*, p. 59.
135. Kūram plates, *op. cit.*, l. 23, pp. 148-49.
136. *SII*, vol. IV, no. 135, p. 11.

The Kendūr inscription of the Western Cāḷukyan king, Kīrtivarman II[137] mentions that his father, Vikramāditya II invaded Kāñcīpuram and after defeating Nandivarman Pallavamalla took possession of some musical instruments called *kaṭumukhavāditra* and *samudraghoṣa* along with his flag, many elephants and a heap of rubies.

One section of the series of historical sculptures found in the Vaikuṇṭhaperumāḷ temple, depict prince Parameśvara seated on his horse marching to Kāñcīpuram for his coronation, with a man just before the horse beating a drum. C. Minakshi has identified this drum as the *kaṭumukhavāditra*.[138] A few panels later, in the same series, a few men have been depicted beating a drum (*kaṭumukhavāditra*) standing in front of Udayacandra, the victorious general of Nandivarman Pallavamalla, proclaiming that he had killed the enemy, Citramāya.

An inscription of Pṛthivīpati, the western Gaṅgā vassal of Parāntaka Coḷa I, mentions his war drum named *paiśāca* (*paiśācadundubhi*).[139]

Camps

Wars were very common in ancient and medieval India and during the course of long drawn out encounters, the kings with their large armies had to move long distances necessitating them to stay at temporary military camps. These military camps were known as *śibira*, *niveśa* and *sainyaniveśa*.[140] The *Arthaśāstra* gives a very detailed outline about the establishment of the *śibira* and devotes an entire section to it.[141] According to Kauṭilya,

> On a site approved by experts in the science of building, the commandant, carpenters and astrologers should cause the camp to be set up, circular,

137. *EI*, vol. IX, no. 28, ll. 31-45, p. 203 (Kendūr Inscription).
138. C. Minakshi, *HSVK*, p. 36.
139. *SII*, vol. II, no. 76, v. 24, p. 384.
140. V.S. Apte, *English-Sanskrit Dictionary*, Delhi, 1963, p. 47.
141. *KA*, X.1.

> rectangular or square, or in conformity with the nature of the ground with four gates, six roads, and nine divisions, endowed with a moat, a rampart, a parapet, gates and towers when there is danger and when the army has to halt.

The inscriptions of the Tamil country reveal that during the frequent wars fought by these kings, the army rested in military camps during their long marches. Some of the early Pallava inscriptions reveal that they were issued from pitched military camps. The Pikira copper-plate grant records that it was issued from Menmātūr which was a Vijayaskandhāvāra (*śrī vijayaskandhāvārān menmātūr*).[142] The Sakrepaṭṇa charter was issued by Siṁhavarman from the victorious camp at Moudgaḷī-taṭa (*vijayaskandhāvārān maudgaḷī-taṭa*).[143] The Oṁgoḍu (II) grant does not refer to the particular name of the camp but just records that it was issued from a victorious camp (*śrī vijayaskandhāvārāt*).[144] The Uruvapaḷḷi charter records that it was issued from "victorious Pallakkaḍa" (*śrī vijaya pallakka-ḍasthānāt*)[145] and the Maṅgalūr inscription mentions that the place of issue was Daśanapura (*śrī vijaya daśanapura*).[146] The Oṁgoḍu (I) grant states that this charter was issued from *śrī vijaya tāmbra-pasthānāt*.[147]

The *Viśvakarma Vāstuśāstra*, while giving a description of the *śibira*, classifies it into seven categories, namely *nigama*, *skandāvāra*, *droṇaka*, *kubja*, *paṭṭaṇa*, *śibira* and *vāhinīmukha*.[148] Of these, the *skandāvāra* is described as a military station or cantonment where the king takes rest after an engagement. It is on top of a hill or slope or in the centre of a big forest, with

---

142. *EI*, vol. VIII, no. 15, p. 161 (Pikira plates).
143. *EI*, vol. XXXVIII, no. 18, p. 104 (Sakrepaṭṇa plates).
144. *EI*, vol. XV, no. 11, p. 251 (Oṁgoḍu II plates).
145. Uruvapaḷḷi plates, *op. cit.*, p. 51.
146. *Ind. Ant.*, vol. V (May, 1876), p. 155 (Maṅgalūr plates).
147. *EI*, vol. XV, no. 11, p. 254 (Oṁgoḍu I plates).
148. K. Vasudeva Sastri and Major N.B. Gadre (ed.), *Viśvakarma Vāstuśāstram*, Thanjavur, 1958, Ch. VIII.

a single gate and fortified with strong ramparts and closed to the general public. The king's palaces and residences of the commander-in-chief and soldiers, with stables for horses and elephants are located therein.

Forts

Forts played a major role in the wars, which were conducted in ancient and medieval India. The *Manusmṛti* mentions the importance of building forts (*pura*) and also gives a list of the types of forts to be constructed.[149] The *Arthaśāstra* names the fort (*durga*) as one of the seven elements constituting the state.[150]

In the Tamil country also, paramount importance was given to the construction of forts at strategic locations as early as the Saṅgam period. The *Kuraḷ* contains many verses on the importance of forts as well as the strategic location and management of forts.[151]

The political instability which prevailed due to constant wars during the period of the Pallavas, Pāṇḍyas and the Coḷas made it necessary for the rulers to build strong forts and also to fortify their capital cities. The inscriptions of this period also provide some information about forts and fortifications during this period.

The Udayendiram plates which record the achievements of Udayacandra, a feudatory of Nandivarman Pallavamalla, state that the former rescued his king from the town of Nandipura which was besieged by the enemies of this king.[152] It is possible that Nandipura was a fortified town and that Udayacandra laid seige to it and captured it. The same epigraph records that this feudatory destroyed the fort of Kāḷīdurga, protected by Goddess Kāḷī (*kāḷībhagavatī paripālita kāḷīdurgām*).[153]

149. *MS*, VII. 70-73.
150. *KA*, VI. 1, 1.
151. *Kuraḷ*, *op. cit.*, Ch. 75, vv. 741-50.
152. Udayendiram plates, *op. cit.*, l. 37, p. 367.
153. *Ibid.*

This account contained in the Udayendiram plates seems to be corroborated by the series of historical sculptures found in the Vaikuṇṭhaperumāḷ temple at Kāñcīpuram. The panels which depict the important events connected with the reign of Nandivarman Pallavamalla, show the Pallava troops attacking a fort. This fort is depicted in the sculpture as having high ramparts with soldiers attacking it and elephants standing near it. C. Minakshi has suggested that this fort could be the fort of Kāḷīdurga.[154]

Another fort is mentioned in the Tiruvālaṅgāḍu grant, which states that the commander of Rājarāja's army captured the fort of Viḷinda (which has been identified with Viḷiñjam near Tiruvanantapuram). This inscription describes this fort as "one whose moat was the sea, whose excessive ramparts were glorious and high and which was impregnable to enemy warriors" (*jalanidhi-parighaṁ viḷindam-uccaiḥ-sphurad-uru-vapram=abhedyam-anya-yodhaiḥ*).[155]

Archaeological excavations have revealed that capital cities such as Kāñcīpuram, Tañjāvūr, and Gaṅgaikoṇḍacoḷapuram were strongly fortified. The Sanskrit inscriptions of this period do not contain any references to the fortifications of these cities. It is, however, possible that the composer of the Tiruvālaṅgāḍu grant while mentioning the town of Tañjāpurī (Tañjāvūr) captured by Vijayālaya refers to the high turrets of the fortifications while describing it as "having reached the skies" (*vyāptāmbarām*).[156]

An inscription of Kulottuṅga Coḷa I found at Cidambaram records that this king "burnt like straw, the fort of Koṭṭara" (*daghdva-koṭṭara-durggān=triṇam-iva*).[157] E. Hultzsch has identified this Koṭṭara as the Sanskritized form of Koṭṭuru near Kanyākumārī.[158]

---

154. C. Minakshi, *HSVK*, p. 42.
155. Tiruvālaṅgāḍu plates, *op. cit.*, v. 79, p. 398.
156. *Ibid.*, v. 45, p. 395-96.
157. *EI*, vol. V, no. 13, p. 103.
158. *Ibid.*, p. 104.

A Pāṇḍyan inscription from Āṉaimalai mentions that a minister (*mantri*) of Parāntaka Neḍuñjaḍaiyan hailed from a place named Karavaṇḍapura (Kaḷakkuḍi).[159] This person is also mentioned in a Sanskrit verse in the Veḷvikuḍi grant as belonging to Karavandapura.[160] This place which has been identified with Uggirankoṭṭai (Tirunelveli district) has also been mentioned in various other bilingual and Tamil inscriptions of the Pāṇḍyas such as the Tirupparakuṉṟam cave inscription,[161] the Daḷavāipuram copper-plates[162] and the Larger Siṉṉamaṉūr plates.[163] Karavandapura, as gleaned from the epigraphs appears to have been an important political and cultural centre and was made into a fortified town during the period of Neḍuñjadaiyan (Jaṭila Parāntakan) in the eighth century AD. The Tamil portion of the Śrīvaramaṅgalam copper-plates of Neḍuñjaḍaiyan gives a beautiful poetic description of Karavandapuram.[164]

According to K.A. Nilakanta Sastri, soon after the conquest of Venād, Neḍuñjaḍaiyan undertook the task of strongly fortifying Karavandapuram probably because it was on the frontier of the newly conquered country.[165]

Navy

The art of ship-building was known to the ancient Tamils and some rulers of the Saṅgam period maintained strong naval forces. The *Śilappadikāram* mentions the naval force of Ceran Senguṭṭuvan.[166]

---

159. *EI*, vol. VIII, no. 33, pp. 319-20.
160. *EI*, vol. XVII, no. 16, v. 18, p. 303.
161. *EI*, XXXVI, no. 15, p. 117.
162. T.N. Subramaniam, *DCVP*, p. 23.
163. *SII*, vol. III, No. XVII, see also K.V. Raman, "Karavandapuram or Uggirankoṭṭati — An Ancient Fortress Town of the Pāṇḍyas," *JIH*, vol. LII, p. 71.
164. *TPC*, Śrīvaramangalam copper-plates of Neḍuñjaḍaiyan, l. 42, p. 58.
165. K.A. Nilakanta Sastri, *The Pāṇḍyan Kingdom*, Madras, 1972.
166. *Śilappadikāram* (Translated into English, *The Lay of the Anklet*), V.R. Ramachandra Dikshitar, Oxford, 1939, XXVII, ll. 119-21.

The inscriptions of the Pallavas, Pāṇḍyas and Coḷas reveal that the art of ship-building was further developed during these periods. Many inscriptions of this age indicate that these kings must have possessed very large naval fleets as many countries off the coast of India were conquered by them.

The Kaśākuḍi plates record that Siṁhaviṣṇu, the father of Mahendravarman I, defeated his enemy, the Siṁhaḷa king.[167] The same inscription records that the son and successor of Mahendravarman I, Narasiṁhavarman I, conquered Laṅkā and thus "surpassed the valour and glory of Rāma" (*laṅkā jayadharita rāma-parākramaḥ*).[168] The conquest of Laṅkā by Narasiṁhavarman I found in the Kaśākuḍi plates is supported by the evidence found in the *Mahāvaṁśa* which gives details about the relationship between Narasiṁhavarman I and a legal claimant to the throne of Sri Lanka named Mānavamma.[169] This chronicle states that Mānavamma sought the help of the Pallava ruler twice and that the second time the latter himself defeated the usurper to the Lankan throne after crossing the sea and installed Mānavamma on the throne.

In the Vāyalūr Pillar inscription of Rājasiṁha the passage, *vahatu raṇajayaḥ śrīnidhir dvīpa lakṣam*[170] has been intepreted in various ways by scholars. According to H. Krishna Sastri, this could be an indirect reference to the conquest of the Lakshadveep (Laccadive) islands by this king.[171] According to T.V. Mahalingam, it is possible that the Pallavas held sway over the islands of South-East Asia.[172]

The practice of maintaining a strong naval force and conquering distant islands continued in the Coḷa period also.

---

167. Kaśākuḍi plates, *op. cit.*, v. 20, p. 348.
168. *Ibid.*, v. 22, p. 349.
169. Wilhelm Geiger, *Cūlavaṁśa being the more recent part of the Mahāvaṁśa*, Colombo, 1953.
170. *EI*, vol. XVIII, no. 17, v. 2, p. 151 (Vāyalūr inscription).
171. *Ibid.*, p. 152.
172. T.V. Mahalingam, "Pallava Rājasiṁha and South-East Asia". *J.M.U.*, vol. XXXII, no. 2 (January 1961), p. 320.

It was during this period that the naval activities of the Tamil country reached its zenith. According to R. Sathianathaier,

> The naval achievements of the Coḷas reached its climax during the reign of Rājarāja and his successor. Not only were the Coromandal and the Malabar coasts controlled by them, but the Bay of Bengal became a Coḷa lake.[173]

Parāntaka I seems to have invaded Laṅkā twice, once before his 32nd regnal year and the next during his 33rd regnal year.[174] The Kanyākumārī (=Cārāla) inscription mentions that Parāntaka "caused his army to cross the seas and defeat the Siṁhaḷa king and thus received the name *Siṁhaḷāntaka*."[175]

Parāntaka's invasion of Laṅkā mentioned in these epigraphs are corroborated in the Tamil literary works of the Coḷa period such as the *Kaliṅgattuparaṇi*,[176] the *Kulottuṅgaśoḷan-ulā*[177] and the *Rājarājaśoḷan-ulā*.[178] However, from the evidence found in the *Mahāvaṁśa*, it appears that his efforts went in vain.[179]

The Tiruvālaṅgāḍu[180] and the Karandai[181] plates mention the conquest of Laṅkā during the reign of Rājarāja I. The naval supremacy of the Coḷas reached its zenith during the rule of Rājendra I. The Karandai plates state that this ruler conquered Sri Lanka.[182]

---

173. R. Sathianathaier, *The Struggle for Empire*, Madras, 1925, p. 251.
174. S. Swaminathan, *The Early Coḷas-History, Art and Culture*, Delhi, 1998, p. 45.
175. Kanyākumārī inscription, *op. cit.*, v. 59, p. 143.
176. *Kaliṅgattuparani*, v. 23, see also S. Swaminathan, *op. cit.*
177. A. Gopala Iyer (ed.), *Mūvarula*, II.45-46, p. 29.
178. *Ibid.*
179. Wilhelm Geiger, *op. cit.*
180. Tiruvālaṅgāḍu plates, *op. cit.*, v. 80, p. 398.
181. K.G. Krishnan, *KTPR*, v. 27, p. 71.
182. *Ibid.*, v. 58, p. 74.

The military sphere of influence of the Coḷas was stretched even up to Kaṭāha (Malaysia). The achievement of Rājendra I in conquering Kaṭāha with the help of his forces are mentioned in a few of the Coḷa inscriptions.[183]

The Pāṇḍyan kings also had a strong naval force and their forces crossed the sea and entered Laṅkā. The Larger Sinnamaṉūr plates record that Śrīmāra Śrīvallabha conquered the Siṁhaḷa king in battle.[184]

It can thus been seen that the rulers of the Tamil country during the period of this study had organized an excellent system of military administration which was the main factor for their numerous convincing victories over their enemies. The personal interest taken by these kings in maintaining an efficient and strong military establishment paved the way for the Pallava, Pāṇḍya and Coḷa dynasties growing from strength to strength in south India.

---

183. Tiruvālaṅgāḍu plates, *op. cit.*, v. 123, p. 400; K.G. Krishnan, *KTPR*, v. 62, p. 74; Kanyākumārī inscription, *op. cit.*, v. 72, p. 146.

184. Larger Sinnamaṉūr plates, *op. cit.*, v. 11, p. 451.

4

Economic Life

THE focus of this chapter will be on the different professions followed by the people of the Tamil country during the period of this study. The Sanskrit inscriptions provide plenty of information about the overall economic condition of the age. The efforts taken by the rulers to help agriculturists, artisans and other people engaged in various trades and activities and which contributed to the general economic prosperity of the period are vividly brought out by these epigraphs.

Agriculture

Agriculture has always been the most important occupation in the Tamil country. An entire chapter in the *Kuraḷ* extolls the glory and greatness of the farmers and their profession.[1] In this section, the focus will be on the kinds of crops cultivated during that time and also on the methods of irrigation which were in vogue to help the agriculturists in their work. The Sanskrit inscriptions of the period of this study throw considerable light on the varieties of crops raised as well as the systems of irrigation employed.

Crops

The earliest Pallava inscription that contains a list of crops grown is the Paḻḻankovil copper-plate grant of the sixth century AD.[2] This inscription describes the rice-fields (*sāli*), the rich

1. P.S. Sundaram (tr. and ed.), *The Kuraḷ*, New Delhi, 1990, Ch. 104, p. 124.
2. T.N. Subramaniam, *PJCG*, v. 5, p. 76.

fields of sugar-cane (*ikṣuvana*), the groves of palm trees (*kramuka*), plantains (*rambha*) and others which grew near the river Kāverī.

The Udayendiram plates which record the exploits of Udayacandra, a vassal of Nandivarman Pallavamalla, who is described as the "lord of the river Vegavatī" (*vegavatyā nadyāḥ pati*) mentions the different varieties of crops which were grown on the banks of this river, such as areca-palms (*kramukha*), coconut trees (*naḷikera*), mango trees (*sahakāra*), palmyras (*tāla*) and various other trees such as *hintāla, tamāla, nāga, puṁnāga, raktāśoka, kuruvaka, mādhavī* and *karṇikāra*.[3]

Again, another record of the Pallavas mentions that "forests of paddy" (*kalama kānana*) and "the brilliant groves of areca palms" (*lasat kramukha maṇḍalāḥ*) were to be found in the Coḷa country.[4]

Another inscription belonging to the Coḷa period also mentions that rice and other grains (*saly-ādi-sasya-bhuṣitam*) and fruit trees such as mango (*āmra*) and jack-fruit (*panasa*) were grown in the Kāverī basin.[5]

Irrigation

The economic prosperity of kingdoms in ancient and medieval India depended to a great extent on agricultural output, which in turn was largely dependent on a sound system of irrigation. South India has always had to rely on rains for agricultural prosperity. While very heavy rainfall could cause floods and destroy the standing crops, thereby causing extreme suffering to the farmers, failure of the monsoon, on the other hand, could result in famine due to the resultant drought conditions.

The rulers of the Tamil country, had, therefore, from the earliest times, to necessarily develop a sound and efficient system of irrigation, which would enable the storage of large quantities of water in case of acute water scarcity in their

3. *SII*, vol. II, no. 74, l. 37, p. 367 (Udayendiram plates).
4. *SII*, vol. II, no. 98, v. 10, p. 508 (Velūrpāḷaiyam plates).
5. *EI*, vol. III, no. 14, p. 82.

kingdoms. The extent to which people in the Tamil country were dependent on rains is brought out by Tiruvaḷḷuvar, "If the heavens dry up, the very Gods will lack festival and worship"[6] and "should rain fail, hunger will rack the wide earth sea-grit."[7]

The kings of the Tamil country were only too well aware of the need to develop a system of irrigation which would fulfil the basic needs of the agricultural classes and also boost the agricultural prosperity of the country. The havoc caused by famines must have been an important factor in drawing the attention of the rulers to render this facility to the farmers.

The numerous works written during the Saṅgam period reveal that plenty of attention was paid to the development of a good system of irrigation. The Sanskrit inscriptions of the Pallava, Pāṇḍya and Coḷa periods provide a clear picture of the importance given to irrigation and the system as it existed in those periods. These epigraphs contain numerous references to wells, tanks, reservoirs and channels which supplied water to the fields.

From these epigraphs it appears that Karikāla Coḷa was the earliest ruler who realized the importance of providing adequate facilities for supplying water to the farmers of the Kāverī delta. The Veḷañjeri,[8] Larger Leiden,[9] Tiruvālaṅgāḍu,[10] Karandai[11] and the Kanyākumārī[12] inscriptions praise Karikāla Coḷa as having raised the embankments for the river Kāverī. The Kanyākumārī inscription states that this king caused the embankments of this river to be raised as it overflowed its banks and did not allow the crops to flourish and that this

6. *Kuraḷ, op. cit.*, Ch. 2, v. 8.
7. *Ibid.*, v. 3.
8. R. Nagaswamy, *TVCP, Veḷāñjeri plates of Parāntaka I*, v. 8, plate II, p. 1.
9. *EI*, vol. XXII, no. 34, p. 239, v. 11 (Larger Leiden plates).
10. *SII*, vol. III, no. 205, v. 42, p. 395 (Tiruvālaṅgāḍu plates).
11. K.G. Krishnan, *KTPR*, v. 13, p. 70.
12. *TAS*, vol. I, no. 34, vv. 48-49, p. 41 (Kanyākumārī inscription).

embankment was constructed "with the earth carried by (insubordinate) kings with baskets in their hands, thereby giving protection to cultivation."[13] Many inscriptions of the Telugu-Coḍa chief Tammusiddhi also record that Karikāla Coḷa built embankments for the Kāverī.[14]

The agricultural prosperity of the Tamil country was mainly due to the rivers flowing through them such as the Vaigai, the Vegavatī and the mighty Kāverī. The Kāverī running through the heartland of the Coḷa empire contributed in no small measure to the bountiful crops yielded in that area and to its subsequent prosperity.

Even the inscriptions of the Pallavas, while referring to the Coḷa country, mention the Kāverī. The Paḷḷankovil inscription poetically describes the land of the Coḷas as that "which has as its garland (*hāra*) the daughter of Kavera (i.e., Kāverī)".[15] The Tirucirāpaḷḷi inscription of Mahendravarman I refers to the Kāverī as "the beloved of the Pallava king" (*pallavasya dayitāmetām*)[16] while the Velūrpāḷaiyam plates state that the Pallava king Siṁhaviṣṇu seized the Coḷa country "embellished by the river Kāverī" (*kavīra-tanay-āñcitaḥ coḷaḥ*).[17]

The Coḷa kings fully realized the potential of utilizing the waters of the Kāverī for irrigation and thereby bringing more lands under cultivation. All the Coḷa rulers, contributing to the betterment of the farmers made the Coḷa empire one of the most fertile areas in south India.

Tanks

The construction and the maintenance of tanks, which were an important source of water supply, was given great importance in ancient India. The construction of tanks was

13. *TAS*, vol. I, no. 34, vv. 48-49, p. 41 (Kanyākumārī inscription).
14. *EI*, vol. VII, no. 17, v. 9, p. 123; no. 17B, v. 7, p. 126; no. 21A, v. 12, p. 150; no. 21B, v. 14, p. 153.
15. T.N. Subramaniam, *op. cit.*
16. *SII*, vol. I, no. 33, p. 29.
17. Velūrpālaiyam plates, *op. cit.*, v. 10, p. 508.

generally considered as a deed of great merit and damage caused to a tank was held as an act of offence.

The kings made arrangements for the construction of tanks in various parts of the country and in many instances also made careful provisions for their upkeep. The Sanskrit inscriptions provide plenty of information about tank-irrigation in this part of the country.

The very first mention of a tank in the Pallava inscriptions appears in the Guṇapadeya plates (*c.* AD 340), which mention a tank named *rājataṭāka* or "king's tank" which was situated in a field.[18] The Pallava queen Cārudevī, is mentioned in this epigraph as having given four *nivartana*s of land near this tank to a temple of God Nārāyaṇa at Dālūra.

An inscription of Mahendravarman I found in a rock-cut temple built by him at Mahendravāḍi (North Arcot district) records that this king caused this temple to be constructed on the banks of the Mahendrataṭāka (tank) in the great city of Mahendrapura.[19]

The Kaśākuḍi plates also mention a tank named *Tīrālaya*, which, together with houses, fields, gardens and groves was included in the *brahmadeya* land called Ekadhīramaṅgalam which was given to a scholary brāhmaṇa named Jyeṣṭhapāda Somayājin by Nandivarman Pallavamalla.[20]

Three more tanks named *Cakratīrta, Uragahrada* and *Sinduvārahrada* are mentioned in the Udayendiram plates in connection with the demarcating of the boundaries of the village which were given to a hundred and eight brāhmaṇas as *brahmadeya*.[21]

A number of tanks having beautiful Sanskrit names like Citramegha-taṭāka, Vairamegha-taṭāka and Parameśvara-taṭāka are mentioned in Tamil inscriptions.[22]

---

18. *EI*, vol. VIII, no. 12, p. 145 (Guṇapadeya plates).
19. *EI*, vol. IV, no. 19, p. 11.
20. Kaśākuḍi plates, *op. cit.*, p. 351.
21. Udayendiram plates, *op. cit.*, l. 65, p. 368.
22. C. Minakshi, *ASLP*, pp. 120-22.

Some of the Sanskrit epigraphs of the Coḷas also contain some references to irrigation tanks. The Anbil charter records that Sundara Coḷa gave to his able and trusted minister, Aniruddha, the village named Karuṇākaramaṅgalam, in which there were a very large number of tanks (*taṭāka*) and ponds (*vāpi*).[23]

The famous Tiruvālaṅgāḍu inscription describes how Rājendra Coḷa I constructed in his own country, as a pillar of victory (a tank), known by repute as *Coḷagaṅgam*, into which the waters of the Gaṅgā were poured (*coḷagaṅgam=iti=khyātyā prathitan=nija maṇḍale, gaṅgā-jala-mayan=devo=jaya-sthambham vyadhatta saḥ*).[24]

A bi-lingual record from Tiruvakkarai (South Arcot district) states that the Kāḍava chieftain, Kopperuñjiṅga constructed a sluice (*praṇātam*) with a feeder-channel (*kulya*) to the tank at Oḻugaṛai. The Sanskrit portion of the epigraph states that the channel was called Tribhuvananṛpanātha.[25]

Maintenance of Tanks

The maintenance of these tanks was also a matter of primary importance to the state. The rulers, officials and others must have certainly contributed to the periodical maintenance of the tanks such as desilting and repairing the embankments, which might have been breached. A bi-lingual inscription of Kopperuñjiṅga from Tribhuvani (near Pondicherry) records that this chief repaired the embankments (*kūlam*), sluices (*pravāham*) and irrigation channels (*parivāha*) of the tank (*taṭāka*) at Tribhuvanamahādevī which had breached at many places (*śitilita-taṭām*).[26]

The Sholingūr inscription of Parāntaka I offers an instance of state help for the maintenance of a tank.[27] According to this

23. *EI*, vol. XV, no. 5, v. 41, p. 63 (Anbil plates).
24. Tiruvālaṅgāḍu plates, *op. cit.*, v. 124, p. 400.
25. *SII*, vol. XII, no. 246, p. 154; *ARE*, 191 of 1904.
26. *SII*, vol. XII, no. 126, p. 63.
27. *EI*, vol. IV, no. 32, p. 224 (Śoliṅgūr inscription).

epigraph, this king granted the entire revenue from a field named Vaṁśavāri (called Mūngīlvāri in the Tamil section) towards the improvement of a tank named Coḷavāridhi. The inscription adds that at the request of Pṛthivīpati II Hastimalla, a vassal of Parāntaka I, this king entrusted him with the work of executing this grant.

Income From Tanks

One source of income for the administrative organizations of the villages was the revenue from tanks by way of sale of fish which was used for the maintenance and repair of the irrigation tanks. We come across a reference to this type of income from a bi-lingual Pāṇḍyan inscription of the thirteenth century AD from Ulagāṇi (Madurai district) which records the order of a chief named Kaṇṭhīrava (Kaṇḍiyadevan in the Tamil portion) assigning the income from the levy called *paśipaṭṭam* (income from fishing) from the tanks in the village to the *sabhā* of Kulaśekharādhipa-caturvedimaṅgalam *alias* Ulagāṇī for the annual dredging of tanks.[28]

Wells

Another source of water for irrigating the fields during the ancient and medieval periods was by means of wells, which were also used for domestic purposes. While a much larger area could be watered by the tanks, the water from wells helped irrigate a much smaller area. However, judging from epigraphical evidence, well irrigation appears to have been widely prevalent in the period of the Pallavas, Pāṇḍyas and Coḷas.

The very first reference is found in the Guṇapadeya charter which mentions a well (*pānīya-kūpa*) in a field containing four *nivartana*s of land which was gifted by the Pallava queen Cārudevī to a temple of God Nārāyaṇa at Dalūra.[29]

---

28. *ARE*, 283 of 1963/64.
29. Guṇapadeya plates, *op. cit.*, p. 145.

The Anbil plates record that the village of Karuṇākaramaṅgalam, which was gifted to Aniruddha, a minister of Sundara Coḷa by the latter himself, contained numerous wells (*kūpa*).[30]

The Daḷavāipuram charter mentions that the composer of the Sanskrit *praśasti* of these plates, a poet named Mādhava was given two fields named Mahāviḷāl and Paruttivayakal including the rights of the wells situated therein.[31] The Sanskrit part of this inscription also states that the poet who composed the Tamil portion of this inscription and the scribe who inscribed it on the copper-plates were given three fields, Kaṇṇankiran Vayakkal, Śiṟukkuḷa Valāḷ and Somayājivayakkal along with the rights to the wells situated therein.[32]

It appears that during the period of the Pallavas, there existed people who practised water-divining as their profession. The Viḻavaṭṭi inscription, while enumerating the list of taxes which were collected by the king, mentions the tax collected from *kūpa-darśaka*s or water-diviners.[33] Thus it appears that these people paid tax to the state regularly.

Channels

The channels, which were dug from the rivers, acted as important sources of irrigation. The tanks which were used to irrigate the fields received water by means of these channels in a few cases. Many copper-plate grants record permission given by the rulers of the Tamil country to the donees of land gifted by them to dig channels from nearby rivers to irrigate their agricultural lands.

Nandivarman Pallavamalla, according to the Kaśākuḍi plates gave a gift of a village as *brahmadeya* to a learned brāhmaṇa named Jyeṣṭhapāda Somayājin along with many exemptions which included the use of water from the rivers

---

30. Anbil plates, *op. cit.*, v. 41, p. 63.
31. T.N. Subramaniam, *DCPV*, p. 18.
32. *Ibid*.
33. *EI*, vol. XXIV, no. 43, p. 303 (Viḻavaṭṭi plates).

Dūrasarit and the Vegavatī by means of digging channels.[34]

In a similar manner, the Udayendiram plates of the same king record that he gave a village named Kumāramaṅgala Veḷḷaṭṭūr, renaming it as Udayacandramaṅgalam to a hundred and eight brāhmaṇas along with the use of the water of the rivers (*nadiḥ*) and canals (*kulyāḥ*) situated therein.[35]

The Karandai charter records that Parāntaka I caused to be excavated hundreds and thousands of deep channels (*nadiḥ*) with clear water (*vimale udakaḥ*) in order to make the earth very fertile (*mahīm-mahā-phalām-kartuṁ*).[36]

An inscription of the period of Rājarāja I from Kappalūr (North Arcot district) mentions the construction of a channel named after the king from the north bank of the river Dūrānadi up to the great tank (*mahātaṭāka*) at Kamapullūr under the orders of the Coḷa ruler by his minister Uttama, the chief of Koṟṟamaṅgalam.[37]

The Karandai plates state that Rājendra I made the *agrahāra* named Tribhuvanamahādevī Caturvedimaṅgalam very fertile "by the flow of enormous and sweet waters of the Kāverī" (*kāverī-sarasa-salila-syanda-sandoha-sāram*).[38] It is possible that this ruler ordered channels to be dug to bring the waters of the Kāverī to this village.

Water-Levers

It appears that implements such as water-levers were used to help in the task of irrigating the fields. The Udayendiram plates mention that a village named Udayacandramaṅgalam was given to a hundred and eight brāhmaṇas along with two water-levers (*jala-yantras*).[39]

---

34. Kaśākuḍi plates, *op. cit.*, l. 102, p. 351.
35. Udayendiram plates, *op. cit.*, no. 74, l. 74, p. 368.
36. K.G. Krishnan, *KTPR*, v. 21, p. 71.
37. *ARE*, 276 of 1938-39.
38. K.G. Krishnan, *op. cit.*, v. 67, p. 75.
39. Udayendiram plates, *op. cit.*, l. 62, p. 368.

The Sanskrit inscriptions also shed some light on the different professions followed by the people and these are given below.

Artisans

The work of artisans such as weavers, goldsmiths, blacksmiths, carpenters and leather-workers is indispensable for the smooth and normal working of any society. These craftsmen seem to have been held in very high esteem in the Tamil country even during the Saṅgam period.

The Sanskrit copper-plate grants and stone inscriptions of the period under study reveal that these artisans enjoyed a very respectable position in society and that these kings gave plenty of encouragement to and showed considerable interest in the artisan community in their highly skilled work.

The inscriptions reveal that the rulers of these dynasties granted special privileges and exemptions from taxes to certain craftsmen. The craftsmen, on their part, fulfilled the material requirements of the people and contributed to the overall economic prosperity of the state.

Goldsmiths

Some information about goldsmiths is available in the Bāhūr plates of Nṛpatuṅgavarman.[40] According to a Sanskrit verse at the end of this inscription, this record was written by a goldsmith (*svarṇakāra*) named Nṛpatuṅga who is described as "the ornament of the family of Uditodita" (*uditodita-kula-tilakaḥ*) and who was a "hereditary servant of the Pallava family" (*pallava-kula-mūla-bhṛtyaḥ*).

A Tamil line following this verse also mentions that this was the writing of Nṛpatunga, the son of Mādevī-perundaṭṭān, and the grandson of Uditodaya-perundaṭṭān.[41] C. Minakshi has opined that this goldsmith was named after his sovereign,

40. *EI*, vol. XVIII, no. 2, v. 32, p. 12 (Bāhūr plates).

41. *Ibid.*, l. 78.

Nṛpatuṅgavarman.[42] Since he was the royal goldsmith he probably assumed the royal prefix after the ruling king.

No other Sanskrit inscription of the period of this study provides any information about goldsmiths. However, it is obvious that these artisans must have been in great demand for making ornaments, especially for royalty, as the sculptures of the kings and queens are shown bedecked with a variety of jewels.

Moreover, the members of the ruling class also gifted gold jewels to temples as seen from a very large number of Tamil epigraphs. The Coḷa inscriptions found at the Bṛhadīśvara temple, Tañjāvūr reveal the names of numerous gold jewels presented to the deities in this temple by Rājarāja I, his queens and other members of the royal family. Some of the gold ornaments inlaid with precious stones are described in great detail in technical language and show that the art of making ornaments of gold and precious stones had reached a great degree of perfection in the Tamil country.

One of the inscriptions from the Tañjāvūr temple refers to the nine varieties of gems (*navaratna*), namely diamond (*vairam*), sapphire (*nīlam*), pearl (*muttu*), topaz (*puṣparāga*), cinnamon-stone (*gomedhakam*), coral (*pavaḷam*), emerald (*pacchai* or *maragatam*), lapis-lazuli (*vaiḍūrya*) and ruby (*māṇikkam*) set in a gold ornament.[43]

An inscription of the thirteenth century AD of the period of Jaṭāvarman Sundara Pāṇḍya I clearly states that the gold taken from the crowns and treasuries of the vanquished enemy kings were used for making ornaments and other items of gold to the temple of Lord Raṅganātha at Śrīraṅgam.[44]

Blacksmiths

The art of the blacksmith is vital to any society as many other artisans such as carpenters, goldsmiths and weavers are

42. C. Minakshi, *ASLP*, p. 75.
43. *SII*, vol. II, no. 93, pp. 428-32.
44. *EI*, vol. III, no. 2, pp. 11-14.

dependent on him for providing them with the necessary tools and implements. Wars being a very common occurrence during the ancient and the medieval periods, the blacksmith must have been in great demand for producing various types of weapons of warfare. Many works of the Saṅgam period show that the blacksmiths played an important role in the society of the time.

The Sanskrit inscriptions of the Tamil country do not provide much information about the blacksmiths and their work. The Daḷavāipuram plates state at the end of the Sanskrit portion that Nakkan of Kuṇṭūr who was the chief blacksmith of the king and the head of the sculptors and who bore the epithet Nṛpaśekhara wrote this grant (*alikhad=idan=niravadyam=rājaniyogād=aśeṣa-śilp-iśaḥ, nakkaḥ kuṇṭūr-prabhavo-nṛpa-śekhara-mukhya-karmmāraḥ*).[45]

A Sanskrit verse following the Tamil section of the same inscription states that the Tamil section of the *praśasti* was composed by the poet Pāṇḍya Dramiḷābharaṇa who was the chief of the *karmāra-śreṇī* (*praśasti śeṣakṛt-pāṇḍya dramiḷ-ābharaṇaḥ kaviḥ, karmāra-śreṇika-mukhyaḥ śivapadāmbhuj=āśṛtaḥ*).[46]

Leather Workers

There is only one reference to workers of leather in the Sanskrit inscriptions of the period under study. The Viḷāvaṭṭi plates, which mention the list of taxes payable by different sections of the society to the state, mention the tax payable by the *carmakāra* or the leather workers.[47] Neither this inscription nor any of the others mention articles made of leather produced during this period.

Barbers

Only one Sanskrit inscription makes a mention of barbers during the period of the Pallavas. The Viḷāvaṭṭi charter

---

45. T.N. Subramaniam, *DCPV*, v. 39, p. 19.
46. *Ibid.*
47. Viḷavaṭṭi plates, *op. cit.*, p. 303.

mentions that the barbers (*nāpita*) had to pay a tax to the state.[48]

Weavers

Weavers have always occupied a very important place in society since very early times since clothing is one of the basic needs of man. References to the skill of the weavers are found in the Saṅgam works and the Sanskrit epigraphs of the succeeding periods point to the high position accorded to them.

The Viḷāvaṭṭi inscription provides some information about weavers. This inscription which gives a list of taxes collected by the state mentions the tax which was collected from weavers (*tantuvāya*).[49]

With regard to the period of the Coḷas, the Madras Museum plates of Uttama Coḷa provide some information about the status of weavers during that period.[50] According to this inscription, Uttama Coḷa Parakesari deposited with two classes of weavers (*paṭṭaśālins*) residing in the quarters of Kaccippeḍu (Kāñcīpuram) known as Karuvuḻāṉpāṭi, Kaṁsahappāṭi, Ātimāṉappāṭi and Eṟṟuvalicceri, two hundred pieces of gold. Since there were no managers (*śrīkāryakṛt*) to supervise the receipts and expenses of the temple of Hari (the Ulagalandaperumāḷ temple) from the income from the gold invested, Uttama Coḷa appointed these weavers from the two quarters, i.e., Atimāṉappāṭi and Karuvuḻāṉpāṭi for the work of temple management (*śrīkārya*). Moreover, this king ordered the residents of another quarter of Kāñcīpuram called Śoḻāniyamam to give to this God, two *prastha* and one *kuḍumbaka* of rice and one *prastha* of oil and thus be exempted from all other taxes payable to the king. The residents of Śoḻāniyamam, together with the managers of the temple, were to write out in turn one after another, the accounts of the income and expenditure of the Viṣṇu temple and show them every month to the weavers of the royal garments living in these four quarters of Kāñcīpuram.

48. Viḻavaṭṭi plates, *op. cit.*, p. 303.
49. *Ibid.*
50. *SII*, vol. III, no. 128, p. 269 (Madras Museum Plates of Uttama Coḷa).

It can thus be seen that the community of weavers was considered trustworthy enough to deposit money with them and also to entrust them with the responsibility of managing the income and expenditure of the temple. This reveals the high status accorded to the community of weavers during this period.

Architects

The prolific building activities of the Pallavas, Pāṇḍyas and Coḷas must have given scope for employing a large number of architects. From the hundreds of beautiful temples that dot the Tamil country, it can be understood that these architects must have been exceptionally skilled in their work. That they were receptive to new fangled ideas can be gleaned from the fact that during the time of Mahendravarman I, who himself bore the title *vicitracitta* or "curious-minded," a "brickless" (*aniṣṭakam*), "timberless" (*adrumam*), "metalless" (*aloham*) and "mortarless" (*asudam*) temple was constructed to Brahmā, Viṣṇu and Śiva (*brahm-eśvara-viṣṇu-lakṣitāyatanam*) for the first time in the Tamil country.[51]

Many of the copper-plate grants of the Pallavas mention that they were engraved by *kāṣṭhakārins*, which literally means carpenters. However, several inscriptions use this term *kāṣṭhakārī* in the sense of *sthapatis*, *śilpins* and architects.[52]

The Kaśākuḍi plates mention that this inscription was engraved by Śrī Parameśvara, the great carpenter (*śrī parameśvara-mahākāṣṭhakāriṇā likhitam*).[53] C. Minakshi has stated that since Parameśvara was also a name of Nandivarman Pallavamalla, this servant of the king was probably named after his sovereign.[54]

The Velūrpāḷaiyam plates record that "this set of (copper) sheets were engraved by the moon in the sky of the family of

51. *EI*, vol. XVII, no. 5, pp. 14-17 (Maṇḍagapaṭṭu inscription).
52. R. Nagaswamy, *ECPR*, p. 10.
53. Kaśākuḍi plates, *op. cit.*, l. 136, p. 353.
54. C. Minakshi, *ASLP*, p. 76.

sthapatis, named Peraya, the son of Śiṟṟaya, who has won (his) reputation for skill in workmanship" (*kara-kauśala-kṛta-yaśasā siṟṟaya-putreṇa patra-saṁgho=yam likhitaḥ perayanāmnā-sthapati-kula-vyoma-candreṇa*).[55] The Tamil portion of the same grant records that this is "the working of Perayan, son of the carpenter (*kāṣṭhakāriṇa*) of Manaicceri in Kaccipeḍu (Kāñcīpuram).[56] It is interesting to find that the words *kāṣṭhakāri* and *sthapati* are used synonymously.[57]

The Sanskrit portion of the Ciṟṟūr plates of Nṛpatuṅgavarman[58] mentions that it was engraved by a person named Naṁpa who belonged to the village named Kūvam and who was a *śilpin*, known for his knowledge of scripts. The Tamil portion of the same record gives his name as *kāṣṭhakāri* Naṁpan Aparājitan. Since it was a popular tradition in those days for the royal servants to bear the name of the ruling king, it appears that before the sixth year of Nṛpatuṅga, Aparājita had become a ruler so as to make the scribe assume the name Aparājita.[59]

A Sanskrit inscription of the eighth century AD, found in the Sundaravaradaperumāḷ temple in Uttaramerūr (Chingleput district) provides some information about the architect (*takṣaka*) named Parameśvara who constructed this shrine.[60] According to this epigraph, "he who understands the measures and architectural details of this (*vimāna*) fully, is an expert among architects versed in *Vāstu Vidyā*" (*asyālaṅkāramānañ ca yathā-lakṣaṇasaṁyutam, yaḥ kaścidvetti sakalaṁ savai vāstuvidāṁ varaḥ*). This shrine, shining as it were, the sun among the shrines (*śrī*

55. Velūrpāḷaiyam plates, *op. cit.*, v. 31, pp. 509-10.
56. *Ibid.*, ll. 68-69.
57. C. Minakshi, *ASLP*, p. 77.
58. T.V. Mahalingam, *IOP*, p. 442.
59. R. Nagaswamy, "The Cirrur Plates of Nṛpatuṅga" *from Studies in Ancient Tamil Law and Society*, Madras, 1978, p. 36, see also R. Nagaswamy, *TVCP*, p. 7.
60. *SII*, vol. VI, No. 333, p. 158, see V. Ganapati Sthapati, "An Interesting Inscription from Uttiramerūr" from R. Nagaswamy (ed.), *Seminar on Inscriptions*, Madras, 1966.

vāstuno bhāskaraḥ) in the village and being "adored by its name" (*nāmnā*) "and class, etc.," (*jātyādina*) "was built in conjunction with the *āgāmikas* of this village, well-versed in āgamic principles and practice" (*yathāgamavidhiḥ grāme prayogānvitaiḥ*) by Parameśvara the architect (*takṣaka*) who hailed from Pāṭaka (a suburb of Kāñcīpuram).

The text which guided Parameśvara *takṣaka* appears to be the *Vaikhānasa Āgama* text, *Marīcisaṁhitā*, as this temple conforms to the codes given in this *Āgama*.[61] Uttaramerūr was an ancient brāhmaṇa settlement (*caturvedimaṅgalam*) and it is not surprising that there were many scholars well-versed in the *āgamas* (*āgāmikas*) in this village who helped this great architect in his endeavour.

In addition to the epigraphical evidence, Sanskrit literature of the Pallava times also provides some information about an architect of this period. The Sanskrit prose work *Avantisundarīkathā* by Daṇḍin, the celebrated court-poet of the Pallava period mentions a famous architect named Lalitālaya who was an expert in building ninety-six kinds of temples (*ṣaṇṇavati-prāsāda-vidhi-viśāradaḥ*), six kinds of mechanical contrivances (*ṣaḍvidhānām yantrāṇām*) and had all the thirty-six qualifications prescribed for an architect (*ṣaṭtriṁśad ācārya-guṇairalaṅkṛtaḥ*).[62] He once requested Daṇḍin to inspect an image of Viṣṇu at Māmallapuram whose broken arm he had refitted. When Daṇḍin saw the image, he was unable to find out where the arm of the statue had been repaired, so well had Lalitālaya done his work.

Some information about the architects of the Coḷa period are also available from their epigraphs. The Veḷāñjeri plates of Parāntaka Coḷa I record that this charter was engraved by Vīra Coḷa, the great architect (*mahātakṣa*) who was "deeply

61. *SII*, vol. VI, No. 333, p. 158, see V. Ganapati Sthapati, "An Interesting Inscription from Uttiramerūr," from R. Nagaswamy (ed.), *Seminar on Inscriptions*, Madras, 1966.

62. K.S. Mahadeva Sastri (ed.), *Avantisundarīkathā*, Trivandrum, 1954, pp. 12-14.

learned in the science of Viśvakarma" (*viśvakarmoktha viśāradaḥ*).[63]

Another Sanskrit epigraph found at the Ādipurīśvara temple at Tiruvoṟṟiyūr mentions a *takṣa* named Vīracoḷa Ravi who constructed the *śrī-vimāna* or the central shrine of this temple with a variety of embellishments.[64] This work was undertaken by the favour of Rājendra Coḷa I. This epigraph also mentions that several black stones were used in the construction (*ati-bahulatārairaśmābhiḥ kṛṣṇavarṇṇaiḥ*). These stones have been identified as belonging to the variety of rock called gneiss (called in Tamil as *karungal*).[65]

This *vimāna* is mentioned as being three-storeyed (*tri-tala*) and built without any fault or defect (*nirggata-dūṣaṇam vimānam*). A number of interesting architectural terms are also mentioned which have been identified by P.R. Srinivasan as follows: *bahuvidha-caraṇaḥ* (various types of pillars and pilasters), *kūṭa-koṣṭhaiḥ* (peaked shrine-like parts and compartments or pavillions), *nidaiḥ* (with a number of cage-like designs with rounded back seen between *śālā*s and *kūṭa*s also called *pañjaras*) *mṛgapati-vadanaiḥ* (with several lion faces), and *nāsikādyaiḥ* (with several nose-shaped designs or vestibules).

An epigraph from the Punnāgeśvara temple at Nemali (North Arcot district) mentions a grant of land to an architect (*sthapati*) called Premaneśa *alias* Coḷamūvenda-takṣa by a great preceptor of Rājendra I (*śrī rājendra-mahā-mahīṣa-guruṇa*).[66] This *sthapati* built the temple at Punna *alias* Arātikulāntaka village, described in this grant as "the village of great brāhmaṇas" (*dvijavara-grāme*).

The Coḷa rulers who were builders of magnificent temples also concentrated their attention on rebuilding the older

63. R. Nagaswamy, *TVCP, Veḷāñjeri plates of Parantaka I*, Plate V, p. 2.
64. *SII*, vol. IV, No. 553, p. 185.
65. P.R. Srinivasan, "A Sanskrit Inscription from Tiruvoṟṟiyūr" *JOR*, vol. XXXII, pp. 11-15.
66. *ARE*, 61 of 1974-75.

temples constructed of brick with stone. A bi-lingual epigraph dated in the second regnal year of Ādirājendra (AD 1068-69), found in the *maṇḍapa* of the Varadarājaperumāḷ shrine inside the Candramauḷīśvara temple at Tiruvakkarai (South Arcot district) mentions the rebuilding of the *vimāna* (*cakreśa-parameṣṭhi vimānam*) in stone.[67] This *vimāna* (*kotacoḷaka vimānam*) was originally built of brick by Kota Coḷa. This Kota Coḷa is considered to be a reference to Koch-Coḷan or Koccenganāṉ, a Coḷa king of the late Saṅgam period who is credited by Tirumaṅgai Āḻvar to be the builder of many Śiva and Viṣṇu temples in the Tamil land.[68]

An epigraph of Māravarman Kulaśekhara I, dated in his 29th regnal year (AD 1298) from the Veṅkaṭācalapati temple in the village of Karisulndamaṅgalam (Tirunelveli district) refers to the rebuilding of the central shrine of this temple by Pittusi Rāhuttar in the thirteenth year of this king. The temple is referred to in this record as the shrine of Veṅkaṭeśātiman, situated on the banks of the river Mauktikavāhinī (Tāmaraparaṇi).[69]

In addition to building beautiful temples, these architects must have also been involved in building palaces for the kings. These architects must have had a thorough knowledge of subjects such as mathematics and several sciences and must have been thoroughly conversant with the *Śilpa* and *Vāstu Sāstra*s to have been able to construct such monuments according to the prescribed rules.

Special Privileges

Certain groups of artisans had the honour to work for the ruler or for the members of the ruling family and thus were more privileged than the others of their community. The Sanskrit inscriptions of the period under study give some examples of such groups of artisans.

---

67. *SII*, vol. XVII, no. 227, p. 83; *ARE*, 205 of 1904.
68. S.R. Balasubrahmanyam, *Early Coḷa Temples*, New Delhi, 1971, p. 202.
69. *ARE*, 568 of 1916.

The Pallava copper-plate inscriptions reveal that some artisans were specially chosen to carry out the work of the rulers, especially the duty of engraving the important copper-plate charters of the kings.

The Kaśākuḍi,[70] the Velūrpāḷaiyam[71] and the Veḷāñjeri[72] plates give the names of the artisans, who were specially commissioned to engrave these edicts of the rulers on copper-sheets for posterity.

Likewise, the goldsmith named Nṛpatuṅga who was the hereditary servant of the Pallava dynasty (*pallava-kula mūla-bhṛtyaḥ*) wrote the Bāhūr charter of the Pallava king Nṛpatuṅgavarman.[73] It appears that the family of this goldsmith must have received special privileges from the royal household.

Again, the Daḷavāipuram charter states that a person named Nakkan was the chief blacksmith (*mukhya karmmāraḥ*) of the king and that he bore the epithet Nṛpaśekhara.[74]

With regard to the period of the Coḷas, the Madras Museum plates of Uttama Coḷa record that the weavers (*paṭṭaśālins*) who lived in the four quarters of Kāñcīpuram, namely Karuvuḷāṉpāṭṭi, Kaṁsahappāṭi, Atimāṉappāṭi and Eṟṟuvalicceri were the weavers of the royal garments (*rāja-vastra-kṛtām=eṣām catur-vyāṭa-nivāsinām*).[75]

Similarly, it can be gleaned from the Larger Leiden,[76] the Tiruvālaṅgāḍu[77] and the Karandai[78] plates that the sculptors (*śilpis*) of the *ovikula* of Kāñcīpuram were granted the special privilege of engraving these edicts during the reign of Rājendra Coḷa I.

70. Kaśākuḍi plates, *op. cit.*, l. 136, p. 353.
71. Velūrpāḷaiyam plates, *op. cit.*, v. 31, p. 510.
72. R. Nagaswamy, *TVCP*, *op. cit.*
73. Bāhūr plates, *op. cit.*, v. 32, p. 12.
74. T.N. Subramaniam, *DCPV*, v. 39, p. 19.
75. Madras Museum Plates of Uttama Coḷa, *op. cit.*, p. 269.
76. Larger Leiden plates, *op. cit.*, vv. 45-48, p. 258.
77. Tiruvālaṅgāḍu plates, *op. cit.*, l. 518, p. 412.
78. K.G. Krishnan, *op. cit.*, p. 76 and p. 193.

Guilds

Guilds, which are corporate organizations of groups such as artisans, traders and merchants played an extremely important role in developing the economy in ancient and medieval India. In the Tamil country, guilds such as the *maṇigrāmam*, *valañjiyar* and the famous *nānādeśa-diśai-āyirattu-aiññuṟṟuvar* contributed substantially to the overall prosperity of the state and even maintained their own armies and have been mentioned in many Tamil epigraphs.

The Daḷavāipuram copper-plates provide some information about a guild.[79] A Sanskrit verse mentions that the Tamil section was composed by the poet Pāṇḍya-dramiḷābharaṇa, who was the chief of the guild of blacksmiths (*karmmāra-śreṇi-mukhyaḥ*).

A bi-lingual record from the Vaḷiviṭṭaiyaṉār temple in Kamudi (Rāmanāthapuram district) belonging to about the tenth century AD, reveals that during that period there existed close contacts between various guilds.[80] This epigraph reveals that there existed an organization consisting of different guilds like the the *paṭṭinam* of the eighteen *nāḍu*, the thirty-two Veḷārpuram and the sixty-four Kaḍigaittavaḷattu Ceṭṭis. The Sanskrit *praśasti* describes the members of this corporation as the original servants (*mūlabṛtya*) of God Vāsudeva and the children of Goddess Śrīvīra-Parameśvarī.

The existance of agricultural guilds called Cittirameḻi or Cittirameḻi-nāṭṭar is seen from a number of inscriptions of the Coḷa period. An eulogy on the organization is first traceable in an eleventh-century inscription of Rājendra II found in the Agnīśvara temple at Tāmaraipākkam (North Arcot district).[81] The Sanskrit verse at the beginning of this epigraph describes the members of this guild as "the sons of the earth" (*śrīmatām*

79. T.N. Subramaniam, *DCPV*, v. 40, p. 31.

80. *ARE*, 96 of 1974-75.

81. *ARE*, 183 of 1973-74 and K.G. Krishnan, "Cittirameḻip-periyanāḍu: An Agricultural Guild of Medieval Tamil Nadu," *JMU*, vol. LIV, no. 1 (January 1982), rpt., 1-20.

bhūmi-putrāṇām), "as belonging to the four castes" (*cātur-varṇya-kulodbhavām*)" and "who dispense justice" (*sarvaloka-hitārthaya citrameḷasya śāsanam*).

Another record of about the twelfth century AD found in the Trivikramaperumāḷ temple at Tirukkoyilūr (South Arcot district) which has two Sanskrit verses at the beginning, gives more details about this organization, describing the members as, "being dependent on cattle and milk for their livlihood" (*śrīmat go-kṣīra-jīvinām*) and as "feeding and strengthening the state" (*pālanam rāṣṭra poṣaṇam*).[82]

Some more inscriptions about this guild, with similar Sanskrit verses differing only in minor details are found in other parts of Tamil Nadu like the Sukhāsīnaperumāḷ temple at Tiṭṭaguḍi (South Arcot district)[83] and the Śokkanātha temple at Pirāṉmalai (Rāmnad district).[84]

The Tamil portion of the Tāmaraipākkam record provides some interesting data about how one guild, called Rājendra Coḷa Cittirameḻi Perukkaḷār, after king Rājendra II, administered justice in a dispute between two brothers in which the elder had died.[85] The record shows that by the eleventh century AD, the arbitrary powers of the guild had extended even to try serious crimes like murder.[86]

Some records reveal that the Cittirameḻi organization had close contacts with the commercial body, the Diśai-Āyirattu-Aiññuṟṟuvar.[87] The Sanskrit *praśasti* of the Pirāṉmalai record mentions that it is an edict of the Cittirameḻi but is followed

82. *SII*, vol. VII, no. 129, pp. 54-55; K.G. Krishnan, *op. cit.*

83. *SII*, vol. VIII, no. 291, p. 160; K.G. Krishnan, *op. cit.*

84. *SII*, vol. VIII, no. 442, pp. 231-34.

85. *ARE*, 183 of 1973-74; R. Nagaswamy, "A Judgement of the Coḷa Period" *from Studies in Ancient Law and Society*, Madras, 1978, pp. 75-78.

86. R. Nagaswamy, *op. cit.*, p. 77.

87. *SII*, vol. VIII, No. 291, p. 160; *SII*, vol. VIII, no. 198, p. 98; *SII*, vol. VIII, no. 442, p. 231; K.G. Krishnan, *op. cit.*

by the expression *pañca-śata-vīra-śāsanam* indicating that it is a joint edict.[88]

The benefactions made by the Cittirameḷi organization includes building temples and making endowments to them[89] and the creation of *caturvedimaṅgalams*.[90]

The Temple as a Socio-Economic Centre

The Sanskrit inscriptions reveal that the temple was not only a place of worship but also played a very active role in the socio-economic sphere. The efficient administration of the temple necessitated the creation of various types of jobs, which gave rise to employment opportunities to people from different walks of life.

The temple, during the Pallava period was a small institution requiring only a few people for its smooth administration, but the gradual increase in the size of the temple and the rituals involved created a demand for more employees and the temple became the hub of the socio-economic life of the villages. The temple needed various employees such as priests, accountants, masons, artisans such as goldsmiths and blacksmiths, cooks and sweepers. The Sanskrit inscriptions of the period provide a few instances of the jobs which the temple provided for the people.

Priests

The most important person involved in the working of the temple was the priest who offered daily worship (*pūja*) to the deities housed therein. Some information about the priests of the temple and the hereditary nature of their duties can be gleaned from a Pallava inscription, namely, the Kūram grant. According to this inscription, the job of worship as well as the responsibilities of carrying out the repairs in the temple of

---

88. K.G. Krishnan, *op. cit.*, p. 14.
89. *SII*, vol. VIII, no. 291, p. 160.
90. *ARE*, 91 of 1941-42.

Vidyāvinīta-Pallava-Parameśvara in the village of Kūram was entrusted to the priests, named Anantaśiva-ācārya and Phullaśarman and their sons and grandsons were also appointed for this purpose.[91]

Accountants

Large sums of money were donated to the temples of the Tamil country by the rulers and by people from different sections of society. The maintenance of proper accounts pertaining to income and the various forms of expenditure incurred by the temple necessitated the appointment of treasurers and accountants. The Madras Museum plates of Uttama Coḷa[92] reveal that a group of weavers (*paṭṭaśālins*) were appointed as managers of the temple of Ūraka at Kāñcīpuram for the purpose of writing the accounts of the income and expenditure of this temple as has already been pointed out in detail earlier in this chapter.

Although these are the only direct data about the temple servants provided by the Sanskrit inscriptions, it can be understood that the daily feeding of devotees, the numerous festivals which were held, and so many of the other innumerable activities with which the temple was concerned made it necessary to employ a host of people to undertake these duties.

Medicine

The science of medicine was in a very advanced state in the ancient Tamil country. Apart from the data seen from the Sanskrit epigraphs, the Tamil inscriptions also reveal the names of numerous Āyurvedic medicines and names of the medicinal texts in Sanskrit studied here. It appears that in every village there were expert medical men and the Udayendiram and Taṇḍantoṭṭam plates of Nandivarman Pallavamalla refer to a share of land for physicians called *vaidyabhoga*.[93]

91. Kūram plates, *op. cit.*, l. 49, p. 154.
92. Madras Museum plates of Uttama Coḷa, *op. cit.*, p. 269.
93. C. Minakshi, *ASLP*, p. 173.

The Larger Siṉṉamaṉūr plates in the Sanskrit portion mention a learned brāhmaṇa called Parāntaka and state that his ancestors who were learned in the Vedas (*ananya-veda-pāragāḥ*) had "established on this earth the extensive work called *Kalpa* written by Āgniveśya."[94] The editor of this inscription has suggested that they were perhaps proficient in the Āgniveśya-kalpa, the doctrine of medicine in which Āgniveśya is said to have been a predecessor of Suśruta.[95]

Many of the Tamil epigraphs mention the hospitals provided for the sick as well as places where the medical sciences were taught. An inscription of the eleventh century AD of the reign of Vīra-Rājendra records that there was a hospital in addition to a Vedic college and hostel attached to the Veṅkaṭeśa Perumāḷ temple at the village of Tirumukkūḍal (Chingleput district).[96] The staff and students of the hostel as well as the temple-servants who fell ill were treated at this hospital named Vīra-Coḷan. This hospital housed a physician, a surgeon, two people for collecting medicinal herbs, three people to prepare medicines, two nurses and a barber for performing minor surgeries.

This lengthy epigraph also provides a list of a number of Āyurvedic medicines such as *brāhmyam-kaḍumbūri, vāsā-harītakī, go-mūtra-harītakī, daśa-mūla harītakī, bhallātaka-harītakī, gaṇḍira, balakeraṇḍa-taila, pañcāka-taila, laśunādy-eraṇḍa-taila, uttama-karṇādi taila, bilvādi-ghṛta, maṇḍūkara-vaṭika, dravatti, vimala, sunetri, tāmrādi, vajrakalpa, kalyāṇaka-lavaṇa and purāṇa-ghṛta.*

Most of the medicines described here are found in the *Caraka-Saṁhitā* (of Caraka) and in the *Aṣṭāṅgahṛdaya* (of Vāghbaṭṭa)[97] thus revealing that the doctors of the time were proficient in these medicinal texts.

---

94. Larger Siṉṉamaṉūr plates, *op. cit.*, v. 22, p. 452.
95. *Ibid.*, p. 458.
96. *EI*, vol. XXI, no. 38, pp. 230-41.
97. *Ibid.*, p. 224.

An inscription of the twelfth century AD belonging to the reign of Vikrama Coḷa refers to the study of medicinal sciences like the *Aṣṭāṅgahṛdaya* and *Caraka-Saṁhitā* at a *maṭha* which was attached to the temple of Tiruvāḍu-tuṟaiyuḍaiyār at Tiruvāḍutuṟai (Tañjāvūr district).[98]

Weights and Measures

The Sanskrit records provide some terms with regard to weights and measures, but it is only the Tamil inscriptions and the Tamil portions of the bi-lingual epigraphs which contain most of these terms as they are the operative part of these records. It is only in some Sanskrit epigraphs which relate to donations of land or money that such terms pertaining to weights and measures can be found.

Land Measures

A number of Pallava copper-plate charters mention the gift of land to temples and to learned brāhmaṇas and some land-measurements are mentioned in them.

NIVARTANA

Nivartana is the most commonly used term for land-measurement and is found in many Pallava records such as the Hīrahadagalli,[99] Guṇapadeya,[100] Uruvapaḷḷi[101] and Kaśākuḍi[102] charters. The term *nivartana* has been stated by V.S. Apte to mean "turning back or returning."[103] According to C. Minakshi it is possible that in the early days, land was measured by an individual starting from a particular point, and after going around the field, returning to the starting point within a certain time and marking the exact boundary

---

98. *ARE*, no. 159 of 1925.
99. Hīrahadagalli plates, *op. cit.*, p. 6.
100. Guṇapadeya plates, *op. cit.*, p. 146.
101. Uruvapaḷḷi plates, *op. cit.*, p. 52.
102. Kaśākuḍi plates, *op. cit.*, p. 351.
103. V.S. Apte, *The Students Sanskrit-English Dictionary*, Delhi, 1986, p. 296.

of the field covered during the course of the round.[104] It was probably later that some fixed unit was invented to define a *nivartana*.[105] A *nivartana* of land was equal to twenty rods.[106]

PAṬṬIKA

The term *paṭṭika* occurs in the Cendalūr plates in connection with a grant of land as *brahmadeya*.[107] C. Minakshi has opined that *paṭṭika* is a Sanskrit term for the measure *paṭṭi* found in the Tamil inscriptions of the Pallavas.[108] From the evidence given by the Kaśākuḍi plates, the term *nivartana* given in the Sanskrit section and the term *paṭṭi* given in the Tamil section are synonymous.[109]

Weights

KAḺAÑJU

The gold weight called *kaḻañju* was prevalent in the Tamil country during the period of this study and is found in some Sanskrit inscriptions which record the gift of gold to temples.

A bi-lingual early Pāṇḍyan record[110] mentions in the Sanskrit part that forty *kṛṣṇakaca* (*catvāriṁśat pramāṇān-kṛṣṇakacān*) were gifted by a person for maintaining a lamp at the temple of Tiruṭṭalīśvara (Rāmanāthapuram district) while in the corresponding Tamil section the amount is mentioned as forty *kaḻañju*. C. Minakshi has mentioned that in early Pāṇḍyan records, there is proof that the *kaḻañju* was the equivalent of the *kṛṣṇakaca*.[111]

---

104. C. Minakshi, *ASLP*, pp. 106-07.
105. *Ibid*.
106. V.S. Apte, *op. cit*.
107. *EI*, vol. VIII, no. 23, p. 235 (Cendalūr plates).
108. C. Minakshi, *ASLP*, p. 107.
109. Kaśākuḍi plates, *op. cit*., p. 359.
110. *SII*, vol. XIV, no. 5, p. 3.
111. C. Minakshi, *op. cit*., p. 111

Dināra

The gold weight called *dināra* also figures in some Sanskrit records of the period of this study. An early Pāṇḍyan bi-lingual epigraph[112] recording an amount paid for maintaining a lamp at a temple mentions the amount as ten *dināra* in the Sanskrit part while in the corresponding Tamil portion the amount is given as ten *kāśu*.

---

112. *SII*, vol. XIV, no. 9, p. 5.

5

Social Life

THE Sanskrit inscriptions of Tamil Nadu of the period of this study throw light on some of the social divisions present at that time, the role of women in society, social customs which were in vogue and also about recreation and pastimes.

Brāhmaṇas

The brāhmaṇas formed a very important section of the society in the ancient and medieval periods in the whole of India. They served mainly as teachers and as priests and held a honoured position in society. The main duties of the brāhmaṇas have been outlined in the *Dharmaśāstras* in a detailed manner. According to the *Manusmṛti*, "teaching, studying, sacrificing for himself, sacrificing for others, making gifts and receiving them are the six acts (prescribed) for a brāhmaṇa."[1]

In the Tamil country also, as early as the Saṅgam age, the brāhmaṇas formed an important section of the society and this practice continued in the later periods also. The Sanskrit inscriptions reveal that the brāhmaṇas, also called as *vipra* and *dvija* in these epigraphs were committed to the ideals enshrined in the *Dharmaśāstras*. The epigraphs reveal that these brāhmaṇas were highly learned in the Śāstras, *Itihāsa* and Purāṇas and formed the highly educated section among the people of the times. They served mainly as teachers and priests, but sometimes followed other occupations such as working as

1. *MS*, 10, 75.

ministers in the government. The brāhmaṇas appear, from the epigraphs, to have been venerated by commoners and royalty alike. The inscriptions such as the Kaśākuḍi plates praise the brāhmaṇas as being "the *devas* on earth" (*bhūdevāḥ*).[2]

Many of the early Pallava copper-plate grants[3] mention the term *deva-dvija-guru-vṛddhopasevinaḥ* (who nourished the Gods, twice-born, i.e., brāhmaṇas, spiritual preceptors and old men) to describe many of the kings of this dynasty which reveals the respect which the rulers gave to the brāhmaṇas.

Again, many of the early Pallava charters like the Vesanta,[4] Sakrepaṭṇa,[5] Udayendiram (I),[6] Cendalūr,[7] Oṁgoḍu (II),[8] Pikira,[9] Mangalūr,[10] Viḻavetti,[11] Cura[12] plates and also the Reyūrū inscription of Rājasiṁha[13] mention the epithet *bappa bhaṭṭāraka-pāda-bhaktaḥ* (devoted to the feet of Bappa Bhaṭṭāraka) while describing the Pallava rulers. According to C. Minakshi, the learned and holy brāhmaṇas were known as bappa bhaṭṭāraka.[14] The Pullūr plates mention that Nandivarman Pallavamalla made a land-grant to a hundred and eight excellent brāhmaṇas (*bappa-bhaṭṭāraka*) hailing from very good families, of good conduct and learning (*nija-vaṁśa-paramparāgatānāṁ śuddhābhijana-vṛtta-vidyānām dvijavara-bappa-bhaṭṭārakānām*).[15]

2. *SII*, vol. II, no. 73, l. 34, p. 347 (Kaśākuḍi plates).
3. *EI*, vol. XV, no. 11, p. 251. (Oṁgoḍu I plates); *Ind.Ant.*, (February 1876), p. 51 (Uruvapalli plates); *EI*, vol. XXXVIII, no. 18, p. 104, (Sakrepaṭṇa plates); *EI*, vol. XXIV, No. 43, p. 302 (Viḻāvaṭṭi plates).
4. N. Ramesan, *VGPS*, pp. 95-96.
5. Sakrepaṭṇa plates, *op. cit.*, p. 104.
6. *EI*, vol. III, no. 23, p. 146 (Udayendiram I plates).
7. *EI*, vol. VIII, no. 23, p. 235 (Cendalūr plates).
8. *EI*, vol. XV, no. 11, p. 254 (Oṁgoḍu II plates).
9. *EI*, vol. VIII, no. 15, p. 162 (Pikira plates).
10. *Ind. Ant.*, vol. V, p. 155 (Mangalūr plates).
11. Viḻāvaṭṭi plates, *op. cit.*, p. 302.
12. *EI*, vol. XXIV, no. 18, p. 141 (Cura plates).
13. *EI*, vol. XXIX, no. 11, p. 96 (Reyūrū plates).
14. C. Minakshi, *ASLP*, pp. 176-77.
15. *EI*, vol. XXXVI, no. 20, p. 153 (Pullūr plates).

The gift of land (*bhūmi-dāna*) has been considered as one of the most meritorious gifts and has been repeatedly highlighted in the *Dharmaśāstras* and other sacred literature. Numerous Pallava inscriptions clearly state that there is no gift greater than the grant of land.[16]

The epigraphs of the Pallava, Pāṇḍya and Coḷa periods are replete with innumerable instances where such donations of land have been made by the rulers and their ministers to the learned brāhmaṇas. The land-grants given by the rulers to the brāhmaṇas were usually made tax-free as the kings considered this as an act of merit which would give them power, prosperity and good health.

Similarly, it was also considered meritorious to feed learned brāhmaṇas. The Sanskrit epigraphs of the period under study record many instances where endowments were created for providing food to brāhmaṇas well-versed in the scriptures. The Anbil plates record that the mother of Aniruddha, who was the trusted minister of Sundara Coḷa, made an endowment for giving sumptuous meals along with side dishes in a silver vessel to a learned brāhmaṇa everyday (*viduṣe dvijāya nityam*).[17] The same epigraph reveals that the great-grandfather of Aniruddha, named Ananta showed great hospitality to all brāhmaṇas (*sarvadvij-ātithyākṛte*).[18] A bi-lingual 10th century Coḷa epigraph found in the Raṅganāthasvāmi temple in Śrīraṅgam records that a certain Somadevabhaṭṭan made an endowment of sixty *kaḻañju* of gold for feeding a brāhmaṇa well-versed in the *Śukla Yajurveda* (*vājasaneya veda viduṣām ādhyaḥ*).[19]

An epigraph of 981 AD from the Anantīśvarasvāmin temple in Uḍaiyārguḍi (South Arcot district) states that a person named Nambieṉbāṉ ceded the village Tuṟaiyūr

16. *EI*, vol. XXXII, no. 9, p. 97 (Vunnaguruvapālem plates); Uruvapaḻḻi plates, *op. cit.*, p. 52; Pikira plates, *op. cit.*, p. 162; Viḻavaṭṭi plates, *op. cit.*, p. 303; Kaśākuḍi plates, *op. cit.*, p. 353.
17. *EI*, vol. XV, no. 5, v. 35, p. 63 (Anbil plates).
18. *Ibid.*, v. 37, p. 63.
19. *SII*, vol. XXIV, no. 11, p. 8.

Kiḷḷikkuḍi to feed a hundred brāhmaṇas everyday at a *sabhā* constructed by him in Ciṟupaṭūr-grāma.[20]

The inscriptions provide the names of different *gotras* and *sūtras* to which the brāhmaṇa donees belonged.[21]

Brāhmaṇas as Administrators and Warriors

Although the brāhmaṇas in ancient and medieval India almost always followed the professions of teaching or officiating as priests, yet there were certain exceptions and there are recorded instances where learned brāhmaṇas strayed into other professions. The *Manusmṛti* states that in case a brāhmaṇa is unable to subsist by these above occupations, he could live according to the law given for the kṣatriyas.[22]

The Sanskrit inscriptions provide instances of brāhmaṇas taking up professions other than that of teaching or officiating as priests. An instance of a brāhmaṇa taking to the profession of a kṣatriya is found in the Pullūr plates of Nandivarman Pallavamalla, in which a brāhmaṇa named Nāgaśarman Brahmādhirāja, who was a minister of this Pallava ruler is described as being well-versed in the use ofarms.[23]

The Anbil charter of Sundara Coḷa records that Aniruddha, who was brāhmaṇa and was the trusted minister of this king,

20. *ARE*, 578 of 1920.
21. Agniveśya, Kāśyapa, Gautama, Kauśika, Kauṇḍinya, Ātreya, Vatsa, Bhāradvāja, Parāśara, Augamedhi, Maudgalya, Rathithara, Jātukarṇa, Vatsa, Vādhula, Viṣṇuvṛddha, Lohita, Vasiṣṭha, Gautama, Parāśara, Harīta, Śāṇḍilya, Nārāyaṇa, Sarvāṇi, Masala, Gārga, Śaunaka, Bhārgava, Salavata, Kutsa, Vārākhya, Kapya, Dhūmrāyaṇa, Paurukutsa, Māṭhara, Padarari, Aṅgīrasa, Devarata, Satha, Aupamanyu, Saṁkṛti, Kokkaṇa, Māśala, Kalayasi, Jāmbavīya, Rauṣyāyaṇa, Nitunḍina, Mitrayu, Śathamarśana, Māṇḍavya, Dhanañjaya, Śārṅgimitra, Halandana, Sraviṣta, Bhādarāyaṇa, Vana, Gavuśu and Aviṣṭa.

    Some of the *sūtras* mentioned are: Āpastamba, Āgniveśya, Āśvalāyana, Bhāradvaja, Chāndogya, Hiraṇyakeśi, Kalaracca, Pravacana, Paviriya and Vaseni.
22. *MS*, 10, 81.
23. Pullūr plates, *op. cit.*, p. 153.

held the title *brahmādhirāja*.[24] This inscription also gives some information about his ancestors. His father is stated to have had many disciples (*śiṣyāḥ*), and it appears that he might have been a teacher.[25] His grandfather and great-grandfather are mentioned as making donations to the temple at Śrīraṅgam and giving gifts to the poor and needy respectively, but no other information is given about them. Thus, it seems that in his family, only Aniruddha was given a very high administrative position in the state by the king; the title *brahmādhirāja* also indicating his prowess as a warrior, thus marking a departure from the traditional professions followed by his forefathers and by the brāhmaṇas of the period in general.

Other Castes

A very interesting epigraph from the Ujjvalanāthasvāmi temple, Uyyakoṇḍān-Tirumalai dated in the 48th year of the reign of Kulottuṅga Coḷa I (AD 1071-1122) records the decision of the *bhaṭṭa*s (learned brāhmaṇas) of Rājāśrayacaturvedimaṅgalam on the basis of the *śāstra*s, the professions which an *anuloma* sect called *rathakāra*s described as the sons of *māhiṣya*s by *karaṇī* women, could follow.[26] On the basis of authorities like Yajñavalkya, Gautama, Kauṭilya, Bodhāyana and others; the *bhaṭṭa*s of this village defined a *māhiṣya* as one born of a kṣatriya father by a vaiśya mother, a *karaṇī* as the daughter of a vaiśya father by a śūdra mother and a *rathakāra* as the son of a *māhiṣya* father by *karaṇī* mother, and were allowed to follow professions in the fields of architecture, building coaches and chariots, constructing temple *gopura*s with images on them, preparation of instruments required by brāhmaṇas in their sacrificial ceremonies like the ladle (*sṛk*), building *maṇḍapa*s and making jewels for the rulers like diadems and bracelets.[27]

24. Anbil plates, *op. cit.*, pp. 58-63.
25. *Ibid.*, vv. 34-37, pp. 62-63.
26. *ARE*, 479 of 1908.
27. *Ibid.*, Pt. II, pp. 94-95.

The *bhaṭṭas* decided that the *anuloma* sect of *rathakāras* was superior to the *pratiloma* sect, to which belonged those who were born of a father of a lower-class and a mother of a higher class. A scripture quoted states that the *rathakāras* were allowed the *upanayana* (sacred-thread ceremony), *ijyā* (performance of sacrifices) and *ādhana* (receiving the sacred fire), while according to another authority, the *anulomas*, who are allowed *upanayanam* are not allowed to peform the *agnihotra* (keeping the sacred fire always alive), *aupāsana* (worshipping the fire thus kindled), *pañcamahāyajña* (the five sacred duties prescribed for the brāhmaṇas), namely *devayajña* (ceremonial worship of the Gods), *pitṛyajña* (ceremonial worship of ancestors), *bhūtayajña* (ceremonial worship of living creatures other than man) and *mānuṣayajña* (ceremonial worship of men) and *adhyayana* (recital of the Vedas), and that their *upanayana* ceremony should not be conducted by reciting *mantras* (sacred hymns).[28] The community of *rathakāras* were not the creation of the brāhmaṇa law-givers, but a class whose profession and intelligence was already noted in the Vedas.

Women

Women have traditionally had a more passive role to play in Indian society than men, both in the north as well as in the south. The Saṅgam classics reveal that women did not occupy equal status with men, but at the same time had attained high levels of excellence in cultural spheres. The chastity of women and their role as devoted housewives have been stressed in the *Kuraḷ*.[29]

The Sanskrit inscriptions of the Pallavas, Pāṇḍyas and Coḷas offer some information regarding the position of women during the ancient and medieval periods of Tamil history. As was the case in the earlier periods, evidence reveals that women continued to occupy a position subordinate to men.

---

28. *ARE*, Pt. II, pp. 94-95.
29. P.S. Sundaram, (tr. and ed.), *The Kural*, New Delhi, 1990, Ch. 6.

The practice of *satī* was prevalent in the Tamil country from the Saṅgam period. However, only one Sanskrit inscription of the period of this study, namely, the Tiruvālaṅgāḍu plates mention this practice.[30] According to this inscription, Vānavaṉmahādevī, the devoted queen of Sundara Coḷa committed *satī* on the death of her husband. A Tamil inscription of Rājarāja I also records this act of Vānavaṉmahādevī.[31]

Some of the Sanskrit epigraphs refer to the custom of wives removing their ornaments on the death of their husbands. The Velūrpāḷaiyam grant refers to this practice in an invocatory verse.[32] The Tiruvālaṅgāḍu plates mention that when Rājendra I defeated and killed Jayasiṁha, the Cāḷukyan ruler, his wives stood bereft of all ornaments.[33]

An inscription of Jaṭāvarman Sundara Pāṇḍya I from the Naṭarāja temple, Chidambaram extolls the valour of this king which brought calamity to the chief ornament (i.e., *tāli* or *maṅgala sūtra*) around the neck of the wives of his enemies.[34]

It appears that the women of the enemies of the Tamil kings were treated very badly. The Karandai plates reveal that when Rājendra I captured and burnt the city of Mānyakheṭa, even the women of the city were not spared and were seen "moving in the open spaces of high palatial residences and appeared to be like the lightening moving frequently in the midst of clouds" (*calantyas=taṭita iva muhur=megha-bṛndodareṣu*).[35]

These inscriptions reveal that the women of these ages from different strata of society made many endowments in their own right. The Anbil plates reveal that the mother of

---

30. *SII*, vol. III, no. 205, v. 65, p. 397 (Tiruvālaṅgāḍu plates).
31. *ARE*, 236 of 1902.
32. *SII*, vol. II, no. 98, p. 507 (Velūrpāḷaiyam plates).
33. Tiruvālaṅgāḍu plates, *op. cit.*, v. 103, p. 399.
34. *SII*, vol. IV, no. 629, p. 192.
35. K.G. Krishnan, *KTPR*, v. 53, p. 73.

Aniruddha, the minister of Sundara Coḷa made an endowment for feeding a learned brāhmaṇa everyday and also gave a big lamp to Hari (Viṣṇu) at Śrīraṅgam.[36]

Other similar stone inscriptions of the Coḷa and Pāṇḍya periods record the names of many ladies who had donated gold or money for installing perpetual lamps in temples.[37]

Queens

The queens of the Tamil country during the ancient and medieval periods did not take an active part in the administration of the kingdom. However, they played important roles in the religious sphere by building shrines, installing images of various deities and making endowments to the temples of the land.

These epigraphs provide the names of the consorts of the Tamil kings and chieftains, eulogise their qualities and reveal their honourable position in the kingdom.

The first inscriptional reference to queens in the Pallava inscriptions occurs in a Prākṛt grant of Cārudevī, the queen of *yuvamahārāja* Vijaya Buddhavarman who made an endowment to a Viṣṇu temple.[38]

A reference to a Pallava queen named Raṅgapatākā, the wife of Rājasiṁha is found in one of the inscriptions at the Kailāśanātha temple built by this ruler at Kāñcīpuram.[39] This inscription describes this queen as having "attained the mighty position of favourite with king Narasiṁhaviṣṇu (Rājasiṁha) and thus seems to have subdued the pride of Puṣkaradevatā (i.e., Lakṣmī)." Raṅgapatākā is described as the favourite mistress of her husband just as Pārvatī is the dear beloved mistress of her husband (Śiva).

Another Sanskrit inscription found at another shrine in

---

36. Anbil plates, *op. cit.*, v. 36, p. 63.
37. *SII*, vol. XIII, no. 340, p. 181; *ARE*, 547 of 1920; *SII*, vol. XIV, no. 9, p. 5; *EI*, vol. XXIII, no. 45, pp. 285-86.
38. *EI*, vol. VIII, no. 12, pp. 145-46 (Guṇapadeya plates).
39. *SII*, vol. I, no. 29, p. 22.

this same temple also offers a description of a lady suggesting that this shrine too was built by a queen belonging to the royal family of the Pallavas.[40] From the description given in this epigraph as "one who was full of loveliness (*lāvaṇya*), softness (*mārdhava*), grace (*vilāsa*) and cleanliness (*mṛja*), and who was charming through genuine sweetness (*akliṣṭa-mādhurya-vilobhanīyam*), who was adorned with grace (*vibhūṣitam-vibhramahāvabhāvaiḥ*), who was like the art of attraction (*ākarṣa-vidyāmiva*) and who appeared to be the master-piece of the first Creator, whose skill had attained perfection at last after he had created thousands of good-looking women" it appears that this description could allude only to one of the queens of the ruling family, possibly Raṅgapatākā.

The Velūrpāḷaiyam plates record that the chief queen of Nandivarman II Pallavamalla was Revā,[41] a Rāṣṭrakūṭa princess, who was the mother of Dantivarman. The same inscription records that this Dantivarman married the daughter of the king of the Kadamba dynasty named Aggaḷanimmaṭī[42] who is described as the chief-queen (*mahiṣī*) of this ruler and the mother of Nandivarman III. The Kumaraḍimaṅgalam plates also mention Dantivarman's marriage to Aggaḷanimmaṭī, the Kadamba princess.[43]

The Bāhūr plates of Nṛpatuṅgavarman record that the queen of Nandivarman III, the son of Dantivarman, was a Rāṣṭrakūta princess named Śaṅkhā.[44] This inscription describes her thus, "full of patience like the earth" (*kṣmāvatī dharitr-iva*), "beloved by the people like a mother" (*mātṛ-vaj=jagataḥ*), "the queen named Śaṅkhā shone as if she were the embodied fortune of the king" (*śrīr=iva=rūpiṇī*).

This queen who is mentioned in this inscription as the

40. *SII*, vol. I, no. 30, p. 24.
41. Velūrpāḷaiyam plates, *op. cit.*, vv. 16-17, p. 508.
42. *Ibid.*, vv. 18-19, p. 508.
43. N. Ramesan, *KPPN*, v. 4, p. 201.
44. Bāhūr plates, *op. cit.*, v. 13, p. 10.

mother of Nṛpatuṅgavarman, is described as possessing "intelligence, beauty, arts, etc." (*mati-kānti-kal-ādimatyām= mānyā*).[45]

The Ciṟṟūr plates of Nṛpatuṅgavarman mention that he was the son of Nandivarman III and his queen who was the daughter of a Rāṣṭrakūṭa king.[46]

The Veḷāñjeri plates of Aparājita Pallava describe the greatness of Vijayā, the wife of Kampavarman. She is described as "being of matchless virtues" (*guṇonurūpa*), "born in the pure Gaṅga family" (*viśuddha-gaṅgānvaya janmamānyā*) and "then becoming the queen of Kampavarman."[47] She is mentioned in this epigraph as the mother of Aparājita.

Some of the epigraphs of the Pāṇḍya rulers also provide information regarding the queens of this dynasty. According to the Veḷvikuḍi grant, the queen of Māravarman Rājasiṁha I was the daughter of the Maḷava ruler and to them was born Jaṭila (Neḍuñjaḍaiyan).[48] The Larger Siṉṉamaṉūr plates record that the queen of Parāntaka Vīranārāyaṇa and the mother of Māravarman Rājasiṁha II was called Vānavaṉmahādevī.[49] She is glorified in this epigraph as being to her husband what Śrī was to Viṣṇu, and Paulomī (Śacī) was to Śatakratu (Indra).

The inscriptions of the Coḷas also furnish some important information about the consorts of the kings of this dynasty. The Anbil plates record that (Parāntaka I) married the daughter of a Keraḷa king called Paḻuveṭṭarayar.[50] This princess whose name is not given in this inscription is described in this record as "resembling glory incarnate" (*rājalakṣmī-iva*). The very next verse mentions that a son named Ariñcika (Ariñjaya) was born to them.[51] The same charter records that

45. Bāhūr plates, *op. cit.*, v. 15, p. 10.
46. T.V. Mahalingam, *IOP*, p. 440.
47. R. Nagaswamy, *TVCP*, *Veḷāñjeri plates of Aparājita*, v. 8, plate II, p. 1.
48. *EI*, vol. XVII, no. 16, v. 14, p. 299 (Veḷvikuḍi plates).
49. *SII*, vol. III, no. 206, vv. 15-16, p. 452 (Larger Siṉṉamaṉūr plates).
50. Anbil plates, *op. cit.*, v. 22, p. 61.
51. *Ibid.*, v. 23, p. 61.

Ariñjaya married a princess of the Vaidumba race named Kalyāṇī, described in this inscription as "a pre-eminent abode of virtues" (*pātram guṇānām param*) and to them was born a son (Sundara Coḷa).[52]

A 10th century bi-lingual inscription from the Nāganāthasvāmi temple, Tirunāgeśvaram (Tañjāvūr district) states that a princess named Ariñjigai-Pirāṭṭiyār, the daughter of Ariñjaya Coḷa and the wife of a Bāṇa chief made an endowment for worship and offerrings and for burning two lamps during the three services daily to the deity Amarasundaradeva installed by her in this temple.[53]

The Tiruvālaṅgāḍu plates record that the queen of Sundara Coḷa named Vānavaṉmahādevī who was like Arundhatī in her devotion to her husband committed *satī* after his death.[54]

One of the queens of Rājarāja I was Vānavaṉmahādevī *alias* Tribhuvanamahādevī, the mother of Rājendra I. The Karandai plates state that Rājendra I granted a whole village in Vīracoḷavaḷanāḍu to a thousand and eighty learned brāhmaṇas by clubbing together fifty-one villages, and that he named the new-found *agrahāra* as Tribhuvaṉamahādevīcaturvedimaṅgalam after his mother.[55]

Some information about the royal ladies of the Hoysala dynasty which ruled over some parts of the Tamil country during the thirteenth and fourteenth centuries AD is forthcoming from a few of their Sanskrit and bi-lingual epigraphs.

An inscription of the Hoysala ruler Someśvara from Kāñcīpuram states that his chief queen was Devikā, born of the Cāḷukya family.[56] Another epigraph from the Raṅganāthasvāmi temple, Śrīraṅgam, dated in the 12th year (AD 1266) of

52. Anbil plate, *op. cit.*, vv. 24-25, p. 61.
53. *SII*, vol. XIII, no. 197, p. 107.
54. Tiruvālaṅgāḍu plates, *op. cit.*, v. 65, p. 397, 55.
55. K.G. Krishnan, *KTPR*, vv. 67-69, p. 75.
56. *ARE*, 602 of 1919.

the reign of Rāmanātha, son of Someśvara records an endowment of garden-land by princess Ponnambala-mahādevī. She is mentioned in this inscription as the daughter of the Hoysala king Vīra-Someśvara and the Cāḷukyan princess Devalamahādevī and the sister (*sahodarī*) of Vīra-Rāmanātha, who succeeded Vīra-Someśvara in the southern part of the Hoysala kingdom.[57]

A large number of Tamil inscriptions mention the numerous gifts to the Raṅganāthasvāmi temple by the Hoysala royal ladies like Devalamahādevī, Somalādevī, Kamalādevī and Chikka Somalā.

A bi-lingual inscription from the Varadarājasvāmi temple, Kāñcīpuram[58] and a long Sanskrit inscription from Śrīraṅgam[59] of the Keraḷa king Ravivarma Kulaśekhara mention that his mother was Umādevī, the queen of Jayasiṁha.

The queens of the vassal chiefs of the imperial rulers are also mentioned in some of the Sanskrit inscriptions. The Ciṟṟūr plates of Pallava Nṛpatuṅga[60] mention a Bāṇa vassal of this king named Parañjaya, who was requested by his queen Pṛthvīmāṇṇikā to grant lands to certain learned brāhmaṇas who had asked her for this favour. Nṛpatuṅga, on the request of Parañjaya acceeded to this and the village named Pṛthvīmahādevī-caturvedimaṅgalam, obviously after this queen was given to the brāhmaṇas.

A Sanskrit epigraph of a Coḷa vassal, Bhūti Vikrama Kesari found at Mūvarkovil in Koḍuṁbāḷūr (Pudukkottai district) mentions that the mother of this chieftain was Anupamā, a daughter of a Coḷa king (*coḷa-rāja-duhitā*).[61] The same record mentions that Bhūti Vikrama Kesari had two wives named Kaṟṟaḷi and Varaguṇā and that the former gave

57. *SII*, vol. XXIV, no. 274, pp. 294-95.
58. *EI*, vol. IV, no. 17, v. 1, p. 146.
59. *Ibid.*, no. 18, v. 1, p. 149.
60. T.V. Mahalingam, *IOP*, vv. 13-15, p. 441.
61. K.A. Nilakanta Sastri, "The Koḍuṁbāḷūr Inscription of Vikrama Kesari," *JOR*, vol. VII, v. 4, p. 9.

birth to two sons, Parāntaka and Ādityavarman.[62] This inscription adds that this chieftain built three *vimānas* (*mūvarkovil*) in his name and in the name of his two wives in which he enshrined Lord Maheśvara (Śiva).

The matrimonial alliances of the Tamil kings with the other ruling powers of south India like the Rāṣṭrakūṭas, Kadambas and Vaidumbas reveal that this was considered essential to increase the power and prestige of the ruling families. Similarly, the marriages of princes and princesses of the imperial Tamil powers with the offspring of their vassal chiefs was done with a view to strengthen their ties and to enlist their support in times of crisis.

The fact that the Tamil kings were polygamists is borne out by the inscriptions wherein the queens are spoken of as "the favourite of the king" or as "the chief queen" thereby indicating that these kings had more than one consort.

The queens of the Tamil country have also been depicted in sculpture and in painting. The Varāha cave in Māmallapuram contains a figure of Mahendravarman I with two of his queens. Many of the Pallava queens are also depicted in the series of historical sculptures found in the Vaikuṇṭhaperumāḷ temple in Kāñcīpuram. Similarly, in the Bṛhadīśvara temple at Tañjāvūr, a mural depicting Rājarāja Coḷa I and his three queens worshipping Naṭarāja has been beautifully depicted.

In sharp contrast to the honourable position given by the kings of the Tamil country to their own consorts, was the treatment meted out to the wives of the kings whom they conquered in battle as seen by the evidence given by some of the Sanskrit inscriptions. An epigraph of Rājarāja I mentions the plight of the queens of the Keraḷa king who was vanquished by this Coḷa ruler and who were forced to take refuge at his feet.[63] The Karandai plates reveal the Rājendra

---

62. K.A. Nilakanta Sastri, "The Koḍuṁbāḷūr Inscription of Vikrama Kesari," *JOR*, vol. VII, v. 9.
63. *ARE*, 572 of 1970-71.

I, having defeated the ruler of Laṅkā, captured even his queen (*mahiṣī*) and his daughter (*putrī*).[64]

The distress experienced by the queens of the Cāḷukyan ruler Jayasiṁha when their husband was killed by the Coḷas is graphically described in the Tiruvālaṅgāḍu plates.[65]

Sports and Pastimes

In any society, it is common for royalty and commoners alike to indulge in some kind of activity such as sports or games. A few of the Sanskrit inscriptions offer a glimpse of some of these activities which were pursued by the people of those times.

Wrestling

Some interesting information about sports is available from the Sanskrit epigraphs. The kings of the Tamil country seem to have been very fond of wrestling (see Chapter III — "Military Administration"). It is possible that these kings learnt wrestling to help them in the numerous battles in which they participated, but it is also likely that they took to it as a sport or as a pastime to reveal their physical prowess. Nandivarman Pallavamalla has been praised in the Kaśākuḍi plates as a master in the "art of gymnastics" (*vyāyāma-vidyā*).[66]

C. Minakshi has drawn our attention to a sculpture in the panel of historical sculptures depicting the various activities of the rulers of this dynasty found at the Vaikuṇṭhaperumāḷ temple at Kāñcīpuram which shows two *malla*s (wrestlers) attacking each other in the court of Narasiṁhavarman I. C. Minakshi has surmised that perhaps this king liked to witness contests among *malla*s which would be an explanation of the name *mahāmalla* by which he is referred to in the Bādāmī stone inscription.[67]

64. K.G. Krishnan, *op. cit.*, v. 58, p. 74.
65. Tiruvālaṅgāḍu plates, *op. cit.*, vv. 102-03, p. 399.
66. Kaśākuḍi plates, *op. cit.*, v. 30, p. 350.
67. C. Minakshi, *HSVP*, p. 26.

Gambling

This pastime appears to have been extremely popular in the Pallava period. The Viḻāvaṭṭi plates, while enumerating the list of taxes collected by the state from the different sections of society, mentions the tax imposed on gambling (*dyūta*).[68] This reveals that gambling must have been a widely prevalent pastime for the state to have imposed a tax on it to enhance its revenue.

It appears from a study of these Sanskrit epigraphs that by and large, the people in the Tamil country led fairly peaceful and comfortable lives. The epigraphs such as the Tiruvālaṅgāḍu[69] and the Karandai plates[70] mention that the people had no grievances, the latter stating very poetically that during the reign of Rājendra Coḷa I, "the people were devoted to *dharma* and their own duties (*lokodharmaparāḥ, svakarma niratāḥ*), free from portentious happenings (*duri-kṛt-opaplavaḥ*), ever wealthy (*nitya-śrīḥ*), were very gay and happy (*niyat-otsavaḥ pramuditāḥ*), took delight in truth (*satyā-bhirāmaḥ*), there were timely rains (*kāle vṛṣṭiḥ*), the rivers had pure water (*śiva-jala nadyo-bhavat*) and the earth was everywhere adorned with varied yields of grains" (*nānā-śasya-vibhūṣitā vasumatī*). Although the accounts given in these epigraphs may be exaggerated versions of the truth and the poets might have attempted to paint an idealistic picture of the society, it may not be wrong to surmise that the people were generally content with their lot since evidence to the contrary is not forthcoming from any source.

---

68. Viḻāvaṭṭi plates, *op. cit.*, p. 303.
69. Tiruvālaṅgāḍu plates, *op. cit.*, v. 58, p. 396.
70. K.G. Krishnan, *op. cit.*, v. 46, p. 73.

6

Education and Literature

THE value of education was realized in India from very early times. The *Manusmṛti* states that it is learning and neither age nor wealth nor descent, which redounds to the glory of a human being.[1] In the Tamil country also learning was held in very high esteem. The *Kuraḷ* states that "the learned alone can be said to possess eyes; the unlettered have but two sores on their head"[2] and "the wealth which never declines is not riches but learning."[3] He adds that "those who have wisdom have all; fools with all have nothing."[4]

Vidyādāna or the gift of knowledge was considered as one of the highest forms of gifts. That the ruling classes made many donations towards educational institutions and scholars for the propagation of learning as revealed by numerous inscriptions makes it clear that *vidyādāna* was indeed considered very auspicious. The kings of the Tamil country considered it their duty to patronize men of learning just as the latter upheld their duty to impart learning to students.

The main source for knowing about the condition of education in the Tamil country in the ancient and medieval periods is epigraphy. The numerous Sanskrit inscriptions of the Pallavas, Pāṇḍyas and Coḷas are a storehouse of information

---

1. *MS*, Ch. II, v. 154.
2. P.S. Sundaram (tr. and ed.), *The Kuraḷ*, New Delhi, 1990, Ch. 40, v. 393.
3. *Ibid.*, v. 400.
4. *Ibid.*, Ch. 43, v. 430.

regarding the type of educational institutions which existed at that time, the role of the kings in promoting education and the encouragement given to scholars.

Education in the Tamil country during this period was religious in nature and was based primarily on the study of the theological and philosophical works written in Sanskrit and in Tamil. A study of the inscriptions of this age reveals that special emphasis was placed on the study of the four Vedas and the Vedāṅgas. Apart from the pursuit of religious education, importance was also given to training in technical education and development of the fine arts.

The copper-plate charters as well as the lithic inscriptions of these periods reveal that these kings themselves were well-educated and cultured and this accounts for their deep-rooted interest in the promotion of learning and the fine-arts.

Education of Princes

The kings in ancient and medieval India were the fountain-head of justice, the head of the entire administrative machinery, and the supreme commander of the army and had to perform various other duties. To be able to perform such onerous tasks in an able and efficient manner, these rulers must have had intensive training in various subjects from a very young age. The law-givers of ancient India such as Manu and Kauṭilya lay emphasis on the education and discipline of the rulers. According to Manu,

> From those versed in Vedas let him learn the threefold (sacred science), the primeval science of government, the science of dialectics, and the knowledge of the (supreme) soul; from the people (the theory of) the various trades and professions.[5]

Kauṭilya in his *Arthaśāstra* says that the prince should learn the three Vedas and philosophy from the learned, economics from the head of the departments and the science of politics from

5. *MS*, Ch. VII, v. 43.

theoretical and practical exponents.[6] Giving a daily timetable of the princes, Kauṭilya adds that the prince was to undergo training in the arts of (using) elephants, horses, chariots and weapons.[7] He should also listen to the Purāṇas, *Itivi̥rtta, Ākhyāyika, Udāharaṇa, Dharmaśāstra* and *Arthaśāstra* which constitute the *Itihāsa*.[8]

Regarding the need for such rigorous education for the princes, Kauṭilya says that only a prince with a disciplined mind and body could carry on the work of administration along sound lines.[9]

While most of the inscriptions do not directly mention the education and training of the princes, they do praise the monarchs of the Tamil country as learned scholars in their own right in literature and in several sciences. The Kaśākuḍi inscription records that all the kings born in the race of the Pallavas were "full of learning" (*ghanāghama*).[10] The early Pallava rulers are described in the same inscription as "those whose are learned" (*paṇḍita-matayaḥ*).[11]

The Hosakoṭṭai plates describe the Pallava ruler Siṁhaviṣṇu as "having attained eminence by the study of Vedic and Āgamic traditions (*sakala mantrā-tantrāntargastasya vividhāgama prakṣālita- viśuddha-buddheḥ*).[12] Vijayaskandavarman is praised in the Oṁgoḍu (I) charter as "one who ably understood the purport of all the *Śāstras*" (*sarva-śāstrārtha-nirṇaya-tattvajñaḥ*).[13] Skandavarman is described in the Mangaḷūr inscription as *vidyāvr̥ddha* (one who grew old in respect of his learning).[14]

---

6. *KA*, I.5, 8.
7. *Ibid.*, I.5, 12.
8. *Ibid.*, I.5, 15.
9. *Ibid.*, I.5, 17.
10. *SII*, vol. II, no. 73, l. 44, p. 348 (Kaśākuḍi plates).
11. *Ibid.*, l. 47.
12. *TPC*, p. 378.
13. *EI*, vol. XV, no. 11, p. 251 (Oṁgoḍu I plates).
14. *Ind. Ant.*, vol. V (May 1876), p. 155 (Mangalūr plates).

The same inscription describes Yuvamahārāja Viṣṇugopa as *vidyāvinītātmanaḥ* (one who was refined due to his learning).[15]

Among all the learned kings of the Tamil country, Mahendravarman I seems to occupy the most exhalted position. The epigraphs of this king reveal that he was a great and talented scholar with interests in many fields including literature, the fine-arts such as music and painting and also art and architecture. The Pallāvaram[16] and Tirucirāpaḷḷi[17] inscriptions of this king mentions his title *mattavilāsa*. Mahendravarman I was the composer of the famous farcical play in Sanskrit named *Mattavilāsaprahasana*, this name being derived from his title. The Māmaṇḍūr inscription of this king mentions the *Mattavilāsaprahasana* (*Mattavilāsādipadam-prahasano-ttamam*).[18] An extract from the play itself proves that it was indeed the composition of this gifted Pallava king. He mentions explicitly in this work that it is a composition of Mahendravikrama of the Pallava family and the son of Siṁhaviṣṇu.[19] Another play in Sanskrit, the *Bhagavadajjukkam* has also been assigned to Mahendravarman I.[20]

A few Sanskrit inscriptions of this king also testify to his love of learning. It appears that this king was a lover of logic. The inscription at the cave temple at Tirucirāpaḷḷi[21] and the Pallāvaram[22] inscriptions mention *anumāna* (logician) as one of his *birudas*. The Pallāvaram inscription also contains the title *upamānaḥ*, which once more reveals his interest in logic.[23]

---

15. *Ind. Ant.*, vol. V (May 1876), p. 155 (Mangalūr plates).
16. *SII*, vol. XII, no. 13, p. 7 (Pallāvaram inscription).
17. *SII*, vol. XII, no. 8, p. 6.
18. *SII*, vol. IV, no. 136, p. 12 (Māmaṇḍūr inscription).
19. N.P. Unni (ed.), *Mattavilāsaprahasana*, Trivandrum, 1974, p. 41.
20. C. Minakshi, *ASLP*, p. 336.
21. *SII*, vol. XII, no. 8, p. 5.
22. *SII*, vol. XII, no. 13, p. 7 (Pallāvaram inscription); see also R. Nagaswamy, "Mahendra's Inscription at Tirucirāpalli" from *Studies in Ancient Tamil Law and Society*, Madras, 1978, p. 84.
23. *Ibid.*

The Māmaṇḍūr inscription of this ruler gives a description of the interest which he evinced in poetry.[24] In the words of T.N. Ramachandran,

> He was an admirer of poets like Vālmīki, Bharata and other kavis and moving as he did in a galaxy of poetical stars, he has given us in his many inscriptions and in the two farces that have luckily been discovered his achievements in the field of poetry.[25]

He was the royal poet-laureate of the day.[26] According to some scholars, Mahendravarman I was the composer of the Tiruciräpaḷḷi cave inscription.[27]

The Kūram plates mention that Parameśvaravarman I was fond of poetry (*kāvya*).[28] An inscription found in the Kailāśanātha temple, Kāñcīpuram describes Rājasiṁha as having mastered many sciences (*vidita bahunayaḥ*)[29] while another epigraph[30] in the same place mentions *śrī itihāsa priyaḥ* (one who is fond of *Itihāsas*) and *śrī kāvya prabodhaḥ* (the reviver of poetry) as the titles of Rājasiṁha thus revealing that this Pallava ruler was very learned.

The inscriptions of Nandivarman Pallavamalla reveal that this king was also of a scholarly bent of mind. The Kaśākuḍi inscription of this king compares him with Bṛhaspati, the preceptor of the *devas* (*tantrālāpa-vidhau svayaṁ nayabharaḥ*)[31] and adds that he resembled Vālmīki in the composition of

---

24. *SII*, vol. IV, no. 136, p. 12 (Māmaṇḍūr inscription).
25. T.N. Ramachandran, "The Royal Artist, Mahendravarman I," *JOR*, vol. 7, p. 308.
26. *Ibid.*
27. P.R. Srinivasan, "Gaṅgādharāṣṭakam in Pallava Inscription from Tiruciräpalli" from *Śrīnidhiḥ* (*K.R. Srinivasan Felicitation Volume*), Madras, 1983, p. 434.
28. *SII*, vol. I, no. 151, p. 148 (Kūram plates).
29. *SII*, vol. I, no. 24, p. 12.
30. *Ibid.*, no. 25, pp. 17-18.
31. Kaśākuḍi plates, *op. cit.*, v. 29, p. 350.

poetry (*kavitā-bandhe sa ādyaḥ kaviḥ*).[32] The Udayendiram plates record that this king was well-versed in poems, dramas and stories (*kāvya nāṭakākhyāyikāsu pravīṇaḥ*). This inscription also mentions that Nandivarman Pallavamalla was skilled in metres such as *bindumati, gūḍacaturthapāda, prahelikā, akṣaracyutaka, mātrācyutaka* and similar verses.[34] Some of the Pallava rulers like Rājasiṁha and Nandivarman Pallavamalla were renowned for their knowledge of elephants and horses as mentioned in an earlier chapter (Administration-Military).

The Tiruvālaṅgāḍu plates describe Āditya Coḷa I as being "equal to Bṛhaspati in learning" (*dhiṣaṇas=tarasvi*) and "the asylum of the wise" (*budhāśrayaḥ*).[35] The Veḷāñjeri plates record that wise men considered Parāntaka I to be Bṛhaspati himself (*dhiṣṇaṁ budhendrāḥ*).[36]

The Tiruvālaṅgāḍu plates praise Rājarāja I as being of "matchless prosperity, majesty, learning, strength of arms, prowess, heroism and courage" (*anupama-vibhava-prabhāva-vidyā-bhuja-bala-vikrama-śaurya-dhairya-rāśiḥ*).[37]

The only inscription which explicitly mentions the education and training given to a prince is the Karandai copper-plates of Rājendra I.[38] This inscription mentions that even when he was a boy, Rājendra was well-versed in all the Vedas and Śāstras (*akhila-veda-śāstra-vit*), well-trained in riding on horses, elephants and chariots (*turaṅga-mātaṅga-rathādhirohaṇe kṛta-śramaḥ*) and also knew the use of arms and weapons very well (*śāstravid=astra kovidaḥ*).[39] The Esālam plates of the same king

---

32. Kaśākuḍi plates, *op. cit.*, v. 29, p. 350.
33. *SII*, vol. II, no. 74, l. 27, p. 365 (Udayendiram plates).
34. *Ibid.*
35. *SII*, vol. III, no. 205, v. 47, p. 396 (Tiruvālaṅgāḍu plates).
36. R. Nagaswamy, *TVCP, Veḷāñjeri plates of Parāntaka I*, v. 13, plate II, p. 2.
37. Tiruvālaṅgāḍu plates, *op. cit.*, v. 76, p. 397.
38. K.G. Krishnan, *KTPR*, v. 42, p. 72.
39. *Ibid.*

describe him as "the ocean into which all the rivers of knowledge flow" (*vidyānadyaḥ jaladhiḥ*).[40] Some Tamil inscriptions record that Rājendra I bore the *biruda paṇḍita coḷa*.[41] Rājarāja II held the title *rāja paṇḍita*.[42]

Some of the kings of the Pāṇḍya dynasty were also very knowledgeable. Māravarman Rājasiṁha I is described as "an ornament of learning" (*vidyācāra-vibhūṣaṇaḥ*) and "a depository of sacred knowledge" (*śruta-dhāraḥ*) in the Veḷvikuḍi charter.[43] The Larger Siṉṉamaṉūr plates mention that a certain Sundara Pāṇḍya was "a helmnsman in the ocean of all *śāstras*" (*samasta-śāstrārṇava-karṇadhāro-yadudbhavaḥ sundara-pāṇḍya-nāmaḥ*).[44]

Many inscriptions of the Keraḷa ruler, Ravivarman Kulaśekhara in Tamil Nadu which consist of the same set of titles record two of his *birudas caturṣaṣṭikalā-vallabha* (the favourite of the sixty-four arts) and *dakṣiṇabhojarāja* (king Bhoja of the south).[45] It is known that Ravivarman Kulaśekhara was a great scholar and composed a Sanskrit drama *Pradyumnābhyudayam*[46] which was written with the specific purpose of being enacted in the Śrī Padmanābhasvāmi temple during the *yātrotsavam*. He was also a scholar in music and poetry. Samudrabandha, the commentator of *Alaṅkārasarvasva* flourished at the court of this king.[47] The composer of these

40. R. Nagaswamy, *ECPR*, v. 16, p. 32.
41. *SII*, vol. II, nos. 12 and 13, pp. 97-99; *SII*, vol. III, p. 127.
42. T.V. Sadasiva Pandarathar, *History of the Later Coḷas*, Annamalainagar, 1949.
43. *EI*, vol. XVII, no. 16, v. 10, p. 229 (Veḷvikuḍi plates).
44. *EI*, vol. III, no. 206, v. 8, p. 451 (Larger Siṉṉamaṉur plates).
45. *EI*, vol. IV, no. 18, vv. 7 and 9, pp. 149-50; *ibid.*, no. 17, l. 6, p. 147, and *EI*, vol. VIII, No. 2, l. 2, p. 8.
46. T. Ganapati Sastri (ed.), *Pradyumnābhyudaya of Ravivarmabhūpa*, Trivandrum, 1910.
47. T. Ganapati Sastri, *The Alankārasūtra of Rājānaka Śrī Ruyyaka (with the Vṛtti, Alaṅkārasarvasva of Śrī Mankhuka and commentary by Samudrabandha on the latter)*, Trivandrum, 1915.

inscriptions, Kavibhūṣaṇa who was also a court-poet of this ruler, probably thought it very apt to compare his learned king who patronized scholars with king Bhoja.[48]

The Kāḍava chieftain, Kopperuñjiṅga was also a great scholar. The Āttūr epigraph describes him as *sāhityaratnākara* (ocean of literature).[49] In some of his epigraphs found at Tripurāntakam[50] and Drākṣārāma[51] in Andhra Pradesh, he is described as *sarasa-sāhitya-sāṁyātrikaḥ* (navigator in the ocean of literature).

This ruler was also a poet as seen from an epigraph from Tirupati which describes him as *kavi-sārvabhauma* (emperor of poetry).[52] His love for the Tamil language is seen from a Tamil record in which he is called *peṇu-sentamiḻ-vāḻappiranda kāḍava* (the Kāḍava born to foster and protect Sentamiḻ).[53]

Kings as Patrons of Education

The kings of the Tamil country being well-educated themselves, strove to spread education in their land. Some of these rulers have been explicitly mentioned in their inscriptions as being great patrons of learning. An early Pallava inscription, the Vesanta charter (*c.* fifth century AD), mentions that Vijayaskandavarman, the father of Siṁhavarman, the donor of this grant, was "a tree of refuge to all learned men" (*vāsa-vṛkṣo vidvaj-janasya*).[54]

---

48. The Paramāra king Bhoja also called Kavirāja who ruled over Mālvā with Dhāra as his capital-city during the first half of the eleventh century AD was renowned as a great scholar, poet and patron of arts and letters. He has been credited with the authorship of books on varied subjects like astronomy, philosophy, grammar, lexicography and poetics. In his court flourished many great scholars and also poets like Padmagupta.
49. *SII*, vol. XII, no. 120, pp. 58-59.
50. *SII*, vol. XII, no. 247, p. 155.
51. *SII*, vol. IV, no. 1352-B, p. 472; 491C of 1893.
52. *TTD* Inscriptions, vol. 1, no. 10, p. 18.
53. *EI*, vol. XXIII, no. 27, ll. 3-7, p. 180.
54. N. Ramesan, *VGPS*, l. 14, p. 95.

Rājasiṁha has been praised as one "who was like Indra in constantly protecting those who followed the path of the three Vedas" (*trayi-patha-niśeviṇām-satata-pālane vāsavaḥ*).[55]

The Coḷa king Āditya I has been praised in the Esālam[56] and the Tiruvālaṅgāḍu[57] plates as "the abode of scholars" (*budhāśrayaḥ*). Āditya's son Parāntaka I bore the title *paṇḍitavatsala*.[58] Sundara Coḷa has been described in the Kanyākumārī inscription as "removing the anguish of learned men" (*jahāra tāpam budha-saṁhatinām*).[59] The Pāṇḍya ruler Arikesari Māravarman I has been mentioned in the Veḷvikuḍi grant as "the patron of the learned" (*sudhiyām-adhipaḥ*).[60]

Sundara Pāṇḍya, the elder brother of Vīra Pāṇḍya is described in the Śivakāśi inscription as "the refuge of the learned" (*vibudh-āśrayaḥ*).[61] Pāṇḍya Vīra-Nārāyaṇa is praised in the Daḷavāipuram plates as "the patron of learned brāhmaṇas" (*vipr-āgre-saratā-juśām*).[62] A Sanskrit term *paṇḍita-vatsalaḥ* (lover of the learned) is used in the Tamil portion of the Veḷvikuḍi grant to describe Parāntaka Neḍuñjaḍaiyan.[63] The Koḍumbāḷūr chief Bhūti Vikrama Kesari, a feudatory of the Coḷas is described as "the wishing tree to the learned" (*vidvat-kalpataru*).[64]

Centres of Education

During the Pallava, Pāṇḍya and Coḷa periods, although the Vedic religion was predominant and the kings strove to propagate the brāhmaṇical system of learning, there also

55. *SII*, vol. I, no. 24, v. 6, p. 12.
56. R. Nagaswamy, *ECPR*, v. 9, p. 31.
57. Tiruvālaṅgaḍu plates, *op. cit.*, v. 47, p. 396.
58. *ASIAR* (1904-05), p. 141.
59. *TAS*, vol. I, no. 34, v. 64, p. 144 (Kanyākumārī Inscription).
60. Veḷvikuḍi plates, *op. cit.*, v. 8, p. 299.
61. T.N. Subramaniam and P.R. Srinivasan, *SCVP*, v. 7, p. 44.
62. T.N. Subramaniam, *DCPV*, v. 18, p. 15.
63. Veḷvikuḍi plates, *op. cit.*, p. 302.
64. KA Nilakanta Sastri, "The Koḍumbāḷūr Inscription of Vikrama-Kesari," *JOR*, vol. VII, v. 8, p. 9.

existed many Buddhist and Jaina systems of learning. The Sanskrit inscriptions of the period under study while supplying a lot of information about the brāhmaṇical centres of education also shed some light on a Jaina seat of learning.

The Paḻḻankovil copper-plate grant of Pallava Siṁhavarman (*c.* AD 550) gives some information about a Jaina hermitage and a seat of learning.[65] This epigraph records that this king gave to a great Jaina ascetic named Vajranandi, at the holy place (*dharma-tīrtha*) of Lord Śrī Vardhamāna (*śrī vardhamāneśvara*) where there was a Nandisaṁgha, an entire village called Śramaṇāśrama (the hermitage of the Śramaṇas) with the purpose of worshipping the Jainendras, Jinendras and Munīndras. The holy place of Śrī Vardhamāneśvara has been described in this inscription as being full of groups of virtuous teachers having many good qualities, wherein lived this Vajranandi who was well-versed in all sacred literature[66] (see Chapter on Religion).

Centres of Brāhmaṇical Learning

Education in ancient and medieval India was, to a great extent, religion-oriented, and this was the case in the Tamil country also. The Pallava, Pāṇḍya and Coḷa rulers, being staunch followers of the Vedic religion knew the value of religious works especially those such as the *Itihāsa*s and the Purāṇas which contain high moral values easily understandable by all and took great efforts for the propagation of such religious works as can be understood from their inscriptions.

Although in ancient India there did not exist many organized public educational institutions as can be understood in the modern context, yet there were a few institutions which helped in the spread of religious education. The inscriptions of the period under study reveal that there were some educational organizations in the Tamil country known as *ghaṭikā*s and *maṭhas*. The *agrahāra*s or the residential areas of

65. T.N. Subramaniam, *PJCG*, pp. 41-83.
66. *Ibid.*, p. 76.

the brāhmaṇas who were the custodians of traditional brāhmaṇical learning and the temples themselves were also great centres of education.

Ghaṭikā

During the Pallava period, an important educational institution was the *ghaṭikā*. Several Pallava Sanskrit inscriptions mention the *ghaṭikā* and the importance given to it by the Pallava kings.[67] The Sanskrit word *ghaṭikā* has been explained by different scholars in various ways. F. Kielhorn has established that the *ghaṭikā* is the same as the *goṣṭhi* and that it was an establishment which comprised groups of holy and learned brāhmaṇas probably in each case founded by the king.[68] S.K. Aiyangar has suggested that it was a settlement of brāhmaṇas.[69] K.A. Nilakanta Sastri has described the *ghaṭikā* as a college of learned brāhmaṇas.[70] C. Minakshi has stated that the word originates from the root *ghaṭ* which in Sanskrit means "to strive after" and that the *ghaṭikā* was an institution where students strove after higher knowledge.[71] According to Bhaṭṭa Someśvara[72] (*c.* AD 1200), the commentator of the *Vārttika* of Kumarilla Bhaṭṭa (seventh century AD), when candidates appeared for examinations in the Vedas, they were asked questions based on different symbols, denoting different portions of the Vedas, written on bits of palm-leaves and placed inside a *ghaṭikā* otherwise known as *kuṁbha* or pot and taken out by lot. It appears that the educational institution *ghaṭikā* derived its name from the vessel *ghaṭikā* by means of which arrangements were made to test the proficiency of the successful candidates in the Vedic examinations.

---

67. *SII*, vol. II, no. 98, v. 13, p. 508 (Velūrpāḷaiyam plates); Kaśākuḍi plates, *op. cit.*, v. 25, p. 349.
68. *EI*, vol. VIII, p. 26 and fn. 1.
69. S.K. Aiyangar, *EHAII*, p. 105.
70. K.A. Nilakanta Sastri, *History of South India*, Madras, 1988, p. 154.
71. C. Minakshi, *ASLP*, p. 224.
72. S. Sankaranarayanan, *The Viṣṇukuṇḍis and Their Times*, Delhi, 1977, p. 237.

The most important *ghaṭikā* of the period of the Pallavas was at Kāñcīpuram. The earliest inscriptional evidence referring to this *ghaṭikā* is the Tāḷagunda Pillar Inscription of the Kadamba king Kākusthavarman which states that his ancestor, Mayūraśarman came to Kāñcī to study at this *ghaṭikā*.[73] Moreas has stated the date of Mayūraśarman to be AD 345-70.[74] The *ghaṭikā* in Kāñcīpuram to which Mayūraśarman sought admission must have been in existance for many years before the middle of the fourth century before it attained the necessary importance for pupils outside the Pallava kingdom to seek admission to it for higher learning.[75]

Many Pallava inscriptions point to the connection between the Pallava kings and the functioning of the *ghaṭikā*. Among the Pallava rulers, Skandaśiṣya, Mahendravarman II, Rājasiṁha and Nandivarman Pallavamalla were closely associated with this institution.

The Velūrpāḷaiyam inscription records that the early Pallava king Skandaśiṣya seized the *ghaṭikā* from Satyasena (*skandaśiṣya tato=bhavat dvijānām ghaṭikām rājñaḥ satyasenāj jahāra yaḥ*).[76] Although there is no unanimity among scholars as to who exactly this Satyasena was, it is obvious that he was an enemy of the Pallavas as the word seized (*jahāra*) in the verse implies. C. Minakshi has stated that when the *ghaṭikā* was in the posession of Satyasena it was disorganized and Skandaśiṣya revitalized it to function effectively after having captured it.[77]

The Kaśākuḍi plates record that Mahendravarman II founded a *ghaṭikā* that housed some deities and brāhmaṇas and that his example was followed by his successors (*yasmāt prabhṛty alam avardhata dharma-karma devadvijanmaviṣayāṁ ghaṭīkāṁ ca dātuḥ*) and adds that Rājasiṁha founded a *ghaṭikā*

73. *EI*, vol. VIII, no. 5, pp. 24-36 (Tāḷagunḍa Pillar Inscription).
74. G.M. Moraes, *The Kadamba Kula*, Bombay, 1931, p. 14.
75. C. Minakshi, *ASLP*, p. 224.
76. Velūrpāḷaiyam plates, *op. cit.*, v. 7, p. 508.
77. C. Minakshi: *ASLP*, p. 230.

of the *cāturvaidyaśāla* type (*cāturvaidyam avīviśat svaghaṭikāṁ bhūdevatā-bhaktitaḥ*).[78] The Velūrpāḷaiyam plates mention that this ruler reorganized the *ghaṭikā* of the twice-born (brāhmaṇas) and built a temple made of stone for Śiva.[79]

Meeting Place of the Ghaṭikā

The information supplied by the Velūrpāḷaiyam plates that Rājasiṁha reorganized the *ghaṭikā* and also built a temple for Śiva are found in one and the same verse. According to C. Minakshi, the construction of the Kailāśanātha temple and the reorganization of the *ghaṭikā* by Narasiṁhavarman II (Rājasiṁha), connecting the *ghaṭikā* with the Kailāśanātha temple indicates that the location of the *ghaṭikā* may be in that temple.[80] It may be presumed that Rājasiṁha constructed the *mahāmaṇḍapa* (big hall) in front of the Kailāśanātha temple to enable the members of the *ghaṭikā* at Kāñcīpuram to meet there to study.[81]

It appears that this *ghaṭikā* continued to function even during the Coḷa period and was located to the east of the Kailāśanātha temple as seen from a Tamil epigraph in this shrine belonging to the period of Rājendra I.[82]

Members of the Ghaṭikā

Some information about the members who constituted the *ghaṭikā* is forthcoming from the inscriptions. This educational institution seems to have been composed of brāhmaṇas well-versed in Vedic and Vedāntic scriptures. The Kaśākuḍi plates refer to this institution as *ghaṭikām bhūdevatām,* i.e., the *ghaṭikā* of the *deva*s of the earth (brāhmaṇas).[83] The Velūrpāḷaiyam

78. Kaśākuḍi plates, *op. cit.*, vv. 23 and 25, p. 349; also see S. Sankaranarayanan, *op. cit.*
79. Velūrpāḷaiyam plates, *op. cit.*, v. 13, p. 503.
80. C. Minakshi, *ASLP*, p. 227.
81. *Ibid.*, pp. 227-28.
82. *ARE*, 240 of 1930.
83. Kaśākuḍi plates, *op. cit.*, v. 25, p. 349.

grant refers to the *ghaṭikā* as *dvijānām ghaṭikām,* i.e., the *ghaṭikā* of the twice-born (brāhmaṇas).[84]

The members of the *ghaṭikā* seem to have played a crucial role in the political sphere also. A Tamil inscription found in the Vaikuṇṭhaperumāḷ temple in Kāñcīpuram records that the *ghaṭikāiyār* (members of the *ghaṭikā*) were instrumental in bringing about the accession of Nandivarman Pallavamalla along with other officials when there was chaos in the Pallava kingdom following the death of Parameśvaravarman II.[85] C. Minakshi has opined that the *ghaṭikāiyār* are shown as participating in the coronation ceremony of Nandivarman Pallavamalla in the series of historical sculptures found in the Vaikuṇṭhaperumāḷ temple.[86]

The esteem in which the *ghaṭikā* and its members were held is brought out by an 8th century epigraph of Cāḷukya Vikramāditya II in the Kailāśanātha temple.[87] The inscription states that this ruler, after his conquest of Kāñcī, did not confiscate the property of the temple but returned it to the God. This inscription adds that "those who destroy these letters and the stability of the king's charity which was thus given, shall enter into the world of those who had killed the great group of men (*mahājana*) of this *ghaṭikā*."

Subjects Taught at the Ghaṭikā

There is no direct epigraphical evidence pinpointing to the subjects taught at the *ghaṭikā*. However, since the brāhmaṇas in the Pallava, Pāṇḍya and Coḷa periods were famous as teachers mainly of the Vedas, Vedāṅgas and other religious texts, and since the epigraphical evidence indicates that the *ghaṭikā* was composed of brāhmaṇas, it may be safely assumed that these were the subjects which were taught in this educational institution.

---

84. Velūrpāḷaiyam plates, *op. cit.*, v. 7, p. 508.
85. *SII*, vol. IV, no. 135, pp. 10-12.
86. C. Minakshi, *HSVK*, p. 33.
87. *EI*, vol. III, no. 48, pp. 359-60.

The Tāḷagunda Pillar inscription also gives some information regarding the nature of study in the *ghaṭikā*. This record mentions that Mayūraśarman, a brāhmaṇa (*dvijottama*), the founder of the Kadamba dynasty came to Kāñcīpuram with his *guru* Vīraśarman to study the whole of the scriptures (*pravacanam nikhilam*) and entered the *ghaṭikā* directly (*āśu*) as an inquirer (*tārkika*). Since Mayūraśarman came to Kāñcī along with his *guru* not as a beginner, but as one who was well-versed in the Vedas, it appears that the *ghaṭikā* must have been a centre of higher studies.

T.N. Subramaniam has opined that military science was also taught at the *ghaṭikā* at Kāñcī, stating that when Mayūraśarman quarrelled with a Pallava horseman, he was able to wield the flashing weapons of warfare with the hand accustomed to handling the *kuśa* grass and other sacrificial oblations and carve out a kingdom of his own.[88]

Some Tamil inscriptions such as the Pārthivaśekharapuram inscription of Karunandaḍakkan the Ay king, reveal that military science was taught at the educational institutions called *śālais*.[89] It is therefore possible that military science was one of the subjects of study at the *ghaṭikā* also.

Apart from the famous *ghaṭikā* at Kāñcīpuram, there existed *ghaṭikās* at other places in the Pallava kingdom as seen from numerous Tamil inscriptions.[90]

Vidyāsthāna

The Bāhūr inscription of the Pallava king Nṛpatuṅgavarman (*c.* AD 877) records a land-grant to a *vidyāsthāna* (seat of learning) at Vāgūr (present-day Bāhūr, near Pondicherry).[91] This centre of learning appears to have been a well-established institution even before the time of this grant.[92]

---

88. *SITI*, vol. III, pt. 2, p. 9.
89. *PCP*, pp. A1-A8 (Pārthivaśekharapuram plates).
90. C. Minakshi, *ASLP*, p. 231.
91. *EI*, vol. XVIII, no. 2, pp. 5-15 (Bāhūr plates).
92. C. Minakshi, *ASLP*, p. 238.

The charter records that three villages were donated to this educational establishment by a chieftain named Mārtāṇḍa of the family of Veśāli whose surname was Nilaitāṅgi, who, in turn, had received them from Nṛpatuṅga. The three villages named Ceṭṭuppākkam, Vilāṅgāṭṭaṅkaḍuvaṇūr, and Iṟaippuṇaicceri were granted to this *vidyāsthāna* as a *brahmadeya* grant and the residents therein to receive the revenues of these villages. The *ājñapti* of this charter was a minister of Nṛpatuṅga named Uttamaśīla who was to carry out the work of the transfer of the villages. This record clearly states that this grant was to be a *vidyā-bhoga* (source of revenue for the promotion of learning). This is perhaps the earliest case on record of a university scholarship or educational endowment.[93]

This inscription also provides information regarding the subjects taught at this institution. H. Krishna Sastri has opined that the *vidyāsthāna* at Bāhūr consisted of fourteen *gaṇa*s (*caturdaśagaṇākula*) and was controlled by the learned men of the village, being organized and maintained by them.[94] C. Minakshi, has stated that the educational institution had a comprehensive curriculum consisting of fourteen *gaṇa*s (branches of learning which include the four Vedas, the six *Vedāṅga*s, the *Purāṇa*s, the *Mīmāṁsā* system of philosophy, the *Nyāya* system and the *Dharmaśāstras*).[95] Another verse in this inscription states that the Sanskrit *praśasti* was composed by a servant of the *vidyāsthāna* named Nāgaya who "knew the truth of sciences" (*śāstra-tattvajñaḥ*).[96]

Maṭhas

Another important centre for the dissemination of the religious and philosophical works in ancient and medieval India was the *maṭha*. The Sanskrit lexicon, *Amarakośa* defines a *maṭha* as "a place where pupils (and their teachers) reside" (*maṭhāscchātrādi-nilayaḥ*).[97] According to P.V. Kane,

93. Bāhūr plates, *op. cit.*, p. 8.
94. *SII*, vol. II, p. 516.
95. C. Minakshi, *ASLP*, p. 238.
96. Bāhūr plates, *op. cit.*, v. 30, p. 11.
97. *Amarakośa*, ed Satyadeva Mishra, Vārāṇasī, 1972, II.2, 8.

> The *maṭhas* were primarily intended for the instruction of pupils or the laity by some great teacher in the tenets of a sect or in the doctrines of some philosophy or in some branch of learning such as grammar, Mīmāṁsā, astronomy and the like.[98]

Some of the Sanskrit inscriptions contain information about the existence or functioning of the *maṭhas*. An epigraph of the tenth century AD in the Ādipurīśvara temple at Tiruvoṟṟiyūr records the existence of a *maṭha* at this place.[99] According to this inscription, a general of the Coḷa prince Rājāditya called Vallabha, who lost interest in worldly pleasures, renounced his worldly life and coming to Tiruvoṟṟiyūr, took his initiation at the cave of Nirañjanaguru. Vallabha who took up the *dīkṣa* name Caturānana, established a *maṭha* at Tiruvoṟṟiyūr, whose successive heads came to be called Caturānana Paṇḍitas after the founder.[100]

A record of the period of Rājendra I, also from the same temple mentions that an architect named Ravi built the *vimāna* of this temple as directed by Caturānana. This Caturānana Paṇḍita must have been one of the successive heads of the Śaiva *maṭha* which was established in the middle of the tenth century AD.[101]

There are a number of Tamil inscriptions which mention the Caturānana Paṇḍitas of this place.[102] One of these states that Rājādhirāja II was present during the Panguni-Uttiram festival in this temple and on the same occasion Caturānana Paṇḍita who owned a *maṭha* in the temple and Vāgīśvara

98. P.V. Kane, *History of Dharmaśāstra*, vol. II, Pt. 2, Poona, 1941, p. 907.
99. *EI*, vol. XXVII, no. 47, pp. 292-303.
100. *Ibid.*, p. 297.
101. *JOR*, vol. XXXII, pp. 11-15.
102. *ARE*, 735 and 739 of 1905; 177 and 181 of 1912; 104 of 1912; *SII*, vol. V, no. 1354, 126 of 1912; *SII*, vol. V, no. 1356; 403 of 1896; 371 of 1911 and 206 of 1912.

Paṇḍita who expounded the *Soma Siddhānta* (doctrine of the Kāpālikas) were also there.[103]

Another *maṭha* of the Kālāmukhas (a sect of Śaiva ascetics following many gruesome practices) is mentioned in an inscription of a chieftain named Bhūti Vikrama Kesari found at the temple of Mūvarkovil at Koḍuṁbāḷūr. The *maṭha* was attached to this temple built by this chieftain.[104]

A bi-lingual record from the Puṇḍarīkākṣa Perumāḷ temple at Tiruveḷḷaṟai (Tiruchirapalli district) dated in the thirteenth century of the period of Kulottuṅga III, mentions that a poet named Sakalavidyācakravartin (also called Dhanvimiśra and Karpaga Villi), who also composed several verses on the Bāṇa chieftain Rājarājadevaṉ Poṉparappināṉ Magadhaipperumāḷ, mentions that this poet established a *maṭha* at Śvetaśaila (Sanskritized form of Tiruveḷḷaṟai)[105] and made an endowment for feeding ninety people everyday for thirty festival days during the year in the temple of Tiruveḷḷaṟai. Another inscription found at the same place mentions that this poet made an endowment for feeding nine-hundred persons in the Karpagavilli *maṭha*, named after him, during the festival in the month of Vaikāśī at Tiruveḷḷaṟai.[106]

Agrahāras

The *agrahāra*s of the Tamil country were places where the brāhmaṇa families lived. The brāhmaṇas were the lawful custodians of the ancient Vedic lore and they earned their living mainly by the professions of teaching and officiating at ceremonies. The Sanskrit epigraphs speak of many villages which were given either to one or groups of learned brāhmaṇas by members of the ruling families to enable them to live in a peaceful manner which would help them in discharging their duties.

103. *ARE*, 371 of 1911.
104. *JOR*, vol. VII, vv. 10-12, p. 9.
105. *ARE*, 208 of 1938-39.
106. *ARE*, 207 of 1938-39.

An endowment to one or a few brāhmaṇas was called *bhaṭṭavṛtti* whereas settlements of a whole village by a large number of brāhmaṇa scholars was known as an *agrahāra*.[107]

The inscriptions of the Pallavas, Pāṇḍyas, and Coḷas reveal that these rulers cared for the welfare of these brāhmaṇas and also for the spread of Vedic education and therefore donated a large number of villages as *agrahāras* to this learned community. The kings of the Tamil country also considered it a meritorious deed to give gifts of land to learned brāhmaṇas. The Oṁgoḍu (II) plates record that the grant of the village of Oṁgoḍu was made by Siṁhavarman to Devaśarman who was "well-versed in all the *śāstras*" (*sarva-śāstra-kuśalayaḥ*) for the increase of the king's life, strength and victory (*asmad-āyur-bala-vijay-ābhivṛddhaye*).[108]

The Cura plates also state that Viṣṇugopavarman made a grant of land in the village of Cura to a scholarly brāhmaṇa named Cesāmiśarman for the increase of this ruler's life, strength and success in exactly the same words as in the Oṁgoḍu (II) charter.[109] The Vunnaguruvapālem plates similarly state that the gift of the village Kubunūru was made to a learned brāhmaṇa named Devaśarman for the augmentation of the king's longivity and health (*asmad-āyur-ārogyābhivṛddhaye*) by Parameśvaravarman I.[110] Rājasiṁha made the gift of a village named Reyūrū as *brahmadeya* to a brāhmaṇa well-versed in the Vedas named Kumāramaṇḍa Śarman for increasing his life, strength, wealth and victory (*āyur-bala-vijaya-aiśvaryābhivṛddhaye*).[111]

Many of these *agrahāras* or *caturvedimaṅgalams* thus donated to brāhmaṇas who taught the sacred scriptures were given as tax-free *brahmadeya* gifts and served as excellent centres of higher education in the Tamil country. It may be assumed

107. C. Minakshi, *ASLP*, p. 233.
108. *EI*, vol. XV, no. 11, p. 255 (Oṁgoḍu II plates).
109. *EI*, vol. XXIV, no. 18, p. 142 (Cura plates).
110. *EI*, vol. XXXII, no. 9, p. 97 (Vunnaguruvapalem plates).
111. *EI*, vol. XXIX, no. 11, p. 96 (Reyūrū plates).

that the students, in the traditional Indian manner lived in the houses of their teachers, this system helping the former to imbibe the high moral values generally followed by their preceptors along with the lessons in the curriculum, since the formation of character has been given great importance by the thinkers of ancient India.

A very large number of copper-plate grants of the Pallavas reveal the gifts of villages as *brahmadeya* to one or more learned brāhmaṇas such as the Prākṛt grant of Viṣṇugopavarma,[112] Cura[113] Oṁgoḍu (I),[114] Vesanta,[115] Sakrepaṭṇa,[116] Udayendiram,[117] Cendalūr,[118] Oṁgoḍu (II),[119] Pikira,[120] Mangalūr,[121] Viḷāvaṭṭi,[122] Reyūrū,[123] Paṭṭattāḷmaṅgalam,[124] Pullūr,[125] Taṇḍantoṭṭam,[126] Kaśākuḍi[127] and Udayendiram plates of Nandivarman II Pallavamalla.[128]

The epigraphs repeatedly mention that the brāhmaṇa donees of the grants were extremely well-read. They are described as masters in the Vedas, the Vedāṅgas, consisting

---

112. A.K.V.S. Reddy and N. Krishna Reddy, "A Newly Discovered Prākṛt Copper Plate Grant of Pallava Viṣṇugopavarman Year I," from *Śāṅkaram, Professor Srinivasa Sankaranarayanan Festschrift*, New Delhi, 2000, pp. 67-70.
113. Cura plates, *op. cit.*, pp. 137-42.
114. Oṁgoḍu plates, *op. cit.*, pp. 251-52.
115. N. Ramesan, *VGPS*, p. 96.
116. *EI*, vol. XXXVIII, no. 18, pp. 104-05 (Sakrepaṭṇa plates).
117. *EI*, vol. III, no. 23, p. 146 (Udayendiram I plates).
118. *EI*, vol. VIII, no. 23, p. 235 (Cendalūr plates).
119. *EI*, vol. XV, no. 11, p. 255 (Oṁgoḍu II plates).
120. *EI*, vol. VIII, no. 15, p. 162 (Pikira plates).
121. *Ind. Ant.*, vol. V (1876), p. 156 (Maṅgalūr grant).
122. *EI*, vol. XXIV, no. 43, p. 302 (Viḷāvaṭṭi plates).
123. *EI*, vol. XXIX, no. 11, p. 96 (Reyūrū plates).
124. *EI*, vol. XVIII, no. 14, pp. 120-21 (Paṭṭattāḷmangaḷam plates).
125. *EI*, vol. XXXVI, no. 20, pp. 152-53 (Pullūr plates).
126. *SII*, vol. II, no. 98, pp. 508-09 (Taṇḍantoṭṭam plates).
127. Kaśākuḍi plates, *op. cit.*, pp. 350-51.
128. Udayendiram plates, *op. cit.*, pp. 361-74.

of Chandakalpa, Vyākaraṇa, Jyotiṣa, Nirukta, Śikṣā and Chandoviciti, Itihāsa, Purāṇa, Sāṅkhya, Yama and Niyama.

The Kaśākuḍi plates in particular, praise the brāhmaṇa donee of this grant in glowing terms. This inscription mentions that the village called Koḍukoḷḷi and renamed Ekadhīra-maṅgalam (after one of the titles of Nandivarman Pallavamalla) after it became a *brahmadeya* was given by this king to a brāhmaṇa named Jyeṣṭhāpāda-Somayājin who had "mastered the Vedas" (*chandapāravārapāragāya*), "who chanted the Sāman (Veda) which are sweet because of their melody" (*svarasamadhura-sāmagāya*), "who has completed the study of the six auxiliary works, namely, the Vedic ritual, grammar, astronomy, etymology, phonetics and metrics" (*chandakalpa-vyākaraṇa-jyotiṣa-nirukta-śikṣā-chandovicitti-ṣaḍaṅga-saṁśita-svādhyāyayanāya*), "who knows the properties of the words and their sentences" (*pada-dharma vākya-dharma vastu-dharma vidhāya*), "who has studied the Śruti and Smṛti" (*śruti-smṛti-rasāyana-pānāya*), "who is proficient in the portion pertaining to the rites and the portion pertaining to knowledge" (*karmakāṇḍa-jñānakāṇḍa paṇḍitāya*), "who is skilled in the ways of the world" (*lokāyukti*), "skilled in the arts" (*kalā-kauśala-peśalāya*), "who is proficient in poems, dramas, stories, epics, and legends" (*kāvya-nāṭakākhyāyiketihāsapurāṇā pariṇatāya*), "learned in all branches of holy and profane knowledge" (*kimbahuna sarvajñāna-vijñana-niṣṇātāya*), "accomplished in the performance of all rites" (*sarvakarmānuṣṭhāna-niṣṭhitāya*), "of good conduct" (*suvṛtāya*) and "who is ranked the first among the brāhmaṇas" (*dvijanmāgragaṇyāya*).[129]

A study of the Sanskrit inscriptions of the Pallavas yields the titles borne by the Sanskrit scholars which reveal their scholarship in their chosen fields of study. Some of the titles of the donees are *caturvedin*,[130] *trivedin*,[131] *somayāgin*,[132]

129. Kaśākuḍi plates, *op. cit.*

130. Taṇḍantoṭṭam plates, *op. cit.*, pp. 531-35.

131. *Ibid.*

132. *Ibid.*

vasantayāgin,[133] *bhaṭṭa*,[134] *sarvkratuyāgin*,[135] *agnicit*,[136] *ṣaḍangavid*[137] and *kramavid*.[138]

Many of the names of the brāhmaṇa scholars are also listed in the inscriptions. Devaśarman,[139] Bhavaskandarata,[140] Cesāmiśarman,[141] Jyeṣṭhapāda Somayājin,[142] Golaśarman,[143] Vilāśarman,[144] Rudraśarman,[145] Dāmaśarman,[146] Yajñaśarman,[147] Bhavakoṭiśarman,[148] Bhartṛśarman,[149] Śivadakta,[150] Ṣaṣṭhikumāra[151] and Viṣṇuśarman[152] are some of the names provided in the epigraphs in the Sanskrit section.

The Coḷa rulers, following the path laid by their predecessors also encouraged the brāhmaṇa scholars of their land by granting them tax-free villages and thereby encouraged the propagation of Vedic learning.

The copper-plate charters of these kings reveal the patronage extended by them in this direction. According to K.A. Nilakanta Sastri, Throughout the hundreds of villages

---

133. Taṇḍantoṭṭam plates, *op. cit.*, pp. 531-35.
134. *Ibid.*
135. *Ibid.*
136. *Ibid.*
137. Paṭṭattāḷmaṅgalam plates, *op. cit.*, p. 124.
138. *Ibid.*
139. Oṁgoḍu (II) plates, *op. cit.*, p. 255.
140. Cendalūr plates, *op. cit.*, p. 235.
141. Cura plates, *op. cit.*, p. 142.
142. Kaśākuḍi plates, *op. cit.*, p. 351.
143. Oṁgoḍu (I) plates, *op. cit.*, p. 251.
144. *EI*, vol. VIII, no. 15, p. 162 (Pikira plates).
145. Udayendiram plates, *op. cit.*, p. 373.
146. *Ibid.*
147. *Ind. Ant.*, (1876 May), p. 155.
148. *Ibid.*
149. *Ibid.*
150. *Ibid.*
151. *Ibid.*
152. Viḻāvaṭṭi plates, *op. cit.*, p. 303.

which flourished in this empire, numerous endowments were created for all kinds of purposes, and several of these were earmarked for the promotion of the study of one Veda or another, a system of philosophy or ritual, grammar, rhetoric and so on and for holding of periodical competitions and the award of prizes for the most proficient among the competitors.[153]

A beautiful Sanskrit verse in an epigraph, probably belonging to the ninth century AD, to the period of Āditya Coḷa I describes an *agrahāra* called Ratnāgrahāra or Ratnagrāma as "being resplendent" and "as an embodiment of the union of the two Goddesses of learning and prosperity," "able to remove distress, of lovely fame and an ocean of all noble qualities."[154] The poetic description of this prosperous *agrahāra* would probably hold true for all such similarly well-endowed villages in the Coḷa empire in which the ancient scriptures were imparted and imbibed, as seen from the other epigraphs which describe them, although probably not so eloquently as this poet.

Parāntaka I has been praised in many epigraphs as having created numerous *agrahāra*s with the purpose of spreading Vedic knowledge. This ruler gave three villages named Tālaiveḍu, Mayangāṟu, and Kilagal in their entirety together with three thousand *kāḍi* of paddy and nine *niśka*s (as tax) to the brāhmaṇas of Meliṟuñjeru village who were great scholars in the Vedas and Vedāṅgas inclusive of the *Sāmaveda* with a thousand *śākhā*s (*sahasraśākhālaṅkr̥ta sāmaveda sahita veda vedāṅga vidbhyaḥ*).[155]

According to the Karandai copper-plates, Parāntaka I established a village named Vīranārāyaṇa *agrahāra* (*cartur-*

153. K.A. Nilakanta Sastri, "Sanskrit Learning in the Coḷa Empire," *JOR*, vol. IX (1937), pp. 1-2.

154. *SII*, vol. III, no. 27, pp. 50-51.

155. R. Nagaswamy, *TVCP*, Veḷāñjeri plates of Parāntaka I, plate III, p. 1.

vedimaṅgalam) named after himself, which is described in this inscription as being "of great wealth, immutable even at the end of the age" (*kalpa*).[156] This charter adds that this ruler founded many other prosperous and great *agrahāras* at various places.[157] The Kanyākumārī inscription also records that Parāntaka I created many *agrahāras* commencing with the name Vīranārāyaṇa, fit to be enjoyed by learned brāhmaṇas, just as Brahmā created *svarga*.[158] The Larger Leiden plates also state that Parāntaka I caused many villages to come into existence.[159] The Udayendiram plates of Pṛthivipati II record among the many meritorious acts of Parāntaka I, the gifts of land for brāhmaṇas (*brahmadeya*).[160]

Parāntaka I obviously made it a pleasure for learned men to live comfortably in the Coḷa country and pursue their studies. A great commentary (*bhāṣya*) on the *Ṛgveda* was composed on the banks of the Kāverī in the reign of Parāntaka Coḷa I, also called Vīra Coḷa. Mādhava, the son of Veṅkaṭārya and Sundarī, and the author of this extensive and important work states expressly that he lived happily in the Coḷa country when he wrote his work: *jagatāmekavīrasya coḷeṣu nivasan sukham, tīram-āśritya nivasan kāveryā dakṣiṇām sukham.*[161]

Sundara Coḷa is glorified in the Anbil plates as giving his able brāhmaṇa minister, Aniruddha, who was well-versed in the *śāstras* (*śruteravasaḥ*) an entire village named Karuṇākara-maṅgalam, which abounded in crops and endowed it with all privileges.[162]

The Karandai plates record that Rājendra I gave to a thousand and eighty brāhmaṇas who were masters in the Vedas, a whole *agrahāra* call Tribhuvaṇamahādevī

156. K.G. Krishnan, *KTPR*, v. 19, p. 70.
157. *Ibid.*, v. 20, pp. 70-71.
158. Kanyākumārī plates, *op. cit.*, v. 60, p. 143.
159. *EI*, vol. XXII, no. 34, v. 16, p. 239 (Larger Leiden plates).
160. Udayendiram plates, *op. cit.*, v. 7, p. 383.
161. *JOR*, vol. IX (1937), p. 2.
162. *EI*, vol. XV, no. 5, vv. 38-41, p. 63 (Anbil plates).

(*caturvedimaṅgalam*) named after his mother, by joining together fifty-one villages in Vīra-Coḷa-vaḷanāḍu, a sub-division of Nityavinoda-vaḷanāḍu.[163] These plates state that "this monarch made this *agrahāra* the most beautiful place on earth by making it fertile with the waters of the Kāverī and reverberating with the loud chants of the Vedas."[164] This inscription also praises the brāhmaṇas (*bhūmidevāḥ*) of this *agrahāra* very eloquently as "unequalled in courage" (*dhairye*), "stability" (*sthairye*), "penance" (*tapasī*), "greatness and humility" (*mahasi praśraye*), "who considered the Vedas a trifle on account of the greatness of their intellect" (*sarvān-vedān-sva-mativibhavāt-svalpam āmanyamānāḥ*), "who were abodes where the wealth of the *śāstras* sported" (*śāstrārtha-śrī-viharaṇa-gṛhāḥ*), "who were the holiest of the holy" (*pāvanaḥ-pāvanānām*) and "who daily displayed their extraodinary intellect" (*nityam-yatra sv-ati-mati-ratim-kurvate*).[165]

The Kanyākumārī inscription states that Vīra-Rājendra Coḷa, the third son of Rājendra Coḷa I, established many villages for brāhmaṇas (*brahmadeyas*) in the Coḷa, Tuṇḍira, Pāṇḍya, Gaṅgavāṭī and Kulūta areas and gave forty thousand brāhmaṇas who were masters in the Vedas gifts of land and made them settle there permanently.[166]

Although we do not find Sanskrit inscriptions which record grants of villages to learned brāhmaṇas during the reign of the later Coḷa rulers, yet some information is forthcoming from literature about the fillip given by these kings for the promotion of Sanskritic learning. The prefactory verses of the Sanskrit lexicon, *Nānārthārṇava Saṁkṣepa*,[167] written by a Chāndoga brāhmaṇa named Keśavasvāmin mention that Kulottuṅga I established a village of Śaiva brāhmaṇas, well-versed in Sanskrit in the Coḷa country. Keśavasvāmin, the

163. K.G. Krishnan, *KTPR*, vv. 65-69, p. 61.
164. *Ibid.*, v. 67.
165. *Ibid.*, v. 66.
166. Kanyākumārī inscription, *op. cit.*, vv. 80-81, pp. 148-49.
167. T. Ganapati Sastri (ed.), *Nānārthārṇava Saṁkṣepa* (*Ekākṣarākāṇḍa*, vv. 1-200), Trivandrum, 1913.

author of this book, belonging to a family of grammarians from this village was in the employment of Rājarāja II at whose instance he wrote this Sanskrit lexicon which is also known as *Rājarājīya*. The *Nanārthārṇava Saṁkṣepa* is the biggest homonymous lexicon known, containing about five thousand eight hundred stanzas, divided into six *kāṇḍa*s according to the number of syllables, with words being arranged after the initial letters in each *kāṇḍa*.[168]

The Pāṇḍya rulers likewise created many brāhmaṇa settlements for the welfare of learned men and for the spread of learning and literature. The Larger Siṉṉamaṉūr plates record that the Pāṇḍyan ruler Parāntaka Vīranārāyaṇa, created many holy brāhmaṇa settlements (*agrahāraiḥ aprameyaiḥ*).[169] The same inscription states that a learned brāhmaṇa named Śrethiśarman received from king Parāṇtaka Vīranārāyaṇa, a very fertile *agrahāra* named Maṇiyāci and that it was renamed Tiśaiccuḍarmaṅgalam. This inscription also states that Śrethiśarman's son Parāntaka received from Pāṇḍya Rājasiṁha III, the *agrahāra* named Naṟceygai-Puttūr, renamed as Maṇḍaragauravamaṅgalam.[170] In the Tamil section this grant of land is called *ekabhoga-brahmadeya*.

The Daḷavāipuram grant refers to Vīra-Nārāyaṇa Pāṇḍya as giving brāhmaṇas many villages such as Śrīvallabhamaṅgala as *ekhabhoga* gifts.[171]

The Śīvakāśi copper-plate grant states that Vīra-Pāṇḍya gave to a brāhmaṇa, Pītāmbara a grant of three *veil*s of land including a hamlet called Vāḻaikoḍu in Nalapura village along with some barren land for residential purposes. This area was separated from the village and renamed as Śāsanamaṅgalam.[172]

---

168. R.C. Majumdar (ed.), *The History and Culture of the Indian People* (vol. V-*The Struggle for Empire*), Bombay, 1989, p. 318.
169. *SII*, vol. III, no. 206, v. 14, pp. 451-52 (Larger Siṉṉamaṉūr plates).
170. *Ibid.*, vv. 25-32, p. 453.
171. T.N. Subramaniam, *DCPV*, pp. 15-16.
172. T.N. Subramaniam and P.R. Srinivasan, *SCVP*, vv. 14-17, p. 45.

Sometimes the names of these *agrahāras* underwent changes over a period of time. The village Maṇimaṅgalam (Chingleput district) also known as Ratnāgrahāra and Ratnagrāma in the Coḷa inscriptions was, in the time of Rājakesarivarman surnamed Lokamahādevī-caturvedimaṅgalam, in the time of Rājādhirāja, Rājendra and Vīra-Rājendra, Rājacūḷāmaṇi-caturvedimaṅgalam and later as Pāṇḍiyanai-irumaḍi-ven-kaṇḍa-śoḷa-caturvedimaṅgalam. In the period of Rājarāja III, it had a new name, Grāmaśikhāmaṇi-caturvedimaṅgalam.[173]

Apart from the royal grants made to promote education, the inscriptions reveal that the common people also took interest in promoting Vedic learning. The method of teaching and learning the Vedas since the ancient days has been by rote and this practice was followed in the period of our study in the Tamil country also. The method of learning religious texts was by memorizing and reciting them, the recital of these works being beneficial to the reciter as well as to the listener.

An interesting bi-lingual inscription belonging to the period of Sundara Coḷa mentions an endowment made for such a purpose.[174] This epigraph, found at the Matsyapurīśvara temple at Koil Tevarāyaṉpeṭṭai (Tañjāvūr district) mentions that a person named Baradayaṉ-Seṉda-Nakkapiraṉbhaṭṭa Sarvakratuyājiyār made an endowment of twenty *karunkāśu* to the temple with the provision that the annual interest of three *kāśu* which would accure from that amount would be given to the best reciter of some portions of the *Jaiminīya Sāmaveda* among all the participants excluding those who had been successful in this competition in the previous years, and that this was to be recited before the God on the night of Tiruvādirai in the month of Mārgaḻi.

This epigraph reveals the importance attached to the learning and recitation of Vedas by students, the proper recital of which was considered to be of paramount importance. This

173. *SII*, vol. III, p. 49.
174. *SII*, vol. XIII, no. 250, p. 133.

record also proves the interest taken by the common people of the time to encourage and promote the learning and recitation of such sacred texts at the temples. The awarding of prizes to the deserving candidates must have greatly encouraged students of Vedic learning.

Temple Colleges

The temples in the Tamil country also served as very important centres of Vedic learning. Although the Sanskrit inscriptions themselves do not reveal any information about the role of the temples in this sphere of activity, some Tamil inscriptions contain important facts regarding the high standard of Sanskritic learning in these religious centres.

An inscription of the ninth century AD records a grant made for a teacher to impart one Veda, including the Bahvṛca and the Āraṇyaka in the Agastyeśvara temple at Ponneri.[175] Provisions were made for the study of Prābhākaram (*Prābhākara Mīmāṁsā*) at the Nāgeśvara temple in Kumbakoṇam according to a record of the tenth century AD.[176] Another epigraph mentions that this same subject was taught in the Bhairava shrine at Tirukkoṣṭiyūr during the reign of Rājarāja I.[177]

A Tamil inscription of the eleventh century AD, belonging to the reign of Rājendra Coḷa I provides a lot of information with regard to the functioning of an educational institution attached to the Aḻagiya Narasiṁhaperumāḷ temple in the village of Eṇṇāyiram in South Arcot district.[178] The subjects taught were *Ṛgveda, Yajurveda, Chandoga-Sāma, Talavakāra-Sāma, Vājasaneya, Baudhāyanīya* (*Gṛhya, Kalpa* and *Kāṭaka*) and *Atharvaveda*. The other subjects taught at this institution were *Rūpāvatāra* (an elementary work on Sanskrit grammar), *Vyākaraṇa, Prābhākara Mīmāṁsā* and *Vedānta*. This institution housed a total of fifteen teachers and three hundred and fifty students among which eleven teachers and two hundred and

175. *ARE*, 15 of 1933-34.
176. *SII*, vol. III, no. 200, pp. 376-77.
177. *ARE*, 333 of 1923.
178. *EI*, vol. XXXIX, no. 34, pp. 223-36 (Eṇṇayiram inscription).

thirty students were involved in Vedic studies alone, thus revealing that this educational centre catered primarily to Vedic learning. The remuneration paid to the teachers and the allowance given to the students are also given in great detail in this epigraph. This inscription is of great importance as it clearly shows that in the ancient temples, not only was the regular conduct of worship maintained, but the study of the Vedas, philosophy, grammar and other subjects were also encouraged by munificient royal gifts.[179]

Two more inscriptions[180] from the Vaikuṇṭhaperumāḷ temple at Uttaramerūr (Chingleput district) belonging to the period of Rājendra Coḷa I record grants of land by the village-assembly for teaching *Bahvṛca* and the *Taittirīya Śākhā* to the students in that village. Some of the other temples where Vedic studies were taught during the reign of this king were at the Bhaktavatsala Perumāḷ temple[181] at Tinnanūr (Chingleput district) and at the Kadambeśvara temple at Turaiyūr[182] (Tirucirāpalli district) where provisions were also made for feeding the students.

An inscription of the period of Rājendra's son and successor, Rājādhirāja I (AD 1048)[183] from the Varadarāja Perumāḷ temple at Tribhuvani (near Pondicherry) mentions that lands were gifted for running a Vedic college in that temple. The subjects taught there included the *Ṛgveda, Yajurveda, Chandoga-Sāma, Talavakāra-Sāma, Apūrva, Vājasaneya, Baudhāyanīya, Satyāśadhasūtra, Mahābhārata, Rāmāyaṇa, Vedānta, Vyākaraṇa, Rūpāvatāra, Manuśāstra* and *Vaikhānasa Śāstra*. The number of teachers and students for these subjects as well as their respective allowances are given in detail in this epigraph which is similar to the one found at Eṇṇāyiram.

179. *ARE*, 1918, pt. II, pp. 146-47.

180. *SII*, vol. VI, nos. 312 and 316, pp. 152-53.

181. *ARE*, 176 of 1937-38.

182. *ARE*, 157 of 1937-38.

183. *ARE*, 176 of 1919.

The Tirumukkūḍal inscription of Vīra-Rājendra (AD 1069) also gives information about Vedic learning pursued at a Vedic college attached to the Veṅkaṭeśa Perumāḷ temple in the village of Tirumukkūḍal (Chingleput district).[184] The teachers of the *Ṛgveda, Yajurveda, Vyākaraṇa* and the *Rūpāvatāra* are mentioned. Sixty persons, including ten brāhmaṇas who studied the *Ṛgveda*, ten brāhmaṇas who learnt the *Yajurveda*, twenty brāhmaṇas and students who studied the *Vyākaraṇa* and the *Rūpāvatāra*, ten Mahā-Pāñcarātras, three Śiva-brāhmaṇas and five Vaikhānasas were fed daily at the hostel attached to this college. Since the hostel also housed a few Mahā-pāñcarātras, Śiva-brāhmaṇas and Vaikhānasas, it may be inferred that the *āgamas* and *tantras* such as *Pāñcarātra, Śaiva* and *Vaikhānasa* were also taught.[185] Apart from being fed, these students were also provided with mats and also with oil for lamps and for bathing. In addition to this, cooks and maid-servants were employed to serve the students and the teachers. All these facilities were intended to help those in pursuit of higher studies to concentrate fully on their work without any disturbance. This inscription also mentions that there was a hospital where the students living in the hostel and temple servants could be treated.

An important and interesting bi-lingual epigraph[186] of the reign of this ruler found at the Kailāśanāthasvāmin temple in Śoḷamahādevī village (Tirucirāpalli district) records the gift of land to a scholar who was teaching a commentary (*vārttika*) titled *Pradīpaka* written by Cidānanda Bhaṭṭāra on a work called *Śārīrakabhāṣya* by a person bearing the title *Bhagavatpāda*. This inscription is the earliest and clearly dated epigraphical reference to Śrī Śaṅkarācārya — that too by his famous title *Bhagavatpāda* — and to his *Brahmasūtrabhāṣya* as *Śārīrakabhāṣya*.[187]

184. *EI*, vol. XXI, no. 38, pp. 220-50 (Tirumukkūḍal Inscription).

185. *Ibid.*, p. 223.

186. S. Sankaranarayanan, "Pradīpaka — A Forgotten Vārttika (From Tamil Nadu on the Śārīrakabhāṣya of Śrī Śankara)", *ALB*, vol. 62, 1998, pp. 109-23.

187. S. Sankaranarayanan, "Sanskrit Education in Ancient Tamil Country (An Epigraphical Survey)," *ALB*, vol. 57, 1993, p. 20.

The very first Sanskrit verse found in this inscription mentions king Vīra Rājendra as humbly requesting (*praśritaḥ prārthayati*) the administrative assembly (*sabhā*) of this village and also the future rulers (*rājñas ca bhāvinaḥ*) to maintain and protect this grant, described as being highly meritorious (*uccair dharmo yam rakṣyatām*). This gift is a *brahmadāna* or *brahmajñānadāna*, i.e., imparting the knowledge of *Brahman*, the Supreme through conducting classes on an Advaita Vedānta treatise.[188]

An inscription of the time of Vikrama Coḷa (AD 1120), mentions that in a *maṭha* which was attached to the temple of Tiruvaḍutuṟaiyuḍaiyār at Tiruvaḍutuṟai, the Sanskrit works, namely, the *Rūpāvatāra* and *Vyākaraṇa* were taught, in addition to the ancient medical texts in Sanskrit such as the *Bāhaḍa* and *Caraka*.[189]

The *Bāhaḍa* mentioned here is either one or both of the *Aṣṭāṅgahṛdaya* of Vṛddha Vāgbhaṭa of *circa* sixth century AD or the *Aṣṭāṅgahṛdaya* of Bāla Vāghbaṭa of *circa* first century AD, and the *Caraka* is the *Saṁhitā* of Caraka of *circa* first century AD.[190]

An inscription from the Varadarājasvāmi temple, Kāñcīpuram belonging to the period of Kulottuṅga Coḷa III records the provisions made for the *Rāmānuja-bhāṣya* to be regularly expounded in the temple *maṭha*.[191]

Another interesting inscription[192] of the period of Kulottuṅga III from the Ādipurīśvara temple, Tiruvoṟṟiyūr states that sixty *velīs* of land was given for the maintenance of a *maṇḍapa* called *Vyākaraṇadāna-Vyākhyāna-maṇḍapa* built in the temple there for the upkeep of the teachers and students who studied Pāṇini's grammar (*vyākaraṇa-śāstra*) in that hall and

188. S. Sankaranarayanan, "Pradīpaka," *op. cit.*, p. 113.
189. *ARE*, 159 of 1925.
190. S. Sankaranarayanan, "Sanskrit Education in the Ancient Tamil Country," *op. cit.*, p. 21.
191. *ARE*, 493 of 1919; K.V. Raman, *Sri Varadarājaswāmī Temple, kanchi*, New Delhi, 1975, p. 65.
192. *ARE*, 201 of 1902.

for the worship of the deity Vyākaraṇadāna-Perumāḷ (Śiva) who was said to have appeared before Pāṇini for fourteen consecutive days and taught him the first fourteen aphorisms (with which begins Pāṇini's grammar) called *Māheśvara Sūtra*s in that very *maṇḍapa*.[193] A later inscription of the thirteenth century AD, of the time of Jaṭāvarman Sundara Pāṇḍya I, provides for the expenses of the upkeep of this *maṇḍapa* where the fourteen *Māheśvara Sūtra*s (or *Pratyāhāra Sūtra*s) were taught to Pāṇini by Śiva.[194]

Śālai

Institutions known as *śālai*s in which Vedic education was imparted to the students or *chātra* (Prākr̥t or Tamil *chattar*) who were also fed at this place are known from some Tamil and Sanskrit inscriptions. The Pārthivaśekharapuram copper-plate grant of AD 869 of the Ay ruler, Karunandaḍakkan, which is in Tamil expect for a few Sanskrit verses at the very end, mentions a *śālai* at Pārthivaśekharapuram or Pārthivapuram (Kanyākumārī district) which consisted of ninety-five students (*chattar*).[195] It appears that the Vedas, as well as *Vyākaraṇa*, *Mīmāṁsā* and *Paurohitya* were taught at this institution. According to T.N. Subramaniam, the students of this *śālai* also had training in military science.[196]

An epigraph of the tenth century AD, records that a brāhmaṇa named Nārāyaṇa who was a *brahmādhirāja* made a grant of twelve *ghaṭa*s of paddy as an offering to the Viṣṇu temple at Pārthivaśekharapuram for feeding the students (*chātra*) there.[197] It is obvious that this feeding endowment made by the brāhmaṇa donor must have been made in connection with this *śālai* mention in Karunandaḍakkan's epigraph which might have continued to flourish till the date of this record.[198]

193. *ARE*, 1913, pt. II, pp. 109-10.
194. *ARE*, 110 of 1912.
195. *PCM*, pp. A1-A8.
196. *SITI.*, vol. III, pt. II, p. 9.
197. *EI*, vol. XLI, no. 1, p. 6.
198. *Ibid.*

Popular Education

Although the pursuit of Vedic and Vedāntic learning was confined mainly to the priestly class, provision was also made in ancient and medieval India for the common people to promote their learning. The epics, the *Rāmāyaṇa* and the *Mahābhārata*, as well as the numerous Purāṇas contain the teachings of the Vedas and the Upaniṣads, but at the same time appeal to the masses. The rulers, therefore, made provisions for the recitation of these sacred texts at temples and at other places so that the common people could inculcate the moral values contained in these works which were presented in a lucid and interesting way.

The acquisition of knowledge by listening to lectures given by the learned has been given importance in India since the earliest times. Tiruvaḷḷuvar, too, has devoted an entire chapter to the importance of listening.[199] He states, "The wealth of wealths is the ear; that well outtops all else"[200] and "though unlettered, listen; you will find this a great help in distress."[201]

It was this system of spreading morality and high values in society, of making laymen listen to the lectures of the wise, that was followed by the kings of the Tamil country. The Kūram copper-plate grant records that Parameśvaravarman I gave a village named Parameśvaramaṅgalam as a divine gift to the God Pinākapāṇi (Śiva) of the temple named Vidyāvinīta-Pallava-Parameśvara in the village of Kūra for the recitation of the *Mahābhārata* (*Bhāratākhyāna*) at this temple.[202]

The Taṇḍantoṭṭam plates, the Sanskrit section of which mentions a grant of land to one hundred and eight learned brāhmaṇas, also gives a long list of the names of these donees at the very end of this epigraph. Among these is mentioned a person who recited the *Bhārata* (*Mahābhārata*) and who received one share of this land-grant.[203]

199. *Kuraḷ, op. cit.*, Ch. 42.
200. *Ibid.*, v. 411.
201. *Ibid.*, v. 414.
202. Kūram plates, *op. cit.*, l. 52, p. 150.
203. Taṇḍantoṭṭam plates, *op. cit.*, p. 534.

The Tamil inscription from Tribhuvani of the reign of Rājādhirāja, mentioned earlier, reveals that the *Rāmāyaṇa* and the *Mahābhārata* were taught along with other subjects at the college here. It seems that works like the *Mahābhārata* and *Rāmāyaṇa* were being expounded to the general audience rather than taught as a regular subject in classes.[204] Another probability is that the college gave regular training to a set of its own capable students in the art of making public and popular discourses on these epics for propagating *dharma*.[205]

Apart from the aim of spreading ethical values among the masses, the exposition of the epics and the Purāṇas helped even the illiterate to understand aspects of India's ancient culture and in this manner it was handed down from one generation to another and preserved for posterity. The underlying unity of India's ancient culture was due, in no small measure to these methods followed by the rulers to spread culture among the people.

Sanskrit Learning in the Tamil Country

Sanskritic studies reached a very high level under the Pallava, Pāṇḍya and Coḷa rulers. Apart from the fact that the educational institutions such the *ghaṭikā*, *maṭha* and the *agrahāras* propagated the ancient Sanskritic texts, many new compositions in chaste and high-flown Sanskrit were composed during these periods. The very inscriptions issued by these kings found on their copper-plate charters as well as on the walls of the temples point to the depth of knowledge and the flowering imagination of the learned men of the time.

The tradition of honouring scholars and poets was in vogue in the Tamil country since the Saṅgam period. The court of the rulers was an important meeting place for the scholars and poets where they could display their extraordinary talent. The Saṅgam works reveal that some poets attained the position of the king's favourites. King Pāri's favourite poet was Kapilar,

204. S. Sankaranarayanan, "Sanskrit Education," *op. cit.*, p. 17.

205. *Ibid.*

Auvaiyār was the favourite poetess of Adihaimān and Talaiyālaṅgānattu Neḍuñjeḻiyan favoured the poet Māṅguḍi Marudanār.[206]

The practice of patronizing learned men continued in the Tamil country in the succeeding periods also. Sanskrit being the court language of the Pallavas, numerous poets and dramatists were patronized by them and Sanskrit learning and literature received considerable encouragement at the hands of these kings.

Among the famous scholars whom the Pallava rulers patronized at their court in Kāñcīpuram were Bhāravi and Daṇḍin. Bhāravi, the author of the famous Sanskrit poem *Kirātārjunīyam* was patronized by Siṁhaviṣṇu and lived in his court for some time.[207] According to some scholars, Daṇḍin, who composed the Sanskrit works, *Daśakumāracaritam*, *Kāvyādarśa* and the *Avantisundarīkathā* lived at Kāñcīpuram during the reign of Rājasiṁha.

Daṇḍin, in his *Kāvyādarśa* mentions a Śaiva ruler, Rājavarma, who judging from the manner in which he is introduced should have been a contemporary of the author and was probably Rājasiṁha, whose inscriptions reveal that he was a devotee of Śiva.[208] Prof. M. Rangachariar has mentioned a tradition with reference to Chapter V of the *Kāvyādarśa* that it was composed by Daṇḍin for giving lessons in rhetoric to a prince at Kāñcīpuram, who was possibly Rājasiṁha's son.[209] According to other scholars, it was probably Rājasiṁha himself who was Daṇḍin's student.[210] From his works it appears that Daṇḍin was well-acquainted with life in

206. N. Subrahmanian, *Sangam Polity*, Madurai, 1980, p. 54.
207. C. Minakshi, *ASLP*, pp. 14-15.
208. R. Narasimhachar, "Bhāmaha and Daṇḍi," *Ind. Ant.*, 1912, p. 92.
209. *Ibid.*
210. R. Gopalan, *History of the Pallavas of Kāñcī*, Madras, 1928, pp. 110-11.

royal courts and that he lived a happy life in affluent circumstances.[211]

Apart from these famous scholars, there were a number of other very talented composers during the Pallava period whose names are known only through the inscriptions which they composed. Some of the Sanskrit epigraphs of the Pallava king Rājasiṁha found on the walls of the Kailāśanātha temple at Kāñcīpuram are of great literary merit.

The Sanskrit (*praśasti*) portions of the bi-lingual copper-plate grants of some of the Pallava rulers are also outstanding compositions in beautiful style replete with similes and metaphors, as found in the Paḷḷankovil, Kūram, Udayendiram, Kaśākuḍi, Pullūr and Taṇḍantoṭṭam plates. While the lithic inscriptions usually do not provide any information about the composer, the copper-plate charters almost always provide the name of the poet-composer along with some details of that individual at the tail-end of the epigraphs. However, the early copper-plate charters of the Pallava kings record only the oral order of these rulers and do not give the name of the composer of the charter.

These *praśasti* portions of the copper-plate inscriptions which are of great importance for the study of their historical contents are of equally great importance for the study of the literary beauty contained therein. A detailed study of these *praśasti*s reveals the knowledge and skill of the poets who showed profound proficiency in the language. The names and accomplishments of these poets are also revealed by these epigraphs.

The Paḷḷankovil epigraph states that the Sanskrit *praśasti* of this record was composed by a great scholar named Medhāvi, who was well-versed in all the *śāstra*s, respectable and who was like Bṛhaspati in intelligence (*samasta śāstra niṣṇāta*

211. M.R. Kale, *Daśakumāracarita of Daṇḍin*, Delhi, 1997, Intro, p. xxi; D.K. Gupta, *A Critical Study of Daṇḍin and His Works*, Delhi, 1970, pp. 96-97.

dhiṣaṇo dhiṣaṇopamaḥ, mānyo nāmāpi medhāvī praśastim kṛtavān=imām).[212]

According to the Kaśākuḍi plates, the composer of the *praśasti* of this charter was the poet Trivikrama, described as "one who was honest, who knew the truth of all sciences" and "who performed sacrifices according to the rules of the three Vedas" (*akṛtimas-trayī vidhi krama kratu-pravartakaḥ, samasta-śāstra tatvavid-praśastikṛt trivikramaḥ*).[213] The Udayendiram plates of Nandivarman Pallavamalla, the major portion of which is in Sanskrit, was composed by the poet Parameśvara, who is mentioned as the son of Candradeva and belonging to the race of Medhāvi.[214] This poet was given the allotment of one share in the village granted by the king.[215]

The poet Parameśvara, surnamed Uttarakaraṇika, the son of Paramottārakaraṇika, "the self-chosen lord of poetry" (*kavitāsvayaṁ-vṛtavaraḥ*) was the composer of the *praśasti* section of the Taṇḍantoṭṭam plates.[216]

Since both the Udayendiram and the Taṇḍantoṭṭam plates record gifts endowed in the same reign (Nandivarman Pallavamalla) and the number of years that separate the two grants is only seven, it may be presumed that the poet Parameśvara who composed the *praśasti* of the Udayendiram plates is the same as Parameśvara surnamed Uttarakaraṇika of the Taṇḍantoṭṭam plates and Candradeva, the poet's father has to be identified with Paramottāra-karaṇika.[217]

Since the Udayendiram plates state that Parameśvara was born in the family of Medhāvi (*medhāvi-kulodbhavaḥ*) it seems clear that the latter should have been an ancestor of the family some generations before and that he was a renowned poet who composed similar *praśasti*s. It is very likely that Medhāvi,

212. T.N. Subramaniam; *PJCG*, v. 9, p. 76.

213. Kaśākuḍi plates, *op. cit.*, v. 31, p. 351.

214. Udayendiram plates, *op. cit.*, v. 8, p. 370.

215. *Ibid.*, p. 373.

216. Taṇḍantoṭṭam plates, *op. cit.*, v. 14, p. 521.

217. C. Minakshi, *ASLP*, p. 78.

the composer of the Paḷḷankovil grant was the ancestor of the composer of the Udayendiram charter.[218]

The *praśasti* of the Velūrpāḷaiyam charter was composed by the poet Maheśvara Manodhīra (*maheśvaro manodhīraḥ praśastim kṛtavāmimām*),[219] while that of the Ciṟṟūr epigraph of Nṛpatuṅga was done by a person named Kumāra.[220] The Bāhūr grant was composed by a poet called Nāgaya who is described in this inscription as pious (*sukṛt*) and a servant of the seat of learning of the residents of the village of Bāhūr (*dāsaḥ sthānasya vidyaya vāgūr grāma juṣām*).[221]

The Veḷāñjeri inscription of Aparājita Pallava was written by a poet named Mahādeva who was the son of a learned brāhmaṇa named Śrī Kumāra "who set aside the eloquence of his rivals" (*vipakṣa-vādi pratibhāva-hartuḥ*) and "was the composer of *mahākāvyas*" (*kartuḥ mahākāvya-nibandhanānām*).[222]

The verse unfortunately does not mention the names of these great works composed by Kumāra. However, since this inscription describes these compositions as *mahākāvyas*, Kumāra must have been a great poet (*mahākavi*) of the Pallava period who was commissioned to write this epigraph. The Sanskrit work *Kāvyamīmāṁsā* by Rājaśekhara[223] which gives a list of different grades of poets mentions *mahākavi* as one of the titles of gifted poets and as one who was very proficient at composing works of prose and poetry (*yaḥ anyataraprabandhe pravīṇaḥ sa mahākaviḥ*).

The Sanskrit verses of the Ciṟṟūr plates of Nṛpatuṅga were composed by the poet Kumāra and the Veḷāñjeri plates of

218. T.N. Subramaniam, *PJCG*, p. 74.

219. Velūrpāḷaiyam plates, *op. cit.*, v. 28, p. 509.

220. T.V. Mahalingam, *IOP*, p. 440 (Ciṟṟūr plates).

221. Bāhūr plates, *op. cit.*, v. 30, p. 11.

222. R. Nagaswamy, *TVCP*, Veḷāñjeri plates of Aparājita, plate V, p. 1.

223. Narayana Sastri Rhiste (ed.), *The Kāvyamīmāṁsā of Rājaśekhara* (Part I), Benaras, 1931, Adhyāya V, p. 63. (The ten grades of poets mentioned in the *Kāvyamīmāṁsā* are *kāvyavidyānāṭakaḥ, hṛdayakaviḥ, anyāpadeśi, sevita, ghaṭamānaḥ, mahākaviḥ, kavirājaḥ aveśikaḥ, aviccedi* and *saṅkrāmayita*).

Aparājita mention that it was composed by Mahādeva, son of Śrī Kumāra. Since both Aparājita and Nṛpatuṅga were contemporaries it is not surprising that Śrī Kumāra composed Nṛpatuṅga's charter and Śrī Kumāra's son Mahādeva composed Aparājita's plates, both father and son obviously serving in the royal court.[224]

The Coḷa rulers continued the impetus given to the promotion of Sanskrit poetry and literature by the Pallava kings. The *praśastis* of the bi-lingual grants of the Coḷa kings such as the Veḷāñjeri, Anbil, Larger Leiden, Tiruvālaṅgāḍu, Karandai, Esālam and Kanyākumārī (=Cārāla) inscriptions provide a glimpse of the high level of Sanskrit language and literature in those days. These epigraphs also provide the names of the composers.

The Veḷāñjeri plates of Parāntaka I mention in the Sanskrit portion at the very end of this epigraph that this charter was composed by a person named Rutsa.[225] The poet-composer of the Śoḷingūr Rock inscription of the same king was sage Kumāra, a *Vaikhānasa* of the Kāśyapa *gotra*.[226]

The Anbil epigraph of Sundara Coḷa was composed by Mādhava Bhaṭṭa, who is mentioned in the very last verse of the Sanskrit portion as being very knowledgeable.[227]

The Larger Leiden plates state that the Sanskrit *praśasti* was composed by a brāhmaṇa named Anantanārāyaṇa who belonged to the lineage (*gotra*) of Vasiṣṭha (*vasiṣṭhānvavāye*).[228] The Sanskrit *praśasti* of the Tiruvālaṅgāḍu grant was composed by a poet named Nārāyaṇa who was the son of Śaṅkara[229] while the Karandai plates also state that the Sanskrit portion was the composition of Nārāyaṇa, son of Śaṅkarārya and a

224. R. Nagaswamy, "The Ciṟṟur Copper Plates of Nṛpatuṅga" from *Studies in Ancient Tamil Law and Society*, Madras, 1978, p. 37.
225. R. Nagaswamy, *TVCP*, *Veḷāñjeri plates of Parāntaka I*, plate V, p. 2.
226. *EI*, vol. IV, no. 32, v. 10, p. 224 (Śoliṅgūr inscription).
227. Anbil plates, *op. cit.*, v. 46, pp. 63-64.
228. Larger Leiden plates, *op. cit.*, v. 39, p. 242.
229. *SII*, vol. III, no. 205, v. 136, p. 401 (Tiruvālaṅgāḍu plates).

resident of Pārśvagrāma.[230] Again, a verse at the end of the Sanskrit part of the Esālam charter states that it was composed by poet Nārāyaṇa Kavi, son of Śaṅkara and a resident of Pārśvagrāma.[231]

K.G. Krishnan has suggested that it is this Nārāyaṇa who was the composer of the Larger Leiden plates.[232] The style of poetry betrays the single authorship of these *praśastis*.[233] It thus seems that from the fifth year of Rājendra to his twenty-fifth year, this poet had been occupying an important position in the court of Rājendra Coḷa I.[234]

The Sanskrit *praśasti* of the Cārāla copper-plate charter of Vīra-Rājendra (which is identical verse for verse with that of the Kanyākumārī lithic inscription of this king, (as mentioned earlier) states that it was composed by Candrabhūṣaṇa-Bhaṭṭa,[235] also called by the paraphrazed name Śaśibhūṣaṇa Paṇḍita in this inscription.[236]

The names of the poets who composed the inscriptions of the Pāṇḍyas such as the Veḷvikuḍi, Larger Siṉṉamaṉūr, Daḷavāipuram and the Śivakāśi epigraphs are mentioned. The fact that these poets belonging to the Pāṇḍyan period too were great scholars in the Sanskrit language and masters in the art of composing poetry can be gleaned from their works.

The Larger Siṉṉamaṉūr plates record that the Sanskrit part of this charter was composed by a poet named Vāsudeva who had "studied the whole science of literature" (*vidita-sakala-vaṅmayaḥ*) and who was "the birth-place of modesty and intelligence" (*vinayanaya=prabhāvaḥ*).[237]

---

230. K.G. Krishnan, *KTPR*, v. 76, p. 76.
231. R. Nagaswamy, *ECPR*, v. 34, p. 33.
232. K.G. Krishnan, *KTPR*, p. 53.
233. R. Nagaswamy, *op. cit.*, p. 28.
234. *Ibid.*, p. 11.
235. *EI*, vol. XXV, No. 25, v. 83, p. 264 (Cārāla plates).
236. *Ibid.*, ll. 207-08.
237. *SII*, vol. III, no. 206, v. 38, p. 454 (Larger Siṉṉamaṉūr plates).

Vārodayabhaṭṭa, who was a performer of all sacrifices (*sarvakratuyājin*) is mentioned as the composer of the *praśasti* of the Veḷvikuḍi grant.[238] According to the Daḷavāipuram epigraph, the *praśasti* portion of this charter was composed by Mādhava, who resided in Śrīvallabhamaṅgalam.[239]

Viṣṇutrāta, who had the epithet *Pārthivakesari* and who was the councillor (*dharmmopadeṣṭaguru*) of Vīra-Pāṇḍya was the composer of the *praśasti* of the Śivakāśi copper-plates.[240] This inscription also states that Vīra-Pāṇḍya appointed a person named Pītāmbara to compose Sanskrit verses (*ślokas*) for his charters and gave him a grant of land.[241]

Some of the Pāṇḍyan inscriptions of the period of Neḍuñjaḍaiyan mention a poet named Madhurakavi. Although he did not compose any of the Pāṇḍyan inscriptions, some details about this poet are available from the records.

A Sanskrit inscription from Āṉaimalai near Madurai mentions this Madhurakavi (Māraṅgāri, who bore the title Mūvendamaṅgaḷapperaraiyaṉ) as a minister of Neḍuñjaḍaiyan[242] (see Chapter II — Administration — Civil). He was apparently an expert in the art of composing poetry and was thus called Madhurakavi.[243] He is mentioned in this epigraph as a learned and illustrious member of the Vaidya family (*śrīmān vaidyaḥ*).

The Veḷvikuḍi inscription of Neḍuñjaḍaiyan mentions that the *ājñapti* (executor) of this grant was this Mārangāri (Maṅgalarāja) and is described in glowing terms as a very sweet (*madhuratara*) poet (*kavi*) and orator (*vāgmi*), who was well-versed in the *śāstras* (*śāstra-vit*), a *vaidya* and belonging to Karavandapura (*karavandapurādhivāstavyaḥ*).[244] In the Tamil

238. *EI*, vol. XVII, no. 16, l. 30, p. 300 (Veḷvikuḍi plates).
239. T.N. Subramaniam, *DCPV*, v. 36, p. 18.
240. T.N. Subramaniam and P.R. Srinivasan, *SCVP*, v. 26, pp. 46-47.
241. *Ibid.*, v. 10, p. 44.
242. *EI*, vol. VIII, no. 33, p. 319.
243. *Ibid.*, p. 318.
244. *EI*, vol. XVII, no. 16, v. 18, p. 303.

portion of the same charter this poet is glorified as *vaidyaka-śikhāmaṇi* (crest-jewel of the *vaidyakas*). It is evident that the members of this family were well-versed in sacred literature as revealed by the term *vaidyaka*.[245]

Apart from the copper-plate charters, some of the lithic inscriptions provide the names of the poet-composers. A long inscription of the Kerala ruler, Ravivarman Kulaśekhara found in the Raṅganāthasvāmi temple, Śrīraṅgam, states that it was composed by Kavibhūṣaṇa, but does not provide any other details about this talented poet.[246] A Sanskrit eulogy of this king by the same poet is found in a bi-lingual epigraph at Tiruppangiḷi (Tirucirapaḷḷi district).[247]

It is interesting to note that some of the very short lithic epigraphs consisting of not more than one or two verses like the inscription of Naralokavīra (the general of Kulottuṅga I) found at a Śiva temple in Siddhaliṅgamaḍam (South Arcot district) and written by Āṇḍapiḷḷai-bhaṭṭan of Tirukkovalūr contain the names of the composers at the very end.[248]

Vidyācakravartins

A large number of Sanskrit and bi-lingual inscriptions in Tamil Nadu contain the names of poets who bore the title *vidyācakravartin*. An analysis of the literary and epigraphical sources have revealed that there was a whole family of composers who had this title and among these, three are very well-known through their literary and epigraphical works.[249]

S.S. Janaki had identified the first of these *vidyācakravartins*, a contemporary of the Hoysala ruler Ballāla II (AD 1173-1220) as the composer of a large number of Sanskrit and bi-lingual

245. *EI*, vol. VIII, no. 33, p. 318 and n. 7; see also K.V. Raman, "Karavandapuram or Uggirankoṭṭai — An Ancient Fortress Town of the Pāṇḍyas," *JIH*, vol. LII, p. 73.
246. *EI*, vol. IV, no. 18, p. 150.
247. *ARE*, 172 of 1938-39.
248. *SII*, vol. XXVI, no. 390, p. 254.
249. S.S. Janaki, *Gadyakarṇāmṛta*, Madras, 1981.

epigraphs of the Bāṇa ruler, Rājarājadevan Ponparapinān̤ Magadhaipperumāḷ (*c.* AD 1181-1213).[250] This poet was also possibly the same as Karpagavilli (Dhanvin or Dhanvimiśra) of the Coḷa records of the early years of the thirteenth century AD of Kulottuṅga III's period from Tiruveḷḷar̤ai who also wrote a commentary *Dīpa* on the *Drahyāyana Śrauta-Sūtra* and lived at Lālguḍi (Tirucirapalli district).

The inscriptions of this Bāṇa ruler from Nāratampūṇḍi[251] (North Arcot district) and Arakaṇḍanallūr[252] (South Arcot district) which consist of the same set of thirteen verses mention that this poet Sakalavidyācakravarti *alias* Kavicakravarti was presented with elephants by this Bāṇa king for composing these verses (*baṇeśvaram prati kavirājarājena sakala-vidyā-cakravartina viracitāni matta-kuñjara=mūlyāni padyāni*).

The two Tiruveḷḷar̤ai epigraphs[253] mention that this poet was called Sakalavidyācakravartin and had the titles *kavirāja* and *tribhuvanakavi-cakravartin*and hailed from Madurāntaka-caturvedimaṅgalam (Ālambākkam, near Lālguḍi). He is described by the Tamil epithet *Tirutter-ponmeynda-perūmāḷ* evidently in deference to his patron, the Bāṇa chief Ponmeynda-perūmāḷ Magadaipperumāḷ of Āragalūr.[254]

This poet was evidently very prosperous as the Tirveḷḷar̤ai records mention that he established a *maṭha* and gave liberal endowments to it (see section on Maṭhas).

Another *vidyācakravartin*, known as Kālakalābha Vidyā-cakravartin was the composer of the Sanskrit historical prose text, *Gadyakarṇāmṛta*, dealing with the historical events associated with the Hoysala and Tamil kings in the thirteenth century AD.[255] This author has been identified with the

---

250. *SII*, vol. VIII, no. 135, pp. 63-64 and *ARE*, 554 of 1902; 482 of 1908, 369, 370 and 371 of 1925, 117 of 1934-35 and 247 of 1941-42.
251. *ARE*, 369, 370, 371 of 1925.
252. *ARE*, 117 of 1934-35.
253. *ARE*, 207 and 208 of 1938-39.
254. *ARE*, 1938-39, pt. II, para 22.
255. S.S. Janaki, *op. cit.*, p. 23.

composer of the two records of the Hoysala ruler Rāmanātha of the thirteenth century from the Raṅganāthasvāmi temple, Śrīraṅgam.[256] These two epigraphs mention the name of this poet as Śokkavilli Bhaṭṭar *alias* Mudaliyār Kaṟiyamaṟi of Pāṭakam who bore the title Salalavidyācakravartin.

Yet another *vidyācakravartin* is known from a Sanskrit epigraph of the Hoysala ruler Ballāla III (AD 1291-1342) from Kāñcīpuram.[257] This poet has been identified with the author of the work *Rukmiṇīkalyāṇa*, commentaries on the *Kāvyaprakāśa* and the *Alaṁkārasarvasva*, the *Prayogadīpikā* and other literary works.[258]

Inscriptions as a Mirror to Sanskrit Literature

The Sanskrit inscriptions of the Tamil country are undoubtedly a very important source for understanding the administrative, social, economic, religious and cultural conditions of the Pallava, Pāṇḍya and Coḷa periods, but these epigraphs have an added value from the viewpoint of language and literature since they clearly reveal the condition of Sanskrit language and literature during those periods. According to A.A. Macdonnel,

> The study of inscriptions is important for the knowledge of the early history of Indian writing and the state of language at that time. It is also valuable for the political, religious and linguistic conditions of the age.[259]

The earliest inscriptions belonging to the Pallava period were written in Prākṛt such as the Mayidavolu, Guṇapadeya and the Hīrahadagalli inscriptions. Later, Sanskrit came to be used in these epigraphs. During the period of the later Pallavas, Pāṇḍyas and Coḷas, many of their inscriptions were bi-lingual,

256. *SII*, vol. IV, no. 498, p. 139; *SII*, vol. XXIV, no. 276, p. 295; *SII*, vol. IV, no. 499; p. 139, *SII*, vol. XXIV, No. 275, p. 295; S.S. Janaki, *op. cit.*
257. *ARE*, 312 of 1954-55.
258. S.S. Janaki, *op. cit.*
259. A.A. Macdonell, *A History of Sanskrit Literature*, Delhi, 1979, p. 14.

i.e., the first or the *praśasti* portion being written in beautiful Sanskrit verses as well as in prose and the latter half being written in Tamil. Most of these inscriptions record the gift of land or money to temples or to brāhmaṇas learned in the Vedic lore.

A detailed study of these Sanskrit inscriptions reveals that the composers of these epigraphs had an excellent knowledge of the epics, the *Rāmāyaṇa* and the *Mahābhārata* and also of many of the Purāṇas. According to D.B. Diskalkar,

> The authors of the south Indian inscriptions were great students of Vedic and classical Sanskrit literature in all its branches and frequently borrowed ideas and even portions from them.[260]

Starting from the Pallava period, the authors of the epigraphs compared their rulers with heroes of the epics, especially those in the *Mahābhārata* known for their valour and statesmanship. The composer of the Kaśākuḍi plates refers to Nandivarman Pallavamalla as being like Yudhiṣṭhira in delighting his subjects (*dharmaḥ prajārañjane*).[261] Rājasiṁha had many *biruda*s like *śrī yuddhārjunaḥ* (he who resembles Arjuna in battle) and *śrī pārthavikramaḥ* (he who resembles Arjuna in valour).[262]

The Kaśākuḍi plates speak of Nandivarman Pallavamalla as being like Arjuna in battle (*saṁgrāme vijayaḥ*).[263] This king is again compared to the Pāṇḍava Nakula (*nakula iva turaṅgameṣu*) who was very adept at managing and training horses.[264] Bhāgadatta, another famous king in the *Mahābhārata* who was an ally of Duryodhana has been mentioned in an inscription wherein Rājasiṁha is described as resembling Bhāgadatta in

---

260. D.B. Diskalkar, "Dravidian and South Indian Inscriptions," *JIH*, vol. XXXIV, p. 194.
261. Kaśākuḍi plates, *op. cit.*, v. 29, p. 350.
262. *SII*, vol. I, no. 25, pp. 15-16.
263. Kaśākuḍi plates, *op. cit.*, v. 29, p. 349.
264. Udayendiram plates, *op. cit.*, p. 366.

his knowledge of elephants (*śrī vāraṇa-bhāgadattaḥ*).[265]

Other heroes, famous in traditional Indian lore have been mentioned in these inscriptions. The story of king Śibi, the ruler of Uśīnara, very famous for his unbounded generosity has been recounted in the *Mahābhārata*.[266] This ruler is mentioned in the Tiruvālaṅgāḍu plates as one of the mythical ancestors of the Coḷa dynasty, and the famous act of this ruler who cut off a part of his body in order to save a pigeon is mentioned therein.[267] This ruler is also mentioned in the Karandai plates.[268]

Bhagīratha

The story of Bhagīratha, ruler of Ayodhyā, who undertook severe penance to bring the river Gaṅgā to the earth so that the souls of his ancestors could ascend to the heavens has been narrated in great detail in the *Rāmāyaṇa* of Vālmīki.[269] The penance of Bhagīratha has been glorified in Hindu lore in association with any sincere or great effort. The story of Bhagīratha and the penance he undertook are often mentioned in the Sanskrit inscriptions and the efforts of these Tamil kings are compared to Bhagīratha's own. The Tiruvālaṅgāḍu,[270] Karandai[271] and the Esālam[272] copper-plate inscriptions compare the effort taken by Rājendra I in bringing the waters of the Gaṅgā to the Coḷa country to the austerities undertaken by Bhagīratha in bringing the Gaṅgā to earth from heaven.

The Kanyākumārī inscription gives a very detailed account

---

265. *SII*, vol. I, No. 25, p. 18.
266. *Mahābhārata*, tr. M.N. Dutt, Vanaparva, Ch. 132.
267. Tiruvalaṅgāḍu plates, *op. cit.*, v. 27, p. 394.
268. K.G. Krishnan, *KTPR*, v. 5, p. 69.
269. *Śrīmad Vālmīki Rāmāyaṇam*, ed. by S. Kuppuswamy Sastrigal, Madras, 1958, Bālakāṇḍa, Sarga 42.
270. Tiruvālaṅgāḍu plates, *op. cit.*, v. 109, p. 400.
271. K.G. Krishnan, *KTPR*, v. 64, p. 74.
272. R. Nagaswamy, *ECPR*, v. 17, p. 32.

of Bhagīratha's penance very much in accordance with the narration of this episode found in the *Rāmāyaṇa*.[273]

Vaiṣṇava Lore

The composers of the Sanskrit inscriptions also display a remarkable knowledge of Vaiṣṇava lore, as a study of their epigraphs shows. Apart from the Vedas and the epics mentioned above, the poets were also very familiar with many Vaiṣṇava Purāṇas. There are many instances where several episodes mentioned in the Purāṇas have been handled by the poets. Viṣṇu is referred to in these inscriptions by many of his names such as Nārāyaṇa, Upendra, Acyuta, Madhusūdana, Hari, Mādhava, Puruṣottama, Śrīdhara, Janārdhana, Śrīpati, Śrīnivāsa, Murāri, Keśava, Indireśa, Padmāpati, Śārṅgin, Madhuripu, Kaṁsadviṣ, Padmanābha, Narakāri, Cakradhara, Kaitabhāri, Mukunda and Pañkajanābha.

Some of the epigraphs offer very vivid descriptions of Viṣṇu. The invocatory verse of the Paṭṭattāḷmaṅgalam plates is in praise of Viṣṇu,

> Let that body of the husband of Śrī (Viṣṇu) which is resplendent with the *kaustubha* jewel on its chest and which, with a hundred *marakata* like arms is lying on the ocean resembling a collection of clouds, lustrous, with the interspersed lightning and settling on the ocean to imbibe its water, grant you welfare.[274]

Other Pallava copper-plate grants containing beautiful invocatory verses in praise of Viṣṇu are the Kaśākuḍi,[275] Bāhūr[276] and the Veḷāñjeri plates of Aparājita.[277] Similarly many of the Coḷa copper-plate records such as the Anbil,[278] Larger Leiden,[279] Karandai[280] and Kanyākumārī[281] records all contain

273. Kanyākumārī inscription, *op. cit.*, v. 21, pp. 134-35.
274. *EI*, vol. XVIII, no. 14, v. 1, p. 120 (Paṭṭattāḷmaṅgalam plates).
275. Kaśākuḍi plates, *op. cit.*, v. 2, p. 346.
276. Bāhūr plates, *op. cit.*, v. 1, p. 9.
277. R. Nagaswamy, *TVCP*, *Veḷañjeri plates of Aparājita*, v. 1, plate I, p. 2.
278. Anbil plates, *op. cit.*, v. 1, p. 58.

benedictory verses praising this deity. Pāṇḍyan epigraphs containing similar verses are the Śrīvaramaṅgalam[282] and the Daḷavāipuram plates of Parāntaka Vīra-Nārāyaṇa.[283]

Some of the copper-plate grants of the vassal chieftains also contain beautiful Sanskrit verses in praise of Nārāyaṇa at the very beginning.[284]

DAŚĀVATĀRA

The Daśāvatāra concept found in many Purāṇas was well known to the poets of the Tamil country as one Sanskrit verse datable to the seventh century AD found in the Ādivarāha cave in Māmallapuram reveals. The Matsya, Kūrma, Varāha, Narasiṁha, Vāmana, Paraśurāma, Rāma, Balarāma, Buddha and Kalki *avatāras* are mentioned in this inscription.[285] It is notable that this description of the ten *avatāras* includes Buddha as the ninth *avatāra* in place of Kṛṣṇa.

VARĀHA

An inscription found at the Varadarājasvāmi temple, Kāñcīpuram dated AD 1316 of the period of the Kākatīya king Pratāparudra II contains a verse in praise of the boar incarnation (Varāha *avatāra*) of Viṣṇu, describing his feat of raising the earth from the waters with his tusks.[286]

TRIVIKRAMA

The Trivikrama *avatāra* so vividly described in the *Bhāgavata* Purāṇa[287] has been beautifully retold by the poet of the Kaśākuḍi charter in the introductory verse:

279. Larger Leiden plates, v. 1, p. 238.
280. K.G. Krishnan , *KTPR*, v. 1, p. 69.
281. Kanyākumārī plates, *op. cit.*, v. 3, pp. 129-30.
282. Śrīvaramaṅgalam plates of Pāṇḍyan Neduñjaḍaiyan, *PCP*, v. 2, p. 56.
283. T.N. Subramaniam, *DCVP*, v. 1, p. 13.
284. *SII*, vol. II, no. 76, v. 1, p. 382; *EI*, vol. III, no. 13, v. 2, p. 75.
285. *ARE*, 1922-23, no. 663.
286. *EI*, vol. VII, no. 18, v. 1, p. 130.
287. *Śrīmad Bhāgavata*, tr. Swami Tapasyānanda, Madras, 1982, Skanda VIII, Chapters 18-22.

> May that blessed Trivikrama (Viṣṇu) grant you prosperity, who, at the sacrifice of Bali asked (only) for three steps (of land), but suddenly expanded and strode thrice thereby appropriating the whole world.[288]

PARAŚURĀMA

The story of Paraśurāma, the sixth incarnation of Viṣṇu, mentioned in the *Bhāgavata Purāṇa*[289] and other ancient texts, is repeatedly mentioned by the poets of these epigraphs. The Tiruvālaṅgāḍu plates state that Rājarāja I conquered the Kerala country which was "the creation of Rāma," i.e., Paraśurāma, whose beloved vow was to annihilate the whole of the *kṣatra* race.[290] Again, in a reference to Rājendra Coḷa I's conquest of Keraḷa, the composer of the charter states,

> Having heard of the humiliation which the rulers of the earth were subjected to by (the sage) Bhārgava (Paraśurāma), on the battlefield, and not being able to meet him (Bhārgava) in battle on earth, the proud king (Madurāntaka) set his mind upon conquering the country called after him.[291]

This inscription also mentions that the Keraḷa country "was protected by the glorious son of the Bhṛgus, i.e., Paraśurāma" (*bhṛgu-kula-tilaka-prabhāva-guptām pṛthvīm*) and that Rājendra I "having conquered the Keraḷa king, took over the country protected by the austerities of the chief of the Bhṛgus" (*jitva keraḷa-bhūpatim bhṛgupateschitva tapo rakṣitam pṛthvīm*).[292] The Karandai inscription also refers to that place as being "protected by the penance of Bhārgava" (*bhārghavasya-tapasābhirakṣitaṁ*).[293]

---

288. Kaśākuḍi plates, *op. cit.*, v. 2, p. 346.
289. *Srīmad Bhāgavata, op. cit.*, Skanda IX, Chapters 15-16.
290. Tiruvālaṅgāḍu plates, *op. cit.*, v. 83, p. 398.
291. *Ibid.*, v. 94, p. 399.
292. *Ibid.*, vv. 95 and 97.
293. K.G. Krishnan, *KTPR*, v. 63, p. 74.

RĀMA

The incarnation of Rāma, made famous by the epic *Rāmāyaṇa* of Vālmīki, has been frequently referred to in the numerous Sanskrit inscriptions of the Tamil country. In many of the epigraphs, the poets compare the kings with Rāma who was a great archer. An inscription of Rājasiṁha describes this king as "resembling Rāma in war" (*śrī saṅgrāma rāmaḥ*),[294] while Nandivarman Pallavamalla is described in the Kaśākuḍi charter as "resembling Rāma in archery" (*kārmukhe rāmaḥ*).[295]

The feat of Rāma in building a bridge to cross over to Laṅkā referred to in the *Yuddhakāṇḍa* of the *Vālmīki Rāmāyaṇa* finds mention in the Tiruvālaṅgāḍu inscription.[296]

The killing of the demons Khara and Dūṣaṇa by Rāma mentioned in the *Vālmīki Rāmāyaṇa* is referred to in an inscription of Aparājita Pallava.[297] According to this inscription, Aparājita destroyed the burden of taxation and hardship in his country just as Rāma destroyed the demons Khara and Dūṣaṇa (*daśarathi-iva janasthāna vinihita kharadūṣaṇau*).

According to the *Vālmīki Rāmāyaṇa*, the four sons of Daśaratha were born as four parts of Viṣṇu. This idea is expressed in the Kanyākumārī inscription.[298] The character of Rāma as an ideal son, brother, husband and ruler as sketched in the *Vālmīki Rāmāyaṇa* has been described in this epigraph,[299] as also Rāma's impassionate adherence to righteous duties.[300]

The act of Rāma accepting back his queen Sītā after she had proved her purity in the fire-ordeal is mentioned in another epigraph.[301]

294. *SII*, vol. I, no. 25, p. 15.
295. Kaśākuḍi plates, *op. cit.*, v. 29, pp. 249-50.
296. Tiruvālaṅgāḍu plates, *op. cit.*, v. 80, p. 393.
297. R. Nagaswamy, *TVCP*, *Veḷāñjeri plates of Aparājita*, plate III, p. 1.
298. *TAS*, vol. I, no. 34, v. 24, pp. 135-36 (Kanyākumārī inscription).
299. *Ibid.*, v. 25, p. 136.
300. *Ibid.*, vv. 26-27, p. 136.
301. *EI*, vol. VII, no. 21, v. 10, p. 150.

KṚṢṆA

Strangely, there are hardly any references to the famous Kṛṣṇa *avatāra* in the Sanskrit inscriptions. Only one epigraph, the Śivanvāyal inscription, in characters of the seventh-eighth centuries AD, mentions a certain Pallava Siṁhavarman as being born "in the race of the Pallavas as God Viśvaksena (Viṣṇu) was born in the Vṛṣṇi race" (*viśvaksena iva vṛṣṇinām*),[302] thereby referring to the incarnation of Kṛṣṇa who was born in the Vṛṣṇi (Yādava) race.

ĀDIŚEṢA

Ādiśeṣa is famed in Vaiṣṇava lore as the serpent on whom Viṣṇu reclines in Vaikuṇṭha and as the one who supports the whole world. Many of the Sanskrit inscriptions contain references to Ādiśeṣa as the supporter of the earth. The Velūrpāḷaiyam plates state in a very poetic manner that the Pallava rulers extended help to Ādiśeṣa "who was fatigued by the labour of (carrying on his head) the burden of the earth."[303]

This same idea of the Tamil kings providing rest to Ādiśeṣa by bearing the burden of the earth is also mentioned in the Coḷa and Pāṇḍya inscriptions such as the Anbil,[304] Tiruvālaṅgāḍu[305] and Veḷvikuḍi plates.[306] The Larger Leiden[307] and Karandai[308] plates state that Rājarāja I bore the heavy burden of the earth on his arm which surpassed the lusture of the lord of serpents, Śeṣa. The Kanyākumārī inscription mentions that the arms of Rājendra II resembled the snake Ādiśeṣa in shape.[309]

---

302. *EI*, vol. XXVII, no. 13, p. 62 (Śivanvāyal inscription).
303. Velūrpāḷaiyam plates, *op. cit.*, v. 4, pp. 507-08.
304. Anbil plates, *op. cit.*, v. 25, p. 61.
305. Tiruvālaṅgāḍu plates, *op. cit.*, v. 63, pp. 396-97.
306. Veḷvikuḍi plates, *op. cit.*, v. 7, p. 299.
307. Larger Leiden plates, *op. cit.*, v. 30, p. 241.
308. K.G. Krishnan, *KTPR*, v. 26, p. 71.
309. Kanyākumārī inscription, *op. cit.*, v. 74, p. 147.

LAKṢMĪ

Lakṣmī, the consort of Viṣṇu, who is extolled as the Goddess of beauty, prosperity and wealth in many Sanskrit texts of ancient India has also been mentioned in the numerous Sanskrit epigraphs of the Tamil country. These epigraphs mention the different names of Lakṣmī such as Śrī, Padmāsanā, Padmā, Puṣkaradevatā, Ramā, Indirā, Kamalā and Sāgarakanyā.

Many of the invocatory verses of the Sanskrit charters are in praise of this Goddess. The Kaśākuḍi plates describe Lakṣmī thus:

> May Padmā (Lakṣmī) regard you with fondness, who is seated on a lotus, whose pair of lotus hands is resplendant with a lotus, (and) whose excellent bath (is poured from) golden jars which are held by the trunks of two female elephants.[310]

The authors of these inscriptions often compare the queens of the Tamil country to Goddess Lakṣmī. An inscription of Rājasiṁha records that his queen named Raṅgapatākā subdued the pride of Puṣkaradevatā (Lakṣmī).[311] The Bāhūr plates compare the queen of Nandivarman III named Śaṅkhā with Lakṣmī,[312] while the queen of Kaṁpavarman called Vijayā is also compared with this Goddess in the Veḷāñjeri plates.[313] The Paṭṭattāḷmaṅgalam inscription states poetically in praise of the Pallava dynasty that "Lakṣmī and the Goddess of the earth (Bhūdevī), having attained the status of the consorts of the kings of this family could not be appropriated by the assemblage of other kings."[314] A Pāṇḍyan queen named Vānavaṉmahādevī, the wife of Parāntaka Vīra-Nārāyaṇa is also compared to Śrī in the Larger Siṉṉamaṉūr plates.[315]

---

310. Kaśākuḍi plates, *op. cit.*, v. 5, p. 346.
311. *SII*, vol. I, no. 29, p. 23.
312. Bāhūr plates, *op. cit.*, v. 13, p. 10.
313. R. Nagaswamy, *TVCP*, *Veḷañjeri plates of Aparājita*, v. 8, plate II, p. 1.
314. Paṭṭattāḷmaṅgalam plates, *op. cit.*, v. 4, p. 120.
315. Larger Siṉṉamaṉūr plates, *op. cit.*, v. 15, p. 452.

Śaiva Lore

A very thorough knowledge of Śaiva lore as found in many Purāṇas and other religious works in ancient India has been exhibited by the composers of the Sanskrit charters in the Tamil country. Śiva is referred to in the epigraphs by many names and epithets such as Īśāna, Īśa, Devadeva, Īśvara, Śaṅkara, Śaṁbhu, Śarva, Hara, Sabhāpati, Pinākapāṇi, Indumauḷi, Rudra, Paśupati, Sadāśiva, Bhavānīpati, Adrisutādipa, Puradviṣaḥ, Candramouḷi, Candrārdhamauḷi, Śrīkaṇṭha, Parameśvara, Dhūrjaṭi, Bhava, Vr̥śāṅka, Vr̥ṣarājaketu, Maheśvara, Purāntaka, Purāri, Gaurīpati, Nr̥ttarāja, Girīśa, Nadipriya and Śūli.

Some of the events in Śaiva mythology are also recorded in these epigraphs. The story of Śiva receiving the river Gaṅgā, falling from the heavens on his own matted locks is mentioned in the Karandai plates.[316] References to Kailāśa, the abode of Śiva, as mentioned in numerous early Sanskrit works are also found mentioned in numerous Pallava epigraphs and also in Coḷa inscriptions such the Tiruvālaṅgāḍu,[317] Larger Leiden[318] and Esālam plates.[319]

Many of the Sanskrit inscriptions commence with invocatory verses in praise of Śiva and are rich in religious fervour. The Kaśākuḍi plates contain the following invocatory verse:

> May Hara (Śiva), the destroyer of Pura, increase your happiness, who bears the moon on his crest, who wears a serpent on his shoulder, who holds Bhavānī on his left, who bears affection to his worshipper, who bears Gaṅgā on his head, who wears ashes on his body, who bears poison in his neck, who wears a braid in his hair and who holds a spear in his hand.[320]

316. K.G. Krishnan, *KTPR*, v. 29, p. 71.
317. Tiruvālaṅgāḍu plates, *op. cit.*, v. 53, p. 419.
318. Larger Leiden plates, *op. cit.*, v. 2, p. 238.
319. R. Nagaswamy, *ECPR*, v. 10, pp. 31-32.
320. Kaśākuḍi plates, *op. cit.*, v. 3, p. 346.

Other invocatory verses praising and describing the form and attributes of Śiva are found in other Pallava inscriptions such as the Udayendiram[321] and the Velūrpāḷaiyam plates,[322] in Coḷa inscriptions such as the Anbil,[323] Esālam[324] and the Kanyākumārī[325] epigraphs and in Pāṇḍyan inscriptions such as the Veḷvikuḍi[326] and the Śrīvaramaṅgalam[327] plates.

The Udayendiram plates of the Bāṇa ruler Vikramāditya II[328] and the Udayendiram plates of Pṛthivīpati II Hastimalla[329] also contain beautiful invocatory verses to Śiva.

Śiva has been described as "eight-formed" (*aṣṭa-mūrti*) in an inscription of Rājasiṁha.[330] Pṛthivīpati's epigraph also describes him in the same manner.[331] This deity has been described in the same way by none less than the celebrated Sanskrit poet Kālidāsa in two of his works, the *Abhijñāna-Śākuntalam*[332] and *Raghuvaṁśam*[333] and it is possible that the poets of these inscriptions familiar with Kālidāsa's works, incorporated this term in their compositions.

PĀRVATĪ

Pārvatī, the consort of Śiva, is referred to in a number of Sanskrit epigraphs by various names such as Umā, Bhavānī,

321. Udayendiram plates, *op. cit.*, v. 1, pp. 365-66.
322. Velūrpāḷaiyam plates, *op. cit.*, v. 2, p. 510.
323. Anbil plates, *op. cit.*, v. 3, p. 59.
324. R. Nagaswamy, *ECPR*, v. 1, p. 31.
325. Kanyākumārī inscription, *op. cit.*, v. 1, p. 129.
326. Veḷvikuḍi plates, *op. cit.*, v. 1, p. 298.
327. Śrīvaramaṅgalam plates, *op. cit.*, v. 3, p. 56.
328. *EI*, vol. III, no. 13, v. 1, p. 75.
329. *SII*, vol. II, no. 76, v. 2, p. 382.
330. *SII*, vol. I, no. 21, v. 6, p. 7.
331. *SII*, vol. II, no. 76, v. 1, p. 382.
332. M.R. Kale (tr.), *The Abhijñānaśākuntalam of Kālidāsa*, Delhi, 1994, Act. I, p. 3.
333. M.R. Kale (tr.), *The Raghuvaṁśa of Kālidāsa* (Cantos I-IV), Bombay, 1925, Canto II, v. 35, p. 37.

Ambikā, Gaurī, Śarvāṇī, Adrisutā, Śāilasutā, Parvatendratanujā, Girijā, Śivā and Āryā. Many inscriptions contain invocatory verses in praise of Pārvatī such as the Kaśākuḍi[334] and the Tiruvālaṅgāḍu[335] plates. Many Pallava inscriptions also compare the queens of the royal family to this Goddess. Raṅgapatākā, the queen of Rājasiṁha[336] and Aggaḷanimmaṭī, the queen of Dantivarman[337] are compared to Pārvatī. Nandivarman III born to this Aggaḷanimmaṭī is compared to Skanda (Kumāra) being born to Ambikā.[338]

GAṆEŚA

The worship of Gaṇeśa was conspicuously absent in the Tamil country during the Saṅgam age. It appears that the cult of Gaṇeśa came into vogue in this area only during the Pallava period. It is believed that it was introduced into Tamiḻagam after the capture of Vātāpī from the Cāḷukyas by the Pallavas.[339] The Gaṇeśa icon brought from Vātāpī (Bādāmī) by Paranjyoti, the general of Narasiṁhavarman I was installed at Tirucenkkāṭānguḍi (Tañjāvūr district) and became famous as Vātāpi Gaṇapati.

The very first mention of Gaṇeśa in the Sanskrit inscriptions of the period of this study appears in the Kaśākuḍi plates. A beautiful invocatory verse praises this deity (Vināyaka) as "one who grants freedom from obstacles, who is as white as the Kailāśa mountain, who has a huge serpent as his girdle, who has the face of an elephant, whose ears are large, who has a single large tusk and whose eyes are half-closed as though under the influence of rut."[340]

334. Kaśākuḍi plates, *op. cit.*, v. 6, p. 346.
335. Tiruvālaṅgaḍu plates, *op. cit.*, v. 1, p. 393.
336. *SII*, vol. I, no. 29, p. 24.
337. Velūrpāḷaiyam plates, *op. cit.*, v. 18, p. 508.
338. *Ibid.*
339. K.K. Pillai, *A Social History of the Tamils*, Madras, 1975, p. 158.
340. Kaśākuḍi plates, *op. cit.*, v. 7, p. 346.

MURUGA

The composers of the Sanskrit records have also described Muruga, the son of Śiva and Pārvatī in many of their records and refer to him by many of his other names like Kumāra, Guha, Ṣaṇmukha, Subrahmaṇya and Mahāsena.

The birth of Kumāra to Śiva and Pārvatī seems to have caught the imagination of the poets of the Pallava charters. They are seen repeatedly comparing the birth of a son to the Pallava kings and queens to this mythological event in many of their inscriptions.[341] The spear or lance called Śakti wielded by this deity is mentioned in an inscription of Rājasiṁha[342] as well as in a Pāṇḍyan epigraph.[343]

It may be mentioned here that the Somaskanda bas-relief sculpture, with Śiva and Pārvatī seated with baby Skanda between them or seated on Pārvatī's lap is found in many of the Pallava monuments. It was characteristic of the periods of Parameśvaravarman I and Rājāsiṁha.[344]

HARIHARA

The concept of Harihara (or Śaṅkaranārāyaṇa), the combined form of Viṣṇu and Śiva seems to have been in vogue in the ancient Tamil country as indicated by many of the verses of the Vaiṣṇava saints, Āḻvars and the Śaiva saints, Nāyaṉmārs. A sculpture of Harihara of the Pallava period is found in the Ādivarāha cave temple in Māmallapuram. References to the Harihara concept are found in a few Pallava and Coḷa Sanskrit inscriptions. The introductory verse of the Kaśākuḍi plates[345] states:

> May Trivikrama and Hara protect you, whose distinct (but) united bodies (respectively) bear on the neck the

341. *SII*, vol. I, no. 24, v. 5, p. 12; Velūrpāḷaiyam plates, *op. cit.*, v. 19, p. 508; R. Nagaswamy, *TVCP*, *Veḷāñjeri Plates of Aparājita*, v. 9, plate II, p. 1.
342. *SII*, vol. I, no. 24, v. 5, p. 12.
343. Śrivaramaṅgalam plates, *op. cit.*, v. 6, p. 57.
344. K.R. Srinivasan, *The Dharmarāja Ratha and its Sculptures, Māmallapuram*, Delhi, 1975, p. 16.
345. Kaśākuḍi plates, *op. cit.*, v. 4, p. 346.

> supreme splendour of two ornaments, the kaustubha (jewel) and the black (poison), hold a discus and spear for the destruction of the *daityas*, black and white in colour, (and) thrill with joy at the expansion (of the eyes) of Śrī and Gaurī (which emit) coquettish glances (resembling) arrows.

The invocatory verse of the Udayendiram plates of Pṛthivīpati II describes Viṣṇu as the master of the universe of whom Śiva himself became one half of the body, thus referring to the Harihara concept.[346]

Brahmā

Brahmā, who according to Hindu mythology is the creator of the universe, is also referred to in many of the inscriptions. The Anbil plates describe Brahmā in a poetic style in the very manner in which this God has been portrayed in the ancient Sanskrit works thus:

> May that light, which is watchful in the sporting act of creating many worlds, which has its sight fixed at the tip of the nose, which has a mass of matted hair with the splendour of lightening, which dwells on the lotus springing out of the navel of the husband of Lakṣmī, which is self-crested and which is in the *svastīkāsana* posture, fulfil your desire for a long time.[347]

The Śrīvaramaṅgalam plates of Pāṇḍyan Neḍuñjaḍaiyaṉ also describe Brahmā in a similar mannar.[348]

Sarasvatī

Sarasvatī, revered down the ages in India as the Goddess of learning, has been referred to only twice by the poets in the epigraphs of the period of this study. The composer of the Tiruvālaṅgāḍu epigraph in an introductory verse very humbly says,

346. *SII*, vol. III, no. 76, v. 1, p. 382.
347. Anbil plates, *op. cit.*, v. 4, p. 59.
348. Śṛīvaramaṅgalam plates, *op. cit.*, v. 1, p. 56.

> The letters (of the alphabet), limited in number are only fifty; (whereas) the virtues of (the kings of) the Solar race are resplendent beyond number. How can I describe these (virtues) with those (letters)? Mother Sarasvatī secure for me (the help of) other letters (*lipi*) also.[349]

In the introductory verse of the Esālam plates, the poet echoes the very same sentiment and requests Sarasvatī to come to his rescue and bestow grace on him.[350]

Indra

Indra, the leader of the celestials (*deva*s) extolled in numerous Sanskrit works for his heroism has been referred to by the poets of the Sanskrit inscriptions by many of his names and epithets like Surendra, Jambāri, Surapati, Mahendra, Kuliśāyuda, Śatakratu, Vāsava, Sūtraman, Hari, Amareśvara, Śakra and Sahasrākṣa.

The composers of these records have time and again compared their kings with Indra. Some of the *biruda*s of Pallava Rājasiṁha were *śrī mahendraparākramaḥ* (he who resembles Mahendra in heroism)[351] and *śrī indralīlaḥ* (one who resembles Indra in grace).[352] Another epigraph of this king states that "like Indra he constantly protected those who followed the path of the three Vedas" (*trayīpātha-niṣeviṇāṁ satata-pālane-vāsavaḥ*).[353]

The Kumaraḍimaṅgalam plates mention that the heroism of Nandivarman III was equal to that of Indra (*vāsava vikramaḥ*)[354] while the Veḷāñjeri plates state that Aparājita Pallava "protected the world like Indra" (*rakṣan-nijendraika-gatiḥ*).[355]

---

349. Tiruvālaṅgāḍu plates, *op. cit.*, v. 3, p. 401.
350. R. Nagaswamy, *ECPR*, v. 2, p. 31.
351. *SII*, vol. I, no. 25, p. 16.
352. *Ibid.*, no. 26, p. 22.
353. *Ibid.*, no. 24, p. 12.
354. N. Ramesan, *KPPN*, v. 2, p. 201.
355. R. Nagaswamy, *TVCP*, *Veḷāñjeri plates of Aparājita*, v. 14, plate II, p. 2.

An epigraph of Tammusiddhi describes Indra as having a thousand eyes (*sahasrākṣa*)[356] and alludes to the famous story of sage Gautama cursing him for trying to covet his wife Ahalyā found in the *Skanda* Purāṇa.[357]

Time and again, the composers of the Sanskrit inscriptions refer to the kings as Narendra (Indra among men).

Indra's consort is also referred to in many of the epigraphs as Śacī, Indrāṇī, Pulomatanayā and Paulomī. Many of the queens are described as being devoted to their husbands as she was to Indra.[358] Another epigraph refers to her as the mother of Jayanta.[359]

Sages

Indian literature abounds with stories of sages, some of whom are considered to be divine. The divine *ṛṣis*, Nārada and Tuṁburu, famed for their musical prowess are mentioned in some Sanskrit epigraphs.

Agastya, a famous sage in Hindu mythology is mentioned in some of the Sanskrit inscriptions. Pallava records such as the Kūram,[360] Kaśākuḍi[361] and the Udayendiram[362] plates mention this sage in connection with his killing of the demon named Vātāpi. However, it is only in the Pāṇḍyan records that this sage is mentioned more often as the Pāṇḍyan rulers considered him as their spiritual preceptor. The Veḷvikuḍi,[363] Larger Siṉṉamaṉūr,[364] Śrīvaramaṅgalam plates[365] and the

356. *EI*, vol. VII, no. 21A, v. 26, p. 151.
357. G.V. Tagare (tr.), *The Skanda Purāṇa*, Delhi, 1977, Ch. 31, vv. 72-75, p. 124.
358. N. Ramesan, *op. cit.*, v. 4, p. 201; Larger Siṉṉamaṉūr plates, *op. cit.*, v. 15, p. 342.
359. Velūrpāḷaiyam plates, *op. cit.*, v. 19, p. 508.
360. Kūram plates, *op. cit.*, l. 17, p. 148.
361. Kaśākuḍi plates, *op. cit.*, v. 22, p. 349.
362. Udayendiram plates, *op. cit.*, l. 14, p. 366.
363. Veḷvikuḍi plates, *op. cit.*, v. 3, p. 298.
364. Larger Siṉṉamaṉūr plates, *op. cit.*, v. 3, p. 451.
365. Śrīvaramaṅgalam plates, *op. cit.*, v. 4, p. 56.

Daḷavāipuram[366] plates all state that Agastya was their family priest. The feats of this sage in preventing the Vindhya mountains from growing further and also drinking the waters of the ocean are also mentioned in the Veḷvikuḍi and the Śrīvaramaṅgalam plates.

The wife of sage Vaśiṣṭha, named Arundhatī, is referred to in many early Indian works such as the *Rāmāyaṇa* as being very devoted to her husband. The Tiruvālaṅgāḍu plates while referring to the performance of *sati* by queen Vanavaṉmahādevī on the death of her husband Sundara Coḷa compares her with Arundhatī in her devotion towards her husband.[367]

The great sage and devotee of Lord Naṭarāja of Cidambaram, Vyāgrapāda (Pulikkāl Munivar in Tamil) so called because he is believed to have had the eyes, feet and claws of a tiger (*vyāghra*) also figures in some of the Sanskrit epigraphs. An inscription of Naralokavīra, the general of Kulottuṅga Coḷa I, mentions that he constructed a temple for God Paśupati (Śiva) whose feet were worshipped by Sage Vyāghrapāda.[368]

Many of the copper-plate charters of the Coḷa kings refer to Cidambaram as Vyāghrāgrahāra, after the name of this sage.[369] Vyāghrāgrahāra is Perumpaṟṟapuliyūr (Puliyūr) in Tamil inscriptions.

The poets of the period under study not only had an excellent knowledge of the epics but also frequently even borrowed some phrases in their works. One of the inscriptions of Narasiṁhavarman I found in the Dharmarāja Ratha at Māmallapuram contains one of his *biruda*s *satyaparākramaḥ* and this very same epithet is found in the *Vālmīki Rāmāyaṇa* to praise Rāma.[370]

366. T.N. Subramanian, *DCPV*, v. 7, p. 14.

367. Tiruvālaṅgāḍu plates, *op. cit.*, v. 65, p. 397.

368. *SII*, vol. XXVI, no. 390, p. 254.

369. Larger Leiden plates, *op. cit.*, v. 17, p. 239; Karandai plates, *op. cit.*, v. 18, p. 70; R. Nagaswamy, *ECPR*, v. 10, p. 31.

370. C. Sivaramamurti, *Epigraphical Echoes of Kālidāsa*, Madras, 1944, p. 9.

The influence of classical Sanskrit poets such as Kālidāsa can be seen very clearly in the works of the poets of the Pallava Pāṇḍya and Coḷa periods. While Ravikīrti, the author of the famous Aihoḷe inscription[371] of the western Cāḷukya king, Pulakeśin II, has openly compared his fame as a poet with Kālidāsa and Bhāravi (*ravikīrtiḥ=kavitāśrita-kālidāsa-bhāravi-kīrtiḥ*), it can be seen that the poets of the Tamil country also admired these classical poets as they have consciously or unconsciously borrowed from their works in many places.

The *Raghuvaṁśam* of Kālidāsa, in particular, seems to have caught the fancy of the composers of some of the Sanskrit inscriptions. A line from the *Raghuvaṁśam*: *saṅgrāma nirviṣṭa-sahasrabāhur=aṣṭādaśa-dvīpa-nikhāta-yūpaḥ* has been incorporated in describing the valorous deeds of Narasiṁhavarman I in the Kūram grant of Pallava Parameśvaravarman thus: *sahasrabāhor=iva samara-śata-nirviṣṭa-sahasrabāhu-karmaṇaḥ*.[372]

A description of the Pāṇḍyan king contained in Kālidāsa's *Raghuvaṁśam: vindhyasya samstambhayitā mahādrer=niḥśeṣa pīto-jjhita-sindhurājaḥ, prīthyāśvamedhāvabhṛt-ārdramūrteḥ sausnātiko yasya bhavaty=agastyaḥ* seems to have been incorporated by the poet-composer of the Veḷvikuḍi grant thus: *aṣṭambhayat=kṣitidharam=pravijṛmbhamāṇam=ambhas=samastam=apibaj=jaladheś=ca yas=saḥ kumbhodbhavo bhavati yasya muniḥ=purodhās=sa śrī-nidhir-jjayati pāṇḍya-narendra-vaṁśaḥ*.[373]

Several verses in the Tiruvālaṅgāḍu copper-plates also bear close resemblence to the ideas expressed by Kālidāsa in his *Raghuvaṁśa*.[374]

Metres

The Sanskrit poets of ancient and medieval India used a large variety of metres in their excellent compositions. A study of

371. *EI*, vol. VI, no. 1, v. 37, p. 7.
372. C. Sivaramamurti, *op. cit.*, p. 29.
373. *Ibid.*, p. 30.
374. Tiruvālaṅgāḍu plates, *op. cit.*, v. 8, p. 393 and v. 118, p. 400 correspond to Canto VI, v. 61 and Canto IV, v. 45 respectively.

the Sanskrit inscriptions reveals that the poet-composers of these epigraphs have also employed numerous metres in their works.

As in the case with classical Sanskrit poetry, most of these Sanskrit inscriptions of the Tamil country were composed in the *anuṣṭubh* metre although a variety of other metres such as *upajāti, pṛthvī, śārdūlavikrīḍita, indravajra, gīti, āryā, vasantatilakā* and others were also employed. Many of the Pallava inscriptions such as the Guṇapadeya,[375] Oṁgoḍu (II),[376] Dalavānūr,[377] Māmaṇḍūr[378] and the Reyūrū inscriptions[379] are composed wholly in the *anuṣṭubh* metre.

The poets have used a very large variety of metres in the bigger epigraphs. The composer of the Kūram plates has used the *sragdharā, śārdūlavikrīḍita, anuṣṭubh, sugītī, āryagīti, prāgīti, gīti, lalitā, vasantatilakā* and *mālinī* in this inscription.[380] In the Paṭṭattāḷmaṅgalam plates, the metres named *śikhariṇī, śārdūlavikrīḍita, indravajra, praharṣiṇi, puṣpitāgrā, rathodhatā* and *āryā* are found used.[381] Similarly, the other large Pallava inscriptions such as the Kaśākuḍi,[382] the Taṇḍantoṭṭam[383] and the Udayendiram[384] plates contain a large variety of metres.

The Veḷvikuḍi copper-plates of the Pāṇḍyas contains metres such as *vaṁśasta, anuṣṭubh, vasantatilakā, śārdūlavikrīḍita, mālabhāriṇī, upendravajrā, drutavilambita* and *āryā*.[385] The Larger Siṉṉamaṉūr plates also contain a large variety of beautiful metres such as *upajāti, vaiśvadevī, upendravajrā, puṣpitāgrā, śālinī,*

---

375. *EI*, vol. VIII, no. 12, pp. 143-47 (Guṇapadeya plates).
376. Oṁgoḍu (II) plates, *op. cit.*, pp. 254-55.
377. *EI*, vol. XII, no. 27, p. 225 (Dalavānūr inscription).
378. *SII*, vol. IV, no. 136, p. 12 (Māmaṇḍūr inscription).
379. Reyūrū plates, *op. cit.*, pp. 95-96.
380. Kūram plates, *op. cit.*, pp. 148-50.
381. Paṭṭattāḷmaṅgalam plates, *op. cit.*, pp. 120-21.
382. Kaśākuḍi plates, *op. cit.*, pp. 346-51.
383. Taṇḍantoṭṭam plates, *op. cit.*, pp. 520-21.
384. Udayendiram plates, *op. cit.*, pp. 265-70.
385. Veḷvikuḍi plates, *op. cit.*, pp. 298-300.

drutavilambita, anuṣṭubh, indravajra, mandākrāntā, śārdūlavikrīḍita, sragdharā and *vasantatilakā*.[386]

The Sanskrit *praśasti* portions of the copper-plate charters of the Coḷas are much longer than those of the Pallavas and the Pāṇḍyas and are composed in a variety of metres. The Sanskrit portion of the Anbil plates, consisting of forty-six verses have been composed in seventeen metres like *mandākrāntā, śārdūlavikrīḍita, sragdharā, vasantatilakā, puṣpitāgrā, hāriṇī, anuṣṭubh, rathoddhatā, mañjubhāṣiṇī, praharśiṇī, upendravajra, āryā, sundarī, vaṁśasta, upajāti, indravajrā* and *svāgatā*.[387]

The bi-lingual Karandai copper-plate record, the biggest among the Coḷa copper-plate grants has seventy-six verses in the Sanskrit portion, composed in seventeen metres like *śārdūlavikrīḍita, sragdharā, anuṣṭubh, vasantatilakā, upajāti, viyoginī, mālinī, puṣpitāgrā, rucirā, mandakrāntā, pramitākṣarā, vaṁśasthavila, mañjubhāṣiṇī, pṛthvi, svāgatā, rathoddhatā* and *praharśiṇī*.[388]

The other large bi-lingual copper-plate grants of the period of Rājendra Coḷa I like the Larger Leiden plates consisting of forty-eight verses,[389] the Tiruvālaṅgāḍu grant composed in a hundred and thirty-seven verses,[390] the Esālam plates consisting of thirty-five verses[391] and also the Kanyākumārī lithic inscription[392] and the Cārāla copper-plates of Vīra-Rājendra[393] consisting of eighty-one verses have all been composed in a variety of metres, revealing the skill of the poet-composers of these *praśasti*s.

A few verses from well-known Sanskrit literary works

---

386. Larger Siṉṉamaṉur plates, *op. cit.*, pp. 451-54.
387. Anbil plates, *op. cit.*, pp. 58-64.
388. K.G. Krishnan, *KTPR*, pp. 69-76.
389. Larger Leiden plates, *op. cit.*, pp. 238-43.
390. Tiruvālaṅgāḍu plates, *op. cit.*, pp. 393-401.
391. R. Nagaswamy, *ECPR*, pp. 31-33.
392. Kanyākumārī inscription, *op. cit.*, pp. 129-49.
393. Cārāla plates, *op. cit.*

are also found inscribed in certain temples. An epigraph found on a pillar in a *maṇḍapa* in the Kacchapeśvara temple in Kāñcīpuram[394] belonging to the tenth century AD, contains six verses from the famous *Sūrya Śataka* (a hymn to the Sun God consisting of about a hundred verses) by the well-known poet, Mayūra who flourished in Harṣavardhana's court in the seventh century AD and who is believed to be the father-in-law of the celebrated Sanskrit writer Bāṇa.[395] It was probably a votive pillar erected in honour of the Sun-God (Sūrya-deva) one of the five Pañcasandhi deities (Aiñjanḍidevar in Tamil) who is installed in a small shrine in the compound of the same temple.[396]

An epigraph from the Udvahanāthasvāmi temple at Tirumaṇañjeri (Māyavaram district) contains some verses from the *Agni* Purāṇa praising Lord Udvahanātha.[397]

Fine-Arts

The pursuit of the fine-arts such as music, dance and painting has always been extremely popular in India since the ancient period. The Vedas mention musicians and several musical instruments such as the lute, flute, conches and drums. The *Sāmaveda* itself is a tribute to the standards achieved in vocal music in ancient India. The epics and the Purāṇas also mention kings like Arjuna and Udayana who were proficient in the fine-arts. The *Arthaśāstra*, while enumerating the different types of training that a king should undergo, states that the ruler should be trained in the arts also.[398]

In ancient India, the arts were divided into sixty-four categories. Every prince and princess, every son and daughter of aristocrats had to gain proficiency in all or most or at least

394. *ARE*, 81 of 1921; see also C. Sivaramamurti, *Indian Epigraphy and South Indian Scripts*, Madras, 1966, pp. 1 and 41.
395. A.B. Keith, *A History of Sanskrit Literature*, Delhi, 1996, p. 201.
396. *ARE*, 1921, Pt. II, para. 78, pp. 115-16.
397. *ARE*, no. 23 of 1914; see also S. Gurumurthy, *Education in South India*, Madras, 1979, p. 157.
398. *KA*, II. 5, 12.

some of these arts failing which he or she would not get a honoured place in society.[399]

References to the sixty-four arts are found in the *Viṣṇu* Purāṇa, *Bhāgavata* Purāṇa and the *Harivaṁśa*.[400]

The *Kāma-sūtra* of Vātsyāyana,[401] the commentary *Jayamaṅgalā* on the *Kāma-sūtra* and Bhoja's *Śṛṅgāra Prakāśa*[402] give detailed lists of these sixty-four arts. Bāṇabhaṭṭa, the court-poet of king Harṣavardhana, in his Sanskrit prose-romance, *Kādambarī* has given a list of the arts in which the hero of this work, prince Candrāpīḍa excelled.[403]

In the Tamil country also, in the Saṅgam period, the fine-arts were pursued with great zeal. Many of the Saṅgam works especially the *Śilappadikāram*, show the high level of attainment of the ancient Tamils in the field of fine-arts.

The interest evinced in the development of the fine-arts in the Saṅgam age was carried on in the subsequent periods in the Tamil country. The inscriptions reveal that encouragement was given to the development of the fine-arts during the period of the Pallavas, Pāṇḍyas and Coḷas and that some of these rulers themselves excelled in certain arts. The Kūram plates describe Parameśvaravarman I as one "who was clever in the sport of the fine-arts" (*caturaḥ kalāvilāse*).[404] The Udayendiram plates state that Nandivarman I was "well-versed in all the fine-arts" (*sakala-kalā-pariṇataḥ*)[405] while Parāntaka I is praised in the Anbil charter as "skilled in all the fine-arts" (*kalā-kuśalatā*).[406] The Karandai epigraph describes Rājendra I as "well-versed in the arts" (*prājñaḥ kalāsu*).[407]

---

399. Anil Baran Ganguly, *Sixty-Four Arts in Ancient India*, New Delhi, 1962, p. 2.
400. *Ibid.*
401. B.N. Basu (tr.), *Kāma-Sūtra of Vātsyāyana*, Calcutta, 1948, pp. 9-10.
402. V. Raghavan, *Bhoja's Śṛṅgāra Prakāśa*, Madras, 1963, pp. 660-61.
403. *Bāṇa's Kādambarī*, ed. M.R. Kale, Delhi, 1968.
404. Kūram plates, *op. cit.*, l. 19, p. 148.
405. Udayendiram plates, *op. cit.*, l. 19, p. 366.
406. Anbil plates, *op. cit.*, v. 20, p. 61.
407. K.G. Krishnan, *KTPR*, v. 75, p. 75.

Ravivarman Kulaśekhara, the Cera ruler has been praised as *catuśṣaṣṭikalā-vallabha* (the favourite of the sixty-four arts) in some of his Sanskrit records found in the Tamil country.[408]

Among the vassal chiefs, Parañjaya, a Bāṇa chieftain under Nṛpatuṅga has been described as being "well-versed in the arts" (*kalājñaḥ*).[409] The Karandai inscription describes the feudatories who always accompanied Rājendra I in a similar way.[410]

Some of the queens of the Tamil country are also mentioned in the epigraphs as being skilled in the fine-arts. The Bāhūr plates mention that the queen of Nandivarman III, a Rāṣṭrakūṭa princess named Śaṅkhā, possessed "intelligence, beauty and the arts" (*mati-kānti-kalādimatyām=mānyā*).[411] Apart from royalty some commoners also had training in the arts. The Kaśākuḍi plates mention that a brāhmaṇa named Jeṣṭhapāda Somayājin "had a knowledge of the arts" (*kalākauśala peśalaḥ*).[412]

Music

Music, which included both vocal (*gītam*) and instrumental music (*vādyam*) were included in the list of the traditional sixty-four arts which were to be cultivated by the refined. The well-known list of sixty-four arts given by Vātsyāyana in his *Kāma-sūtra* includes both vocal and instrumental music.[413]

Bhoja's *Śṛṅgāra Prakāśa* and the commentary *Jayamaṅgalā* on the *Kāma-sūtra*, while sometimes differing from Vātsyāyana's list also mention vocal music (*gītam*) and instrumental music (*vādyam*) among the sixty-four arts.[414] Bāṇabhaṭṭa mentions in his *Kādambarī* that prince Candrāpīḍa had mastered the science of music (*gāndharvaveda*),[415] thus

408. *EI*, vol. IV, no. 17, l. 6, p. 147; *Ibid.*, no. 18, l. 4, p. 149.
409. T.V. Mahalingam, *IOP*, p. 441 (Ciṟṟūr plates).
410. K.G. Krishnan, *KTPR*, v. 56, p. 74.
411. Bāhūr plates, *op. cit.*, v. 15, p. 10.
412. Kaśākuḍi plates, *op. cit.*, l. 83, p. 350.
413. B.N. Basu, *op. cit.*
414. V. Raghavan, *op. cit.*
415. *Bāṇa's Kādambarī*, *op. cit.*

showing that it must have been mandatory for kings and princes of ancient India to learn this art.

The Sanskrit inscriptions of the Tamil country reveal that many of the kings of the Pallava, Pāṇḍya and Coḷa dynasties patronized music and that some of them were outstanding musicians. Of all the musical-minded kings of south India, Mahendravarman I must be ranked as the topmost, so great was his contribution to the field of music.

One of the *biruda*s of Mahendravarman I was *saṅkīrṇajāti* which appears in his Pallāvaram[416] and Tirucirāpaḷḷi[417] cave inscriptions. According to Krishna Sastri, *saṅkīrṇajāti* is the name of a variety of musical time and that Mahendravarman held it because he was the inventor of this type of *tāla*.[418]

The famous musical inscription in Sanskrit in Pallava-Grantha characters of the seventh century AD, found on a rock behind the Śikhanāthasvāmi temple at Kuḍimiyāmalai (Pudukottai)[419] which contains groups of musical notes arranged for the benefit of his disciples by a Śaiva ruler, who was the disciple of a certain Rudrācārya (*śrī rudrācārya śiṣyeṇa paramamāheśvareṇa rājña śiṣya-hitārtham kṛtaḥ svarāgamaḥ*) has been assigned by scholars like C. Minakshi[420] and T.N. Ramachandran[421] to Mahendravarman I. K.A. Nilakanta Sastri has opined that this epigraph, which consists of exercises to be practised on stringed instruments has been without good reason assigned to Mahendravarman I.[422] Several scholars have commented on the great importance of this epigraph in the history of Indian music, the earliest among them being P.R.

416. *SII*, vol. XII, no. 13, p. 7 (Pallāvaram inscription).
417. *SII*, vol. XII, no. 8, p. 4 (Tirucirāpaḷḷi inscription).
418. C. Minakshi, *ASLP*, p. 264.
419. *EI*, vol. XII, no. 28, pp. 231-37 (Kuḍimiyāmalai inscription).
420. C. Minakshi, *ASLP*, pp. 269-70.
421. T.N. Ramachandran, *op. cit.*, p. 303.
422. K.A. Nilakanta Sastri, *A History of South India*, Madras, 1988, p. 364.

Bhandarkar[423] and B. Sambamurthy.[424] More recently other scholars like S. Ramanathan[425] and V. Premalatha[426] have also analysed this epigraph in great detail and therefore the technical details are not presented here.

Another inscription of Mahendravarman I from Māmaṇḍūr mentions the *Gāndharvaśāstra* in the first line.[427] C. Minakshi has stated that in this damaged inscription, the king has recorded his composition of the Kuḍimiyāmalai music and his experiments with it on an instrument.[428]

While P.R. Bhandarkar[429] has suggested that the instrument for which the music of the inscription was intended was the *vīṇā*, C. Minakshi holds the view that it was the *parivādinī* or a seven-stringed instrument similar to the *vīṇā* that was used, a small label containing the reading *parivādinī* found on the Valampuri Gaṇeśa shrine at Kuḍimiyāmalai confirming this view.[430]

Another epigraph which contains information about music is the Tirumayyam inscription found on the rock-cut cave temple of Śiva at Tirumayyam in Pudukoṭṭai district.[431] This inscription also contains musical notations similar to that of the Kuḍimiyāmalai epigraph. The instrument *parivādinī* is also mentioned in this inscription.

The Pallava ruler, Rājasiṁha also appears to have been an accomplished musician. Some of the titles of Rājasiṁha found at the Kailāśanātha temple at Kāñcīpuram are *śrī*

---

423. Kuḍīmiyāmalai inscription, *op. cit.*
424. C. Minakshi, *ASLP*, pp. 278-307.
425. S. Ramanathan, "Music from Inscriptions," from *Seminar on Inscriptions* ed. R. Nagaswamy, Madras, 1966, pp. 32-35.
426. V. Premalatha, "Inscription on Music," from *Seminar on Inscriptions*, ed. R. Nagaswamy, Madras, 1966, pp. 29-31.
427. *SII*, vol. IV, no. 136, p. 12 (Māmaṇḍūr inscription).
428. C. Minakshi, *ASLP*, p. 271.
429. *EI*, vol. XII, p. 228.
430. C. Minakshi, *ASLP*, p. 272.
431. *Ibid.*, p. 275.

vādyavidyādharaḥ (a *vidyādhara* on the instrument), *śrī ātodya tumburu* (he who resembles Tumburu in the knowledge of musical instruments), and *śrī vīṇā nāradaḥ* (he who resembles Nārada in the playing of the *vīṇa*).[432]

Nandivarman Pallavamalla also appears to have been proficient in music. The Kaśākuḍi plates compare this ruler with the king of Vatsa who is famous in Sanskrit literature as having excelled in the field of music (*vādyaviṣaye vatseśvaraḥ*).[433]

The Pāṇḍyan ruler Parāntakan Neḍuñjaḍaiyaṉ seems to have been an excellent musician. The Tamil portion of the Veḷvikuḍi charter praises this king using the Sanskrit term *gīta kinnaran* (a *kinnara* in music).[434]

The Coḷa ruler, Rājendra III held the *biruda*s *gāna-vidyā-vallabha*[435] (one who is fond of music) and *rāja-gāna-vidyā-vallabha* (the best among those who are fond of music).[436]

Dance

Dance (*nr̥tyam* or *nr̥ttam*) was considered to be one of the sixty-four arts and is mentioned next only to music in the lists provided by Vātsyāyana, the commentary *Jayamaṅgalā* and the *Śr̥ṅgāra Prakāśa*.

The art of dance was very popular in the ancient Tamil country and various types of dances are mentioned in many of the Saṅgam works such as the *Śilappadikāram*.

The Sanskrit inscriptions of the Pallava period do not throw any light on the art of dancing during that age. However, the sculptures adorning the walls of the Kailāśanātha temple in Kāñcīpuram depict Lord Śiva in many of the dance-poses enumerated in the *Nāṭya-Śāstra*. A queen of Rājasiṁha, Raṅgapatākā, who was associated with the construction of the Kailāśanātha temple in Kāñcīpuram may

432. *SII*, vol. I, no. 25, pp. 14-18.
433. Kaśākuḍi plates, *op. cit.*, p. 349.
434. Veḷvikuḍi plates, *op. cit.*, p. 302.
435. *ARE*, 515 of 1922.
436. *ARE*, 77 of 1913.

be presumed to have been an expert Bharatanāṭyam dancer as her name indicates.[437]

The Coḷas following in the footsteps of their predecessors encouraged this fine-art. Large numbers of dancing girls were dedicated to temples to perform as part of the devotional services to the Lord as can be gleaned from numerous Tamil inscriptions. The numerous *karaṇa*s depicted in Bharata's *Nāṭya-Śāstra* have been beautifully sculpted in the temples at Tañjāvūr, Kuṁbakoṇam, Cidambaram, Paḻayārai and other places.[438]

The western *gopura* of the Cidambaram temple has sculptures of the *karaṇa*s which bear inscribed labels below each of them indicating the name of the *karaṇa*.[439] J.C. Harle has opined that the west *gopura* is the oldest of the four *gopura*s of the Naṭarāja temple.[440] According to B. Natarajan, the western *gopura* is the most ancient one in this temple and belongs to the reign of Vikrama Coḷa and was perhaps completed during the period of his successor Kulottuṅga Coḷa II.[441]

Similarly the eastern *gopura* of this temple has sculptures depicting various Bharatanāṭya *karaṇa*s with accompanying inscriptions[442] (see Appendix). Kopperuñjiṅga, the Kāḍava ruler was a patron of dance as can be seen from his *biruda bharatamalla* found in an inscription of this ruler from Āttūr.[443] His Tamil inscription from Tiruvaṇṇāmalai[444] mentions several more of

437. C. Minakshi, *ASLP*, p. 311.
438. B. Venkatraman, *Rājarājeśvaram — The Pinnacle of Coḷa Art*, Madras, 1985, pp. 132-33.
439. *ARE*, 368 of 1913.
440. James C. Harle, *Temple Gateways in South India*, New Delhi, 1995, pp. 65-66.
441. B. Natarajan, *Tillai and Naṭarāja*, Madras, 1994, pp. 154-55.
442. *ARE*, 343 of 1913.
443. *SII*, vol. XII, no. 120, pp. 58-59; *ARE*, 286 of 1921.
444. *SII*, vol. VIII, no. 69, pp. 38-40; *ARE*, 480 of 1902.

his *biruda*s such as *bharatamvaḷḷaperumāḷ* and *bharatamvaḷḷan* which testify to his knowledge of the *Nāṭya-Śāstra*.

Several Sanskrit records of this ruler found outside Tamil Nadu reveal his interest in this art. The Drākṣārāma[445] (Andhra Pradesh) inscription describes Kopperuñjiṅga as *nāṭyākhyavedāmbudhiḥ* (the ocean of the art of dancing or the *Nāṭya-Śāstra*) and as *bharatārṇavapāriṇaḥ* (one who has crossed the ocean of Bharatanāṭyam).[446] In his Sanskrit epigraph from Tripurāntakam, (Andhra Pradesh) he is called *bharatārṇava-karṇadhāraḥ* (the helmsman in the ocean of Bharata's *Nāṭya-Śāstra*).[447] The same record mentions that this ruler built the eastern *gopura* of the Naṭarāja temple and the decorations on the four sides of this *gopura* are said to have been made with the booty acquired from his enemies.[448]

According to B. Natarajan, the gateway portion of this *gopura* was constructed in the days of the Coḷa king, Kulottuṅga II in the twelfth century AD and that the *karaṇa*s with the inscribed labels belong to the period of the later Coḷas, Kopperuñjiṅga having merely added the embellishments to the east *gopuram* with his booty.[449]

Some of the panels depicting dancing figures around the eastern *gopura* of the Śārṅgapāṇi temple in Kuṁbakoṇam also bear labels describing these dance-poses in *grantha* script of about the twelfth century AD.[450] The names of the different *karaṇa*s depicted are *vikṣiptam, uromaṇḍalikam, gṛddhravalīnakam, sucīvṛtam, vaiśākarecitam, bhramarakam, caturam, ākṣiptam, vṛścikarecitam, vartitam, ardhamaṭṭali, ardhasūci, cakramaṇḍalam, vṛścikakuṭṭitam, kuñcitam, viṣṇukrāntam, vikṣiptakṣiptakam, kaṭibhrāntam, nikuñcitam, daṇḍapakṣam, samanakham, svastikarecitam, maṇḍalasvastikam, nāgapāśārpitam, arggalam, tālapuṣpapuṭam, lalātatilakam* and *nūpuram*.

445. *SII*, vol. IV, no. 1341, pp. 471-72; *ARE*, 419 of 1893.
446. *SII*, vol. IV, no. 1342B; *ARE*, 419C of 1893.
447. *SII*, vol. XII, no. 247, p. 155.
448. *SII*, vol. XII, no. 247, pp. 154-55; *ARE*, 198 of 1905.
449. B. Natarajan, *op. cit.*, p. 157.
450. *ARE*, 279 of 1964-65.

A label below a panel built into the *maṇḍapa* near the tank in the Kumbheśvarasvāmin temple, Kumbakoṇam contains the name of one *karaṇa, udvṛttam*.[451]

Some of the scholar-composers of the Sanskrit epigraphs also seem to have been conversant with Bharatanāṭyam. One of the poets having the honorofic title Salalavidyācakravartin, identified with Śokkavilli of the Śrīraṅgam records of the period of Hoysala Vīra-Rāmanātha and the author of the *Gadyakarṇāmṛta* reveals clearly in this work his knowledge and familiarity with this dance form.[452]

Another Vidyācakravartin who composed an epigraph of Ballāla III found in Kañcīpuram was the author of many literary works, including the *Bharatasaṁgraha*.[453]

Painting

The art of painting (*citram* or *citravidhiḥ*) was again, like music and dance considered to be one of the sixty-four arts fit to be cultivated by the refined. Painting developed to a high degree of perfection during the Saṅgam age. In the succeeding periods of Tamil history also, the art of painting continued to flourish. The Pallava court played an important part in the development of the art of painting and patronizing skilled painters who were attracted to it by royal patronage.[454]

Mahendravarman I bore the title *citrakārapuli*[455] (tiger among artists), which reveals his interest and proficiency in the art of painting. The Māmaṇḍūr inscription of this ruler mentions that he caused to be compiled a commentary (*vṛtti*) known as *Dakṣiṇacitra* (south Indian art or painting) following the methods and rules laid down for such a work (*yathāvidhi*),

---

451. *ARE*, 280 of 1964-65.
452. S.S. Janaki, *op. cit.*, p. 137.
453. V. Raghavan, "The Bharatasaṁgraha of Vidyācakravartin," *ABORI*, vol. XIV, pp. 256-57.
454. C. Minakshi, *ASLP*, p. 320.
455. Pallāvaram inscription, *op. cit.*, p. 7.

after classifying the subject from an old work.[456] It is evident that he analysed the subject of painting that was laid down in an earlier work (*kalpa*) which was probably cumbrous or not clear or which had perhaps to be revised in the light of later inventions in the field.[457]

The paintings belonging to the period of the Pallavas such as the traces of paintings found in the Kailāśanātha temple at Kāñcīpuram reveal the talent of the painters of that period.

The murals found in the Bṛhadīśvara temple at Tañjāvūr convey the depth of talent of the painters of the period. Some of the paintings such as those of Dakṣiṇāmūrti, Rājarāja and the three queens worshipping Naṭarāja, Rājarāja and Karuvūr Devar and the thematic panel representing the episodes in the life of Sundaramūrti Nāyanār are well-known exquisite masterpieces of Coḷa painting.

Sculpture

It appears that sculptors (*śilpin*) were sometimes made to engrave the royal orders on copper-plates. The Veḷañjeri plates of Aparājita Pallava record that a person named Vijayaṇṇa, "foremost of *śilpins*" (*śilpāgragaṇyaḥ*), "hailing from Kāñcī" (*kāñcīpurāvāptabhavaḥ*), "a connoisseur of art" (*kalāvat*) and "who was well-known, inscribed this *praśasti*" (*praśastimetām-alikhatpraśasti*).[458]

The Larger Leiden plates state in the Sanskrit section that this record was engraved by Rājarāja-Mahācārya (Rājarājapperācāryaṉ in the Tamil section), otherwise called Vāsudeva, son of Kṛṣṇan, his brothers, Śrīraṅga and Dāmodara, the son of Vāsudeva named Kṛṣṇa and the son of Āravamuta named Puruṣottama, the five artists (*citrakāriṇaḥ*) who "were the forehead marks of the Hovya family" (*hovy-ānvavāya-tilakaḥ*) and who were born at Kāñcīpuram (*kāñcīpura-*

456. Māmaṇḍūr inscription, *op. cit.*, p. 12.
457. T.N. Ramachandran, *op. cit.*, p. 237.
458. R. Nagaswamy, TVCP, *Veḷāñjeri Plates of Aparājita*, v. 20, plate V, p. 1.

samudbhavaḥ).[459] The Tamil portion of the same grant describes these artists as *oviyaccittirakāri*.[460]

The Sanskrit term *citrakāriṇaḥ* literally means painters and *oviya* in Tamil means painting. It appears that the inscriptions were first painted on stone or metal by painters, though the incising might have been done by carvers on stone or metal but it is also likely that both painting and carving were done by the same individuals.[461]

The term *hovya* and *oviya* used in this record may not be the proper name of a family or caste, but the name of the profession followed which we know from this inscription to be painting.[462]

The Tiruvālaṅgāḍu plates, in the Sanskrit portion at the end of the charter also refer to this family of artists. However, only four members of the family who engraved this edict are mentioned namely, Ārāvamṛta, his two younger brothers, Raṅga and Dāmodara and Ārāvamṛta's son Puruṣottama.[463] This record describes them as masters in the art of sculpture (*śilpa-kovidaḥ*).

Likewise, the Karandai plates, also issued in the reign of Rājendra I record that it was engraved by two members of the same family namely, Araṅgam (Śrīraṅga) and Puruṣottaman, who held the titles Tribhuvanamahādevī-mahācārya (Tribhuvanamahādevī-perācāryaṉ in the Tamil section) and Rājendrasiṁha-perācarya (Rājendrasiṁha-perācāryaṉ) respectively.[464] Although these persons are mentioned in the Larger Leiden and Tiruvālaṅgāḍu records, the titles are not mentioned there. It seems that these titles might have been conferred on them, if their absence in the other grants was not an omission, sometime in the intervel

459. Larger Leiden plates, *op. cit.*, vv. 45-48, p. 243.
460. *Ibid.*, l. 108.
461. *Ibid.*, p. 223 and n. 4.
462. *Ibid.*, p. 223.
463. Tiruvālaṅgāḍu plates, *op. cit.*, l. 518, p. 412.
464. K.G. Krishnan, *KTPR*, v. 76, p. 76.

between the Tiruvālaṅgāḍu and Leiden grants and the Karandai plates.[465] They are mentioned in the Sanskrit verse as expert sculptors (*śilpāgama-tattva-kuśalau-dvau*).[466] The Tamil section of the same grant describes them as *kāṣṭhakāri*.[467] *Kāṣṭhakāri* is a Sanskrit coinage of the word *takṣaka* which actually means *śilpins* and not carpenters.[468] Since both the Tiruvālaṅgāḍu and Karandai epigraphs describe the members of this family as *śilpins*, the word *kāṣṭhakāri* used to describe Araṅgam and Puruṣottaman in the Tamil section of the Karandai plates should be understood in the sense of *śilpins* or sculptors although the literal meaning of the word *kāṣṭhakāri* is a worker on wood or carpenter.

The last portion of the Esālam grant mentions that this charter was engraved by Ulagalanta-Coḷa Ācārya (*alikat-praśastiṁ etām ulagalanta-coḷa ācāryaḥ*).[469] The name Vāsudeva also occurs at the very end of this Sanskrit part. The Leiden plates mention a certain Vāsudeva, son of Kṛṣṇan who had the title Rājarājaperācāryan but it is difficult to say whether the engraver of this charter was identical with or related to the Vāsudevan of the Leiden grant.[470]

Art of Theft

Interestingly, according to Indian tradition, the art of theft was included in the list of fine-arts in which a prince had to attain proficiency. Daṇḍin, who lived in the Pallava court mentions in the *Pūrvapīṭhikā* of his Sanskrit drama *Daśakumāracarita* that princes had to learn different arts including the arts of thieving and gambling.[471] *Kalavum kaṟṟu mara* (even thieving must be learnt as an art and later forgotten) is an ancient Tamil proverb.

465. K.G. Krishnan, *KTPR*, p. 54.
466. *Ibid.*, p. 76.
467. *Ibid.*, p. 193.
468. R. Nagaswamy, *ECPR*, p. 10.
469. *Ibid.*, v. 35, p. 33.
470. *Ibid.*, p. 10.
471. M.R. Kale, *Daśakumāracarita of Daṇḍin*, Delhi, 1997, Pūrvapīṭhikā.

The composer of the Kaśakuḍi plates describes Nandivarman Pallavamalla as being like Karṇīsuta in acquaintance with the arts (*kalāparicaye karṇisutaḥ*).[472] This is a reference to Mūladeva *alias* Karṇīsuta believed to be the first propounder of the science of thieving.[473] The *Hārāvaḷi* of Puruṣottama Deva mentions Karṇīsuta, Kharapaṭa, Mūladeva and Kalaṅkura as synonyms.[474]

Karṇīsuta and his skill in the art of thieving are mentioned in many Sanskrit works like the *Harṣacarita*[475] and *Kādambarī*.[476] In some Sanskrit works, Karṇīsuta is also described as a master of all the fine-arts. The *Bhāṇa Padmaprābhṛtaka* believed to have been written by Śūdraka mentions that Karṇīsuta was proficient in all the arts.[477] The *Kalāvilāsa* of Kṣemendra states that Mūladeva was a teacher of the arts.[478]

Karṇīsuta was also well known in the ancient Tamil country. The *Śilppadikāram* contains a reference to a work on the science of theft by Mūladeva.[479] Daṇḍin in his *Daśakumāracarita* refers to Karṇīsuta.[480] In the *Avantisundarī-kathā*, the same author describes Karṇīsuta as a teacher of the art of thieving.[481]

Many Sanskrit works mention a thieves' manual known as the *Cora-Śāstra* or the *Steya-Śāstra*. In the Sanskrit play

---

472. Kaśākuḍi plates, *op. cit.*, v. 29, p. 349.
473. M. Bloomfield, "Character and Adventures of Mūladeva," *Proceedings of the American Philosophical Society*, LII, 616-50.
474. Pandit G. Harihara Sastri, "Kharapata and Mūladeva," *Asutosh Memorial Volume*, Patna, 1926-28, p. 225.
475. *Harṣacharita of Bāṇabhaṭṭa*, ed. P.V. Kane, Delhi, 1965.
476. *Bāṇa's Kādambarī*, *op. cit.*
477. Pandit G. Harihara Sastri, *op. cit.*, p. 226.
478. Aryendra Sharma (ed.), *Minor Works of Kṣemendra*, Hydrabad, 1961, p. 200.
479. V.R. Ramachandra Dikshitar, *Studies in Tamil Literature and History*, Madras, 1983, p. 76.
480. *Daśakumāracarita*, *op. cit.*, pp. 76 and 102.
481. K.S. Mahadeva Sastri (ed.), *Avantisundarīkathā*, Trivandrum, 1954; see also Pandit. G. Harihara Sastri, *op. cit.*, p. 225.

Mattavilāsaprahasana, Mahendravarman I refers to Kharapaṭa as the author of *Cora-Śāstra* (science of theft).[482] According to a commentator on the *Daśakumāracarita*, Karṇīsuta authored the *Steya-Śāstra*.[483]

It is only natural that the poet of Nandivarman Pallavamalla's inscription, who must have been familiar with the traditional story of Karṇīsuta *alias* Mūladeva being an expert in all the arts, wished to compare his patron Nandivarman Pallavamalla who was also well-versed in various arts with Karṇīsuta. However, Karṇīsuta was most well known as an expert in the art of burglary and since the works written in the Pallava period like the *Mattavilāsaprahasana*, *Daśakumāracarita* and the *Avantisundarīkathā* refer to him only in the context of stealing or burglary it is also possible that the composer of the Kaśākuḍi plates might have wanted to compare his king with this arch-thief as the art of thieving was, in any case, one of the many arts to be learnt by princes.

482. *Mattavilāsaprahasana*, ed N.P. Unni, Trivandrum, 1974.

483. *Daśakumāracarita*, *op. cit.*, p. 76.

7

Religion

THE importance of religion in ancient and medieval society can hardly be exaggerated. The Sanskrit inscriptions of the period of this study provide plenty of information regarding the religious activities of this age. The copper-plate as well as the lithic inscriptions are extremely useful in showing the personal devotion of many of the rulers and the immense contribution made by them in the sphere of religion. The spirit of tolerance towards faiths other than their own as well as the contribution of the common people in the sphere of religion are vividly brought out by a study of these epigraphs.

The construction of temples was considered to be a very sacred and meritorious act and the Tamil rulers in their religious zeal built a number of shrines in various parts of their kingdom as attested to by a large number of their epigraphs. These records also mention the immense royal patronage which these temples received in the form of land, gold and jewels. The land donated to the temples were called *devadāna* or *devabhoga*. Even some of the royal grants made in favour of learned brāhmaṇas as *brahmadeya* mention that the *devabhoga* were excluded from this.

The earliest Pallava inscription which mentions an endowment to a temple is the Guṇapadeya copper-plate grant of the Pallava queen Cārudevī which states that this queen made a gift of four *nivartana*s of land to the God Nārāyaṇa of

Kūḷi-Mahātāraka temple at Dalūra and that it was to be exempted from all immunities.[1]

The Uruvapaḷḷi charter of Yuvamahārāja Viṣṇugopavarman records that he granted two hundred *nivartana*s of land as *devabhoga* in the village of Uruvapaḷḷi to the temple of God Viṣṇuhāradeva which had been founded by a military officer (*senāpati*) named Viṣṇuvarma in the village of Kaṇḍukura, and that this land was granted immunity from taxation.[2] Yuvamahārāja Viṣṇugopavarman is mentioned in the Neḍuṅgarāya grant as a devotee of Viṣṇu (*paramabhāgavataḥ*).[3] Kumāraviṣṇu II is described in the Cendalūr plates as one "who meditates at the feet of Viṣṇu" (*bhagavad-pādānudhyātaḥ*) and also as *parama-bhāgavataḥ*.[4] Siṁhavarman is referred to in exactly the same manner in another early Pallava record.[5] The Cura charter of king Vijaya Viṣṇugopavarman also mentions that this king "enjoyed all auspiciousness due to his devotion to Viṣṇu" (*bhagavad-bhakti-sadbhāva (sambhā)vita-sarva kalyāṇa-saṁdogaḥ*), that he meditated at the feet of Viṣṇu (*bhagavad-pādānudhyātaḥ*) and that he was an ardent devotee of Viṣṇu (*paramabhāgavataḥ*).[6] The Vesanta[7] and the Udayendiram (I)[8] charters also describe Siṁhavarman II and Nandivarman I respectively as *paramabhāgavataḥ*.

Mahendravarman I appears to have been a devotee of Śiva as seen from numerous epigraphs. Many of his inscriptions such as the Kuḍimiyāmalai[9] and the Tirumayyam[10] epigraphs begin with the auspicious term *namaḥ śivāya* or "salutations to

---

1. *EI*, vol. VIII, no. 12, pp. 143-47 (Guṇapadeya plates).
2. *Ind. Ant.*, (1876 February), pp. 50-53 (Uruvapaḷḷi plates).
3. T.V. Mahalingam, *IOP*, p. 50 (Neḍuṅgarāya plates).
4. *EI*, vol. VIII, no. 23, p. 235 (Cendalūr plates).
5. *EI*, vol. VIII, no. 15, p. 162 (Pikira plates).
6. *EI*, vol. XXIV, no. 18, p. 141 (Cura plates).
7. N. Ramesan, *VGPS*, p. 96.
8. *EI*, vol. VIII, no. 23, p. 146 (Udayendiram I plates).
9. *EI*, vol. XII, no. 28, p. 231 (Kuḍimiyāmalai inscription).
10. *SII*, vol. XII, no. 7A, p. 8 (Tirummayam inscription).

Lord Śiva." The very first verse in both the *Mattavilāsa-prahasana* and *Bhagavadajjukam* are also in praise of Śiva, the former to Kapāli and the latter to Rudra. In the Kuḍimiyāmalai inscription[11] this king is called as a *paramamāheśvara*.

During the reign of Mahendravarman I many rock-cut cave temples dedicated to Śiva were excavated, called after several of the titles (*biruda*s) which this ruler assumed. The Tirucirāpaḷḷi Rock inscription reveals that this king caused a temple of Girīśa (Śiva) to be built on a mountain, and placed in it a matchless stone figure of Hara (*śailiṁ harasya tanum=apratimām=anēna kṛtvā*).[12] He is described in this inscription as Puruṣottama, who bore Śiva fixed in his mind (*śivam śirasi dhārayat=ātmasaṁstham*). He is referred to as a worshipper of the *liṅga*.[13] Mahendravarman's cave-temple in Tirucirāpaḷḷi is called Lalitāṅkura-Pallaveśvaragṛham[14] after his title Lalitāṅkura.

An inscription in the rock-cut cave at Dalavānūr (South Arcot district) of the period of Mahedravarman I records that the (cave) temple on this hill was made at the order of this king called in this record as Narendra and Śatrumalla and named (after himself) as *Śatrumalleśvarālaya*, i.e., the Īśvara (Śiva) temple of Śatrumalla.[15]

Another inscription of Mahendravarman I found at the Śiva temple at Śīyamaṅgalam (North Arcot district) states that this temple named *Avanibhajana Pallaveśvara*, called after his *biruda* Avanibhajana, was caused to be made by this king in order to obtain merit in future life.[16]

Although Mahendravarman I was a devout Śaivite, he also built temples in honour of other Gods. The Mahendravāḍi inscription of this ruler records that he excavated a spacious

---

11. Kuḍimiyāmalai inscription, *op. cit.*, p. 237.
12. *SII*, vol. I, no. 34, p. 30.
13. *SII*, vol. I, no. 33, p. 29.
14. *SII*, vol. XII, no. 9, p. 6.
15. *EI*, vol. XII, no. 27, p. 225 (Dalavānūr inscription).
16. *EI*, vol. VI, no. 32, p. 320 (Śīyamaṅgalam inscription).

temple of Murāri (Viṣṇu) called Mahendra-Viṣṇugṛha, after his own name, out of rock on the banks of the Mahendrataṭāka in the city of Mahendrapura.[17] An epigraph of this ruler found in a rock-cut cave-temple in Maṇḍagapaṭṭu (South Arcot district) states that "the brickless (*aniṣṭakam*), timberless (*adrumam*), metalless (*aloham*) and mortarless (*asudham*) temple, which is a mansion for the (Gods) Brahmā, Īśvara and Viṣṇu was caused to be made by the king Vicitracitta (*vicitracittena nirmāpitam*)."[18] This cave temple, called Lakṣitayatana is named after one of Mahendravarman's *birudas* Lakṣita.

According to tradition, Mahendravarman I was originally a Jain who persecuted the Śaiva saint Appar. C. Minakshi has opined that this act of his would appear doubtful in view of his tolerant attitude towards all religious sects, including Vaiṣṇavism.[19]

The Ciṟṟūr plates of Nṛpatuṅga mention that Narasiṁhavarman I created a temple (*sayyagṛha*) for Viṣṇu made of stone (*aśmābhiḥ*) on the sea-shore.[20]

Parameśvaravarman I was a devotee of Śiva. He is described as a staunch follower of Maheśvara (Paramamāheśvara) in the Vunnaguruvapālem plates.[21] The Kūram plates record that this ruler gave a village named Parameśvaramaṅgala as a divine gift to Lord Pinākapāṇi (Śiva) of the temple of Vidyāvinīta-Pallava-Parameśvara in the village of Kūra (near Kāñcīpuram) in order to provide for the worship (*pūjā*), bathing of the idol (*snāpana*), flowers (*kusuma*), perfumes (*gandha*), incense (*dhūpa*), lamps (*dīpa*), oblations (*havir-upahāra*), conches (*śaṅkha*), drums (*paṭaha*) and also for the recitation of *Mahābhārata* at this temple (*Bhāratākhyāna*).[22]

17. *EI*, vol. IV, no. 19, pp. 152-53 (Mahendravāḍi inscription).
18. *EI*, vol. XVII, no. 5, p. 17 (Maṇḍagapaṭṭu inscription).
19. C. Minakshi, *ASLP*, p. 206.
20. T.V. Mahalingam, *IOP*, p. 440.
21. *EI*, vol. XXXII, no. 9, p. 97 (Vunnaguruvapālem plates).
22. *SII*, vol. I, no. 151, p. 150 (Kūram plates).

An inscription of this ruler found in the Gaṇeśa temple at Māmallapuram records that this temple was caused to be built by this king, surnamed Atyantakāma to be the abode of Śaṁbhu (Śiva).[23] This epigraph which commences with two verses in praise of Śiva, describes Parameśvaravarman I as one who "bears Śiva in his mind" (*bhakti-prahveṇa manasā-bhavaṁ bibharti*), and who "assiduously worships Hara" (*hara-ārādhana-saṅginaḥ*) and ends with the imprecatory verse "Six times be cursed be those, in whose hearts does not dwell Rudra (Śiva), the deliverer from walking on the evil path" (*dhik=teṣām=dhik=teṣām=punar=api dhig=dhig=astu dhik=teṣām, yeṣām=na vasati hṛdaye ku-patha gati-vi-mokṣako-rudraḥ*).

A duplicate of this same inscription of Parameśvaravarman I along with this imprecatory verse is found in the Dharmarāja Maṇḍapa at Māmallapuram[24] and inscriptions of this king consisting of this imprecatory verse alone are found in the Rāmānuja Maṇḍapa cave-temple[25] and the Ādivarāha cave-temple[26] at the same place.

Rājasiṁha was an ardent devotee of Śiva as can be seen from several of his epigraphs. An inscription of this ruler found at the Atiraṇacaṇḍeśvara temple at Śāḷuvaṅkuppam near Māmallapuram records that this king, who bore deep devotion to Īśāna caused this house of Śaṁbhu (Śiva), which resembles Kailāsa and Mandara to be made.[27]

The two Śiva shrines of the Shore temple at Māmallapuram, Rājasiṁha-Pallaveśvara and Kṣatriyasiṁha-Pallaveśvara were built by Rājasiṁha.[28] An epigraph of six verses containing many of the *biruda*s of Rājasiṁha of which one of the verses is

---

23. *SII*, vol. I, no. 18, p. 4.
24. *SII*, vol. I, no. 19, p. 6.
25. *SII*, vol. I, no. 20, p. 6.
26. T.V. Mahalingam, *IOP*, no. 51, p. 167; see K.R. Srinivasan, *The Dharmarāja Ratha and its Sculptures, Mahābalipuram*, Delhi, 1975, p. 96.
27. *SII*, vol. I, no. 21, p. 7.
28. *EI*, vol. XIX, no. 18, p. 106; see also C. Sivaramamurti, *Mahābalipuram*, New Delhi, 1978, p. 31.

identical with an inscription of this king from the Kailāśanātha temple, Kāñcīpuram[29] is found in this Shore temple.[30]

Rājasiṁha also built the famous Kailāśanātha temple at Kāñcīpuram. One of the inscriptions found therein states that this temple named Rājasiṁheśvara and "which robbed Kailāśa of its beauty" (*kailāśa-līlām=apaharati*) was built by this king who had "Śiva as his crest jewel" (*śivacūḍāmaṇiḥ*).[31]

The Velūrpāḷaiyam plates mention that this ruler built of stone a temple for Śiva which was comparable with (the mountain) Kaiḷāśa (*śilāmayam veśma śaśāṅka-mauleḥ kailāśa-kalpañ=ca mahendra kalpaḥ*)[32] and the Ciṟṟūr plates of Nṛpatuṅgavarman also repeat the same facts, adding that this temple was constructed at Kāñcīpuram (*kāñcyām=mahad-aśma-veśma vidadhe śailopamaṁ-śūlinaḥ*).[33]

Another inscription found in this temple mentions several of his *biruda*s such as *śrī iśānaśaraṇaḥ* (he whose refuge is Śiva), *śrī devadeva bhaktaḥ* (the devotee of Devadeva), *śrī śaṅkara bhaktaḥ* (the devotee of Śaṅkara) and *śrī īśvara bhaktaḥ* (the devotee of Īśvara).[34] Rājasiṁha is also referred to as one "who (gained glory) in the path of Śaiva Siddhānta and had, because of that, got rid of all impurities" (*kṣatasakalamalaḥ*).[35] This is probably the earliest datable reference to the Śāiva Siddhānta mārga, "the school of Śāiva Siddhānta philosophy."[36]

Several other epigraphs also proclaim him to be a staunch follower of Śiva. The Vāyalūr inscription states that his crown was resplendent with the crest-jewel, viz., Maheśvara (*maheśvara-śikhāmaṇi-dīpta-mauḷiḥ*) and as "one who is

---

29. *SII*, vol. I, v. 12, p. 13.
30. *EI*, vol. XIX, no. 18A, v. 3, p. 107.
31. *SII*, vol. I, pp. 12-13.
32. *SII*, vol. II, no. 98, v. 13, p. 508 (Velūrpāḷaiyam plates).
33. T.V. Mahalingam, *IOP*, no. 152, p. 440 (Ciṟṟūr plates).
34. *SII*, vol. I, no. 25, pp. 14-15.
35. *SII*, vol. I, no. 24, v. 5, p. 12.
36. S. Sankaranarayanan, "A Pallava Inscriptional Poem in Sanskrit," *ALB*, vol. 55, 1991. p. 77.

excessively devoted ever to serve at the pair of lotus feet of Śaṁbhu (*Śaṁboḥ pādāravinda-dvaya-paricaraṇe nityam=atyantakāmaḥ*).[37] He is described in an inscription in the Tāḷagirīśvara temple at Panamalai as one "in whose mind Mṛgāṅkamauḷi (Śiva) rests his foot" (*citte sadā sambhṛta-bhakti-pūte dhatte padam yasya mṛgāṅkamauḷiḥ*).[38]

The Udayendiram plates refer to him as a devout worshipper of Śiva (*paramamāheśvara*),[39] while in the Kaśākuḍi plates he is described as "a complete incarnation of Śiva" (*śrī parameśvarasya sakalsy=āṅga-avatāraḥ*).[40] It is interesting to see that this great devotee of Śiva is also described as a devotee of Viṣṇu (*paramabhāgavata*) in the Reyūrū plates.[41]

The Āgamas which prescribe the rules for worship in temples appear to have gained popularity in the period of the Pallavas. Rājasiṁha's titles *śrī āgama priyaḥ* (lover of the *Āgamas*)[42] and *śrī āgamānusārī* (one who follows the path laid down by the *Āgamas*)[43] shows that the Pallavas rulers must have keenly adhered to the Āgamic codes in temple rituals.

Mahendravarman III, son of Rājasiṁha, also appears to have been a devotee of Śiva. An inscription of his found in the shrine of Mahendravarmeśvara in front of the central shrine in the Kailāśanātha temple at Kāñcīpuram states that this shrine was built by him and was named after him as *mahendravarmeśvaragṛhaṁ*.[44]

Nandivarman Pallavamalla's religious disposition can also be seen from several epigraphs. The Kaśākuḍi plates describe him as one "who worships the feet of Viṣṇu" (*hari caraṇa*).[45]

---

37. *EI*, vol. XVIII, no. 18, p. 151 (Vāyalūr inscription).
38. *EI*, vol. XIX, no. 18, p. 107 (Panamalai inscription).
39. Udayendiram plates, *op. cit.*, l. 19, p. 366.
40. Kaśakuḍi plates, *op. cit.*, v. 25, p. 349.
41. *EI*, vol. XXIX, no. 11, pp. 95-96 (Reyūrū plates).
42. *SII*, vol. I, no. 25, p. 17.
43. *Ibid.*
44. *SII*, vol. I, no. 27, p. 22.
45. Kaśākuḍi plates, *op. cit.*, v. 30, p. 350.

The Taṇḍantoṭṭam plates record the sentiments of this ruler thus: "May his pair of feet dwell on this (my) head which never knew of bowing down to others excepting to the pair of the worshipful feet of Mukunda" (*mūrdani=atra=mukunda=vandhya=caraṇa-dvandvaṁ-vihāy=āpareṣu=ajñāna-praṇatou*).[46] He was the builder of the famous Vaikuṇṭhaperumāḷ temple (*Parameśvara-viṇṇagaraṁ*) in Kāñcīpuram. Despite the fact that this ruler was such a great devotee of Viṣṇu, many of his epigraphs[47] contain invocatory verses in praise of Śiva also. Such instances reveal the eclectic religious outlook of the Pallava kings.

Nandivarman III was a devotee of Śiva as revealed by the Velūrpāḷaiyam plates which describe this ruler as "one whose head is marked by the head-jewel, viz., the lotus feet of Hara (Śiva)" (*hara-caraṇa-sarojaotaṁsa-cihnena*).[48] This inscription also begins with an invocatory verse in praise of Śiva.

Aparājita Pallava was a great devotee of Ṣaṇmukha (Muruga) of Tiruttani. In the Tiruttani copper-plate inscription, this king is mentioned as gifting with great devotion to Subrahmaṇya, the village of Pudūr as a *devadāna brahmadeya*.[49] The gifted village named Pudūr was combined with a great *agrahāra* (*mahāgrahāra*) named Meliṟuñjeru and the village *sabha* was ordered to pay a thousand *kāḍi* of paddy to Lord Subrahmaṇya. In the Sanskrit portion of this epigraph, this god is mentioned as "Ṣaṇmukha, the son of Maheśvara (*maheśvara sūnave ṣaṇmukhākya*)." In the Tamil part of the same inscription he is referred to as "Subrahmaṇya who is pleased to stand on Tiruttani hill (*tirumalayil niṇdraruḷina*)" and also as Subrahmaṇya, the Lord of Tiruttani hill (Tirumalai Piranār).

The Sanskrit inscriptions reveal that some of the Pallava kings worshipped Śiva while others had leanings towards

46. *SII*, vol. II, No. 99, p. 520 (Taṇḍantoṭṭam plates).
47. Kaśākuḍi plates, *op. cit.*, p. 346; Udayendiram plates, *op. cit.*, pp. 365-66; *EI*, vol. XXXVI, no. 20, p. 152 (Pullūr plates).
48. Velūrpāḷaiyam plates, *op. cit.*, v. 29, p. 509.
49. R. Nagaswamy, *TVCP Velāñjeri plates of Aparājita*, plate III, p. 2.

Vaiṣṇavism. According to C. Minakshi, the bull being the symbol of the Pallavas significantly portrayed the prevailing religion of the state. The bull was the favourite of Śiva, his vehicle and usher and the fact that the Pallavas throughout their rule used *vṛṣabha-lāñchana* as one of the insignia of royalty irrespective of the personal faith of the individual king indicates that the state religion was nothing but Śaivism.[50]

During the Coḷa period the Śaiva-Vaiṣṇava polarization had emerged quite strongly. Even then the ruling monarchs were generally never hostile to any particular sect, although each king had a special devotion to a particular deity. According to K.A. Nilakanta Sastri,

> Generally speaking, the religious temper of the period, particularly in the first half of it was by no means narrow or sectarian. Not only did the kings, as a rule tolerate religions and sects other than their own, but they often patronized all persuations in equal measure.[51]

Vijayālaya, the founder of the line of imperial Coḷas, is mentioned in the Tiruvālaṅgāḍu inscription as having consecrated an image of Goddess Niśumbhasūdanī at Tañjāvūr and that he ruled the kingdom with her grace.[52]

Regarding Āditya I, the son and successor of Vijayālaya, the Anbil plates record that this king built a row of large stone temples of Śiva (*puramathana-mahādhāma-mālā śilābhis=tuṁga yena vyadhāyi*) on either bank of the river Kāverī starting from the Sahāya mountains up to the sea.[53] According to T.A. Gopinatha Rao, there are a number of temples dedicated to Śiva situated on the banks of the Kāverī which might be assigned to the reign of Āditya I and of which the construction continued even in the reign of his son Parāntaka I.[54]

---

50. C. Minakshi, *ASLP*, p. 55.
51. K.A. Nilakanta Sastri, *The Coḷas*, Madras, 1984, p. 643.
52. *SII*, vol. III, no. 205, v. 46, p. 396 (Tiruvālaṅgāḍu plates).
53. *EI*, vol. XV, no. 5, v. 18, p. 60 (Anbil plates).
54. *Ibid.*, p. 50.

Parāntaka I, the son and successor of Āditya I and probably the greatest conqueror among the early Coḷa rulers was a great devotee of Śiva and held special reverence for God Naṭarāja of Cidambaram as revealed by several Sanskrit inscriptions. The Larger Leiden[55] and the Karandai plates[56] state that this king covered the temple of Indumauḷi (Śiva) at Vyāghrāgrahāra (Cidambaram) with pure gold acquired by him in various wars. The Tiruvālaṅgāḍu plates also record that this ruler was a devotee of Śiva, the composer of this epigraph describing Parāntaka I poetically as "a bee at the lotus feet of Śiva" (*purāntaka-angri-dvaya-padmabr̥ṅgaḥ*) and states that he built for Purāri (Śiva) who was before (this) on the silver mountain (Kailāśa), a golden house, Dabhra-Sabha and thus put to shame his (Śiva's) friend the Lord of wealth (Kubera) by his immense riches.[57] The Esālam plates also describe Parāntaka I's devotion to Naṭarāja of Cidambaram in exactly the same manner.[58] Thus Cidambaram became Hema-Sabhā, Hiraṇya-Sabhā, Kanaka-Sabhā or Ponnambalam and Parāntaka acquired the title of "Pon Veinda Perumāḷ," one who covered with gold the roof of the Dabhra or Cit-Sabhā at Cidambaram.[59] The Udayendiram plates of Pr̥thivīpati II record among the many meritorious acts of Parāntaka I, the building of many temples (*surālayāḥ*).[60]

Gaṇḍarāditya, the son and successor of Parāntaka I, who was also a great devotee of Śiva and author of the *Tiruviśaippā* which contains a hymn on the temple at Cidambaram mentions in this hymn that Parāntaka covered the temple of Naṭarāja with gold.[61]

Madhurāntaka Uttama Coḷa, the son of Gaṇḍarāditya Coḷa was also a staunch Śaivite. The Tiruvālaṅgāḍu plates record

55. *EI*, vol. XXII, no. 34, v. 17, p. 239 (Larger Leiden plates).
56. K.G. Krishnan, *KTPR*, v. 18, p. 70.
57. Tiruvālaṅgāḍu plates, *op. cit.*, v. 50, p. 396.
58. R. Nagaswamy, *ECPR*, v. 10, pp. 31-32.
59. S.R. Balasubrahmanyam, *Early Coḷa Temples*, Madras, 1971, p. 3.
60. *SII*, vol. II, no. 76, v. 7, p. 383.
61. K.A. Nilakanta Sastri, *The Coḷas*, p. 152.

that Uttama Coḷa, "applying his mind to the devotion of Śiva" (*manaś=śarve kurvan*), "utilizing his wealth in the act of performing his worship" (*dhanam=api tad-abhyarcana-vidhau*), "employing all his retinue in the construction of temples for him" (*tad-āvās-ārambhe-parijanaṁ=aseṣam*) and "directing his subjects to regularly perform his festive processions" (*sarvan=tasy=otsava-vidhiṣu*), ruled the earth.[62] The Madras Museum plates of this ruler give details about his orders to some residents of Kāñcīpuram in connection with the management of the temple of Ūraka (Ulagalandaperumāḷ temple).[63]

Rājarāja I, continuing in the religious traditions of his forefathers was also a staunch Śaivite. His greatest claim to fame was the construction of the colossal temple to Śiva at his capital city, Tañjāvūr, although many other Śiva temples were constructed during his reign all over the Coḷa country. The only reference to the Bṛhadīśvara temple at Tañjāvūr in the Sanskrit inscriptions of this period is found in the Esālam copper plates.[64] According to this charter, Aruḷmoḻivarman (Rājarāja) erected a very great temple for Śiva (*śambor atyuttamān*) called Rājarājeśvaram at Tañjāvūr with the wealth obtained from his conquests. The benefactions made to this temple by Rājarāja are mentioned in numerous Tamil inscriptions found there.

Although Rājarāja was a devotee of Śiva and bore the title *śivapādaśekhara* (he who bears the feet of Śiva on his head) his liberal outlook towards Vaiṣṇavism can be clearly seen from some Tamil inscriptions found at the Bṛhadīśvara temple which state that he gave to this temple, a gift of silver icons of Vāsudeva[65] and a copper image of Mahāviṣṇu with four hands.[66]

62. Tiruvālaṅgāḍu plates, *op. cit.*, v. 71, p. 397.
63. *SII*, vol. III, no. 128, p. 269 (Madras Museum plates of Uttama Coḷa).
64. R. Nagaswamy, *ECPR*, v. 13, p. 32.
65. *SII*, vol. II, no. 91, pp. 418-19.
66. *SII*, vol. II, no. 52, pp. 217-18.

The Someśvara and the Nelliappar temples (Tirunelveli district) contain shrines dedicated to Viṣṇu (*Paḷḷikoṇḍa Perumāḷ*) which were built by this king.[67]

The epigraphs of Rājendra I reveal his devotion to Śiva. The Esālam charter of this king mentions that he established the city of Gaṅgaikoṇḍacoḷapuram after his name (Gaṅgaikoṇḍa Coḷa) and built a temple for Śiva out of great devotion, which was also named after the king himself (Gaṅgaikoṇḍacoḷīśvaram), adding that this king "was deeply attached to the lotus feet of that Lord, like a bee ever humming over a pārijāta flower" (*tan-nāmnā-vara-bhavanaṁ maheśvarasya bhaktyā tad-pada-yuga-pārijāta-bhṛṅgaḥ*).[68]

The Esālam plates also record that Rājendra I, by clubbing together two villages named Nannāḍu and Erpākkam into one unit and renaming it Vikramacoḷanallūr, donated it tax free to the temple of Lord Śiva which his preceptor Śarvaśiva Ārya had built at Eydar, a suburb of Rājarājacaturvedimaṅgalam in Jayaṁkoṇḍacoḷamaṇḍalam.

The Tiruvālaṅgāḍu plates of this king record that he deputed his minister named Jananātha to give the prosperous village named Purāṇagrāma to the temple of Śiva, known by the name Ammayappa in that village (Tiruvālaṅgāḍu).[69] The Sanskrit portions of both the Esālam and the Tiruvālaṅgaḍu plates commence with a verse in praise of Lord Śiva. Many Tamil records reveal that Rājendra I constructed numerous Śiva temples in the Coḷa country.

Rājendra I, like his father, was tolerant of the Vaiṣṇava faith, as proved by many Viṣṇu temples built during his reign. The Śiva temple at Polannaruva (Sri Lanka) named Vānavaṉ-Mahādevī Īśvaram, after the queen of Rājarāja I and the mother of Rājendra I contains a shrine for Viṣṇu in his recumbent

---

67. S.R. Balasubrahmanyam, *Middle Coḷa Temples*, Haryana, 1975, pp. 185-86.
68. R. Nagaswamy, *ECPR*, v. 18, p. 32.
69. Tiruvālaṅgāḍu plates, *op. cit.*, vv. 125-28, p. 401.

form (*paḷḷikoṇḍar*). It was built either by Rājarāja or, more likely by his son Rājendra I when he was a viceroy there.[70]

A Tamil inscription of this king found at the Aḻagiya Narasiṁha Perumāḷ temple at Eṇṇayiram (South Arcot district) which also had a Vedic college attached to it, records that this ruler granted forty *veli*s of land to this temple for food offerings to the God and festivals and also for the recitation of the Tiruvāymoḻi (hymns of the Tamil Vaiṣṇava saint Nammāḻvār) and maintenance of the Vedic college.[71]

Some information about the religious leanings of Vīra-Rājendra, son of Rājendra I is forthcoming from the Sanskrit portion of the Kanyākumārī (= Cārāla) inscription of this ruler.[72] The devotion of this king towards Lord Naṭarāja of Cidambaram just like his predecessors is revealed in this epigraph which records that Vīra-Rājendra gave an invaluable precious ruby called *Trailokya-sāra* to the God Dabhra Sabhāpati (Naṭarāja of Cidambaram), which was placed on the crown of the Lord.

The fact that this devotee of Śiva also made endowments to Viṣṇu temples is seen from his Tamil inscription found at the Veṅkaṭeśa Perumāḷ temple in Tirumukkūḍal (Chingleput district) in which a Vedic college, hostel and hospital were also housed. This epigraph states that Vīra-Rājendra made a grant to this temple for the maintenance of worship to the God and also for the upkeep of the other three institutions attached to this temple.[73]

A record of Kulottuṅga I found in the temple dedicated to the Sun God (Sūrya) at Sūryanārkovil (near Kumbakoṇam), the only temple exclusively dedicated to Sūrya in Tamil Nadu refers to this shrine as Kulottuṅga-Coḷa-Mārttāṇḍālayam, i.e., "the temple of the Sun God named after Kulottuṅga I in whose

70. K.V. Raman, "Religious Trends in Rājarāja's Time" from *Rājarāja, the Great* (Seminar proceedings), Bombay 1987, p. 109.
71. *EI*, vol. XXXIX, no. 34, pp. 228-36 (Eṇṇayiram inscription).
72. *TAS*, vol. I, no. 34, v. 79, p. 148 (Kanyākumārī inscription).
73. *EI*, vol. XXI, no. 38, pp. 230-41 (Tirumukkūḍal inscription).

reign it was built."[74] It appears that this Coḷa ruler and the Gāhaḍavāla kings of Kanauj who were great devotees of Sūrya were on very friendly terms. An inscription of Kulottuṅga I dated in the 41st year (AD 1110-11) but in a damaged state inscribed on the west wall of the central shrine in the Bṛhadīśvara (Gaṅgaikoṇḍacoḷīśvara) temple at Gaṅgaikoṇḍa-coḷapuram[75] contains a few Sanskrit verses which are interestingly, a verbatim copy of a portion of the introduction of a copper-plate record of the Gāhaḍavāla rulers.[76] Since the date of the Tamil portion is AD 1110-11, the incomplete, damaged inscription in the Coḷa temple could belong to either Madanapāla or his son Govindacandra. It is possible that either Madanapāla or Govindacandra or some other person of the Gāhaḍavāla family came to Gaṅgaikoṇḍacoḷapuram, the capital city of the Coḷas on a friendly visit to Kulottuṅga I and wishing to make a grant to this temple, got the genealogy inscribed.[77] Perhaps, the grant for some reason was not made or it was not engraved in full on stone. The close connection between the Gāhaḍavālas and the Coḷas during the time of Kulottuṅga I would point to the reason for the spread of Sun worship in the Tamil country during this period.[78]

Kulottuṅga II (Anapāya) was also a great devotee of the deity at Cidambaram. In one of his inscriptions found at Tiruvārūr, he is described as "one whose head glitters when placed at the feet of the Lord of the Golden Hall" (*hema-sabhā-ādhinātha-caraṇa-nyāsollasan-mastakaḥ*) and as "the bee at the lotus feet of Naṭeśa at the golden hall in Vyāghrāgrahāra (*vyāghrāgrahāra-vara-hema-sabhā-naṭeśa-pād-āravinda madhupaḥ*)."[79]

The Sanskrit records also provide some information about the religious leanings of Kulottuṅga III. An inscription of this

74. S.R. Balasubrahmanyam, *Later Coḷa Temples*, Madras, 1979, p. 131.
75. *ARE*, 29 of 1908.
76. *EI*, vol. IV, no. 11A, p. 100.
77. *ARE*, 1908, pt. II, p. 66.
78. S.R. Balasubrahmanyam, *op. cit.*
79. *SII*, vol. II, pp. 153-54.

ruler found at the Kaṁpahareśvara temple at Tribhuvanam, records that he made benefactions to various Śiva temples.[80] He built the *mukha-maṇḍapa* for Sabhāpati (Naṭarāja) and *gopuras* over the shrines of Śrīpati (Viṣṇu), Girijā (Pārvatī) and an enclosing verandah (*prākāra harmya*) evidently at Cidambaram. He is described as an unequalled devotee (*ekabhakta*) of the God at Cidambaram. This ruler built (or made additions to) the temples of Ekāmreśvara (at Kāñcīpuram) for Halasya (at Madurai), for Madhyārjuna (at Tiruviḍaimarudūr) and for Valmīkeśvara (at Tiruvārūr). This ruler also built the temple of Tribhuvaneśvara at Tribhuvanam along with several shrines and *vimānas*, the God and Goddess in this temple being consecrated by his *guru*, Someśvara.

Rājendra III following in the tradition of his Coḷa ancestors was a devotee of Śiva as seen from his *birudas rājaparameśvara* and *rājaparamamāheśvara*.[81] His special reverence for Lord Naṭarāja of Cidambaram is reflected in his *birudas vyāghrapura-kanaka-sabhāpati-divya-śrīpāda-pīṭhārādhaka* and *vyāghrapura-kanaka-sabhāpati-divya-śrīpāda-padma-ārādhaka*).[82]

The contributions of the Pāṇḍyan kings to the temples was also enormous. A long epigraph of the thirteenth century AD of the reign of Jaṭāvarman Sundara Pāṇḍya I, consisting of thirty beautiful verses found in the Raṅganātha temple at Śrīraṅgam mentions his bountiful benefactions to this temple.[83]

He covered the main shrine of Lord Raṅganātha with gold which he had given by frequently performing the *tulābhāra* ceremony and having done so, placed in it an image of Lord Viṣṇu made of gold "to the tips of the nails." As a result of this he assumed the title *hemācchādanarāja* or "the king who covered the temple with gold"[84] and called the golden image of Viṣṇu (Hari) installed in the main shrine after his own name i.e., *hemācchādanarāja*.

---

80. *SII*, vol. XXIII, no. 190, p. 147.
81. *ARE*, 77 of 1913 and 515 of 1922.
82. *Ibid*.
83. *EI*, vol. III, no. 2, pp. 11-14.
84. *Ibid*., p. 11.

Sundara Pāṇḍya also built a shrine for Lord Narasiṁha and a shrine for Viśvaksena, both covered with gold. He covered the inner walls of the main shrine with gold and in front of it built a dining-hall for the Lord (*abhyavahāra maṇḍapa*) filled with golden vessels. He arranged for two dining weeks (*abhyavahāra vāras*) and called it after his own name.

He celebrated the procession festival (*yātrotsava*) for the God in the month of Caitra and in order to celebrate the festival of "the sporting of the God with Lakṣmī" (*vihārotsava*) he built a new ship of gold. He constructed three golden domes over the image of Hemaccādanarāja-Hari, for Garuḍa and the hall which contained the couch of the Lord.

In addition to these, this king gave some more invaluable gifts to this temple. A garland of emeralds which this king had taken from the king of Kāṭhaka's treasure was given to this God. According to E.Hultzsch, it is this gift of emeralds (*marakata*) which made the king adopt the uncommon surname of "emerald king" (*marakatapr̥thvībhr̥t*).[85] He also gave to this God, a crown of jewels (*maṇimayamakuṭa*), an image of Ādiśeṣa covered with golden skin (*kanakacharmacāditam*), a golden arch (*makara-toraṇa*) adorned with many jewels, a pendant garland of pearls (*muktāsraja*), a canopy (*vitāna*) of pearls and many kinds of fruits like areca-nut (*kramukha*), jack-fruit (*panāśa*), plantains (*moca*), coconuts (*nālikera*) and mangoes (*āmra*) made of pure gold. In addition to this he also presented a car (*śatāṅga*), a trough (*prapa*), an image of Garuḍa, an inner-garment (*antarīyam*), an aureola (*prabhāvalaya*), a pedestal (*pīṭhi*), an armour (*tanutram*), many vessels (*pātrāṇi*), a throne (*siṁhāsana*) and a ship (*nāva*) all made of pure gold.

One more Sanskrit record of this king in the same temple records some more benefactions of this ruler to this temple such as the guilding of the *vimāna*, a gift of a couch (*śayyā*) to the God, gateway (*dvāra*) and canopy (*vitāna*) which he had wrested from his enemies.[86]

85. *EI*, vol. III, no. 2, p. 14.

86. *SII*, vol. IV, no. 507, p. 146

The fact that Jaṭāvarman Sundara Pāṇḍya I was also a great devotee of Naṭarāja of Cidambaram can be seen from several inscriptions of his at this temple which record that the gold against which he weighed himself in the *tulābhāra* ceremony was gifted to this God.[87]

An inscription found in the *maṇḍapa* in the Vijayarāghava-perumāḷ temple at Tirupputkuḻi near Kāñcīpuram, datable to the period of Jaṭāvarman Sundra Pāṇḍya I mentions that this *maṇḍapa* was built for the merit of a Pāṇḍya called Kulaśekhara.[88] K.A. Nilakanta Sastri has opined that this king could possibly be Jaṭāvarman Kulaśekhara II.[89]

An epigraph from the Nelliappar temple, Tirunelveli, mentions the benefactions of gifts of ornaments and the construction of buildings by Sundara Pāṇḍya to this temple called Veṇuvaneśvara (Lord of the bamboo forest) and Vrīhivṛtīśvara (Lord of the paddy-hedge) in this epigraph.[90]

Another record in the Raṅganāthasvāmi temple, Śrīraṅgam mentions that a gift of a crown embedded with rubies (*dīpta-ratna makuṭa*) and two fly-whisks (*cāmara dvandva*) were presented to Lord Raṅganātha by a person named Śokavilli Bhaṭṭa *alias* Mudaliya Kariyamāri who held the title Sakalavidyācakravarti who received this gift from Perumāḷ Vīra Pāṇḍyadeva who may be identified with Jaṭāvarman Vīra Pāṇḍya I.[91] This Sakalavidyācakravartin has been identified with the author of the Sanskrit work *Gadyakarṇāmṛta* named Kālakalāba Sakalavidyācakravartin.[92]

A few Sanskrit and bi-lingual records of the Hoysala kings who ruled over some parts of the Tamil country also mention their benefactions to religious institutions. A sister of Vīra-Rāmanātha, named Ponnambaladevī made an endowment to

---

87. *SII*, vol. IV, nos. 628-30, pp. 191-92.
88. *ARE*, 19 of 1899.
89. K.A. Nilakanta Sastri, *The Pāṇḍyan Kingdom*, Madras, 1972, p. 152.
90. *SII*, vol. V, no. 407, p. 135 and *ARE*, 118 of 1894.
91. *SII*, vol. XXIV, no. 275, p. 295.
92. S.S. Janaki, *Gadyakarṇāmṛta*, Madras, 1981, p. 23.

the Śrīraṅgam temple in the twelfth year of this king (see Chapter V for details).

A bi-lingual record from Madagoṇḍapaḷḷi (Dharmapuri district) of the reign of Vīra-Viśvanātha, son and successor of Rāmanātha registers the gift of the village named Kuḍaimalam for providing food, offerings and other services to god Tiru-Arigaḷuśvaram-uḍaiyanāyanār for the welfare and victory of the king.[93]

A partly damaged epigraph of the Keraḷa ruler, Ravivarman Kulaśekhara in the Varadarājasvāmi temple in Kāñcīpuram records that this king gave to Aruḷālaperumāḷ (Varadarāja) various requirements such as offerings and ornaments for daily worship and also many such requirements for a festival day to be celebrated in the month of Āvaṇi.[94] Another long Sanskrit inscription of this Cera ruler found at the Raṅganāthasvāmi temple, Śrīraṅgam gives a list of his benefactions to this Viṣṇu shrine. According to this epigraph, this king worshipped with matchless diadems and other gifts his tutelary deity Lord Raṅganātha and built there a shrine for the Lord. He also celebrated here an auspicious festival of lights for Raṅganātha and provided for the payment on a particular day every year a sum of a hundred *paṇa*s each to fifty learned men.[95]

Both of the above records as well as the Sanskrit portion of a bi-lingual record of this ruler from Tiruvaḍi[96] mention *śrī padmanābha-pādakamala=paramārādhaka* (the devout worshipper of the lotus-feet of the holy Padmanābha) as one of the *biruda*s of this king, obviously referring to Lord Padmanābha of the temple at Thiruvanantapuram, Keraḷa. Ravivarman Kulaśekhara's devotion to Lord Padmanābha is also seen in the prelude to the Sanskrit drama *Pradyumnābhyudaya*

93. *ARE*, 202 of 1971-72.
94. *EI*, vol. IV, no. 17, p. 147.
95. *EI*, vol. IV, no. 18, pp. 149-50.
96. *EI*, vol. VIII, no. 2, p. 8.

composed by the ruler himself in which Padmanābha is described as the "family deity of the Yādava king," i.e., Ravivarma (*yādavanr̥pakuladaivata*).[97] The prelude also mentions that this king composed this work for being enacted in the Padmanābhasvāmi temple in connection with the *yātrotsava*.

Apart from the well-known rulers, many of the chieftains and vassals contributed to the construction and endowments of temples as seen from their epigraphs. The various gifts and benefactions made to temples by the famous Kāḍava chief Kopperuñjiṅga (Mahārājasiṁha in Sanskrit), who was a vassal of the Coḷas but who became virtually independent since AD 1243, are known from his numerous inscriptions.

A bi-lingual record of Kopperuñjiṅga from the Śiva temple at Vr̥ddācalam[98] mentions that this ruler gave to God Śiva of this temple a gift of a gold forehead plate encrusted with jewels in expiation of the sin of having killed many generals (*daṇḍanāyaka*) of the Hoysala king and for having seized their ladies and treasures. This ornament called Avani-āḷapirandān was placed on the image of the God to the chanting of a verse in Sanskrit: *cāru-ratnamayam paṭṭam=avany-avana-saṁbhavaḥ, dideśa=tridaś-eśāya-śrī-vr̥ddhagiri-vāsine*).

According to a bi-lingual epigraph from the Varadarāja-perumāḷ temple at Tribhuvani[99] (near Pondicherry) this ruler constructed a temple for Heramba Gaṇapati on the banks of a tank at Tribhuvanamahādevī.

Kopperuñjiṅga's devotion to Lord Naṭarāja of Cidambaram is evident from many of his records. His Āttūr inscription describes him as *kanaka-sabhāpati-sabhā-sarvakārya-sarvakāla-nirvāhakaḥ* (a servant of Lord Naṭarāja, wholly devoted to Him at all times and in all the services of the Lord).[100]

97. *Pradyumnābhyudaya of Ravivarmabhūpa*, ed. T. Ganapati Sastri, Trivandrum, 1910.

98. *ARE*, 73 of 1918.

99. *SII*, vol. XII, no. 126, p. 63.

100. *Ibid.*, no. 120, pp. 58-59.

Numerous Tamil inscriptions of this ruler describe his munificient gifts to this temple and one of these records mentions that he gave the village of Āttūr as a gift for constructing a seven-storeyed *gopura* at the southern entrance of the Naṭarāja temple at Cidambaram called *tiruvāśal sokkaciyān tirunilai eḻu gopuram.*[101]

A Sanskrit record of Kopperuñjiṅga mentions that this ruler constructed a *maṇi-maṇḍapa,* a pedestal (*pīṭha*) and a garden (*upavana*) for the deity at Sonācalendranilaya (Aruṇācaleśvara) of Tiruvaṇṇāmalai.[102] The munificient gifts made by Kopperuñjiṅga to this temple are well known from numerous Tamil inscriptions.

A long Sanskrit inscription of this ruler found at Tripurāntakam (Andhra Pradesh), praises him as a devotee of Naṭarāja of Cidambaram[103] and records that he built the eastern *gopura* at Cidambaram resembling Mount Meru from the riches got from defeating his enemies and named it after himself. From the booty he acquired from his conquests and from the riches used in his *tulāroha* ceremony, he ordered the decorations to be made on the four sides of this *gopura*. This record also mentions that he made gifts to various temples including the ones at Drākṣārāma, Ekāmra (Kāñcīpuram), Vīraṭṭana, Svetajaṁbu (Jambukeśvaram), Madurai and Kāḷahasti.

Many of the lesser-known chiefs and vassals of the imperial rulers contributed to the construction and endowment of temples. An epigraph of an Atiya chieftain, datable to the eighth century AD,[104] discovered at a rock-cut cave temple dedicated to God Raṅganātha at Nāmakkal (Salem district) reveals that this cave-temple called *atiyanātha-viṣṇu-gṛham* and *atiyendra-viṣṇu-gṛham* was caused to be excavated by the Atiya chief named Guṇaśīla also called Soma. The inscribed portion on

101. *SII*, vol. XII, no. 119, pp. 56-57.
102. *ARE*, 65 of 1974-75.
103. *SII*, vol. XII, no. 247, pp. 154-55.
104. *EI*, vol. XXXVI, no. 18, pp. 137-38.

the beam above the corbels of the pillars of the inner sanctum mention the names of gods, demi-gods and demons like Mārkaṇḍeya, Parṇṇa (Suparṇa, i.e., Garuḍa), Varuṇa, Brahmā, Īśa, Dakṣa, Śaśi, Sūrya, Tuṁburu, Nārada, Guru, Bṛgu, Śārṅga, Kaumodakī, Cakra, Nandaka, Pāñcajañya, Śrī, Madhu and Kaiṭabha. It is interesting that the figures found on the wall of the sanctum behind the figure of Raṅganātha are in almost the same order as those given in this inscription which also describes this cave-temple with the technical term *śayyā-gṛham*.

A Sanskrit inscription of the Koḍumbāḷūr chief, Bhūti Vikrama Kesari found at the Mūvarkovil shrine in Koduṁbāḷūr mentions that this chief erected three *vimāna*s (*vimāna traya*) in his name and in the names of his two wives, Kaṟṟaḷī and Varaguṇā and enshrined Maheśvara therein.[105]

Another inscription of a Koḍuṁbāḷūr chief, a vassal of Sundara Coḷa, named Siruveḷa (Siriya Veḷa) found at the Śivayoganāthasvāmi temple at Tiruviśalūr, records that this chief gave some gold for rice offering and the revenue from the village Niṁba or Niṁbāgrahāra for repairs and a lamp to this temple.[106]

Some information about the religious activities of a Milāḍu chief is forthcoming from a bi-lingual record of the period of Rājendra Coḷa II, dated in the 6th year of his reign (AD 1057-58). This chief named Narasiṁhavarman, surnamed Raṇakesari Rāma, who resided at Śrīkovalūra (Tirukkovalūr) gave to Lord Vāmana (Trivikrama) at that place a great *maṇḍapa* made of stone, with pitchers of shining gold, a surrounding wall adorned with excellent buildings and a canopy of pearls.[107]

The Tamil portion of the same inscription gives several more details about this grant. It records that this chief, having seen that the central shrine of the temple at Tirukkovalūr which had formerly been built of bricks and had become old and

105. K.A. Nilakanta Sastri, "Koḍuṁbāḷūr Inscription of Vikrama Kesari," *JOR*, vol. VII, p. 9.

106. *SII*, vol. III, pt. 3, pp. 157-58.

107. *SII*, vol. VII, no. 20 (K), pp. 145-46.

cracked pulled down this temple, rebuilt the central shrine as well as the *maṇḍapa* with granite, placed there five golden pitchers, constructed a surrounding wall along with a *maṇḍapa* in front of it and presented a canopy of pearls. This chief also caused to be re-engraved on the stones of the central shrine, all the endowments from copies of the former engraving on stone.

A few Sanskrit inscriptions mention the gifts to temples given by Tammusiddhi of the lineage of the Telugu Coḍas, vassals of Kulottuṅga Coḷa III, to several temples in the Tamil country. Tammusiddhi, soon after his anointment as king in the town of Nellūr, gifted the village of Muṭṭiyaṁpākka to Lord Varadarāja (Hastiśaileśvara) of Kāñcīpuram as recorded in an inscription in that temple.[108]

A record of this ruler mentions the gift of the income from all levies due to the king from Tiruverkāḍu to the Śiva temple at Satyāraṇya (Tiruverkāḍu)[109] and also gave to Lord Ādipurīśvara at Tiruvoṟṟiyūr (Chennai), all the revenue due to him in the villages belonging to this temple.[110]

An inscription of a Gaṅga chieftain of Kolār (near Mysore) named Śīyagaṅga, a vassal of Kulottuṅga III, records that he constructed the shrine of Anantāḻvār (Ādiśeṣa) in the Varadarājasvāmi temple at Kāñcīpuram.[111]

Another vassal of Kulottuṅga III was the Bāṇa chief called Rājarājadevaṉ Magadhaipperumāḷ who held the title Poṉparappināṉ since he covered the roof of the temple at Tiruvaṇṇāmalai with gold. A Sanskrit inscription of this ruler found at Tiruvaṇṇāmalai records this benefaction of this king.[112] The composer of this inscription states poetically that this ruler

108. *EI*, vol. VII, no. 21B, pp. 153-54.

109. *ARE*, 395 of 1958-59.

110. *EI*, vol. VII, no. 21-A, pp. 149-50.

111. *ARE*, 589 of 1919; K.V. Raman, *Śrī Varadarājaswāmī Temple, Kāñcī*, Delhi, 1975, p. 46.

112. *ARE*, 554 of 1902 and *SII*, vol. VIII, no. 135, pp. 63-64.

(Bāṇeśvara) took away the Pāṇḍyan crown (*pāṇḍyāt=saṁyati saṁhṛtāni makuṭāni*) six times (*pūrvam pañcakam=adya caikam*) and that he presented only one of these to his Coḷa king (*ekañ=coḷakṛte vitīrṇam*). He offered the other five crowns to Lord Aruṇācala of Tiruvaṇṇāmalai (*aparāṇ=ady=aruṇā-khyāyate śāilendraya samarpitāni*) and had nothing to offer to his supplicants (*bhavata kim va=arthine dāsyate*).

Another verse in the same poetic vein states that with his bounties, this Bāṇa chief covered Aruṇādri with gold and thus the sun mistook it for mount Meru.

The officials of the Tamil kings also donated liberally to the temples as seen from many epigraphs. A bi-lingual record of the reign of Uttama Coḷa states that Aṁbalavān Paḻuvūr Nakkaṉ a nobleman of the king's council who received the title Vikrama-Coḷa-Mahārāja from his king, built a Śiva temple of stone called Vijayamaṅgalattu-Mahādeva at a *brahmadeya* called Periya Śrī Vānavaṉmahādevī-caturvedimaṅgalam. He also made an endowment of the village of Neḍuvāyil along with its nearby hamlets for offerings, worship and other needs of the temple, having purchased it tax-free from the assembly.[113]

Naralokavīra, one of the most famous generals of Kulottuṅga Coḷa I, who also served his son and successor, Vikrama Coḷa, is known for his various benefactions to a large number of temples. His numerous inscriptions recorded on the walls of various temples, some in very chaste Sanskrit verses, enumerate his gifts to these shrines.

A long inscription found at the Naṭarāja temple at Cidambaram reveals that Naralokavīra made substantial gifts to the God Naṭarāja of this temple.[114] According to this epigraph, Naralokavīra, also known as Mānāvatāra made arrangements for many street lamps (*vīthidīpa*) to dispel the darkness, arranged for the sprinkling of the streets with holy

---

113. *SII*, vol. XIX, no. 357, pp. 183-86.

114. *SITI*, vol. III, Pt. 2, pp. 1304-24.

water during the festivals of Lord Śiva (*ssekam kartum mudita-bhuvaneś-ūtsaveṣu smarāreḥ*), planted fifty thousand areca-palms (*kramuka-daśa-saha-śrī-pañcakam-tatra cakre*), created a sacred garden (*druma-vanam=anurūpaṁ tatra paty=ābyadhatta*), erected a *maṇḍapa* for Śiva (*śambor maṇḍapam*) on the sea-shore and created a large tank full of fresh and sweet sacred water (*madhura-pāvana-bhūri-toyam toyāśayam*) near the *maṇḍapa*. He also constructed around the Naṭarāja temple a great wall (*śālam=mahāntam*) named after himself, a pair of tall towers (*gopura*), a hall with a hundred pillars (*śata-śilā-stambha-sthiram maṇḍapam*), caused the deepening of the tank and also made provision for setting up of lamps (*maṅgala dīpa*) on either side of the golden gateway on the south side of the temple. The priests of this temple were given rich endowments by him and he constructed a hall of gold for the constant recitation of *Kumāra-stotra*. According to T.N. Subramaniam, this *Kumāra-stotra* refers to the *Tevāram* of Tirujñānasambandar.[115]

Naralokavīra also covered the great *sabhā* (*mahatīm sabhām*) with copper, constructed a golden vehicle with a bull (*vṛṣabha*) mounted on it on which the God was taken in procession during the *bhikṣātana yātrās*, presented a bugle (*kāhala*) inlaid with gold, made arrangements for a regular supply of fresh flowers (*navam=iva puṣpam*) for the Lord, gave precious jewels (*mautikaiḥ bhūṣaṇāni*) and also arranged for the offering of the nectar of milk with sugar-candy (*kṣīram sa-khaṇḍam amṛtam*) to Śiva (*gaurīpati*). He endowed the temple with ten perpetual lamps (*nitya-dīpa*) of fragrant camphor, gave to the God a beautiful water pot (*kalaśa*) and other vessels made of gold, presented one thousand milch cows for conducting the *abhiṣeka* of milk to the God and set up images of Nandi and the Goddess, presented many beautiful jewels set with precious stones (*tad-bhūṣaṇāni bahuratnavicitrāṇi*) and gave one village making it free of tax to meet the expenses of *arcana*.

This devout general also made arrangements to perform *abhiṣeka* every year to the God in the sanctum-sanctorum

115. *SITI*, vol. III, Pt. 2, p. 1311.

(*mūlasthāna*) with one thousand measures, set up a golden image of Tirujñānasambandar and also an image of Bhaṭṭācārya, who is described in this inscription as an important person of the *brāhmaṇa-kula* and who had earlier defeated in debate, opponents of religious other than those who followed the Vedas and established Śaivism in this world. T.N. Subramaniam has suggested that this Bhaṭṭācārya was probably a priest of the temple at that time and that he was probably Sundaramūrti Nāyanār.[116]

Naralokavīra also constructed a *prākāra* and a *maṇḍapa* to the shrine of Goddess Pārvatī, adorned her image with jewels from head to foot (*bhūṣaṇam mauḷipūrvam*) and presented a yellow robe of gold to this Goddess (*pītāmbaram kāñcanameśa devyā*). This record adds that he erected a high outer wall (*śālam*) constructed of stone (*śilābhiḥ*) to the shrine of this Goddess (Śivā) and also gave a perpetual endowment for supplying oil (*taila*) and milk (*kṣīra*) daily for children.

The Tamil portion of this epigraph repeats all these details and also adds that Naralokavīra created an *agrahāra* for the brāhmaṇas to live in, constructed a sluice to the big tank for irrigating the lands of the brāhmaṇas known as the "three thousand of Tillai" (*Tillai-mūvāyiravar*), covered many parts of the *sabhā* with gold, gave an elephant to the temple and also built out of stone the temple of *Śuḍalai-y-amarndān* (he who took his abode at the crematorium at Tillai (Cidambaram).

Vikrama Coḷa who was also served by Naralokavīra was a devotee of Lord Naṭarāja of Cidambaram. It seems that Vikrama Coḷa's buildings and gifts in Cidambaram were meant to complete an extensive remodelling of the temple, begun by Naralokavīra in the closing years of Kulottuṅga's reign and that this chieftain had much to do with the planning and execution of Vikrama Coḷa's projects in the holy city.[117]

---

116. *SITI*, vol. III, Pt. 2, p. 1320.
117. K.A. Nilakanta Sastri, *Studies in Coḷa History and Administration*, Madras, 1932, p. 176.

Naralokavīra's gifts to the Varadarājasvāmi temple in Kāñcīpuram are known from a long inscription written in chaste and beautiful Sanskrit found in this temple. This record mentions the construction by Naralokavīra of the kitchen-room, a *maṇḍapa*, and the high *prākāra* wall and the setting-up of a recumbent image of Hari. He made a gift of a gold pinnacle to this new shrine and made an endowment for perpetual lamps and a flower-garden.[118]

An inscription found in the Vyāghrapādeśvara temple in Siddhamaṅgalam (South Arcot district) records that Naralokavīra, called in this inscription as Nartakka and Mānāvatāra, the ruler of Manavil, built a stone temple (*vimāna*) along with a *prākāra* and a *maṇḍapa* to Lord Śiva (Paśupati) at Siddhaliṅga, described as a beautiful and prosperous *agrahāra*, during the reign of Kuḷottuṅga I.[119] The very same facts are recorded in another inscription in the same temple.[120]

Similarly, he made a gift of a gold aureola and money for two lamps to the temple of Somanātheśvara in Āttūr (Tirunelveli district), as attested by a Sanskrit epigraph in this shrine.[121] Naralokavīra's Tamil inscriptions also reveal his benefactions to numerous other temples in the Tamil country.

A minister of Kulottuṅga I (*colendra-mantri*) called Maliruñjolai erected a *maṇḍapa* in the Varadarājasvāmi temple at Peṇṇaḍam (South Arcot district) as stated in an inscription in the same shrine.[122] An epigraph from the Raṅganāthasvāmi temple, Śrīraṅgam states that another minister of Kulottuṅga Coḷa called Vāṇādhirāja constructed a *prākāra* in this temple.[123]

A *sāmanta* (feudatory) of Kopperuñjiṅga named Gāṅgeya is stated to have excavated a tank, constructed a *maṇḍapa* and

118. *ARE*, 473 of 1919; K.V. Raman, *op. cit.*, p. 14.
119. *SII*, vol. XXVI, no. 390, pp. 253-54.
120. *Ibid.*, no. 388, pp. 252-53.
121. *ARE*, 405 of 1930.
122. *ARE*, 271 of 1928-29.
123. *SII*, vol. XXIV, no. 26, p. 21.

gifted chariots to the temple of Aruṇācaleśvara at Tiruvaṇṇāmalai.[124]

With regard to the period of the Pāṇḍyas, a few Sanskrit inscriptions provide some information about the contribution of Pāṇḍyan officials in the sphere of religion. An inscription found in the rock-cut Narasiṁha shrine at Āṉaimalai near Madurai mentions that a minister (*mantri*) of Pāṇḍyan Neḍuñjaḍaiyaṉ called Madhurakavi set up an image of Viṣṇu in the cave (*śilāgṛham viṣṇoḥ*) in the year AD 770.[125] A Tamil inscription in the same place records that this Madhurakavi, whose actual name was Māraṅgāri and who bore the title Mūvendamaṅgaḷapperaraiyaṉ, excavated the cave at Āṉamalai, but passed away before its consecration. His younger brother Māṟaṉ Eyiṉaṉ *alias* Pāṇḍimaṅgala-viśaiyaraiyaṉ, who became the minister after him constructed the *maṇḍapa* in front of the shrine and performed the consecration ceremony.[126]

A Pāṇḍyan Sanskrit inscription of the eighth century AD from the rock-cut cave of Subrahmaṇya at Tirupparaṅguṉṟam (near Madurai) mentions the excavation of an abode for Śaṁbhu (Śiva) and the consecration of the image by Gaṇapati *alias* Sāmanta Bhīma, who is described as chief of the *vaidya*s (*vaidya mukhyaḥ*).[127] A Tamil inscription found at the same shrine provides some more details on the same subject and mentions the excavation of the temple and a tank by Śāttaṉ Gaṇapati who bore the title Pāṇḍi-amṛtamaṅgalavaraiyaṉ who was the *mahāsāmanta* of Parāntaka Neḍuñjaḍaiyaṉ and a resident of Karavandapura.[128] His wife (*dharmapatnī*), named Nakkaṉ Koṟṟi caused to be excavated the shrines for Durgā and Jyeṣṭhā in the same place.

A bi-lingual inscription of the thirteenth century AD, found in the Ninra-Nārāyaṇa shrine at Tiruttaṅgal (Rāmnāḍ district)

124. *ARE*, 65 of 1974-75.

125. *EI*, vol. VIII, no. 33, pp. 319-20.

126. *Ibid.*, p. 320.

127. *EI*, vol. XXXVI, no. 15, p. 117.

128. *Ibid.*

records that a minister of Māravarman Sundara Pāṇḍya I named Gurukulaṭṭaraiyaṉ built of stone the *garbha-gṛha, ardha-maṇḍapa* and the *mahā-maṇḍapa* of this temple. This person also known as Śoṟan Uyyaṉiṉṟāḍuvāṉ in the Tamil section, set apart his village Ānaiyūr *alias* Teṉṉavan-Śiṟṟūr for maintaining the service called Sundara Pāṇḍyan *sandi* in this temple in the 7th regnal year (AD 1227) of this king.[129]

Āḻvārs and Nāyaṉmārs

There appear to be a few references to the Vaiṣṇava and Śaiva Tamil saints, the Āḻvārs and Nāyaṉmārs in the Sanskrit inscriptions of this study. Māraṅgāri or Madhurakavi mentioned earlier as the minister of the Pāṇḍyan ruler, Neḍuñjaḍaiyaṉ from Karavandapura and who set up the image of Viṣṇu in the cave-temple at Āṉaimalai has been identified by some scholars with Madhurakavi Āḻvār, one of the twelve Āḻvārs and who hailed from Pāṇḍyanāḍu and who was a disciple of Nammāḻvār.[130] His only work was a hymn on Nammāḻvār who interestingly was called Kāri Māṟaṉ and was possibly a chieftain of Kurugūr in Pāṇḍyanāḍu.[131]

The Pattattāḷmaṅgalam plates state that a person named Maṅgalarāṣṭra-bhartṛ (the lord of the district called Maṅgala) and called Maṅgalanāḍāḷvan in the Tamil portion requested his king Nandivarman Pallavamalla to give a land-grant to some learned brāhmaṇas.[132] K.V. Subrahmanya Aiyer has identified Maṅgala-nāḍu as a sub-division of Aruḷmoḻideva-vaḷanāḍu in which the village of Maṅgalam now called Maṅgal was situated.[133]

This ruler of Maṅgalarāṣṭra has been glorified in this epigraph as the store-house of austerities and virtues

129. *ARE*, 554 of 1922.

130. K.A. Nilakanta Sastri, *The Pāṇḍyan Kingdom*, Madras, 1972, p. 86.

131. K.V. Raman, "Karavandapuram or Uggirankoṭṭai — An Ancient Fortress Town of the Pāṇḍyas," *JIH*, vol. LII, p. 70.

132. *EI*, vol. XVIII, no. 14, v. 10, p. 121 (Paṭṭattāḷmaṅgalam plates).

133. *Ibid.*, p. 119.

(*parantapo-guṇanidhiḥ*) heroic (*vīraḥ*), highly distinguished (*variṣṭaḥ*), whose wealth was honour (*māna dhanaḥ*), whose spreading fame enveloped the interior of all quarters (*sva kīrti-visara vyāpt-ākhilāś-āntaraḥ*) and who was a relative of the world (*jagat bāndhavaḥ*). These references bear a close resemblence to the epithets which Tirumaṅgai Āḻvār has applied to himself in his Periya Tirumoḻi and it is possible that Maṅgalanāḍāḻvan subsequently became the celebrated Vaiṣṇava saint Tirumaṅgai Aḻvār.[134] It is known from his work that this great Vaiṣṇava saint was a contemporary of Nandivarman Pallavamalla.[135]

The Anbil plates mention that the Sanskrit *praśasti* was composed by Mādhava Bhaṭṭa who is called as the disciple of Śrīnātha.[136] T.A. Gopinatha Rao had identified this Śrīnātha with Nāthamuni the Vaiṣṇava *ācārya*, who collected and codified the hymns of the Āḻvārs.[137]

Apart from the benefactions made to the main deities in the temples, gifts in the form of land, gold and jewels were made to the images of the Āḻvārs and the Nāyaṉmārs which were consecrated in the temples.

An inscription of the twelfth century AD, of the reign of Kulottuṅga II (Anapāya) found in the Tyāgarājasvāmi temple at Tiruvārūr mentions that he made gifts of land, gold, brass, silver and other excellent treasures (*bhūmi-hiraṇya-kaṁsa-rajatān=anyān-dhanān sa uttamān*) to the images of Brahmapurīśa (Tirujñānasambandar), Vāgādhipati (Tirunāvukkaraiyar) and Svasvāmimitra (Sundaramūrti) at the shrine of the Lord of Ārūr (Tiruvārūr).[138] This record also mentions that the mother of Sundaramūrti called Ñāni was born at Tiruvārūr (called Kamalālaya and Lakṣmyālaya in this epigraph) in the family of Nānāśivācārya and in the Gautama *gotra*.

---

134. *PCM*, p. xvii.
135. C. Minakshi, *ASLP*, p. 231.
136. Anbil plates, *op. cit.*, v. 46, p. 64.
137. *Ibid.*, p. 54; see also K.A. Nilakanta Sastri, *The Coḷas*, p. 638.
138. *SII*, vol. II, pp. 153-54.

Similarly, there are some records registering benefactions made for worshipping the images of the Āḻvārs. A bi-lingual epigraph from the Karivaradarāja Perumāḷ temple from Komāraliṅgam dated AD 1231 in the reign of Tribhuvanacakravartin Konerinmaikoṇḍaṉ records a gift of land for offerings to the ten Āḻvārs in the temple of Aḻagar at Tirumāliruñjolai (Aḻagarkovil) near Madurai.[139]

Another bi-lingual inscription from the Vijayarāghava Perumāḷ temple in Tirupputkuḻi (near Kāñcīpuram) of the thirteenth century AD, belonging to the period of Jaṭāvarman Sundara Pāṇḍya I records the gift of the village of Dadhipākkam (Tayirpākkam in Tamil), a hamlet of Dāmar for offerings to the Āḻvārs set up in the temple by Pallavarāyaṉ of Tuñjalūr.[140]

A Tamil inscription of Rājendra I from the Aḻagiya Narasiṁhaperumāḷ temple at Eṇṇāyiram (South Arcot district), mentions an endowment, among other things, for the recitation of the Tiruvāymoḻi (of Nammāḻvar) in this temple as mentioned earlier.[141] Apart from this record, there are numerous other epigraphs which record grants made for the singing of Tiruppadīyam and Tiruvāymoḻi in temples.

Temple Gardens

Apart from the benefactions in the form of buildings, gold and jewellery to the temples, the rulers and other officials deemed it an act of great merit to donate garden-lands called as *nandavana* and *upavana* in the Sanskrit inscriptions to these shrines.[142] Various kinds of flowering plants and fruit-bearing trees were raised in these gardens and their produce offered to the deities in the temples. The Sanskrit inscriptions provide a number of instances where such donations of garden-lands have been made.

---

139. *ARE*, 135 of 1909.
140. *ARE*, 176 of 1916.
141. *EI*, vol. XXXIX, no. 34, p. 230.
142. *ARE*, 144 of 1894; *SII*, vol. IV, no. 225, pp. 31-34; *ARE*, 473 of 1919; *ARE*, 65 of 1974-75; *SII*, vol. XXIV, No. 274, pp. 293-94; *ARE*, 578 of 1920.

In addition to royalty and state officials, there are a very large number of Sanskrit and bi-lingual epigraphs which register the gifts made by commoners to temples in the form of gold, livestock and paddy. An analysis of these records reveals that people from all walks of life such as brāhmaṇas, women, headmen of villages and many others gave various types of gifts to the temples of their choice. These donations were usually done as an act of merit and for the welfare of the donor and they helped in the upkeep and maintenance of the temple.

Pāśupatas, Kālāmukhas and Kāpālikas

Apart from the two main branches, Śaivism and Vaiṣṇavism, there also existed followers of various sub-sects such as the Pāśupatas, Kāpālikas and the Kālāmukhas who followed certain practices which were very gruesome such as eating food in a skull and smearing their bodies with ashes of a corpse. They appear even to have practised human sacrifices.[143]

The fact that these sects lived in the ancient Tamil country is seen from the literary as well as the epigraphical data of the period. The Sanskrit play, *Mattavilāsaprahasana* of Mahendravarman I mentions that the Kāpālikas and Pāśupatas lived in the Pallava capital, Kāñcīpuram. They are also ridiculed in the work for their life style.[144]

An inscription of the Koḍumbāḷūr chief, Bhūti Vikrama-Kesari from the Mūvarkovil temple at Koḍumbāḷūr, reveals that these sects thrived in the Coḷa period also.[145] According to this epigraph, Vikrama Kesari gave to a chief of the Kālāmukha sect, named Mallikārjuna a big *maṭha* (*bṛhan-maṭham*) attached to this temple of Śiva and also gave eleven villages for the maintenance of that *maṭha* and for the enjoyment of fifty *asita-vaktra* (Kālāmukha ascetics). This chief

143. T.A. Gopinatha Rao, *Elements of Hindu Iconography*, Delhi, 1985, vol. II, pt. 1, p. 28.

144. N.P. Unni, *Mattavilāsaprahasana*, Trivandrum, 1974.

145. K.A. Nilakanta Sastri, "Koḍumbāḷūr Inscription of Vikrama Kesari,"

of the Kālāmukha sect, Mallikārjuna has been described in this epigraph as master of the Vedas (*vedapāragaḥ*) and a student of Vidyārāśi.

From some Tamil inscriptions it is known that Tiruvoṟṟiyūr was also an important centre of Kāpālika Śaivism where the work "*Somasiddhānta*" which dealt with the doctrines of the Kāpālika school was propagated.

Ritual Sacrifices

The performance of sacrifices (*yajñas*) has been traditionally held to be one of the duties of the kings. The Saṅgam works speak of the performance of various sacrificial ceremonies by the rulers.

The Pallava kings who were strict followers of the Vedic faith, conducted numerous sacrifices such as the *aśvamedha*, *rājasūya* and the *soma yajña* as revealed by many of the copper-plate charters, especially those of the early Pallava kings.

The Mañcikallu inscription mentions that Siṁhavarman performed the *śānti* and *svastyāyana* rites for his victory and for increasing his merits and prowess.[146] *Śānti* was a rite for eradicating evil and *svastyāyana* for the attainment of prosperity.[147]

The Hīrahadagalli inscription states that Śivaskanda-varman performed the *agnīṣṭoma*, *vājapeya* and *aśvamedha* sacrifices and is described as *aggitthomavājapeyassa-medhayāji*.[148]

That the *aśvamedha yajña was* also performed by the Pallava ruler Kumāraviṣṇu, is known from the Oṁgoḍu (I) grant.[149] Many early Pallava charters praise the kings of the Pallava dynasty as "having performed many horse sacrifices according to rule" (*yathāvadāhṛt-anek-āśvamedhānāṁ*).[150]

146. *EI*, vol. XXXII, no. 2, pp. 87-90 (Mañcikallu inscription).
147. *Ibid.*, p. 88.
148. *EI*, vol. I, no. 1, p. 5 (Hīrahadagalli plates).
149. *EI*, vol. XV, no. 11, p. 251 (Oṁgoḍu I plates).
150. Uruvapaḷḷi plates, *op. cit.*, p. 51, Cendalūr plates, *op. cit.*, p. 235; Pikira plates, *op. cit.*, no. 15, p. 162; *EI*, vol. XXIV, no. 43, p. 302 (Viḷāvatti plates).

The Vunnaguruvapālem plates record that the Pallava kings performed many sacrifices inclusive of the *aśvamedha* according to the rules of the *śāstras* (*yathāvad-āhṛt-aśvamedh-ādy-aneka-kratu yājinām*).[151] Another epigraph records that Parameśvaravarman I performed the horse-sacrifice and many other sacrifices according to rule (*yathāvad-ābhṛt-aśvamedh-ādy-aneka-kratu-yājinaḥ*).[152]

The fragmentary Śivanvāyal Pillar inscription of a Pallava king (name lost) praises one Siṁhavarman, obviously an ancestor, as a performer of ten *aśvamedhas* (*daśāśvamedha*) and *bahusuvarṇa* sacrifices in characters of about the seventh-eighth century AD.[153] The *soma* sacrifice also seems to have been performed during this period. The Kūram inscription records that in the race of the Pallavas, all the kings performed the *soma* sacrifice.[154]

A reference to an *aśvamedha* sacrifice conducted by a Niṣāda chief is also mentioned in the Udayendiram plates.[155] According to this epigraph, Udayacandra, a general of Nandivarman Pallavamalla chased the Niṣāda chief named Pṛthivīvyāghra who was following the *aśvamedha* horse and defeated him.

The information regarding the *aśvamedha* sacrifices given in the Sanskrit inscriptions of the Pallavas are corroborated by the some of the sculptures depicting the historical events of this dynasty found in the Vaikuṇṭhaperumāḷ temple, Kāñcīpuram. C. Minakshi has identified at least three panels which depict the performance of the *aśvamedha* sacrifice and which correspond to the information supplied by the copper-plate charters.[156] The sculptures depict the *yūpa* or the sacrificial post, the beautifully decorated horse tied to this *yūpa* and the rulers and their queens who were to perform the sacrifice.

151. Vunnaguruvapalem plates, *op. cit.*, p. 96.
152. Reyūrū plates, *op. cit.*, p. 95.
153. *EI*, vol. XXVII, no. 13, p. 62 (Śivanvāyal pillar inscription).
154. *SII*, vol. I, no. 151, p. 148 (Kūram plates).
155. Udayendiram plates, *op. cit.*, l. 37, p. 368.
156. C. Minakshi, *HSVK*, p. 59.

The inscriptions of the Coḷas also record some of the sacrifices performed by the rulers of this dynasty. However, it seems that compared to the Pallava period, the sacrifices conducted by the royalty during this age were fewer in number. According to K.A. Nilakanta Sastri, "More emphasis seems to have been laid in this period on *dāna* (gift) in preference to *yāga* (sacrifice)."[157]

Only one Coḷa Sanskrit record, the Kanyākumārī inscription of Vīra Rājendra mentions that Rājarāja I caused several sacrificial rites to be performed.[158] However, this epigraph does not give any details about these sacrifices.

The inscriptions of the Pāṇḍyas also mention the performance of such Vedic sacrifices. The Larger Siṉṉamaṉūr plates mention that many of the rulers of the Pāṇḍyan dynasty performed numerous *rājasūya* and *aśvamedha* sacrifices.[159]

It is interesting to note that many of the poet-composers of the Sanskrit inscriptions are praised as performers of Vedic sacrifices. The poet Trivikrama, the composer of the Kaśākuḍi plates is described as "one who performed sacrifices according to the Vedas" (*trayi-vidhi-krama-kratu-pravartakaḥ*).[160] The poet Vidyācakravartin who composed the Bāṇa records as well as some of the Coḷa epigraphs of the period of Kulottuṅga III and who earlier seems to have enjoyed the patronage of Ballāla II (see Chapter VI) is mentioned in the Tiruveḷḷaṟai inscriptions[161] as the performer of the *vājapeya* sacrifice (*vājapeyayājin*). The Sanskrit work *Rukmiṇikalyāṇa*, authored by another Vidyācakravartin, a scion of the same family whose patron was Ballāla III, mentions that the family of Vidyācakravartins were *vaidikas* and performers of sacrifices.[162]

157. K.A. Nilakanta Sastri, *The Coḷas*, Madras, 1984, p. 451.
158. Kanyākumārī plates, *op. cit.*, v. 66, p. 145.
159. *SII*, vol. III, no. 206, v. 9, p. 451 (Larger Siṉṉamaṉūr plates).
160. Kaśākuḍi plates, *op. cit.*, v. 31, p. 351.
161. *ARE*, 207 and 208 of 1938-39.
162. S.S. Janaki, *Gadyakarṇāmṛta*, Madras, 1981, p. 23.

Mahādānas

The gift of certain items of great value was considered as *mahādāna*.[163] Many of these *mahādānas* were practised by the kings of ancient and medieval India with the intention of distributing wealth and acquiring religious merit.

The inscriptions of the Pallavas, Coḷas, and Pāṇḍyas reveal that these kings gave *mahādānas* to deserving people on a number of occasions. The Oṁgoḍu (II) charter records that Skandavarman made gifts of numerous cows, gold and land (*aneka-go-hiraṇya-bhūmi-ādi-pradānaiḥ*).[164]

During the Coḷa period, the *tulābhāra* ceremony seems to have been popular and was performed by many rulers. Parāntaka I, according to the Veḷāñjeri plates, performed the *tulābhāra* with the gold acquired by his valour (*hemnāvīryañcitena*) at three places namely at Śrīrāmatīrtha (Rāmeśvaram), Kanyātīrtha (Kanyākumārī) and at Śrīraṅgam.[165] The Udayendiram plates of Pṛthivīpati II mention that Parāntaka I performed many meritorious acts such as the *hemagarbha* and *tulābhāra*.[166] The Tiruvālaṅgāḍu plates record that after he was anointed king, Rājarāja I was weighed against gold pieces in the scales (*tulā*) in the *tulābhāra* ceremony.[167]

Many of the epigraphs of the Pāṇḍyas reveal that the kings of this dynasty frequently performed many *mahādānas*, especially the *tulāpuruṣa* or *tulābhāra*. A Tamil inscription of the Pāṇḍyan king Cendaṉ or Jayantavarman of the seventh century AD contains some Sanskrit expressions which refer to

---

163. The sixteen *mahādānas* traditionally known are: *tulāpuruṣa, hiraṇyagarbha, brahmāṇḍa, kalpavṛkṣa, gosahasra, kāmadhenu, hiraṇyāśra, hiraṇyāśvaratha, hemnāstiratha, pañcalaṅga, dhāradāna, viśvacakra, kalpalatā, saptasāgara, ratnadhenu* and *mahābhūtagata*.

164. *EI*, vol. XV, no. 11, p. 254 (Oṁgoḍu II plates).

165. R. Nagaswamy, *TVCP Velāñjeri plates of Parāntaka*, I, v. 14, plate II, p. 2.

166. Udayendiram plates, *op. cit.*, v. 7, p. 383.

167. Tiruvālaṅgāḍu plates, *op. cit.*, v. 75, p. 397.

this king as having performed numerous *mahādānas* such as *hiraṇyagarbha, gosahasra* and *tulābhāra*.[168] The Tamil portion of the Veḷvikuḍi record states that Pāṇḍyan Arikesari Māravarman performed the *hiraṇyagarbha* and *tulābhāra* ceremonies and gave the gifts to brāhmaṇas and to the infirm. Māravarman Rājasiṁha I also performed the *gosahasra, hiraṇyagarbha* and *tulābhāra* countless times.[169]

The famous Sanskrit record of Jaṭāvarman Sundara Pāṇḍya I at Śrīraṅgam mentions that he built a shrine for Lord Raṅganātha with the gold which he had given frequently by performing the *tulābhāra*, termed in this epigraph as *tulādhirohaṇa* (ascending of the scales).[170] The composer of this epigraph states in a poetic vein that this king, who repeatedly performed the "ascending of scales everyday at the shrine of Lord Raṅga, would have doubtlessly broken up (Mount) Meru for the sake of its gold, if that mountain had not borne the emblem of the fish which was the crest on his banner."[171] The Tamil literary work, *Koiloḻugu*,[172] a chronicle of the Śrīraṅgam temple, corroborates this inscriptional evidence and states that Sundara Pāṇḍya built twenty-four *tulāpuruṣa maṇḍapa*s in the four inner enclosures of this temple in which he performed the *tulābhāra*s. This work also mentions the performance of a rare *tulābhāra* in which gold and jewels were weighed against his state-elephant and given to the temple.

Several inscriptions of Jaṭāvarman Sundara Pāṇḍya I found at the Naṭarāja temple in Cidambram record that he performed the *tulābhāra* at this temple also. One of these epigraphs states that the gold from the *tulābhāra* ceremony of this ruler was utilized for gilding the *vimāna* of the Naṭarāja temple,[173] while another inscription records the gift of all the gold and pearls by the king after weighing himself against

168. *EI*, vol. XXXVIII, no. 4, p. 32.
169. Veḷvikuḍi plates, *op. cit.*, p. 301.
170. *EI*, vol. III, no. 2, v. 2, pp. 12-13.
171. *Ibid.*, v. 27, p. 14.
172. *Koiloḻugu*, Published by Puttur Krishnaswami Iyengar, Trichi, 1976.
173. *SII*, vol. IV, no. 628, p. 191.

them to Lord Sabhāpati (Naṭarāja).[174] Yet another epigraph reveals that this ruler gave the gold of several *tulābhāra* ceremonies to this God for remodelling the hall (*sabhā*) extensively.[175]

An inscription from Tripurāntakam (Andhra Pradesh) records that the Kāḍava chieftain, Kopperuñjiṅga used the riches acquired from his *tulābhāra* ceremony for benefactions to the Naṭarāja temple at Cidambaram.[176]

Although the rulers gave away gifts very regularly, certain astronomical days were specially chosen for this purpose. The authors of the *Dharmaśāstra*s have specified that grants made on certain occasions such as during the solar and lunar eclipses, on new-moon and full moon days, on the first day of each *ayana* (the sun's passage to the north or south) like *uttarāyaṇa* and *dakṣiṇāyana* would bear special benefits.

Inscriptional evidence reveals that these codes were followed by the Tamil kings. An early Pallava grant, the Oṁgoḍu (II) plates, mention that Siṁhavarman made a grant of the village of Oṁgoḍu to a brāhmaṇa, well-versed in the *śāstra*s on the occasion of an eclipse (*grahaṇa-nimittam*) for the increase of the king's life, strength and success (*āyur-bala-vijay-ābhivṛddhaye*).[177]

Another early Pallava inscription, the Cura plates record that Vijaya Viṣṇugopavarman gave a gift of land and a house-site with a garden in the village of Cura to a learned brāhmaṇa named Cesāmiśarman on the occasion of the *uttarāyaṇa* (*uttarāyaṇa-nimittam*) for the increase in the life, strength and success of the king in exactly the same words.[178] The Reyūru plates mention that Rājasiṁha gave a land-grant to a brāhmaṇa on a full-moon day (*pūrṇamāsyām*) and lunar-eclipse (*soma-grahaṇa-nimitte*).[179]

174. *SII*, vol. IV, no. 629, p. 192.
175. *SII*, vol. IV, no. 630, p. 192.
176. *SII*, vol. XII, no. 247, p. 155.
177. *EI*, vol. XV, no. 11, p. 225 (Oṁgoḍu II plates).
178. *EI*, vol. XXIV, no. 18, p. 142 (Cura plates).
179. Reyūrū plates, *op. cit.*, l. 18, p. 96.

Rivers

In India, since the Vedic age, some rivers have been considered to be very holy and bathing in them or performing penance on their banks was believed to be very efficacious. Traditionally, rivers like the Gaṅgā, Yamunā, Sarasvatī, Sindhu (Indus), Narmadā, Godāvarī and Kāverī have been considered to be among the holiest in this country.

The inscriptions of the period of this study describe some of these sacred rivers. The Kāverī, the life-line of the mighty Coḷa empire which has been extolled in the *Rāmāyaṇa*[180] and *Mahābhārata*[181] finds mention in these epigraphs.

The Tirucirāpaḷḷi Rock inscription[182] of Mahendravarman I mentions in a poetic vein that Pārvatī, afraid that Śiva, who is fond of rivers (*nadīpriyaḥ*), having perceived the Kāverī, who is pleasing to the eye (*nayanābhirāmām*), who wears a garland of gardens (*ārama mālādharām*) and who possesses lovely qualities (*priyaguṇām*), might fall in love with her, left her father's family and resided permanently on this mountain, calling this river the beloved of the Pallava king (*pallavasya dayitāmetām*).

The Kanyākumārī inscription[183] mentions that people bathe in the Gaṅgā (*amara-sarit*) and do penance in order to obtain heaven (*svarga*), but a bath in the Kāverī and severe penance on her bank (*snānam ghoram tapaśca*) would take those who do them to regions higher even than the abode of the Gods (*surālayād=api*). The same epigraph states very poetically that the Kāverī carries on earth, in the form of water, the very nectar (*pīyūṣa*) obtained by the Gods (*suraiḥ avāptam*) from the ocean of milk (*kṣīr-āṁbhonidhi-mathanāt*).[184]

---

180. *Śrīmad Vālmīki Rāmāyaṇam*, ed. Kuppuswami Sastrigal, Madras, Kiṣkindhā Kāṇḍa, Sarga 41, v. 15.
181. *The Mahābhārata*, tr. M.N. Dutt, vol. I, Sabha Parvā, Ch. 9, v. 20.
182. *SII*, vol. I, no. 33, p. 29.
183. *TAS*, vol. I, no. 54, v. 35, p. 138.
184. *Ibid.*, v. 32.

The Kāḍava ruler, Kopperuñjiṅga bore the title *kāverī-kāmukha* (lover of the Kāverī),[185] thus revealing that this river had captured the sentiments of the Tamil kings.

In the two inscriptions of Mahendravarman I from Tirucirapaḷḷi, the river Kāverī is recorded as Kāvīrī.[186] In many of the Saṅgam works also, this river has been called Kāvīrī, meaning in Tamil, "the river which enriches the gardens."[187] In the Sanskrit epigraphs of the Coḷas, this river is called the Kāverī. In many of the Pallava and Coḷa inscriptions, this river is called Kavīra-tanayā,[188] Kavera-tanayā,[189] Kavera-kanyakā[190] and Kavera-kanyā.[191]

Likewise, India's most sacred river, the Gaṅgā, also called Bhāgīrathī and Mandāginī in a few Sanskrit records has been extolled in some of the Pallava and Coḷa epigraphs.

An inscription of Rājasiṁha found in the Kailāśanātha temple, Kāñcīpuram, contains a beautiful invocation to the holy river Gaṅgā in the very first verse.[192] This is probably the earliest south Indian invocation of the Gaṅgā.[193]

The Pallava rulers seem to have been fascinated by the Gaṅgāvataraṇa (descent of the Gaṅgā) theme. The Tiruciräpaḷḷi cave inscriptions of Mahendravarman I reveal that this ruler set up an image of Śiva as Gaṅgādhara.[194] The Kailāśanātha

---

185. *SII*, vol. XII, no. 120, p. 58.
186. *SII*, vol. I, nos. 33 and 34, pp. 29-30.
187. N. Subrahmanian, *Pre-Pallavan Tamil Index*, Madras, 1990, pp. 267-68.
188. Velūrpāḷaiyam plates, *op. cit.*, v. 10, p. 508.
189. T.N. Subramaniam, *PJCG*, p. 76 and *EI*, vol. VII, no. 21A, v. 12, p. 150.
190. Tiruvālaṅgāḍu plates, *op. cit.*, v. 35, p. 395.
191. Larger Leiden plates, *op. cit.*, v. 22, p. 240.
192. *SII*, vol. I, No. 24, v. I, p. 12.
193. S. Sankaranarayanan, "A Pallava Inscriptional Poem in Sanskrit," *ALB*, vol. 55, 1991, p. 73.
194. *Ibid.*, P.R. Srinivasan, "Gaṅgādharāṣṭakam in Pallava Inscription from Tirucirapalli" from *Śrīnidhiḥ* (*Śrī K.R. Srinivasan Felicitation Volume*), Madras, 1983, pp. 431-35.

temple, in Kāñcīpuram built by Rājasiṁha has many sculptures depicting Gaṅgāvataraṇa and this is found in Māmallapuram also.[195]

The Kaśakuḍi plates mention that the descent of the powerful and spotless race of the Pallavas (*vaṁśāvatāraḥ*) which resembled a partial incarnation of Viṣṇu (*viṣṇor=aṁśāvatāra iva*) purified the whole world like the descent of the Gaṅgā (*gaṅgāvatāra iva*).[196]

The Gaṅgā is also frequently mentioned in the Coḷa copper-plate inscriptions. The Tiruvālaṅgaḍu plates mention that Rājendra I wished to sanctify his own country with the waters of the Gaṅgā (*gaṅgā-jalaiḥ pāvayitum svakīyām-iyeṣa pr̥thvīṁ ravivaṁśa-dīpaḥ*) carried there by the strength of his arm.[197] The next few verses state that he accomplished this by sending his army to vanquish the kings on the banks of the Gaṅgā and that his general got the waters of this river carried to his king. Rājendra I, who assumed the title Gaṅgaikoṇḍacoḷa to commemorate this victory, constructed a tank called Coḷagaṅgam, composed of the waters of the Gaṅgā in his capital-city, Gaṅgaikoṇḍacoḷapuram.[198]

The Esālam plates, recording the same event, mention that having brought the pure waters of the Gaṅgā to his country, Rājendra I surpassed Bhagīratha in this effort (*gaṅgām tuṅga-payodharām guṇavatīm nītva svadeśam prati prāptaśrīḥ sa bhagīratham vyajayat=akr̥cchrāpta-gaṅgājalaḥ*).[199] The Karandai[200] and the Kanyākumārī[201] plates also mention the effort taken by Rājendra I to bring the Gaṅgā to his country.

195. S. Sankaranarayanan, *op. cit.*
196. Kaśākuḍi plates, *op. cit.*, ll. 34-37, pp. 347-48.
197. Tiruvālaṅgāḍu plates, *op. cit.*, v. 109, p. 400.
198. *Ibid.*, vv. 110-24, p. 400.
199. R. Nagaswamy, *ECPR*, v. 17, p. 32.
200. K.G. Krishnan, *KTPR*, v. 64, p. 74.
201. Kanyākumārī Inscription, *op. cit.*, v. 71, p. 146.

Cows

According to the Vedic religion cows (*paśu*) were considered as very sacred animals. The kings and the majority of the people of the Tamil country practised the Vedic religion and hence considered the cows to be very sacred. The reverence in which these animals were held is clearly brought out by some of the Sanskrit inscriptions. The Taṇḍantoṭṭam plates state,

> May the sacred cows whose every limb is purifying and whose purity is demonstrated as it were, in the form of white milk which they yield, grant your desires.[202]

Again, many of the imprecatory verses at the end of the copper-plate charters mentioning land-grants state that those who confiscate the land thus given would incur the sin of killing a hundred thousand cows.

Spiritual Preceptors

The kings of the Tamil country were very pious and followed one or the other of the various sects of Hinduism, according to the tenets of which initiation by a spiritual preceptor (*guru*) is deemed necessary. Some of the Sanskrit inscriptions reveal the respect and devotion shown by these kings to their teachers.

Many of the copper-plate inscriptions of the early Pallava kings such as the Oṁgoḍu (II),[203] Viḻāvaṭṭi,[204] Uruvapaḻḻi[205] and Pikira[206] plates employ the phrase *deva-dvija-guru-vṛdh-opasevinaḥ* (those who nourished the Gods, twice-born, spiritual preceptors and old men) to describe the kings of this dynasty.

It is known from the numerous Tamil inscriptions of the Coḻas, that these kings received advice on religious matters

202. *SII*, vol. II, no. 2, v. 13, pp. 520-21 (Tāṇḍantoṭṭam plates).
203. *EI*, vol. XV, no. 2, p. 254 (Oṁgoḍu (II) plates).
204. Viḻāvaṭṭi plates, *op. cit.*, p. 302.
205. Uruvapaḻḻi plates, *op. cit.*, p. 51.
206. *EI*, vol. VIII, no. 15, p. 161 (Pikira plates); the Uruvapaḻḻi and Pikira plates read — *opacāyino*.

from their spiritual preceptors. A Sanskrit inscription which contains information regarding such a teacher is the Esālam copper-plates of Rājendra I.[207] According to this inscription, a spiritual-preceptor named Sarvaśiva Ārya, who was well-versed in all the Āgamas was the *guru* of Rājendra Coḷā. This preceptor built a temple to Rāmeśvara (Śiva) with great devotion at a place named Eydār, which was a suburb of Rājarājacaturvedimaṅgalam. Rājendra I with respect and devotion to his *guru* gave land to this temple, asking his subordinates to demarcate the land. Nannāḍu and Erpākkam, two villages in Paṇaiyūrnāḍu were grouped into one village, renamed Vikramacoḷanallūr and given to this temple. The *vijñapti* or executor of this order was this *guru* himself.

A Tamil epigraph of the 19th regnal year of Rājendra I from the Bṛhadīśvara temple, Tañjāvūr gives some information about this *rājaguru*, Śarvaśiva Paṇḍita.[208] This record refers to him as the *guru* of Rājendra (*nam uḍaiyār śarvaśiva paṇḍita*). He was given the *ācāryabhogam* in the Rājarājeśvaram (Bṛhadīśvara) temple in Tañjāvūr. The inscription states that only those who deserve it among his students (*śiṣya*) and his student's students (*praśiṣya*) hailing from Āryadeśa, Madhyadeśa and Gauḍadeśa were entitled to receive the teacher's share of two-thousand *kalam* of paddy annually. The record adds that this endowment was to be safeguarded by the *Śaiva-ācārya*s of this lineage (*vaṁśa*).

Some Tamil inscriptions from the Bṛhadīśvara temple mention another royal preceptor of Rājarāja I and Rājendra I known as Īśānaśiva Paṇḍita. One of these mention that he gave gilt copper-pots (*stūpi kalaśa*) to be placed on the subsidiary shrines in this temple in the 29th year of Rājarāja I and that he was the *gurukkaḷ* of this king.[209] The same inscription mentions that he gifted a silver receptacle for sacred ashes during the second year of Rājendra I. Another record dated

207. R. Nagaswamy, *ECPR*, v. 19, p. 32.

208. *SII*, vol. II, no. 20, pp. 106-07; R. Nagaswamy, *ECPR*, p. 11.

209. *SII*, vol. II, no. 90, p. 414.

in the sixth regnal year of Rājendra states that this preceptor gave money for burning camphor (*karpūra*) in the main shrine of Rājarājeśvaram for daily worship and during the annual festivals.[210]

E. Hultzsch has suggested that Īśānaśiva Paṇḍita and Śarvaśiva Paṇḍita were perhaps identical.[211] According to R. Nagaswamy, they should be considered as two different *gurus*, Śarvaśiva succeedingĪśānaśiva to become the *guru* of Rājendra Coḷa sometime after his sixth regnal year (AD 1018).[212] Īśānaśiva acted as *rājaguru* under Rājarāja I till his death and continued to be the *guru* of Rājendra also. Possibly, after Īśānaśiva's death, Śarvaśiva became his preceptor. It is this Śarvaśiva Paṇḍita, the royal preceptor of Rājendra I who built the Esālam temple.[213]

A *guru* of Kulottuṅga Coḷa III named Someśvara (also called Īśvara Śiva) is mentioned in one of the inscriptions of this ruler from Tribhuvanam (Tañjāvur district).[214] This teacher, the son of Śrīkaṇṭha Śaṁbhu is described in this epigraph as a great scholar and well-versed in the eighteen *vidyā*s and the *Śaiva darśana*s and capable of expounding the glory of Śiva as taught in the Upaniṣads. Kulottuṅga Coḷa III who built the Śiva temple of Tribhuvanavīreśvara (at Tribhuvanam) got the God and Goddess consecrated at this temple by this *guru*, who is stated in this inscription as having written a work called *Siddhātaratnākara*.

It is interesting to note that a few records of Jaṭāvarman Sundara Pāṇḍya I from the Naṭarāja temple, Cidambaram which speak of the Sarasvatī-bhaṇḍāra (library) of the temple mention the work *Siddhāntaratnākara* in the library collection.[215] Although these records do not mention the name of the author,

210. *SII*, vol. II, no. 9, pp. 90-91.
211. *Ibid*., no. 4, p. 109.
212. R. Nagaswamy, *ECPR*, p. 12.
213. *Ibid*.
214. *SII*, vol. XXIII, no. 190, p. 147.
215. *EI*, vol. XL, no. 47, pp. 223-24.

it seems identical with the work of the same name that figures in the Tribhuvanam record of Kulottuṅga III who ruled till about AD 1218, i.e., just about thirty-two years before the accession of Sundara Pāṇḍya I, the king of the Cidambaram records.[216]

In support of the above identification, it is interesting to see that the Tribhuvanam epigraph in which Īśvara Śiva is said to be the author of this work, contains the passage *sthānor=yena viviktam aupaniṣadam viśvādhikatvam vibоḥ* and it is significant that the land granted for the maintenance of the *bhaṇḍāra* in the Cidambaram inscription was named *viśvādhikaviveka-maṅgalam* which is evidently connected with the expressions *viśvādhikatvam* and *viviktam* of the verse.[217]

Both Śrīkaṇṭha Śaṁbhu and Īśvaraśiva were the *rājagurus* of the Coḷa kings from the time of Vikrama Coḷa to Kulottuṅga Coḷa III, Śrīkaṇṭha Śaṁbhu being called Uḍaiya Svāmidevar, epithets used in respect of Coḷa preceptors in those days.[218] The name Śrīkaṇṭha Śaṁbhu reminds us of the name Śrikaṇṭha Śiva who was the author of *Śaivabhāṣya* (*Śrīkaṇṭhabhāṣya*) on Bādarāyaṇa's *Brahmasūtra* and who was perhaps a southerner, i.e., of the Tamil country of around AD 1122 and hence a contemporary of Kulottuṅga III.[219]

The famous spiritual preceptor of Rājarāja I was Karuvūr Devar who figures prominently along with this king in paintings at the Bṛhadīśvara temple, Tañjāvūr. Unfortunately, the Sanskrit inscriptions do not contain any information about this teacher.

A Hoysala inscription from the Candracūḍeśvara temple in Hosūr (Dharmapuri district), records that on the thirteenth day after the death of the Hoysala ruler, Vīra-Rāmanātha,

216. S. Sankaranarayanan, "Sanskrit Learning in Ancient Tamil Country (An Epigraphical Survey)," *ALB*, vol. 57, p. 30.

217. *EI*, vol. XL, no. 47, p. 221.

218. *Ibid*.

219. S. Sankaranarayanan, *op. cit.*, p. 31.

Tapodhirāja, the royal preceptor (*guru*) of this king set-up an image of Lord Śiva (Śambhu) in the garden-land there.[220]

Jainism

The presence of Jainism in the Tamil country during the Saṅgam period is attested by some literary works such as the *Śilappadikāram*.

Jainism continued to thrive during the Pallava period also, although the information provided by the Sanskrit epigraphs is very scanty. The bi-lingual Paḷḷankovil inscription of Siṁhavarman datable to about AD 550, provides some important data about the Jain settlements at Tirupparuttikuṉṟu near Kāñcīpuram.[221] According to the Sanskrit portion of this grant, there existed a Jaina monastery named Nandisaṁgha at the holy place (*dharmatīrtha*) of Lord Śrī Vardhamāna consisting of many virtuous teachers among whom Vajranandi who was well-versed in all sacred literature was one. Siṁhavarman gave the village of Śramaṇāśrama (the hermitage of the Śramaṇas) to this ascetic for the worship of the groups of Jinendras, Jainendras and the Munīndras.

The Tamil portion of the same grant mentions that Siṁhavarman, in the sixth year of his reign gave the village Amaṇśerkkai in Perunagara-nāḍu as a *paḷḷiccandam* to the religious teacher named Vajranandi of Paruttikuṉṟil. This inscription also mentions the gift of another sixteen and a half *paṭṭi*s of land in Dāmar village to this Jain teacher.

The temple of Vardhamāna at Paruttikuṉṟil is the same as the one at Tirupparuṭikkuṉṟil near Kāñcīpuram.[222] This record makes it clear that this temple of Śrī Vardhamāna was considered a sacred place for Jains even in the sixth century AD.[223] Later inscriptions from Tirupparutikuṉṟil show that the

220. *ARE*, 275 of 1969-70.
221. T.N. Subramaniam, *PJCG*, pp. 41-83.
222. *Ibid.*, p. 73.
223. K.V. Raman, "Jainism in Toṇḍaimaṇḍalam," *BITCM* (1974 January-June), p. 17.

Nandi-saṁgha continued to be there for a long time under a succession of teachers among whom many names like Candrakīrti, Ananta Vīrya Vāmana, Puṣpasena, etc., occur.[224]

An inscription of the tenth century AD from Kiraipākkam (Chingleput district) mentions the construction of a Jain temple called Deśāvallabha-Jīnālaya to the north of this village by Amara-mudalguru, a disciple of Mahāvīraguru (*mahavīraguro-śiṣyaḥ*) of the Yāpanīya-saṁgha and Kumiḻi-gaṇa who also made a provision for feeding the members of the saṁgha.[225]

Buddhism

Buddhism was also a popular religion in the Tamil country during the Saṅgam period as seen from the evidence gathered from the literature of that age.

Buddhism continued to thrive in the Tamil country even during the subsequent periods, albeit in a limited way since the kings of the Pallava, Pāṇḍya and Coḷa dynasties patronized the Vedic religion which gained ascendency during this period. However, a few Sanskrit epigraphs of this age reveal that these kings were very tolerant of Buddhism and even made endowments towards several Buddhist institutions.

One of the earliest Pallava inscriptions which contain some reference to Buddhism is the Amarāvatī Pillar inscription (Andhra Pradesh).[226] This epigraph records that while returning from an expedition to the north, Siṁhavarman II visited a place which was sacred to the Buddha (Vītarāga) named Dhānyaghaṭa or Dhānyaghaṭaka (Dhānyakaṭa or Dhānyakaṭaka, the well-known old name of Amarāvatī in Andhra Pradesh). Although this inscription is incomplete it appears that the last part must have recorded a donation this king made to Buddha at this place.

---

224. K.V. Raman, "Jainism in Toṇḍaimaṇḍalam," *BITCM* (1974 January-June), p. 18.
225. *ARE*, 22 of 1934-35.
226. *SII*, vol. I, no. 32, pp. 25-38.

This king prayed to the tutelar deities responsible for the protection of that place (*kṣetra*) and also listened to a discourse on the law (*dharma*). Although this inscription is incomplete, it appears that this king was desirous of erecting a statue of the Buddha there, ornamented with gold, silver and jewels.

During the Coḷa period also, Buddhism was prevalent in the Tamil country. The tolerant attitude adopted by the Tamil kings is clearly reflected by the information contained in the bi-lingual Larger Leiden plates.[227] According to this inscription, Rājarāja I, in his twenty-first regnal year (AD 1005), gave the village named Āṉaimaṅgalam to the Cūḷāmaṇivihāra at Nāgapaṭṭinam built by Māravijayottuṅgavarman of the Śailendra dynasty, and the Lord of Śrī Viṣaya (Śrī Vijaya) and Keṭah (Kaḍāram) in the name of his father Cūḷāmaṇivarman. This *vihāra* has been praised in glowing terms in this inscription as being "surpassingly beautiful" (*atiramaṇīyam*) and "equalling the mountain Meru in loftiness" (*kanakagiri-sammunati-vibhavam*). After the death of Rājarāja I, his son Rājendra I issued an enduring edict to be made for this village which had previously been granted by his father. This inscription poetically states that this king ordered that "as long as Śeṣa, the Lord of all serpents holds the entire earth, so long may this *vihāra* last in this world as endowment."

It appears that the Sanskrit portion of this record was composed much after the Tamil portion.[228] According to the Tamil part of this inscription, this *vihāra* was in the process of being built by the ruler of Kaḍāram, Cūḷāmaṇivarman at the time of the grant, i.e., in the twenty-first year of Rājarāja I. However, the Sanskrit portion of this record states that it was built by Māravijayottuṅgavarman, the son of Cūḷāmaṇivarman in his father's name. It appears that the construction of the Cūḷāmaṇivihāra was undertaken by the Kaṭāha king, Cūḷāmaṇivarman himself in the twenty-first year

227. Larger Leiden plates, *op. cit.*, pp. 213-59.

228. *Ibid.*, p. 238.

of the reign of Rājarāja I, but was completed by Cūḷāmaṇi-varman's son Māravijayottuṅgavarman in the reign of Rājarāja's son, Rājendra I.[229]

A Tamil inscription, the Smaller Leiden plates of Kulottuṅga I record that an embassy from the king of Śrī Vijaya consisting of two ambassadors petitioned him to issue a copper-plate grant containing the name of the village granted as *paḷḷiccandam* at Nāgapaṭṭinam built by the king of Kaḍāram and that this was duly done.[230]

229. Larger Leiden plates, *op. cit.*, pp. 238-39.

230. *EI*, vol. XXII, no. 35, pp. 276-79 (Smaller Leiden plates).

Conclusion

THE Sanskrit inscriptions which have been analysed in this study have clearly shown that they are a mine of information, giving details about aspects of administration, both civil and military, economic and social life, education and literature, and religious and cultural conditions as they existed during the time of the Pallavas, Pāṇḍyas and Coḷas.

A detailed analysis of these Sanskrit epigraphs has revealed that they provide data about some topics which do not find such detailed mention in the Tamil inscriptions which are much more copious in number nor in any other source. Thus, the nature of data gleaned from the Sanskrit records are of two types — primary and secondary. As a primary source they supply information which is not forthcoming from any other source. For example, it is in the Sanskrit epigraphs that a reflection of some of the rules laid down in the *Dharmaśāstras* such as the *Manusmṛti* and also the *Arthaśāstra* can be found. Moreover, the names of some of the government officials, some aspects of military organization, details about education of princes, about the educational institutions such as the *ghaṭikās* and *maṭhas* and the contribution of brāhmaṇas in this sphere as well as details about the state of religion and some religious ceremonies such as the *aśvamedha* are known only through the Sanskrit inscriptions.

In addition to this, these Sanskrit records also serve as secondary sources in corroborating the evidence given by the Tamil inscriptions in many instances. Attention has also been drawn to many newly discovered Sanskrit epigraphs which are rich in historical content.

The Sanskrit records provide the names of many of the territorial divisions which existed in the Tamil country and which were found in other parts of south as well as north India and also serve to corroborate the data supplied by the Tamil inscriptions on this topic.

Many of the names of government officials such as *amātya*s, *saciva*s and *mantri*s gleaned from the Sanskrit records reveal that these types of officials existed in the Tamil country as they did in other parts of India also. The Sanskrit records which have been analysed also provide a wealth of data on the various aspects of the administrative machinery as it existed during the periods of the Pallavas, Pāṇḍyas and Coḷas. Similarly, a study of the military organization as can be gleaned from the Sanskrit epigraphs show the special features of the armies of the rulers of the Tamil country.

The overall economic and social conditions have also been reflected in the Sanskrit inscriptions and much light, especially on education and literature are provided by the Sanskrit inscriptions which are not provided in such great detail by any other source.

The manner in which religion was patronized by the rulers and the religious fervour of the kings and the masses and the fillip given to cultural activities are other aspects on which interesting data has been supplied by the Sanskrit records.

Thus, it can be seen that, overall, the Sanskrit records, both lithic as well as the copper-plate inscriptions of the Tamil country of the period of this study, which have not been utilized to their full extent earlier, are indeed a great storehouse of information for the historical and cultural study of the Tamil country. Therefore an analysis of these Sanskrit records has shown that they are an invaluable source for the study of the ancient Tamil country and are almost indispensable as historical data for providing clarity and a better understanding of several aspects of our history.

Appendix I

BHARATA Nāṭya Panels in the East Gopuram, Naṭarāja temple, Cidambaram Extracts (Reproduction) from *ARE*, 1914, pp. 74-81.

No. 920, Public, 4th August 1914

[1]**Descriptive list of different dancing postures from Cidambaram; illustrated in Plates I to IV (opp. p. 80, below)**

No. of sketch on plate	Name	Description in Sanskrit verse	Corresponding no. of verse in the *Bhāratīya Nāṭyaśāstra*
1	Vr̥ścikarecitam	वृश्चिकञ्चरणं कृत्वा स्वस्तिकौ च करावुभौ [।*] रेचितौ विप्रकीर्णौं च [2]कुर्य्याद्दि्वृश्चिकरेचिते [॥*]	099
2	Vr̥ścikam	बाहुशीर्षाञ्चितौ हस्तौ पादः पृष्ठाञ्चितस्तदा [।*] दूरसन्नतपृष्ठञ्च [वृश्चिकं] [तत्प्रकीर्तितम्*] [॥*]	100
3	Vyaṁsitaṁ	आलीढं स्थानकं यत्र करा वक्षसि रेचितौ [।*] ऊर्ध्वाधो विप्रकीर्ण्णौं च व्यंसितं करणञ्च तत् [॥*]	101
4	Pārśvanikuṭṭakam	हस्तौ तु स्वस्तिकौ पार्श्वे तथा पादो निकुट्टितः [।*] यत्र तत् करणं ज्ञेयम् बुधैः पार्श्वनिकुट्टकम् [॥*]	102
5	Lalāṭatilakam	वृश्चिकञ्चरणं कृत्वा पादस्यांगुष्ठकेन तु [।*] ललाटे तिलकं कुर्य्याल्ललाटतिलकञ्च तत् [॥*]	103

No. of sketch on plate	Name	Description in Sanskrit verse	Corresponding no. of verse in the *Bhāratīya Nāṭyaśāstra*
6.	Krāntakam	पृष्ठतः कुञ्चितं कृत्वा व्यतिक्रान्तक्रमन्ततः [।*] आक्षिसौ [च क]रौ कार्य्यौ क्रा[न्तकं] करणे द्विजाः [॥*]	104
7.	Kuñcitam	आद्यः पादो नतः कार्य्यस्सव्यहस्तश्च कुञ्चितः [।*] उत्तानो वामपार्श्वस्थस्तत् कुञ्चितमुदाहृतम् [॥*]	105
8.	[3]Cakramaṇḍalam	प्रलम्बिताभ्याम्बाहुभ्याम् यत् गात्रेण नतेन च [।*] अभ्यन्तरापविद्धं स्यात्तद्ज्ञेयञ्चक्रमण्डलम् [॥*]	106
9.	Bhramarkam	आक्षिप्तस्स्वस्तिकः पादः करौ चोद्वेष्टितौ तथा [।*] त्रिकस्य घलनाच्चैव ज्ञेयम् भ्रमरकञ्च तत् [॥*]	91
10.	Caturam	अञ्चित स्यात् करो वामस्सव्यश्चतुर एव तु [।*] [द]क्षिणः कुट्टितः पादश्चतुरन्तत् प्रकीर्त्ति[तम्] [॥*]	92
11.	Bhujaṅgāñcitakam	भुजंगत्रासितः पादो रेचितो दक्षिणः करः [।*] लताख्यश्च करो वामो भुजंगाञ्चितकम् भवेत् [॥*]	93
12.	Daṇḍakarecitam	विक्षिप्तं हस्तपादञ्च समन्ताद्यत्र दण्डवत् [।*] रेच्यते तद्धि करणं ज्ञेयन्दण्डकरेचितम् [॥*]	94
13.	Vṛścikakuṭṭitam	वृश्चिकञ्चरणं कृत्वा द्वावप्यथ निकुट्टितौ [।*] विधातव्यौ करौ तत्तु ज्ञेयं वृश्चिककुट्टितम् [॥*]	95

14.	Kaṭibhrāntam	सूचीन्दत्वापविद्धञ्च दक्षिणञ्चरणन्न्यसेत् [।*] रेचिता च कटिर्य्यत्र कटिभ्रान्तन्तदुच्यते [॥*]	96
15.	Latāvr̥ścikam	अञ्चितः पृष्ठतः पादः कुञ्चितोर्द्ध्वतलांगुलि [।*] लताख्यश्च करो वामस्तल्लतावृश्चिकम् भवेत् [॥*]	97
16.	Chinnakaraṇam	अलपत्मः कटीदेशे छिन्नपर्य्यायशः कटीन [।*] वैशाखस्थानकनेह तच्छिन्नकरणं भवेत् [॥*]	98
17.	Pādāpaviddhakam	कार्य्यौ नाभितटे हस्तौ प्राङ्मुखौ खटिकामुखौ [।*] सूचीविद्धावपक्रान्तौ पादौ पादापविद्धके [॥*]	87
18.	Valitam	अपविद्धो भवेद्धस्तस्सूचीपादस्तथैव च [।*] तथा त्रिकं विवृत्तञ्च वलितन्नाम तत् भवेत् [॥*]	88
19.	Ghūrṇitam	वर्त्तिताघूर्णितस्सव्यो हस्तो वामश्च डोलितः [।*] स्वस्तिकापसृतः पादः करणं घूर्णितञ्च तत् [॥*]	89
20.	Laḷitam	करिहस्तो भवेद्वामो दक्षिणश्च विवर्तितः [।*] बहुशः कुट्टितः पादो ज्ञेयन्तल्ललितम् बुधैः [॥*]	90
21.	[4]Daṇḍapakṣam	ऊर्द्ध्वजानु विधायाथ तस्योपरि लतान्न्यसेत् [।*] दण्डपक्षञ्च तत् प्रोक्तं करणन्त[त्त्व] वेदिभिः [॥*]	
22.	Bhujaṁgatra- starecitam	भुजंगत्रासितं कृत्वा यत्रोभावपि रोचितौ [।*] वामपार्श्वस्थितौ हस्तौ भुजंगत्रस्तरेचितम [॥*]	
23.	Nūpuram	त्रिकं सुवलितं कृत्वा लतारेचितकौ करौ [।*] नूपुरञ्च तथा पादं करणे नूपुरे न्य[से]त् [॥*]	

No. of sketch on plate	Name	Description in Sanskrit verse	Corresponding no. of verse in the *Bhāratīya Nāṭyaśāstra*
24.	Vaiśākharecitam	रेचितं हस्तपादञ्च कटिग्रीवा च रेचिता [।*] . . . . . स्थानकेनैतत् भवे [द्वै]शाखरेचितम् [॥*]	
25.	Arddhasvastikam	स्वास्तिकौ चरणौ कृत्वा कटिहस्तश्च दक्षिणम [।*] वक्षस्थाने तथा वाममर्द्धस्वस्तिकमादिशेत् [॥*]	79
26.	Añcitam	व्यावृत्तपरिवृत्तस्तु स एव तु करो यदा [।*] अञ्चितो नासिकाग्रे तु तदाञ्चितमुदाहृतम् [॥*]	80
27.	Bhujaṁgatrāsitam	कुञ्चितं पादमुत्क्षिप्य त्र्यश्रमूरुं विवर्त्तये[त्] [।*] कटीजानुविवृत्त्या च भुजंगत्रासितम् भ[वेत्] [॥*]	81
28.	Ūrddhvajānu	कुञ्चितम् पादमुत्क्षिप्य जानु स्तनसमन्न्यसेत् [।*] प्रयोगवशगौ हस्तावूर्द्ध्वजानु प्रकीर्त्तितम् [॥*]	82
29.	[Ni]kuñcitam	[वृश्चिकं चरणं कृत्वा करं पार्श्वे निकु*]श्चयेत् [।*] [नासाग्रे दक्षिणश्चैव ज्ञेयं तत्तु*] [नि]कुञ्चितम् [॥*]	83
30.	Mattalli	वामदक्षिणपादाभ्यां घूर्ण्णमानोपसर्प्पणैः [।*] उद्वेष्टितापविद्धैश्च हस्तैर्म्मत्तल्लयुदाहृतम् [॥*]	84
31.	Arddhamattali	स्खलितापसृतौ पादौ वामहस्तश्च रेचितः [।*] सव्यहस्तः कटिस्थ स्यादर्द्धमत्तल्लि तत् स्मृतम् [॥*]	85
32.	Recitanikuṭṭitam	रेचितो दक्षिणो हस्तः पादस्सव्यो निकुट्टितः [।*] डोळा चैव भवेद्वामस्त[द्रे]चितनिकुट्टितम् [॥*]	86

33.	[5]Diksvastikam	पार्श्वयोरग्रतश्चैव यत्र श्लिष्टकृतो भवेत् [।*] [स्वस्ति]को हस्तपादाभ्यान्तद्दिक्स्वस्तिकमुच्यते [॥*]	74
34.	Alātakam	अलातश्चरणं कृत्वा व्यंसयेद्दक्षिणं करम् [।*] ऊर्द्ध्वजानुक्रमं कुर्य्यादलातकमिति स्मृतम् [॥*]	75
35.	[Kaṭīsamam]	स्वस्तिकापसृतः पादः करौ नाभिकटिस्थि[तौ] [।*] पार्श्वमुद्वाहितञ्चैव [करणन्तत्कटीसमम्*] [॥*]	76
36.	Ākṣiptarecitam	हस्तो हृदि भवेद्वामस्सव्यश्चाक्षिप्तरेचितः [।*] रेचितश्चापांविद्धश्च तत् स्यादाक्षिप्तरेचितम् [॥*]	77
37.	Vikṣiptākṣiptakam	विक्षिप्तं हस्तपादञ्च तस्यैवाक्षेपणम् पुनः [।*] यत्र तत् करणं ज्ञेयं [वि]क्षिप्ताक्षिप्तकं [द्वि]जाः [॥*]	
A.	[6]Nikuṭṭakam	निकुट्टितौ यदा हस्तौ स्वबाहुशिरसोन्तरे [।*] पादौ निकुट्टितौ चैव ज्ञेयन्तत्तु निकुट्टकम् [॥*]	67
B.	Arddhanikuṭṭakam	अञ्चितो बा[हु]शिरसि हस्तस्त्वभिमुखांगुलिः [।*] निकुट्टितार्द्ध[य]ोगेन भवेदर्द्धनिकुट्टकम् [॥*]	68
38.	Kaṭicchinnam	पर्य्यायशः कटिच्छिन्ना बाहू शिरसि पल्लवौ [।*] पुनः पुनश्च करणं कटिच्छिन्नन्तु तत् भवेत् [॥*]	69
39.	Arddharecitam	अपविद्धः करस्सूच्या पादश्चैव निकुट्टितः [।*] सन्नतं यत्र पार्श्व[न्तु] तत् भवेदर्द्धरेचितम् [॥*]	70
40.	Yakṣasvastikam	स्वस्तिकौ चरणौ यत्र करौ वक्षसि रेचितौ [।*] निकुञ्चितन्तथा वक्षो वक्षस्वस्तिकमेव तत् [॥*]	71

No. of sketch on plate	Name	Description in Sanskrit verse	Corresponding no. of verse in the *Bhāratīya Nāṭyaśāstra*
41.	Unmattam	अञ्चितेन तु पादेन रेचितौ तु करौ यदा [।*] उन्मत्तं करणं तत्तु विज्ञेयं [नृ]त्तकोविदैः [॥*]	72
42.	Svastikam	[7]हस्ताभ्यामथ पादाभ्याम् भवतस्स्वस्तिकौ यदा [।*] तत् स्वस्तिकमिति प्रोक्तं करणं करणार्त्थिभिः [॥*]	73
43.	Pṛṣṭhasvastikam	विक्षिप्तोत्क्षिप्तबाहुभ्यां स्वस्तिकौ चरणौ यदा [।*] अपक्रान्तार्द्धसूचीभ्यां तत् पृष्ठस्वस्तिकम भवेत् [॥*]	
[8]44.	Talapuṣpapuṭam	वामे पुष्पपुटः पार्श्वे पादोग्रतलसञ्चरः [।*] तथा च सन्नतम् पार्श्वन्तलपुष्पपुटम् भवेत् [॥*]	59
45.	Vartitam	कुञ्चितौ मणिबन्धे तु व्यावृत्तपरिवर्त्तितौ [।*] हस्तौ निपतितौ चोर्वोर्वर्त्तितं करणन्तु तत् [॥*]	60
[9]46.	Valitoru	शुकतुण्डौ यदा हस्तौ व्यावृत्तपरिवर्त्तितौ [।*] [ऊरू] च वलितौ यस्मि[न्] वलितोरु तदुच्यते [॥*]	61
47.	Apaviddham	आवर्त्त्य शुकतुण्डाख्यमूरुपृष्ठे निपातयेत् [।*] वामहस्तश्च वक्षस्थो ह्यपविद्धन्तु तत् भवेत् [॥*]	62
48.	Samanakham	श्लिष्टौ [स]मनखौ पादौ करौ चापि प्रलंबितौ [।*] देहस्स्वाभाविको यत्र भवेत् समनखन्तु तत् [॥*]	63

49.	Līnam	पताकाञ्चलि वक्षस्थम् प्रसारितशिरोधरम् [।*] [10]नि[भ]ञ्चितांसकूटञ्च तल्लीनं करणं स्मृतम् [॥*]	64
50.	Svastikarecitam	स्वस्तिकौ रेचिताविद्धौ विश्लिष्टौ कटिसंस्थितौ [।*] यत्र तत् करणं ज्ञेयम् बुधैस्स्वस्तिकरेचितम् [॥*]	65
51.	Maṇḍalasvastikam	स्वस्तिकौ तु करौ कृत्वा प्राङ्मुखोर्द्ध्वतलौ समौ [।*] तथा च मण्डलं स्थानम्मण्डलस्वस्तिकन्तु तत् [॥*]	66
52.	Sūcīviddham	पादसूच्या यदा पादो द्वितीयस्तु प्रविध्यते [।*] कटिवक्षस्थितौ हस्तौ सु[चीवि]द्धन्तदुच्यते [॥*]	130
53.	[Hariṇaplutam]	अतिक्रान्तक्रमं कृत्वा [स][मुत्प्लुत्य निपात*]येत् [।*] जंघाञ्चिता परिक्ष[प्ता] [तद्विन्द्याद्धरिणप्लुतम्*] [॥*]	135
54.	Atikrāntam	अतिक्रान्तक्रमं कृत्वा पुरस्तात् सम्प्रसारयेत् [।*] प्रयोगवशगौ हस्तावतिक्रान्ते प्रकीर्त्तितौ [॥*]	119
55.	Viṣṇukrāntam	पुरः प्रसारितः पादः कुञ्चितो गगनोन्मुखः [।*] करौ च रेचितौ यत्र विष्णुक्रान्तन्तदुच्यते [॥*]	152
56.	[11]Āvartam	प्रसार्य्य कुञ्चितम् पादम् पुनरावर्त्तये[द्द्रु]तम्[12] [।*] [प्र]योगवश*]गौ हस्तौ तदावर्त्तमुदाहृतम् [॥*]	112
57.	[13]Ḍoḷāpādam	कुञ्चितम् पादमुत्क्षिप्य पार्श्वात्पार्श्वन्तु डोलयेत् [।*] प्रयोगवशगौ हस्तौ डोळापादं प्रकीर्त्तितम् [॥*]	113
58.	[14]Vivṛttam	आक्षिप्तं हस्तपादञ्च त्रिकंचैव विवर्त्तयेत् [।*] रेचितौ च तथा हस्तौ विवृत्ते करणे द्विजाः [॥*]	114

No. of sketch on plate	Name	Description in Sanskrit verse	Corresponding no. of verse in the *Bhāratīya Nāṭyaśāstra*
59.	Pārśvakrāntam	पार्श्वक्रान्तक्रमं [कृ]त्वा पुरस्तादथ पातयेत् [।*] प्रयोगवशगौ हस्तौ पार्श्वक्रान्तन्तदुच्यते [॥*]	116
60.	Ardhasūci	[15]अलपत्मशिशरोहस्तस्सूचीपादश्च दक्षिणः [।*] यत्र तत् करणं ज्ञेयमर्द्धसूचीति नामतः [॥*]	129
61.	Nāgāpasarpitam	[16]स्वस्तिकापसृतो पादो शिरश्च परिवाहितम् [।*] रेचितौ च तथा हस्तौ स्यातान्नागापसर्पिते [॥*]	157
62.	Talasaṁsphoṭitam	द्रुतमुत्क्षिप्य चरणम् पुरस्तादथ पातयत् [।*] तलसं[स्फो]टितौ हस्तौ तलसंस्फोटिते म[तौ] [॥*]	122
63.	[Vṛ]ṣabhakrīḍitam	[प्रयुज्यातालकं पूर्वे*] हस्तौ चापि हि रचेयेत् [।*] [कुञ्चितावञ्चितौ चैव*] [वृ]षभक्रीडिते सदा [॥*]	156
64.	Daṇḍapādam	[नू पुर*]श्चरणं कृत्वा दण्डपादम् प्रसारयेत् [।*] [क्षिप्त*]विद्धकरश्चैव दण्डपादन्तदुच्यते [॥*]	134
65.	Niveśa-karaṇam	करौ वक्षःस्थितौ कार्य्यावुरो निर्भुग्नम् एव च [।*] मण्डलं स्थानकञ्चैव निवेशकरण[ञ्च] तत् [॥*]	148
66.	Premkhoḷitam	डोळापादक्रमं कृत्वा समुत्प्लुत्य निपातयेत् [।*] परिवृत्तन्त्रिकञ्चैव तत् प्रेंखोळितमुच्यते [॥*]	136
67.	Gṛddhrāvalī[nakam]	[पृष्ठप्रसा*]रितः पाद किञ्चिदञ्चितजानुकः [।*] [यत्र प्रसारितौ बाहू तत्*] [स्यात्]गृद्धावली[नकं] [॥*]	126

68.	[17]Nitambakaraṇam	[भुजा*][वूद्धर्व][विनिष्का*]न्तौ हस्तौ चाभिमुखांगुली [।*] [बद्धा चारी तथा*]चैव नितम्बे करणे भवेत् [॥*]	137
69.	[18][Loḷitam]	रेचिताववञ्चितौ हस्तौ लोळितं . . . . [।*] . . . . . श्च/ . . . ल्लोळि . . [॥*]	
70.	Skhalitam	डोळापादक्रमं कृत्वा हस्तौ तदनुगावुभौ [।*] रेचितौ घूर्ण्णितौ चापि स्खलितं करणं [भ]वेत् [॥*]	138
71.	[Sarpi]tam	[19]अञ्चितापसृतः पादश्शिर[श्च]परिवाहितम् [।*] [रोचि]तौ च तथा [हस्तौ तत्स*][र्पि]तमुदाहृतम् [॥*]	133
72.	Vidyutbhrāntam	पृष्ठतो वलितम् पादं शिरो घृष्टम् प्रसारयेत् [।*] सर्व[तोमण्डर्ला*]बद्धं विद्युत्भ्रान्तन्तदुच्यते [॥*]	118
73.	Sannatam	उत्प्लुत्य चरणौ कार्य्यावग्रतस्स्वस्तिकस्थितौ [।*] सन्नतौ च [त]था हस्तौ सन्नतन्तदुदाहृतम् [॥*]	127
74.	Vivarttitakam	आक्षिप्तं हस्तपादञ्च त्रिकञ्चैव विवर्त्तितम् [।*] [द्वितीयो रोचितो हस्तो विवर्त्तितकमेव तत्*] [॥*]	120
75.	Sūci	कुञ्चितं पादमुत्क्षिप्य कुर्य्यादग्रस्थितम् भुवि [।*] [प्रयोगवशगौ हस्तौ] तत् सूचि परिकीर्त्तितम् [॥*]	128
76.	Siṁhavikṛḍitam	अल[तञ्च*]पुरस्कृत्य द्वितीयञ्च व्रुतक्रमम् [।*] ह[स्तौ पादानुगौ चै]व सिंहविक्रीडितम् [स्मृतम्] [॥*]	141
77.	Arggaḷam	पृष्ठतः प्रसृतः पादो द्वौ [20]तालावर्द्धमेव च [।*] तथैव चानुगो हस्तः [पु]रतस्त्वर्ग्गळं तु तत् [॥*]	110

No. of sketch on plate	Name	Description in Sanskrit verse	Corresponding no. of verse in the *Bhāratīya Nāṭyaśāstra*
78.	Uromaṇḍalikam	स्वस्तिकापसृतौ [21]पादावपविद्धक्रमौ यदा [।*] उरोमण्डलिनौ हस्तावुरोमण्डलिकन्तु तत् [॥*]	107
79.	Karihastakam	वामो वक्षस्थितो हस्तः प्रोद्वेष्टित[तलो परः*] [।*] अञ्चितश्चरण[श्चैव प्रयोज्यः करिहस्तके] [॥*]	139
80.	Siṁhakampitakam	पृष्ठप्रसर्प्पितः पादश्स्तथा हस्तौ निकुञ्चितौ [।*] पुनस्तथैव कर्तव्यौ [22]सिंहाक [र्षि]त[के] द्विजाः [॥*]	142
81.	Udghaṭṭitam	पादावुत्घट्टितौ काय्यौं [23]तलसंघट्टितौ करौ [।*] [24]नतं तु पार्श्वे कर्तव्यं बुधैरूत्घट्टि[ते[25] सदा*] [॥*]	155
82.	[26][Maṇikākrīḍitam]	तलसञ्चरपादभ्यामुत्प्लुत्य प [तनं भ*] वेत् [।*] सन्नतं वलितं गात्रम् [मनिका][क्रीडितं तु तत्*] [॥*]	149
83.	[27]Saṁbhrāntam	[करमा*] [वर्त्तितं कृ]त्वा ह्यूरूपृष्टे(ष्ठे) निकुञ्चयेत् [।*] [ऊरू*][श्चै*]व तथा विद्धस्समुभ्रान्तं करणन्तु तत् [॥*]	153
84.	Janita	एको पक्षस्थितो हस्तो द्वितीयश्च प्रलम्बितः [।*] तलाग्रसंस्थितः पादो जनिते करणे भवेत् [॥*]	146
85.	[28]Upasṛtakam	आक्षि[प्तश्चर*]णः काय्यों हस्तस्तस्यैव [चानुगः*] [।*] [आनतं च तथा गात्रं तथोपसृतकं भवेत्*] [॥*]	144
86.	Pārśvajānu	एकस्समस्स्थितः पाद ऊरुपृष्ठे स्थितोपरः [।*] मुष्ठिहस्तश्च वक्षस्थः [पा]र्श्वजानु तदुच्यते [॥*]	125

87.	[Madaskhalitakam]	करौ प्रलम्बितौ [कार्यौ*]शिरश्च परिवाहितम् [।*] पादौ च वलि [ताविद्धौ मदस्खलित*]के द्विजाः [॥*]	151
C.	[Viṣkambham]	[अप*]विद्धः करस्सूच्या [पा][दश्चैव निकुट्टि*]तः [।*] [वक्षस्थश्च करो वामो विष्कंभे करणे भवेत्*] [॥*]	154
[29]88.	Vikṣiptam	विक्षिप्तं हस्तपादञ्च पार्श्वतः पृष्ठतोपि व [।*] एकमार्ग्गगतं यत्र तद्विक्षिप्तमुदाहृतम् [॥*]	111
89.	Udvṛttam	[आ]क्षि[प्तह]स्तमाक्षिप्तदेहमाक्षिप्तपादकम् [।*] [उद्धत्य गात्रमि*]त्येतदुद्वृत्तं करणं स्मृतम् [॥*]	143
90.	Ūrūdvṛttam	करमावृत्तकरणमूरुपृष्ठेञ्चितन्न्यसेत् [।*] जंघाञ्चिता तथोद्वृत्ता हुरूह्येद्वृत्तन्तु तत् भवेत् [॥*]	150
91.	[Ākṣiptam]	आक्षिप्तं हस्तपादन्तु क्रियते यत्र वेगतः [।*] [आक्षिप्तं करणं नाम विज्ञेयं तद्दिवजोत्तमाः*] [॥*]	108
92.	[30]Śakaṭāsyam	निषण्णांगस्तु चर[ण]म् प्रसा[र्य्य] तलसंचय*]म् [।*] [31]उद्वाहितमुरः कृत्वा शकटास्यम् प्र[योज]येत् [॥*]	158
93.	[32]Gaṅgāvataraṇam	ऊर्द्ध्वांगुलितलः पादस्त्रिपताकाववोमुखौ [।*] हस्तौ [33]शिरस्सन्नतश्च गंगावतरणन्त्विति [॥*]	159

References

1. The list includes 93 figures numbered consecutively and three others numbered A, B and C. Sketches of the three latter figures were omitted by mistake and consequently do not appear on the plates. The *Bhāratīya Nāṭyaśāstra* while it enumerates 108 postures in vv. 33 to 53 of the printed Bombay Edition, describes only 101, thus omitting seven postures. Of those latter

six are supplied by Nos. 21 to 24, 42 and 69 of the Cidambaram sculptures. It may be noted that the *Bhāratiya Nāṭyaśāstra* makes a mistake in the description of Pṛṣṭhasvastika (No. 43) quoting wrongly the second half of v. 42 (in the list) and the first half of v. 43. The Cidambaram labels also are defective inasmuch as they do not supply us with the description of eleven postures, viz., Talavilāsita, Vinivṛtta, Niśumbhita, Gajakrīḍitaka, Garuḍapluta, Gaṇḍasūcī, Apakrānta, Mayūralalita, Prasarpitaka, Talaghaṭṭitaka and Bahistrika which are found in the *Bhāratīya Nāṭyaśāstra*. Illustrative pictures which may correspond to these are, however, found in the compartments of the pillars of the E. Gopura of the Cidambaram temple without bearing any labels above them. The dance Parivṛtta is omitted both in the Cidambaram labels and in the descriptive verses of the *Bhāratīya Nāṭyaśāstra*. The numbers attached to the verses in the inscriptions follow the order in which the postures are enumerated in the *Nāṭyaśāstra*. The order is correct (read from left to right) on the seven projecting pillars of the inner wall of the *Gopura*, on the right side; but the corresponding figures on the left side are much deranged. This may have been due to the ignorance of the masons whose work was not properly supervised.

2. Read कुर्य्याद्दृ°.
3. The enumeration in *Bhā. Nāṭ*. gives the name as Vaktramaṇḍalam but as Cakramaṇḍalam, correctly, in the description.
4. This and the next three are enumerated in the printed work *Bhāratīya Nāṭyaśāstra* in vv. 39 and 40, but not described.
5. Two compartments, bearing sculptures, next to this do not belong to the series. One of them has an unfinished picture not distinct on the original and the other the modern image of a devotee.
6. This and the next compartment bear figures with labels on their sides. Sketches of these were not prepared by mistake.
7. In the *Bhāratīya Nāṭyaśāstra*, no. 43 is described with the first half of 42 and the second half of 43, but in the enumeration two separate postures called Svastika and Pṛṣṭhasavastika are mentioned. The omission of Svastika (No. 42) thus made in the printed work is supplied by the list before us.
8. This begins with the phrase स्वस्ति श्रीः and is marked as 1. The *Bhāratīya Nāṭyaśāstra* also begins with this verse. But the subsequent numbering of the verses on the stones are much worn out and cannot, consequently, be compared with the numbering in the printed work. Where, however, the stones are clearly numbered the numbers of the verses do mostly agree with those of the *Bhāratīya Nāṭyaśāstra*.
9. The printed work calls this Calitoru.
10. *Bhā. Nāṭ*., reads निकुञ्चि°.
11. *Bhā. Nāṭ*., calls this Ārtava in the enumeration.

12. *Bhā. Nāṭ.*, reads °येद्रतम्.
13. *Bhā. Nāṭ.*, reads Ḍolapādakam in the enumeration.
14. *Bhā. Nāṭ.*, reads Vivṛta.
15. *Bhā. Nāṭ.*, reads has वामपादश्शिरोदेशे.
16. Here the printed copy of *Bhā. Nāṭ.*, omits the first half, reads नेंचितावञ्चितौ हस्तौ in the beginning of the second half and calls the dance sāmāpasarpita.
17. *Bhā. Nāṭ.*, calls this Nitānta in the description but, correctly, Nitamba in the enumeration.
18. This is perhaps Loḷitam omitted after v. 156 of the *Bhā. Nāṭ.*, though enumerated in v. 52.
19. *Bhā. Nāṭ.*, reads अन्तरापसृतौ पादौ.
20. *Bhā. Nāṭ.*, reads तलावूर्ध्वमेव च.
21. *Bhā. Nāṭ.*, reads पादावर्धक्रमो.
22. *Bhā. Nāṭ.*, reads सिंहकपितके.
23. *Bhā. Nāṭ.*, reads तिल°.
24. *Bhā. Nāṭ.*, reads नितंब°.
25. *Bhā. Nāṭ.*, reads °रूद्धाटिते.
26. *Bhā. Nāṭ.*, reads Maulikākrīḍam in the enumeration.
27. *Bhā. Nāṭ.*, reads Saṅkrāntam in the enumeration
28. *Bhā. Nāṭ.*, reads Apasritakam in the enumeration
29. One compartment below No. 88 is occupied by two modern pictures which do not belong to the series. People consider them to be the sculptors who out the dancing figures.
30. *Bhā. Nāṭ.*, gives the name as Śakaṭākhyam.
31. *Bhā. Nāṭ.* has उद्धाटित.
32. *Bhā. Nāṭ.* gives the name as Raṅgāvataraṇam.
33. *Bhā. Nāṭ.*, reads शिरः सकत्तं/ त्त.

Sanskrit inscription of Pallava Rājasiṁha (AD 691-728) in Nāgari script, Atiraṇacaṇḍēśvara Cave Temple Śāḷuvankuppam, Māmallapuram

(*Source: E.I.*, Vol. X; *Courtesy*: Archaeological Survey of India)

Sanskrit inscription of Pāṇḍyan Parantaka Neḍuñjaḍaiyaṉ (770 AD) from a Cave-Temple at Āṇamalai (near Madurai)

(in Grantha script)

(*Source: E.I.*, Vol. VIII; *Courtesy*: Archaeological Survey of India)

A portion of the Sanskrit praśasti of the Tiruvālaṅgāḍu Copper-Plate Grant of Rājēndra Chōḷa I (AD 1018)

(in Grantha script)

ib

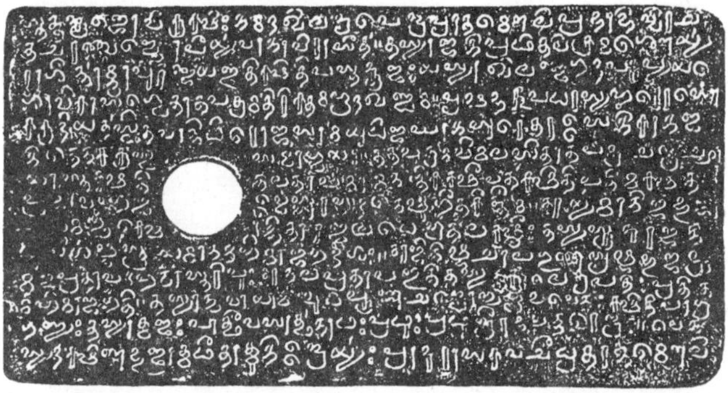

iia.

(*Source: S.I.I.*, Vol. III; *Courtesy*: Archaeological Survey of India)

Bibliography

Epigraphical Sources

Annual Reports on Epigraphy.

Epigraphia Indica.

Pallavar Ceppetukal Muppatu (Thirty Pallava copper-plates), Madras, 1967.

Pandiyar Ceppedukal Pattu (Ten Pandyan copper-plates), Madras, 1967.

South Indian Inscriptions.

South Indian Temple Inscriptions.

Travancore Archaeological Series.

Literary Sources

SANSKRIT

Abijñānaśākuntalam of Kālidāsa, tr. M.R. Kale, Delhi, 1994.

Alaṅkārasūtra of Rājānaka Śrī Ruyyaka (with the *vṛtti Alaṅkārasarvasva* of Mankhuka and commentary by Samudrabandha on the latter), ed. T.S. Ganapati Sastri, Trivandrum, 1915.

Amarakośa, ed. Satyadeva Mishra, Varanasi, 1972.

Avantisundarīkathā, ed. K.S. Mahadeva Sastri, Trivandrum, 1954.

Avantisundarīkathāsāra, ed. G. Harihara Sastri, Madras, 1957.

Bāṇa's Kādambarī, ed. M.R. Kale, Delhi, 1968.

Daśakumāracarita of Daṇḍin, tr. M.R. Kale, Delhi, 1997.

Gadyakarṇāmṛta of Sakala Vidyācakravartin, Madras, 1981.

Gajaśāstra of Pālakāpya Muni, ed. K.S. Subrahmanya Sastri, Tanjavur, 1958.

Kāmasūtra of Vātsyāyana, tr. B.N. Basu, Calcutta, 1948.

Kauṭilīyam Arthaśāstram, ed. K.P. Kangle, New Delhi.

Kāvyamīmāṁsa of Rājaśekhara (Part I), ed. Narayana Sastri Rhiste, Banaras, 1931.

Mahābhārata, tr. M.N. Dutt, Calcutta, 1964.

Manu-Smṛti., ed. Ganganatha Jha, Delhi, 1992.

Mattavilāsaprahasana, ed. N.P. Unni, Trivandrum, 1974.

Nānārthārṇava-Saṁkṣepa, ed. T. Ganapati Sastri, Trivandrum, 1913.

Pradyumnābhyudaya of Ravivarmabhūpa, ed. T. Ganapati Sastri, Trivandrum, 1910.

Śrīmad Bhāgavata, tr. Swami Tapasyananda, Madras, 1982.

Śrīmad Vālmikī Rāmāyaṇa ed. Kuppuswami Sastrigal Madras, 1958.

The Raghuvaṁśa of Kālidāsa (Cantos I-V), tr. M.R. Kale, Bombay, 1925.

Viśvakarmā Vāstuśāstram, ed. K. Vasudeva Sastri and Major N.B. Gadre, Tanjavur, 1958.

TAMIL

The Kuraḷ, (tr. and ed.) with an introduction by P.S. Sundaram, New Delhi, 1990.

Kalingattuparani, ed. A. Gopala Iyer, Madras, 1924.

Maduraikkāñci, ed. U.V. Swaminatha Iyer, Madras, 1920.

Mūvarula, ed. A. Gopala Iyer, Madras, 1926.

Nalāyira Divya Prabandham, ed. K. Venkataswami Reddiyar, Madras, 1981.

Paṭṭinapālai, ed. U.V. Swaminatha Iyer, Madras, 1918.

Puraṇānūru, ed. U.V. Swaminatha Iyer, Madras, 1923.

Śilappadikāram, Tr. V.R. Ramachandra Dikshitar, Oxford, 1939.

Tolkkāpiam, ed. V.U. Chidambaram Pillai, Madras, 1941.

Secondary Sources

Appadurai, A., *Economic Conditions in Southern India (AD 1000-1500)*, 2 vols, Madras, 1991.

Altekar, A.S., *Education in Ancient India*, Banaras, 1951.

———, *State and Government in Ancient India*, Delhi, 1984.

Begde, Prabhakar V., *Forts and Palaces of India*, New Delhi, 1982.

Bühler, George, *The Laws of Manu*, Delhi, 1993.

Coomaraswamy, Ananda K., *The Indian Craftsman*, New Delhi, 1989.

Das, Shukla, *Crime and Punishment in Ancient India*, New Delhi, 1977.

Das, S.K., *Educational System of Ancient Hindus*, Calcutta, 1930.

Ganguly, D.K., *Aspects of Ancient Indian Administration*, New Delhi, 1979.

Gieger, Wilhelm (ed.), *Cūlavaṁśa being the most recent part of the Mahāvaṁśa*, Colombo, 1953.

Gopalan, R., *History of the Pallavas of Kāñci*, Madras, 1928.

Govindasamy, M.S., *The Role of Feudatories in Later Coḷa History*, Annamalainagar, 1979.

———, *The Role of Feudatories in Pallava History*, Annamalainagar, 1965.

Gupta, D.K., *A Critical Study of Dandin and his Works*, Delhi, 1970.

Gupta, V.K., *Kautilyan Jurisprudence*, New Delhi, 1987.

Gurumurthy, S., *Education in South India*, Madras, 1979.

Hall, Kenneth, *Trade & Statecraft in the Age of the Coḷas*, New Delhi, 1980.

Harle, James C., 'Temple Gateways in South India,' New Delhi, 1995.

Kane, P.V., *History of Dharmaśāstra*, vol. II, Poona, 1941.

Kangle, R.P., *The Kauṭīlīyam Arthaśāstram*, Delhi, 1992.

Keith, A.B., *History of Sanskrit Literature*, Delhi, 1996.

Krishnan, K.G., *Studies in South Indian History and Epigraphy*, Madras, 1981.

———, *Karandai Tamil Sangam Plates of Rajendra Cola-I* (*MASI, No. 79*), New Delhi, 1984.

———, *Inscriptions of the Early Pandyas* (*c. 300* BC *to 984* AD), New Delhi, 2002.

Krishnaswami, Aiyangar, S., *Evolution of Hindu Administrative Institutions in South India*, Madras, 1931.

Lorenzen, David, N., *The Kapalikas and the Kalamukhas* (*Two Lost Śaiva Sects*), Delhi, 1991.

Macdonell, A.A., *A History of Sanskrit Literature*, Hyderabad, 1935.

Mahalingam, T.V., *South Indian Polity*, Madras, 1955.

———, *Kancipuram in Early South Indian History*, Madras, 1969.

———, *Inscriptions of the Pallavas*, New Delhi, 1988.

Minakshi C., *Administration & Social Life Under the Pallavas*, Madras, 1975.

———, *The Historical Sculptures of the Vaikunṭhaperūmāl Temple, Kāñcī (Memoirs of the Archaeological Survey of India)*, New Delhi, 1940.

Mookerji, R.M., *Ancient Indian Education*, London, 1947.

Nagaswamy, R., *Tiruttani and Velanjeri Copper Plates*, Madras, 1979.

———, *The Esalam copper-plates of Rajendra Cola I*, Bulletin De L'Ecolencaise, D'Extreme-Orient, Tome LXXVI, Paris, 1987.

———, *Studies in Ancient Tamil Law and Society*, Madras, 1978.

Natarajan, B., *Tillai and Nataraja*, Madras, 1994.

Nilakanta Sastri, K.A., *History of Sri Vijaya*, Madras, 1949.

———, *The Pāṇḍyan Kingdom (From the Earliest times to the sixteenth century)*, Madras, 1972.

———, *The Coḷas*, Madras, 1984.

———, *Development of Religion in South India*, New Delhi, 1992.

———, *A History of South India*, Madras, 1988.

———, *Foreign Notices of South India*, Madras, 1939.

———, *Studies in Coḷa History and Administration*, Madras, 1932.

Pal, M.K., *Crafts and Craftsmen in Traditional India*, New Delhi, 1978.

Pandeya, B.K., *Temple Economy under the Coḷas*, New Delhi, 1984.

Pillay, K.K., *A Social History of the Tamils*, Madras, 1969.

Raghavan, V., *Bhoja's Sṛṅgāra Prakāśa*, Madras, 1963.

Ramachandra Murthy, S.S., *A Study of Telugu Place-Names*, Delhi, 1985.

Ramachandra Dikshitar, V.R., *Hindu Administrative Institutions*, Madras, 1929.

———, *Studies in Tamil Literature and History*, Madras, 1983.

———, *Cilappatikaram*, Madras, 1997.

———, *War in Ancient India*, New Delhi, 1987.

———, *The Mauryan Polity*, Delhi, 1993.

Ramachandran, C.E., *Ahananuru in its Historical Setting*, Madras, 1974.

Raman, K.V., *Early History of the Madras Region*, Madras, 1959.

———, *Some aspects of Pāṇḍyan History in the light of new discoveries*, Madras, 1974.

———, *History of the Pāṇḍyas* (Tamil), Madras, 1977.

———, *Śrī Varadarājaswāmī Temple, Kanchi*, New Delhi, 1975.

Ramesh, K.V., *Indian Epigraphy*, New Delhi, 1984.

Sankaranarayanan, S., *The Vishnukundis and their Times*, Delhi, 1977.

Sathianathaier, R., *Studies in the Ancient History of Tondaimandalam*, Madras, 1987.

Shanmugam, P., *The Revenue System of the Coḷas (850-1279)*, Madras, 1987.

Sharma, R.S., *Political Ideas and Institutions in Ancient India*, Delhi, 1968.

Singh, Sarva Daman, *Ancient Indian Warfare*, Delhi, 1997.

Singh, D.C., *Ancient Indian Warfare*, Delhi, 1997.

Sircar, D.C., *The Successors of the Satavahanas in Lower Deccan*, Calcutta, 1939.

———, *Indian Epigraphy*, Delhi, 1965.

———, *Indian Epigraphical Glossary*, Delhi, 1966.

———, *Inscriptions of Aśoka*, Delhi, 1966.

Sivaramamurti, C., *Epigraphical Echos of Kālidāsa*, Madras, 1944.

———, *Indian Epigraphy and South Indian Scripts*, Bulletin of Madras Government Museum, vol. 3, no. 4, Madras, 1966.

———, *Mahabalipuram*, New Delhi, 1978.

———, *Naṭaraja in Art, Thought and Literature*, New Delhi, 1994.

Srinivasan, C.R., *Kañcīpuram Through the Ages*, New Delhi, 1979.

Srinivasan, K.R., 'The Dharmarāja Ratha and its scuptures, Māmallapuram,' Delhi, 1975.

Srinivasan, T.M., *Irrigation and Water Supply in South India (200 BC to 1300 AD)*, Madras, 1997.

Subbarayalu, Y., *Political Geography of the Coḷa Country*, Madras, 1973.

Subrahmanian, N., *Sangam Polity*, Madurai, 1980.

Subrahmanya Aiyer, K.V., *Historical Sketches of Ancient Dekhan*, Coimbatore, 1967.

Subrahmanyam, Padma, *Bharata's Art, Then and Now*, Bombay, 1979.

Sundararajan, S., *Ancient Tamil Country: its Social and Economic Structure*, New Delhi, 1991.

Swaminathan, S., *The Early Coḷas: History, Art and Culture*, Delhi, 1998.

Venkataraman, B., *Rajarajesvaram: The Pinnacle of Coḷa Art*, Madras, 1985.

Articles

Arokiaswamy, M., "Social Developments under the Imperial Coḷas," *TASSI*, 1956-57, vol. 2, pp. 1-7.

Balasubramanyam, S.R., "Conquests of Kulottunga-III," *JOR*, vol. 5, 1931, pp. 167-78.

———, "Kopperuñjiṅga-His Life and Times," *JMU*, vol. IX, no. 3 and vol. X, no. 1, pp. 40-98.

Bühler, G., "The Indian Inscriptions and the Antiquity of Indian Artificial Poetry," *Ind. Ant.*, 1913 February.

Desayar, M., "Irrigation in Medieval Tamil Nadu," *QJMS*, vol. LXXXVI (86) no. 2, April-June, 1995, pp. 15-28.

Diskalkar, D.B., "Dravidian or South Indian Inscriptions," *JIH*, vol. XXXIV, p. 173.

Gurumurthy, S., "Popular Education in Ancient South India from Inscriptions," *JMU*, vol. LI, no. 1, 1979 January, pp. 19-28.

Harihara Sastri, G., "Kharapata and Mūladeva from Asutosh Memorial Volume," Patna, 1926-28, pp. 224-27.

Krishnan, K.G., "Sanskrit in Inscriptions of Tamil Nadu," from *Svasti Sri B. Ch Chabbra Felicitation Volume*, New Delhi, 1984.

———, "Cola Charters: Socio-Economic Aspects, Tamil Civilization," *Journal of the Tamil University*, vol. 3, no. 1-2, 1985, pp. 71-74.

Mahalingam, T.V., "The Accession of Nandivarman Pallavamalla," *JIH*, vol. XXXVI, Part-II, 1958 August.

———, "Pallava Rajasimha and South East Asia," *JMU*, 1961 January, vol. XXXII, pp. 317-30.

———, "Udayacandra — A Great Pallava General from Ācārya-Vandana," *D.R. Bhandarkar Birth Centenary Volume*, University of Calcutta, 1982, pp. 286-96.

———, "An Interregnum in Pallava History" *JIH*, vol. XLI, Part I, 1963 April.

———, "The Banas in South Indian History," *JIH*, vol. XXIX (1951), pp. 153-81 and 277 to 305.

Minakshi, C., "The Khaṭvāṅga of the Pallavas," *IHQ*, vol. XIII, no. 4, 1937, pp. 717-19.

Nagaswamy, R., "Mahendra's Inscription at Tirucirapalli — A Study," *JOR*, vol. 7, pp. 135-38.

Natarajan, D., "Śaivism under Rājarāja — A Study," from *Rājarāja the Great — Seminar Proceedings*, Bombay, 1987.

Nilakanta Sastri, K.A., "The Koḍumbāḷūr Inscription of Vikrama-Kesari," *JOR*, vol. 7, 1933, pp. 1-10.

———, "Sanskrit Learning in the Coḷa Empire," *JOR*, vol. 9, Part I, 1937, pp. 1-2.

———, "Education in the Tamil Country," *Indian Culture*, vol. I (Part-I), pp. 85-88.

———, "The Kaliṅga Wars of the reign of Kulottunga," *JOR*, vol. 10, 1936, pp. 295-301.

Raghavan, V., "Sanskrit and Epigraphy," *The Mysore Orientalist*, vol. 4 (no. 1), 1971 March, pp. 1-7.

———, "Adult Education in Ancient India," *Memoirs of the Madras Library Association*, Madras 1944, pp. 57-65.

———, "Methods of Popular Religious Institution in South India," Article from *The Cultural Heritage of India*, vol. 14, Calcutta, 1969.

———, "The Bharatasaṁgraha of Vidyāchakravartin," *ABORI*, vol. XIV, pp. 256-57.

Ramachandra Dikshitar, V.R., "A Hindu University at Kanchi, from Studies in South Indian History and Culture," *Prof. V.R. Ramachandra Dikshitar Centenary Volume*, Chennai, 1997, pp. 164-67.

Ramachandran, T.N., "The Royal Artist, Mahendravarman I," *JOR*, vol. 7, pp. 219-45 and 303 ff.

Raman, K.V., "Jainism in Toṇḍaimaṇḍalam," *BITC*, 1974 January-June, pp. 13-23.

———, "Karavandapuram or Uggirankoṭṭai — An Ancient Fortress Town of the Pandyas," *J.I.H.*, vol. LII, pp. 69-74.

Ramesh, K.V., "A Pallava Charter and Two Copper Medallions from Peddamudiyam" from *Sri Rama Chandrika* (*Prof. Oruganti Ramachandraiya Festschrift*), Delhi, 1993, pp. 117-21.

Ramesan, N., "The Vesanta Grant of Pallava Simhavarman," *TASSI*, 1960-62 (vol. 6, Silver Jubilee Volume), pp. 85-96.

———, "The Kumaraḍimangalam Plates of the Pallava King Nandivarman III," *Shri Mallampalli Somasekara Sarma Commemoration Volume*, Hyderabad, 1976, pp. 193-205.

Reddy, A.K.V.S., and Krishna Reddy, N., "A Newly Discovered Prakrit Copper-plate Grant of Pallava Vishnugopavarman, Year I," *Professor Srinivasa Sankaranarayanan Festschrift*, New Delhi, 2000.

Sampath, M.D., "A note on the Velanjeri plate of Pallava Aparājita," from *Sri Ramachandrika* (*Prof. Oruganti Ramachandraiya Festschrift*), New Delhi, 1993, pp. 67-70.

Sankaranarayanan, S., "The Kāñcīpuram Inscription of Jaṭā-Coḷa Bhīma and Rājarāja in Rangavalli," *S.R. Rao Felicitation Volume*, Delhi, 1983, pp. 95-99.

———, "A Pallava Inscriptional Poem in Sanskrit," *ALB*, vol. 55, 1991, pp. 71-90.

———, "Sanskrit Education in Ancient Tamil Country (An Epigraphical Survey)," *ALB*, vol. 57, 1993, pp. 7-33.

———, "Pradīpaka: A Forgotten Vārttika from Tamil Nadu on the Śārīrakabhāṣya of Śrī Śaṁkara," *ALB*, vol. 62, 1998, pp. 109-23.

———, "The Bhagavatpādīyam Śārīraka Bhāṣyam in the Coḷamādevī Epigraph: More Light," *ALB*, vol. 64, 2000, pp. 105-35.

Sircar, D.C., "South Indian Epigraphy — Its Value as Source Material in South Indian Studies," *Dr. T.V. Mahalingam Commemoration Volume*, Mysore, 1990, pp. 183-90.

Srinivasan, P.R., "Gaṅgādharāṣṭakam in Pallava Inscription from Tirucirapalli from *Srinidhih — Perspectives in Indian Archaeology, Art and Culture*," *Shri K.R. Srinivasan Festschrift*, Madras, 1983, pp. 431-35.

———, "A Sanskrit Inscription of the time of Rājendra Coḷa I from Tiruvorriyur," *JOR*, vol. 32, 1962-63, pp. 11-15.

———, "Rare Sculptures at Kumbhakonam," *TASSI*, (1958-59), pp. 35-36.

Subrahmanian, V.S., "Characteristic Features of Sanskrit Inscriptions, (South Indian Studies," *Dr. T.V. Mahalingam, Commemoration Volume*, Mysore, 1990, pp. 191-205.

Subramaniam, T.N. & Srinivasan, P.R., "The Sivakasi Copper-plate Grant of Vira Pandya," *TASSI* (1962-65), pp. 33-52.

Subramaniam, T.N., "The Dalavaypuram Copper-Plate Grant of Parāntaka Vira Narayana Pandya," *TASSI* (1962-65), pp. 1-31.

———, "Paḷḷankoil Jaina Copper-plate Grant of Early Pallava Period," *TASSI*, 1958-59, vol. IV, pp. 41-83.

Journals

Journal of Ancient Indian History, Calcutta.

Journal of the Epigraphical Society of India, Mysore.

Journal of Indian History, Trivandrum.

Journal of the Madras University, Madras.

Journal of the Orient Institute, Baroda.

Journal of Oriental Research, Madras.

Journal of Tamil Civilization, Tanjavur.

Sri Venkatesvara University Oriental Journal, Tirupathi.

The Indian Historical Quarterly, Calcutta.

Quarterly Journal of the Mythic Society, Bangalore.

Felicitation/Commemoration Volumes

Ācarya Vandana (*D.R. Bhandarkar Birth Centenary Volume*), Calcutta, 1982.

Indian History and Epigraphy (*Dr. G.S. Gai Felicitation Volume*), Delhi, 1990.

Raṅgavalli, Recent Researches in Indology (*S.R. Rao Felicitation Volume*) Delhi, 1983.

Śāṅkaram (*Professor Srinivasa Sankaranarayanan Festschrift*), New Delhi, 2000.

Shri Malampalli Somasekhara Sarma Commemoration Volume, Hyderabad, 1976.

South Indian Studies (*Dr. T.V. Mahalingam Commemoration Volume*), Mysore, 1990.

Śri Nidhiḥ, Perspectives in Indian Archaeology (*Sri K.R. Srinivasan Felicitation Volume*), Madras, 1983.

Studies in South Indian History and Culture (*Prof. V.R. Ramachandra Dikshitar Centenary Volume*), Chennai, 1997.

Svasti Śrī (*B.Ch. Chhabra Felicitation Volume*) New Delhi, 1984.

Index